国家级一流本科专业建设配套教材

新编 英国文学

A NEW SURVEY OF ENGLISH LITERATURE

左金梅 主编

清华大学出版社
北京

内 容 简 介

《新编英国文学》以英国文学发展为主线，介绍了古英语时期、中古英语时期、文艺复兴时期、英国资产阶级革命和复辟时期、古典主义时期、浪漫主义时期、现实主义时期、现代主义时期以及后现代主义时期等各个时期的历史背景、文学流派及特点、代表作家及作品，并附有经典作品选读和注释。本书内容详实、逻辑清晰、层次分明、重点突出、文字流畅，便于学生了解英国文学发展历史，学习文学相关知识与技能，培养文学批判性思维，提升人文素养。

本书适合普通高校英语专业学生和具有一定英语基础、对英国文学感兴趣的读者使用。

版权所有，侵权必究。举报：010-62782989，beiqinquan@tup.tsinghua.edu.cn。

图书在版编目（CIP）数据

新编英国文学：英文 / 左金梅主编. —北京：清华大学出版社，2024.3
国家级一流本科专业建设配套教材
ISBN 978-7-302-61643-6

Ⅰ.①新… Ⅱ.①左… Ⅲ.①英语—阅读教学—高等学校—教材②英国文学—文学史 Ⅳ.①H319.4：I

中国版本图书馆CIP数据核字（2022）第145456号

责任编辑：杨文娟
封面设计：李伯骥
责任校对：王凤芝
责任印制：宋　林

出版发行：清华大学出版社
网　　址：https://www.tup.com.cn，https://www.wqxuetang.com
地　　址：北京清华大学学研大厦A座　　邮　编：100084
社 总 机：010-83470000　　邮　购：010-62786544
投稿与读者服务：010-62776969，c-service@tup.tsinghua.edu.cn
质量反馈：010-62772015，zhiliang@tup.tsinghua.edu.cn
印 装 者：三河市龙大印装有限公司
经　　销：全国新华书店
开　　本：185mm×260mm　　印　张：21　　字　数：417千字
版　　次：2024年4月第1版　　印　次：2024年4月第1次印刷
定　　价：79.00元

产品编号：098495-01

前 言

文学就是人学,是作家以独特的语言艺术表达客观世界和心灵世界的手段,是不同地域、不同时期社会文化的表现形式,代表着人类社会进步、发展的智慧。英国文学作为人文学科研究的重要领域之一,发端于中世纪,从古英语时期的《贝奥武甫》、中古英语时期的韵文体骑士传奇《高文骑士与绿衣骑士》、文艺复兴时期的莎士比亚、英国资产阶级革命和复辟时期的弥尔顿、19世纪的浪漫主义、现实主义文学,到20世纪乃至21世纪的现代主义和后现代主义,经历了一千多年的积累与沉淀,取得了举世瞩目的成就。多年来,国内外学者就英国文学的研究众多,撰写的专著、教材层出不穷。我们吸取中外研究的精华,于2004年编纂出版了《英国文学》,以简明、条理清晰、重点突出为特点,深受广大师生和西方文学爱好者的好评。

《新编英国文学》以《英国文学》为基础,结合一线教师多年来在英国文学教学中的实践经验和同行专家的一些建议,就各个章节的内容和阅读文本做了相应的补充和调整。本书分为九个章节。第一章是古英语时期的文学,其特点是歌颂英雄主义,该时期出现了英国的第一部史诗《贝奥武甫》;第二章是中世纪时期的文学。中世纪虽然为神学时代,但其最为流行的文学体裁是骑士传奇,赞扬骑士的勇敢、忠诚、礼仪和荣誉感,同时诗人乔叟也写下了英国现实主义的开山之作《坎特伯雷故事集》;第三章是文艺复兴与宗教改革时期的文学,该时期的文学主流是反对神权、宣扬人权的人文主义,最突出的成就是莎士比亚的诗歌和戏剧;第四章是英国资产阶级革命和复辟时期的文学,该时期最伟大的作品是弥尔顿反映英国资产阶级革命精神的史诗《失乐园》；第五章是18世纪古典主义时期的文学，这个时期的英国文学以古希腊、古罗马以及法国作者为楷模，追求理性和艺术形式的完美，最为杰出的代表是约翰·德莱顿的三一律戏剧和亚历山大·蒲伯的英雄双韵体诗歌；第六章是浪漫主义时期的文学，其文学宗旨是对作者内心情感的自由表达，反映普通人的生活，巅峰之作是华兹华斯的《抒情歌谣集》；第七章是维多利亚现实主义时期的文学，以劳苦大众的生活命运为主题背景，批判资本主义制度的拜金、不平等、腐朽等各种弊端。批判现实主义小说是该时期的主流文学体裁，最伟大的代表作者有狄更斯和哈代；第八章和第九章是现代主义时期的文学，该时期意识流、荒诞派等各种文学作品和流派纷纷出现，反映现代和后现代社会人类的迷茫、困惑与无奈，乔伊斯的《尤利西斯》是现代主义小说的巅峰。

  本书从编写到出版得到了中国海洋大学外国语学院的大力支持，外国语学院院长杨连瑞教授亲自组织编写团队，督促、把关每一个环节，付出了大量心血。英语系刘秀玉教授、金浩副教授、辛彩娜副教授在收集资料、文字整理、内容校对等方面都花费了大量时间，给予了许多帮助。在此，向他们表示衷心的感谢和敬意。

  书中有不妥、疏误之处，恳请读者予以指正，欢迎同行不吝赐教。

左金梅

2023年12月25日

Contents

Chapter One Old English Literature

1.1 Historical Background 1
1.2 The Development of the English Language 2
1.3 Literary Features 2
1.4 Representative Writers and Works 3
1.5 *Beowulf* and the Heroic Epic Tradition 4

Chapter Two Middle English Literature (1066–1510)

2.1 Historical Background 7
2.2 Literary Features 9
2.3 Romance and *Sir Gawain* 12
2.4 Popular Ballad 13
2.5 Medieval Drama 14
2.6 William Langland and *Piers Plowman* 15
2.7 Geoffrey Chaucer (1942/43–1400) 16
2.8 Reading 22

Chapter Three — Literature of Renaissance and Reformation (1510–1620)

- 3.1 Historical Background 25
- 3.2 Literary Features 27
- 3.3 Renaissance Poetry 28
  - 3.3.1 Sir Phillip Sydney (1554–1586) 28
  - 3.3.2 Edmund Spenser (1552–1599) 29
- 3.4 Renaissance Prose 31
- 3.5 Renaissance Drama 33
- 3.6 William Shakespeare (1564–1616) 37
- 3.7 Reading 55

Chapter Four — Literature of Revolution and Restoration (1620–1690)

- 4.1 Historical Background 60
- 4.2 Literary Features 61
- 4.3 Seventeenth-Century Prose 62
  - 4.3.1 Francis Bacon (1561–1626) 62
  - 4.3.2 John Bunyan (1628–1688) 65
- 4.4 Seventeenth-Century Drama 66
- 4.5 Seventeenth-Century Poetry 70
  - 4.5.1 John Donne (1572–1631) 71
  - 4.5.2 John Dryden (1631–1700) 74
- 4.6 John Milton (1608–1674) 75
- 4.7 Reading 82

Chapter Five The Eighteenth-Century Literature (1690–1780)

5.1 Historical Background 90
5.2 Literary Features 92
5.3 Eighteenth-Century Poetry 93

    5.3.1 Alexander Pope (1688–1744) 93
    5.3.2 James Thomson (1700–1748) 95
    5.3.3 Thomas Gray (1716–1771) 96

5.4 Eighteenth-Century Prose 97

    5.4.1 Jonathan Swift (1667–1745) 98
    5.4.2 Joseph Addison (1672–1719) and Sir Richard Steele (1672–1729). 100
    5.4.3 Samuel Johnson (1709–1784) 101
    5.4.4 Edward Gibbon (1737–1794) 102

5.5 Eighteenth-Century Novel 103

    5.5.1 Daniel Defoe (1660–1731) 104
    5.5.2 Samuel Richardson (1689–1761) 105
    5.5.3 Henry Fielding (1707–1754) 106
    5.5.4 Laurence Sterne (1713–1768) 109
    5.5.5 Tobias Smollett (1721–1771) 110
    5.5.6 Oliver Goldsmith (1730–1774) 111

5.6 Eighteenth-Century Drama 112

    5.6.1 Oliver Goldsmith (1730–1774) 112
    5.6.2 Richard Brinsley Sheridan (1751–1816) 112

5.7 Reading 114

Chapter Six The Literature of the Romantic Period (1780–1831)

6.1 Historical Background 122
6.2 Literary Features 124

6.3 Romantic Poetry 125
 6.3.1 William Blake (1757–1827) 126
 6.3.2 William Wordsworth (1770–1850) 127
 6.3.3 Samuel Taylor Coleridge (1772–1834) 129
 6.3.4 Robert Burns (1754–1796) 131
 6.3.5 Walter Scott (1771–1832) 132
 6.3.6 George Gordon Byron (1788–1824) 133
 6.3.7 Percy Bysshe Shelley (1792–1822) 136
 6.3.8 John Keats (1795–1821) 141

6.4 Romantic Essayists 146
 6.4.1 Thomas De Quincey (1785–1859) 146
 6.4.2 William Hazlitt (1778–1870) 147
 6.4.3 Charles Lamb (1775–1834) 147

6.5 Romantic Novels 148
 6.5.1 Jane Austen (1775–1817) 150
 6.5.2 Walter Scott (1771–1832) 156

6.6 Reading 157

Chapter Seven Victorian Literature (1832–1900)

7.1 Historical Background 168
7.2 Literary Features 169
7.3 Victorian Novel 170
 7.3.1 Charles Dickens (1812–1870) 172
 7.3.2 William Makepeace Thackeray (1811–1863) 179
 7.3.3 The Brontë Sisters (1818–1848, 1820–1849) 184
 7.3.4 George Eliot (1819–1880) 187
 7.3.5 Elizabeth Gaskell (1810–1865) 190
 7.3.6 George Meredith (1828–1909) 193

7.3.7 Wilkie Collins (1824–1889) 194
7.3.8 Anthony Trollope (1815–1882) 196
7.3.9 Thomas Hardy (1840–1928) 198
7.3.10 George Gissing (1857–1903) 204
7.3.11 George Moore (1852–1933) 204
7.3.12 Samuel Butler (1835–1902) 205
7.3.13 William Morris (1834–1896) 206
7.3.14 Robert Louise Stevenson (1850–1894) 207
7.3.15 Henry James (1848–1916) 208
7.3.16 Rudyard Kipling (1865–1936) 210

7.4 Victorian Poetry 211

7.4.1 Alfred Lord Tennyson (1809–1892) 211
7.4.2 Robert Browning (1812–1889) 214
7.4.3 Elizabeth Barrett Browning (1806–1861) 216
7.4.4 Mathew Arnold (1822–1888) 217
7.4.5 Algernon Charles Swinburne (1837–1909) 219
7.4.6 Dante Gabriel Rossetti (1828–1882) 220
7.4.7 Christina Rossetti (1830–1894) 220

7.5 Victorian Critics and Historians 221

7.5.1 Thomas Carlyle (1795–1881) 221
7.5.2 Thomas Babington Macaulay (1800–1859) 223
7.5.3 John Ruskin (1819–1900) 224

7.6 Victorian Drama 225

7.6.1 Oscar Wilde (1854–1900) 225
7.6.2 George Bernard Shaw (1856–1950) 227

7.7 Reading 230

Chapter Eight The Twentieth-Century Literature (1900–1945)

8.1 Historical Background **237**

8.2 Literary Features **238**

8.3 Modern Poetry **239**

    8.3.1 Thomas Hardy (1840–1928) 240

    8.3.2 William Butler Yeats (1865–1939) 241

    8.3.3 Thomas Stearns Eliot (1888–1965) 243

    8.3.4 Edward Thomas (1871–1917) 245

    8.3.5 Wilfred Owen (1893–1918) 247

    8.3.6 Wystan Hugh Auden (1907–1973) 248

8.4 Modern Drama **249**

    8.4.1 John Millington Synge (1871–1909) 250

    8.4.2 Sean O'Casey (1880–1964) 251

    8.4.3 Noël Coward (1899–1973) 251

    8.4.4 John Boynton Priestley (1894–1984) 252

    8.4.5 William Somerset Maugham (1874–1965) 253

8.5 Modern Novels **253**

    8.5.1 John Galsworthy (1867–1933) 255

    8.5.2 Herbert George Wells (1866–1946) 256

    8.5.3 Arnold Bennett (1867–1931) 257

    8.5.4 Edward Morgan Forster (1879–1970) 257

    8.5.5 Joseph Conrad (1857–1924) 260

    8.5.6 David Herbert Lawrence (1885–1930) 263

    8.5.7 James Joyce (1882–1941) 268

    8.5.8 Virginia Woolf (1882–1941) 272

    8.5.9 Dorothy Richardson (1872–1957) 274

    8.5.10 May Sinclair (1863–1946) 275

    8.5.11 Katherine Mansfield (1888–1923) 275

    8.5.12 Aldous Huxley (1894–1963) 277

    8.5.13 Evelyn Waugh (1903–1966) 278

8.5.14 Henry Green (1905–1973) 279

8.5.15 Graham Greene (1904–1991) 280

8.5.16 Christopher Isherwood (1904–1985) 280

8.5.17 George Orwell (1903–1950) 281

8.6 Reading **281**

Chapter Nine English Literature (Since 1945)

9.1 Historical Background **288**

9.2 Literary Features **289**

9.3 Drama **290**

9.3.1 Samuel Beckett (1906–1989) 292

9.3.2 John Osborne (1929–1994) 293

9.3.3 Harold Pinter (1930–2008) 294

9.3.4 Arnold Wesker (1932–) 296

9.3.5 Joe Orton (1933–1967) 296

9.3.6 Tom Stoppard (1937–) 297

9.3.7 Alan Ayckbourn (1939–) 297

9.3.8 Edward Bond (1934–) 298

9.3.9 David Hare (1947–) 298

9.3.10 Howard Brenton (1942–) 299

9.3.11 Caryl Churchill (1938–) 299

9.4 Novel **300**

9.4.1 William Golding (1911–1993) 301

9.4.2 John Fowles (1926–2005) 302

9.4.3 Augus Wilson (1913–1991) 302

9.4.4 Alan Sillitoe (1928–2010) 303

9.4.5 Kingsley Amis (1922–1995) 304

9.4.6 Martin Amis (1949–) 304

9.4.7 Salman Rushdie (1947–) 305

9.4.8 Doris Lessing (1919–2013) 306

  9.4.9 Antonia Susan Byatt (1936–2023) 306
  9.4.10 Muriel Spark (1918–2006) 307
  9.4.11 Iris Murdoch (1919–1999) 308
  9.4.12 Angela Carter (1940–1992) 308

9.5 Poetry **309**
  9.5.1 Dylan Thomas (1914–1953) 310
  9.5.2 Philip Larkin (1922–1985) 310
  9.5.3 Ted Hughes (1930–1998) 311
  9.5.4 Tony Harrison (1937–) 311
  9.5.5 Seamus Heaney (1939–2013) 312

9.6 Reading **313**

References **321**

Chapter One
Old English Literature

1.1 Historical Background

In the middle of the fifth century, several Germanic tribes invaded the British Isles inhabited by the Celts and established permanent settlements there. They brought with them there a language, a religion, and a poetic tradition. In time, their culture was transformed by natural processes from inside and by invasions and other influences from outside, the most important single force being the conversion of the island to Christianity.

The invaders consisted of three Germanic tribes—the Angles, the Saxons, and the Jutes. The origins of the three are clouded in obscurity and controversy, and it is said that distinctions between Angles and Saxons had been blurred even before their migration to England. The term "Anglo-Saxon" originally differentiated the English from the continental Saxons, but it came to include all the Germanic invaders, possibly because of the overwhelming prominence of the Saxons. Yet, surprisingly enough, "England" and "English" are derived from the word "Angle". At any rate, by the end of the sixth century the Jutes occupied Kent (in the southeast); the Saxons held Sussex and Wessex (in the south); the Angles settled in East Anglia (north of Kent), Mercia (in central England) and Northumbria (in the north, bordering on Scotland). Tribal affiliations soon gave way to somewhat loose political units, small kingdoms based upon new geographic ties.

The social unit of the Germanic tribes was the family or clan. Each member bore responsibility for any wrongs inflicted or suffered by his kinsmen; included among his duties was the obligation to execute revenge or to arrive at a peaceful settlement through the payment of a predetermined value in money or property. A youth would attach himself to a strong leader. In exchange for economic and legal protection, the young man offered military service. The chief fought for victory, and the followers fought for their chief. If the young man retreated from the field after his leader had been killed, he would suffer reproach and infamy for the rest of his life. This kind of social culture can be seen in *Beowulf* and in other Old English poems.

1.2 The Development of the English Language

English, like other languages, has continually changed and continues to change in response to fresh influences. New habits slowly develop among those who use the language, and drastic modifications take place as a result of contact with foreign cultures through trade, migration, and war. Sometimes a new field of learning catapults into public recognition—nuclear physics or rocket science, for instance—with the eventual result that portions of a highly specialized vocabulary filter down into popular usage.

The present-day English language is the product of several thousand years of such evolution. English is a member of a large and ancient family of languages—the Indo-European Family of Languages, and it falls into three major periods: Old English or "Anglo-Saxon" (449–1066), Middle English (1066–1485), and Modern English (1485 to the present day). Old English differs from Modern English in spelling, pronunciation, and grammar. Yet the most formidable difference between Old English and Modern English is in vocabulary. Old English was essentially unilingual: Instead of borrowing from other languages, it formed new words out of its own native resources. Modern English was enriched by foreign importations, especially French. Yet it proceeded to evolve largely from London English.

1.3 Literary Features

Behind the literary products of the Anglo-Saxons, especially the poetry, lays a long oral tradition which developed during the time when the Germanic tribes still inhabited the European continent. Early Germanic poetry was composed and recited by the scop, a professional bard who might have often wandered from court to court hoping to acquire the patronage of some generous lords. At court feasts, the scop would celebrate the deeds of real or legendary heroes out of the remote past with songs.

But with the conversion of England to Christianity, the subject matter of poetry underwent a crucial change. Poetry and prose were committed to religious writing, and, with the Church virtually monopolizing the art of copying old works and creating new ones, the clerics generally preserved only such material as was considered serviceable to Christianity. The Old English poets either used Christian material from Scripture or the liturgy, or they tried, with varying degrees of success, to get subjects of pagan derivation into the framework of the

Christian universe. Beowulf could be comprehended as an ideal Christian king who had not been entirely divested of the thirst for worldly glory that motivated the Germanic warriors.

The verse patterns utilized by Old English poets also represented an accumulation of centuries of oral tradition. The poetic line, which was really two half-lines separated by a distinct pause, contained four accented syllables and a varying number of unaccented syllables. It was once thought that each of the four stressed syllables was accompanied by chords struck by the scop on a small harp.

Old English poets rarely used end rhyme, but they regularly used a system of alliteration. This alliteration involved the initial sounds, whether vowels or consonants, of the four stressed syllables. As a rule, three of the stressed syllables were alliterated, and it was the initial sound of the third accented syllable that normally determined the alliteration.

Rhythm and alliteration were not the only poetic devices. In order to achieve variety, as well as to suggest important attributes of his subject, the scop would frequently introduce a kind of metaphor called the "kenning", a compound of two terms used in place of a common word. The sun, for example, could be referred to as "world candle"; the prince as "ring giver"; the ocean as "sea-monster's home" or "gannet's bath". The "kenning" in the hands of a talented poet could provide a fresh appeal to the imagination of the audience.

Many of the earliest works written by English churchmen were in Latin. And throughout the Old English period, as well as during the Middle Ages and thereafter, a number of English writers—John Milton, to cite a distinguished example—continued to produce sizable quantities of Latin verse and prose. Anglo-Latin literature in the Old English period was often didactic, with its principal functions being to provide religious instruction or inspiration, but Anglo-Latin literature boasts a few writings which combine charm with piety and still others which can almost be called secular. Judged merely as literature, the Latin writings of the Anglo-Saxons may not rank high. But as a measure of the level of culture achieved and sustained in Anglo-Saxon England, they are extremely valuable.

1.4 Representative Writers and Works

A tremendous amount of Old English literature has perished, and much of that which has survived is in a fragmentary form. Among the most substantial surviving Old English poems is *Beowulf*, which will be dealt with later.

The prose division of Anglo-Saxon literature is of less literary interest than the verse. But it is more abundant in quantity. The man most responsible for the development of literary prose during the Old English period is Alfred the Great (849–899), who, as part of his systematic efforts to make Wessex a center of English culture, translated into English certain important Latin texts, among which is Bede's *History*. King Alfred's representative work is the *Anglo-Saxon Chronicle*, the most important monument of Anglo-Saxon prose, carrying us to contemporary vernacular history from the middle of the eighth century to the middle of the twelfth century, preserving amid drier annals some exceedingly interesting fragments of composition of the more original kind both in prose and verse, manifesting an ability to manage the subject that was only much later shown in other vernacular languages, and bridging for us the gulf between the ruin of Anglo-Saxon even before the Conquest and the rise of English properly more than a century subsequent to it.

The outstanding representative of Anglo-Latin culture was Bede (673–735). In his monastery at Jarrow, Northumbria, Bede encompassed many areas of intellectual accomplishments. He wrote Latin treatises on medicine, astronomy, mathematics and philosophy. He was also a biographer. His immortal achievement, however, was in the field of history. Bede's monumental *Historia Ecclesiastica Gentis Anglorum* (*Ecclesiastical Histories of the English People*) traces the history of England from Caesar's invasion, in 55 B.C., to 731, the year in which the *Historia Ecclesiastica Gentis Anglorum* was completed. The first writer to conceive of the English as one people with a single destiny, Bede would have his readers become more familiar with the actions and sayings of former men of renown. To make his narrative still more attractive, he introduced anecdotes, dramatic speeches, and miracles—all designed to show the Christian ideal as the most compelling force in the universe.

1.5 *Beowulf* and the Heroic Epic Tradition

Sometime between the year 700 and 900, the first great English epic poem *Beowulf* was composed. It tells the song of Beowulf, a warrior prince from Geatland in Sweden, who goes to Denmark and kills the monster Grendel that has been attacking the great Hall of Heorot, built by Hrothgar, the Danish King. Grendel's mother, a water monster, takes revenge by carrying off one of the King's noblemen, but Beowulf dives into the underwater lair in which she lives and kills her, too. Returning home, in due course, Beowulf becomes the King of the Geats. The poem then moves forward about fifty years. Beowulf's kingdom is ravaged by a fire-breathing dragon that burns the royal hall. Beowulf, aided by a young warrior, Wiglaf, manages to kill the dragon, but is fatally wounded in the course of the fight. He pronounces Wiglaf his successor. The poem ends with Beowulf's burial and a premonition that the kingdom will be overthrown.

Structurally, *Beowulf* is built around three fights. Each of these involves a battle between those who live in the royal hall and a monster; the monsters are dangerous, unpredictable, and incomprehensible forces that threaten the security and well-being of those in power and the way of life they represent. This is a pattern that is specific to the Anglo-Saxon period, but which also echoes down through the whole history of English literature. Time and time again, literary texts deal with an idea of order. There is a sense of a well-run state or a settled social order, and, for the individual a feeling of existing within a secure framework. In *Beowulf*, a sense of security is linked with the presence of the great hall as a place of refuge and shared values; it is a place for feasting and celebrations, providing warmth and protection against whatever might be encountered in the darkness outside. Over and over again, however, literary texts focus on threats to such a feeling of security and confidence. There might be an external threat, such as a monster or a foreign enemy, or an enemy within, such as the rebellious noblemen in Shakespeare's history plays who challenge the authority of the King. The Anglo-Saxon period is essentially a warrior society, a tribal community with people clustering together in forts and settlements, fearing attack. The land is farmed, and there are centers of learning, but the overwhelming fact of life is invasion by outside forces. *Beowulf* reflects and expresses the anxieties that would have dominated such a society.

Beowulf belongs to a tradition of heroic or epic poetry. This tradition can, indirectly, be traced back to Ancient Greece and Rome. An epic is a long narrative poem (there are 3,182 lines in *Beowulf*) that operates on a grand scale and deals with the deeds of warriors and heroes. As is the case in *Beowulf*, while focusing on the deeds of one man, epic poems also interlace the main narrative with myths, legends, folk tales, and past events; there is a composite effect, the entire culture of a country cohering in the overall experience of the poem. *Beowulf* belongs to the category of oral, as opposed to literary, epic, in that it was composed to be recited; it was only written down much later as the poem that exists today, possibly as late as the year 1000.

In epic poetry there are always threats and dangers that have to be confronted, but even more important is the sense of a hero who embodies the qualities that are necessary in a leader in a hierarchical, masculine, warrior society; the text is concerned with the qualities that constitute his greatness, the poem as a whole amounting to what we might regard as a debate about the nature of the society and its values. Central to those values is the idea of loyalty to one's lord: The lord provides food and protection in return for service. He is the "giver of rings" and rewards, and the worst of crime is betrayal. This impression of a larger purpose in *Beowulf* is underlined by the inclusion of decorous speeches and passages of moral reflection, and by the inclusion of quasi-historical stories of feuds and wars that echo and support the main narrative. The fact that *Beowulf* exists within a literary tradition is also apparent in its use of the alliterative meter, which is the most notable feature of Germanic prosody; in *Beowulf*, as in Old English verse generally, there are two or three alliterating stressed syllables in each line, reflecting the pattern of speech and so appropriate for oral performance. The effect is to link the two halves of the lines into rich interweaving pattern of vocabulary idea. The convention may seem strange to modern readers, but in its distinctive way it serves, like rhyme, to reinforce the poem's theme of the search for order in a chaotic world. Observe the following sample describing the monster Grendel's approach to the Danish hall:

> From the stretching moors, from the misty hollows,
> Grendel came creeping, cursed of God,
> A murderous ravager minded to snare
> Spoil of heroes in high-built hall.
> Under clouded heaven she held his way
> Till there rose before him the high-roofed house
> Wine-hall of warriors gleaming with gold.

(Beowulf)

The pounding rhythm, in conjunction with the alliteration, conveys an impression of unrelenting strength.

Chapter Two
Middle English Literature (1066–1510)

2.1 Historical Background

The Middle English period, an age which in time produced Chaucer and witnessed the birth of modern drama, began in 1066, the year of the Norman Conquest. The Normans, originally a band of Scandinavian pirates, conquered England and brought it into the orbit of French culture. Under the leadership of William, Duke of Normandy, the Norman invaders proceeded to reshape the destiny of England. Anglo-Saxon *political institutions* were overhauled by Norman administrators; the English language was remolded through contact with French; society at large underwent great changes, often reflected in the literature of the period.

After the Norman victory at the Battle of Hastings, William II was crowned King William I of England. The new monarch systematically embarked upon an economic and social reorganization of the conquered country. He rewarded his Norman followers with the lands of the defeated English nobility and thereby introduced feudalism into England. On the relationship between the ecclesiastical and secular arms of the government, the King had definite views. Although he cooperated with the Pope in seeking monastic reform and drew England generally closer to Rome, he insisted upon a separation of the secular from the ecclesiastical courts and firmly upheld the independent authority of the former. The King, William maintained, should hold the highest position and make the major appointments. William managed to exercise personal control over the affairs of state, and even when he delegated powers to his justifiers (political and judicial officers appointed by the King), he kept himself fully informed as to what was going on throughout England.

The Norman Empire, which was built by William I and his immediate successors, began to decline near the end of the twelfth century. In 1204, the ineffectual King John lost Normandy to France (an event of special significance for the history of the English language), and in 1215 his domestic powers in England were seriously challenged by the rebellious barons. The fourteenth and fifteenth centuries were marked by the exhausting

Hundred Years' War (1337–1453) between England and France; England not only lost the war, but was torn by civil strife, particularly the Wars of the Roses (1455–1485) between the rival houses of Lancaster and York. At last, however, at the battle of Bosworth (1485), the Wars of the Roses came to a military end. The Duke of Richmond gained the English throne and, reigning as Henry VII, ushered in the era of the Tudors. With this event, the Middle English period may be said to have ended.

Although the political implications of the Norman Conquest were of exceptional importance, the most significant effect of the conquest consisted in the impact it had upon the structure and future growth of the English language. The conquest led in time to an expansion of the literary potentialities of English beyond anything the language had previously known.

After the cultural leadership of Alfred's Wessex receded in the face of almost constant social and military pressures, English and French began a long struggle for linguistic supremacy. Naturally enough, the masses, who had been born in England, continued to speak English, while the new nobility, which had its roots in France, read and wrote in French. English was the language of day-by-day utilitarian discourse; French was the language of belles-lettres (intellectuals). But the loss of Normandy to France weakened the allegiance of the Anglo-Norman lords to the continent and gave a fresh stimulus to English nationalism. By about 1250, English had begun to supplant French, and to a large extent Latin, in nearly all areas. The displacement of French was further accelerated by the wave of patriotism that accompanied the Hundred Years' War. By the end of the fourteenth century, a literature had been created in English that surpassed what was produced in French. After about 1450, a "standard" English emerged from the welter of local Middle English dialects.

Spelling, pronunciation, and grammar changed strikingly between Old English and Middle English, which can be seen in a page of the Old English *Beowulf* in the original, and a page of the Middle English *The Canterbury Tales*. Some of the changes were in the direction of simplicity—for example, the substantial loss of inflections. Others complicated the language, as in the frequently revolutionary spelling conventions introduced by the Anglo-Norman scribes. But the most prominent feature of Middle English was its new and enlarged vocabulary. Besides additional prefixes and suffixes, more than ten thousand French words found their way into the English language.

Chapter Two
Middle English Literature (1066–1510)

2.2 Literary Features

The Christian view of the universe permeates the most enduring literature of the Middle English period. The bulk of the extant literature of the Middle English period is concerned, explicitly or implicitly, with the problem of sin and redemption. One insistent theme recurs: the vanity and treachery of transitory world as opposed to the perfect bliss of the world to come. Death is seen not as an affliction, but rather as the culmination of a long journey—the release from all the shortcomings attendant upon man in his mortal state and the deliverance into eternal joys. God himself was absolute perfection. His greatness was manifest throughout His great universe. Consequently, some authors, for figurative purposes, chose to speak of the world as symbol. By the visible forms and motions of everyday life could be expressed intangible spiritual mysteries. The red rose, for example, was a convenient figure for the blood of the martyrs; the twelve months could be used to represent the apostles. This kind of symbolizing can be readily seen in the Middle English *Pearl*, *Piers Plowman*, *Everyman*, and, to a certain extent, *The Canterbury Tales*. In Dante's *The Divine Comedy* (1307–1317), the most sublime poem of the Middle Ages, the poet's journey from the forest of Error through Inferno (Hell), Purgatorio (Purgatory), and Paradiso (Paradise) stands symbolically for the gradual accent of mankind to the divine presence and the seat of grace.

Medieval literature is also frequently concerned with clarifying the duties of each member in the hierarchal feudal society. The feudal king had the commanding position and expected complete allegiance and devotion from his subjects. He rewarded his followers with the lands of displaced English nobles, but these lands remained in his jurisdiction. The lords and their descendants held the estates in perpetuity so long as they furnished the king with knights, young men who were trained to fight on horseback, for his military campaigns. The lords would meet their military commitments by similarly subinfeudating, or subleasing, part of their estates to lesser nobles in return for military service. This vassalage continued down the social scale. The serfs were obligated to provide physical labour on the manor of their immediate lord in exchange for food and protections on which they lived. Each member of hierarchy, from king to serfs, thus had definite responsibilities.

Medieval literature constantly stressed the doctrine of chivalry and courtly love. Chivalry was the elegant ideal of knighthood, initially a practical means of supplying cavalrymen for the king's wars. But soon it was not enough for the true knight to be merely a capable horseman. He was expected, like the knight in *The Canterbury Tales*, to exemplify courage, piety, generosity, and above all, courtesy. In theory, chivalry was identified with virtue; later, with increasing emphasis placed upon the protection of the weak, the chivalric ideal became as compelling in peace as in war. One development conventionally associated with chivalry is the highly controversial doctrine known as courtly love. According to the rules of courtly love, true love is impossible between husband and wife, but under no circumstance is marriage to be considered an exercise for not loving. The courtly lover is required to worship at the shine of a beautiful lady, generally the wife of somebody else. After being singled out for the favours of his mistress, he must swoon, send her the appropriate gifts, and obey her every whim. Moreover, he risks anything—even his life—to defend her reputation. The passion is, by definition, adulterous, and secretly becomes imperative in the relationship; medieval romance abounds in references to "derne (secret) love", a phrase Chaucer frequently makes fun of. At one point, courtly love seems to be partially reconciled with the chivalric ideal. This kinship appears that the courtly lover is never promiscuous. He remains faithful to his one lady; she, in turn, inspires him to perform acts of courtesy on behalf of all womanhood.

Though medieval literature has some specific religious, political, and social-aesthetic ideals as mentioned above, the reader approaching it for the first time will be most impressed by its enormous diversity. There are about sixteen major literary types in the Middle English period. There is also considerable metrical variety in it. Old English verse was almost without exception unrhymed, nonstanzaic, and alliterative; Middle English poets, on the other hand, frequently utilized complicated rhyme schemes and stanza forms. Although writers, especially in the North, did not altogether abandon Old English literary conventions, they nevertheless imported French genres and prosody, and they often tried to imitate the elegance of polite French literature. Chaucer, for one period, absorbed many lessons from his study and imitation of French and Italian poetic masters. The Middle English period was one of experiment and discovery in literature.

The following is a list of the dominant types and verse forms employed by Middle English writers:

Allegory: the more or less extended use of metaphor, symbol, or personification for the purpose of communicating indirectly a hidden meaning—often a veiled personal identity, political opinion, or religious or moral doctrine.

Dream Allegory: an allegory set in the framework of a dream or vision.

Exemplum: a moralized tale that usually embellishes a sermon or homily.

Fabliau: a short, humorous, and sometimes bawdy story, usually in verse, which deals with middle- or lower-class life.

Lay: a short poem, usually a romantic narrative, intended to be sung or recited by a minstrel.

Miracle Play: a dramatization of some extraordinary power exhibited by a saint. The term, in English usage, is also applied to a play based upon the Bible scenes (e.g. *The Second Shepherds' Play*).

Morality Play: an allegorical drama in which some or all of the characters are abstractions, frequently, of particular virtues and vices who struggle for possession of the soul of man (e.g. *Everyman*).

Mystery Play: a term, in French usage, designating a play based upon the Scripture or sacred history. In English usage, however, this kind of play is more often called "miracle".

Romance: a tale of chivalric adventure, in verse or prose. Romances in verse are sometimes called "metrical romances".

Satire: a work in verse or prose, aiming to expose, and sometimes to correct, personal, social or spiritual follies or vices.

Couplet: a pair of successive lines that rhyme *aa*, *bb*, *cc*, *dd*.

Heroic Couplet: a pair of successive lines, in iambic pentameter (regularly five feet, or ten syllables), that rhyme.

Octosyllabic Couplet: a pair of successive lines, in iambic tetrameter (regularly four feet, or eight syllables), that rhyme.

Rhyme Royal: a stanza of seven iambic pentameter lines that rhyme *ababbcc*.

Terza Rima: three-line stanzas with interlocking rhyme *aba*, *bcb*, *cdc*, *ded*.

Ballade: sometimes spelled "balade" and not be confused with the folk ballads, a poem consisting of one or more three-stanza groups, each group within a given ballade usually ending with the same refrain.

Envoy: usually a half-stanza that frequently appears at the end of a ballade.

2.3 Romance and *Sir Gawain*

The most widely read and enjoyed of all literary genres employed during the Middle Ages was the romance. Within the highly palatable framework of daring deeds performed by knights in shining armor, the authors of the romances (almost all of whom were anonymous) gave expression, often in prose but still more often in verse, to some of the most cherished religious, political, and courtly ideals of the Middle English period. According to national themes, or "matters", medieval romances can be classified into several groups. The "matter of Greece and Rome", for example, deals mainly with the exploits of Alexander the Great and with the Trojan War and its aftermath, as treated by Homer and Virgil; the "matter of France" includes romances about Charlemayne and his Frankish Knights; the "matter of England" treats the careers of English and Germanic heroes of history and legend; the "matter of Britain" centers upon King Arthur and the knights of the Round Table. There are, in addition, countless other romances which do not fit into any of the major cycles. By far the most important focus of the romances, both in English literature and elsewhere, has been the mysterious, partly historical, partly mythical figure of King Arthur. King Arthur received his fullest treatment in Middle English in an important prose work by Sir Thomas Malory, published in 1485 under the title *Le Morte d'Arthur* (*The Death of Arthur*). The tales surrounding King Arthur illustrate the curious web of history and fable which entangles nearly all folk heroes. A real Arthur apparently lived during the sixth century, and he seemed to have been renowned for his valiant leadership of the Welsh in their hopeless defense of the island against the invading Anglo-Saxon. He eventually became a legend.

Sir Gawain and the Green Knight is the most enjoyable of Middle English Arthurian romances. The story begins at Camelot, King Arthur's court. On New Year's day, a figure enters the King's hall; he is gigantic in stature and green in colour. The Green Knight issues a challenge: A member of the Round Table will be permitted to strike a blow with the massive axe the Green Knight carries, but in a year's time this challenger must seek out the Green Knight and receive a blow in return. Arthur attempts the challenge, but Gawain begs for the contest to be his. He strikes his opponent's head off but the Green Knight picks up his severed head, reiterates his challenge, and departs. A year later, seeking the knight, Gawain stays at a lord's castle, and, during a further test, embarks upon an amorous relationship with his hostess. He then finds the Green Knight, who, after mocking Gawain, delivers nothing more than a light blow on Gawain's neck. The Green Knight then reveals himself as the lord of the castle. He contrives the challenge and the amorous temptation to test Gawain's integrity as a knight. Gawain passes the test in every respect except one; he has kept silent about a gift of a magical green lace belt that he receives from the lady.

There are various layers of meaning in *Sir Gawain,* but the major issue is the testing of a knight; it is a double test of Gawain's courage and honour. There is a courtly and chivalric ideal he must live up to. The tension in the story is provided by sex; it is possible that Gawain will be tempted by and yield to his hostess. And to a certain extent he is tempted. Here we can see the gap between the courtly, and literary, ideal and the reality of physical desire. It is as if mundane reality challenges the whole received structure of medieval culture. In the process, the poem explores the nature and limitations of personal integrity, culminating in the hero's acquisition of self-knowledge. In some general terms, though, the experience of the poem might be described as contest between the romance literary form, with its emphasis on elaborate courtly behavior imported along with French language, and a vernacular voice that is consistently ill at ease with his imposed narrative structure.

2.4 Popular Ballad

English literature in the fifteenth century witnessed the flourish of popular ballad. Ballad belongs to the folk literature, the literature of the common people, just as romance is the literature of the upper classes. Ballads are anonymous narrative poems designed for singing or oral recitation and composed in usually four-line stanzas, the first and the third lines having four feet each, the second and the fourth lines having three feet each and rhymes falling on the second and the fourth lines. Usually a ballad deals with a single episode and the beginning is often abrupt, without any introduction to the characters and background information. The themes of ballads are various in kind, from war and bloodshed and superstition to domestic life, particularly with the relations between different members of a family or between lovers.

The history of ballads can be dated back to the thirteenth century and they were not collected and published until much later. The best-known of the earliest collections was given by Thomas Percy (1729–1811), entitled *Reliques of Ancient English Poetry*. Among the ballads published, the Robin Hood ballads are of special significance. Robin Hood, the famous outlaw welcomed by the poor, was a half-historical and half-legendary hero. He and his men lived in the forest, fighting with the oppressors and protecting the poor and the oppressed.

2.5 Medieval Drama

The two basic types of medieval drama are the miracle plays and morality plays of the fourteenth and fifteenth centuries.

The miracle plays deal with the Christian history of the world from the Creation to the last Judgment. Each play focuses on one major event from the Bible, such as the fall of Adam and Eve or the birth of Christ, and forms part of a series or cycle of plays named after the town where they are performed: York, Chester, and Wakefield are the most important. Such plays can be seen as didactic drama intended to explain the mysteries of Christianity. Yet there is always a gap in the plays between the ideal of God's divine order and the violent, often grotesquely comic actions or the characters. For example, *The Crucifixion*, a York play, is the contrast between Christ's silent suffering and obedience to God and the noisy, bungling workmanship of the soldiers as they try to nail him to the cross.

This gap between religious ideal and worldly disorder is also present in the morality plays. Unlike the miracle plays, the morality plays focus on the moral dilemma that confronts man as he journeys from birth to death. These are allegorical plays in which both plot and character are used to illustrate an absent moral lesson. In *Everyman,* for example, the most famous of the morality plays, God instructs Death to tell the hero he must die. Everyman looks for someone to accompany him, but only Good Deeds will do so. The moral of the play is that everyone should be prepared for death and look to his/her good deeds, but what strikes us most is the sheer confusion and panic of Everyman, and how difficult religious ideals are to live up to. The same is true in *The Castle of Perseverance,* where the hero Mankind is torn between his desire for salvation and his desire for wealth and pleasure. As in Marlowe's *Dr. Faustus,* Mankind is accompanied by a good and bad angel to guide or mislead him, and indeed the whole of Elizabethan and Jacobean drama owes a lot to the morality-play tradition, especially in the figure of the Vice who underlines the presentation of such characters as Iago in Shakespeare's *Othello* (1603).

2.6 William Langland and *Piers Plowman*

William Langland, the author of *Piers Plowman*, strikes us as a writer who, working in a traditional form, looks at the world and sees things that give him serious cause for concern. *Piers Plowman,* a religious allegory in alliterative verse, is a series of extraordinary visions concerning the way in which man can attain salvation. In the opening vision, the poet William clothes himself as a hermit and falls asleep by the bank of a brook on Malvern Hillside. There he dreams of a crowd of people in a field, one that is bounded by a tower, the dwelling of truth, and by a dungeon, the house of Wrong. Every kind of person is in the field: honest, dishonest, generous, mean-spirited, and so on. A beautiful woman, who represents the Holy Church, explains certain things to the dreamer. For example, he asks her what Christ's will is, and the woman tells him to love the Lord, to do good work, and to be on guard against duplicity and guile. The poem then moves on with illustrations of corruption. He subsequently has another vision. He visions a sermon preached by conscience back in the original field. So moving is this exhortation to repentance that even the seven Deadly sins begin to confess—all but Gluttony. After the confessions, he, in his role as Everyman seeking salvation, continues with his pilgrimage to Truth with a huge mob of pilgrims. No one, however, knows where Truth lives. At this stage of the poem, Piers the Plowman makes his first appearance. He knows where Truth is and will gladly serve the pilgrims as a guide as soon as he finishes plowing his half-acre. At the end of the poem, the dreamer is preparing for the supreme encounter, but it is at this moment that he awakens from his sleep, and realizes, to his grief, that the world is as it ever has been.

Piers Plowman can be read simply as a religious allegory, but what we really encounter in the poem is Langland's problems with an increasingly complex and corrupt society. It is essentially a deeply conservative poem; shocked by what he encounters, Langland wants to reassert the value of traditional attitudes and the importance of a straightforward moral fame. But it is not the force of its religious message that impresses the reader of *Piers Plowman* so much as the sense of a tension that is conveyed: the quest for coherence in a world that no longer feels coherent. After 1250, as the Anglo-Norman hold over England slackens, there is an increasing sense of a gap between an idea of order, including religious order, and the actual state of the country; it is as if in the three elements that constitute the nation—the church, the court, and the people—the people are becoming more and more visible and assertive. *Piers Plowman* offers us a dismayed vision of the diversity of English life at this time, of a loss of moral and social direction, but also, paradoxically, by virtue of its mixture of dream vision and social protest, biblical narrative and poetic symbol, as well as its own vigorous use of English. It actually adds to this sense of diversity.

2.7 Geoffrey Chaucer (1942/43–1400)

1. Life and Career

Everything about Chaucer's life suggests someone at the heart of the established order. Chaucer was born around 1340, the son of a wealthy London wine merchant with good court connections. When young, he served in the household of Prince Lionel, the son of the King, Edward III. Subsequently, he studied law, and visited Spain on diplomatic mission. From 1367, he was an esquire to the royal household. He was with the King's army in France in 1359, and later, in 1372–1373, he was in Italy, where he might have met Petrarch and Boccaccio. He sat in Parliament, and held various appointments under Richard II. Chaucer lived his last years pretty much in obscurity, devoting the bulk of his energies to *The Canterbury Tales*. He died on October 25, 1400.

Chaucer's literary creation has been conveniently assigned to three periods: the French (1365–1372), Italian (1372–1386), and English (1386–1400) periods. Chaucer came early under the spell of French dream allegory, especially the extremely popular *The Romance of the Rose,* a long poem which was to exert a lasting influence upon his verse, and which he translated and added something of his own to. His chief work during this time is *The Book of the Duchess,* an allegorical lament written in 1369 on the death of Blanche, wife of John of Gaunts.

Then Chaucer began to look towards Italian influences. He drew heavily upon Boccaccio and Dante. The major works of the second period include *The House of Fame*, recounting the adventures of Aeneas after the fall of Troy; *The Parliament of Fowls*, which tells of the mating of fowls on St. Valentine's Day and is thought to celebrate the betrothal of Richard II to Anne of Bohemia; a prose translation of Beothius's *De Consolatione Philosophiae*. Also among the works of this period are the unfinished *Legend of Good Women*, a poem telling of nine classical heroines, which introduced the heroic couplet into English verse, and *Troilus and Criseyde,* based on Boccaccio's *Filostrato*, one of the great love poems in the English language. In *Troilus and Criseyde*, Chaucer perfected the seven-line stanza later called rhyme royal.

During the English period, to which much of *The Canterbury Tales* belongs, Chaucer broke the mould of what he inherited from earlier foreign writers, concentrated to a large extent upon contemporary English life and manners, and achieved his fullest artistic power.

Geoffrey Chaucer was the greatest English poet of the Middle Ages in that he brought into focus all the tendencies, characteristics, and ideals of the literature of the age. He was also the first of the major English writers, who would rise above the limitations of his generation and create what any future generation can understand and appreciate, that is, the universal. In Chaucer's works are represented virtually all types of Middle English literature—romance, vision, fabliau, satire, homily, saint's life, sacred and secular lyric—written both singly and in various combination. Moreover, his strong, bracing reality of touch, his amazing powers of observation, his pungent humor and pathos, and his human insight and graceful personality have appealed to all who have come to know him well. He virtually established the modern English language and the forms and development of English literature.

2. Thoughts

Despite the manifest political and social disruptions of his age, Chaucer's poetry both expresses and embodies a firm sense of order. This is true as much of his twin masterpieces, *Troilus and Criseyde* and *The Canterbury Tales*, as of his more modestly conceived "minor" poems and surviving prose works. This sense of order is evident not simply in his reflections on the nature and working of the cosmos but also in his steady affirmations of an orthodox Christian belief in divine involvement in human affairs.

Chaucer also recognized that the natural and the human worlds could be seen as interrelated in the divine scheme of things, and, like the kingdom of heaven, ordered in hierarchies. In the witty, elegantly formed *The Parliament of Fowls,* he presents a vision of birds assembled on St. Valentine's Day in order to choose their proper mates. The birds have gathered before the goddess of Nature, and in accordance with "natural" law, they pay court, dispute, and pair off in a strictly stratified way. The royal eagles, seated in the highest places, take precedence, followed in descending order by other birds of prey until we reach the humblest and smallest seed eaters. The debate in this avian parliament about how to properly secure a mate may remain unsolved, but it is clear that the nobler the bird, the more formal are the rituals of courtship accorded to it.

The question of degree, and of the social perceptions conditioned by rank, also determines the human world that Chaucer variously delineates in *The Canterbury Tales*. The General Prologue presents the pilgrims to us, as far as is feasible, according to their estate.

Despite his intellectual delight in the concept of cosmic, natural, and human order, Chaucer subverts certain received ideas of degree and utters new views. Most crucially, he effectively undermines the commonly held medieval idea of the natural inferiority of women to men by representing articulate and intelligent women at the center of human affairs rather than on the periphery. He stresses a distinctive self-assurance and dignity in women and gives his evident sympathy with women and his admiration for what he seems to have identified as feminine generosity of spirit. The wife of Bath in *The Canterbury Tales* asserts a distinctly ungentle opposition to anti-feminist stereotypes. She is certainly no model of meekness, patience, and chastity. She opens her discourse with the word "experience", and from that experience of living with five husbands she builds up a spirited case against conventional, theoretical, and clerically inspired anti-feminism. Her stridency, we realize, is a direct consequence of over-rigid patriarchal ways of thinking and acting.

3. Style

Chaucer's contemporaries and successors thought that Chaucer's finest accomplishment was his high style. The style was partly a matter of diction, with a heavy use of Latin and French borrowings and partly a matter of versification, including the elegant "rime royal" stanza, which became the standard for elegant verse in the centuries that followed. But even more important was the skilled use of the arts of a matter of "rhetoric" which was understood to be not the art of persuasion as we usually define it today, but the art of producing elegantly adorned verse. The style was suitable for writing to kings and writing about them. Other obvious marks of the high style are the elaborate rhetorical descriptions of characters, which Chaucer employed in early works like *The Book of the Duchess* and used as a kind of referential frame for some of the descriptions in the General Prologue, the use of catalogues, such as the long list of trees in *The Knight's Tale*, and a heavily Latinate diction.

Another thing that is reflected in his works is Chaucer's realistic point of view. Chaucer prefers not to take sides and does not overtly judge the characters he presents, but he allows the reader a new degree of interpretative freedom, based on the recognition of an ironic gap between how the characters see themselves and how others see them. By neutralizing and diminishing himself as a narrator, Chaucer insists that his narrative representation of others' words and narratives might shine with a greater "truth" to God's nature. To reinforce his realistic presentation, Chaucer uses the device of irony effectively. For example, a gentle irony surrounds the Nun in *The Canterbury Tales*. She is a sensual woman, one who enjoys the pleasures of the senses. Hanging from the bracelet around her wrist, there is not a cross (as the reader might expect) but a "brooch" with the motto in Latin, "Love conquers all". Love of Christ and sensual love are brought together in one very vivacious female character. Such a gentle mocking of heroic courtly values is compatible with Chaucer's religious beliefs: Perfection is the exclusive preserve of heaven; human weakness is inevitable, and the appropriate response is laughter. Chaucer's laughter is warm and generous, but actually a fairly harsh laughter is directed at anybody who might be judged to be a threat to the established order. This stance reveals that Chaucer's intention is more than just to describe the world in which he lived. Although himself conservative, he examines and wants the reader to see the changes that society is undergoing. There is a sense of shifting emphasis as older values are questioned and new rules affirmed.

In metrical skill, Chaucer stands high among the greatest English writers. He introduced the heroic couplet into English verse, and he handled the decasyllabic with a mastery which was the envy of the following century.

4. Major Works

Troilus and Criseyde, written in rhyme royal, is Chaucer's only complete long poem and his greatest sustained narrative. It has an intellectual and psychological range unprecedented in the English language and rarely equaled anywhere. It is a love story set against the background of the Trojan War. Troilus, Nestor's valiant brother, openly scoffs at love until he catches his first glimpse of Criseyde, a lovely widow who has lived in Troy under Nestor's protection ever since her father, Calchas, deserted the Trojans and joined the Greek camp. While Troilus suffers all the prescribed agonies of the courtly lover, his friend Pandarus, who is Criseyde's uncle, acts as a go-between. A series of cleverly executed moves by Pandarus finally unite the lovers. All goes well for several years until, in exchange of prisoners, Criseyde is returned to the Greek camp. Although she has pledged herself eternally to Troilus and promised to come back at the first opportunities, Criseyde soon becomes the mistress of her Greek military escort, the "sudden" Diomede who takes his pleasure where he finds it. Troilus, at last aware of the betrayal, dies in battle and ascends to the eighth sphere. From this celestial vantage point he looks down upon the world and laughs.

The story based on Boccaccio's *Il Filostruto* is originally a tale of courtly love, with the familiar complication that human sexual desire is at odds with a noble ideal. But the freshness of Chaucer's poem is to a large extent a consequence of the way in which he moves towards a sense of Troilus and Criseyde as fully developed individuals, the poem as a whole articulating an idea about the psychological realities of love with its remarkable probing of motive and insight into character. The first parts of the poem account how Criseyde, having been pressured into responding to a man's over-enthusiastic love for her, is driven from one relationship to another.

The Canterbury Tales tells the story that the premise of *The Canterbury Tales* is that pilgrims on their way to Thomas Becket's tomb at Canterbury divert themselves with the telling of tales; the twenty-four stories told constitute less than a fifth of the projected work. Each tale told is, however, a vivid exploration of the personality of the speaker, and the General Prologue also provides an often amusing reflection of the pilgrims' characters. The result is an extremely lively picture of the diverse range of people who lived in England during the late Middle Ages. The framework of the pilgrimage is a colourful cross-section of the main English social classes (there are three "estates" or groups—lords, priests and labourers, and Chaucer adds urban and professional people), but however varied the figures may be, they are united by their sense of religious purpose in life. In terms of the separate tale, each belongs to an established mode, for example, romance, exemplum, fabliau and sermon. But the stories are often told in such a vigorous manner, and so often focus on human weakness, that we are left with an overwhelming impression of the gap between polite literary forms and the rude untidiness of everyday life. This echoes the pattern in the

Chapter Two
Middle English Literature (1066-1510)

conception of the work as a whole: the gap between the religious ideal of the pilgrimage and the all-too-human reality of the pilgrims. This disparity shows us the social and religious aspirations of fourteenth-century English people and secular and religious failings that are distinctively characteristic of the English society at this time. This poem seeks to articulate the particular desires and weaknesses of the time in certain set of circumstances. However, Chaucer seems to present the weaknesses with a comic and tolerant tone, as if he is only amused, and never outraged, by human conduct.

In *The Canterbury Tales*, there is a profound sense of the importance of hierarchy, as in his other works. The knight, who tells the first story, is at the top of the social pyramid, followed by his son the Squire, and his attendant Yeoman. The knight is duly succeeded by representatives of the church: the fastidious Prioress with an accompanying Nun, personal chaplain, and three other priests; the Monk who holds the office of outrider in his monastery; the equally worldly and mercenary Friar. The third estate is represented by a greater variety of figures, rich, middling, and poor, beginning with a somewhat shifty Merchant, a bookish Oxford Clerk, a Sergeant of the Law, and a Franklin. We move downwards socially to urban guildsmen (Haberdasher, Carpenter, Weaver, Dyer, and Tapicer), to the skilled tradesmen (Cook, Shipman, Doctor of Physic), and to a well-off widow with a trade of her own (the Wife of Bath). Chaucer relegates his Parson, his Ploughman, his Manciple, and his reprobates (the Reeve, the Miller, the Summoner, and the Pardoner) to the end of his troupe (though he also modestly includes himself a high-ranking royal official, at the end of the list). It is with this last group that he seems to want to surprise his readers by contrasting paragons of virtue with those whose very calling prompts periodic falls from grace (the Reeve strikes fear into his master's tenants while feathering his own nest; the Miller steals corn and overcharges his clients; the lecherous Summoner makes parade of his limited learning; the Pardonder trades profitably in patently false relics).

In spite of the various failings, what emerges in the poem overall is a rather reassuring and essentially positive picture of the late Middle Ages. This is aided by the fact that Chaucer excludes uncomfortable evidence that might unsettle things. This was a bloody and violent period, in which no King would ever feel safe or established on the throne, but the poem offers no real sense of unrest in England. On the contrary, it does not just endorse but actually helps establish an idea of a certain kind of ordered England.

2.8 Reading

The Canterbury Tales
The General Prologue

By Geoffrey Chaucer

When the sweet showers of April fall and shoot

Down through the drought of March to pierce the root.

Bathing every rein in liquid power

From which there springs the engendering of the flower;

When also Zephyrus[1] with his sweet breath

Exhales an air in every grove and heath

Upon the tender shoots, and the young sun

His half-course in the sign of the Ram[2] has run,

And the small fowls are making melody

That sleep away the night with open eye

(so nature pricks them and their hearts engages)

Then people long to go on pilgrimages

And palmers long to seek the stranger strands[3]

Of far-off saints, hallowed in sundry[4] lands,

And especially, from every shire's end

In England, down to Canterbury they wend[5]

To seek the holy blissful martyr[6], quick

In giving help to them when they were sick.

It happened in that season that one day

In Southwark, at The Tabard[7], as I lay

Ready to go on pilgrimage and start

For Canterbury, most devout at heart,

At night there came into the hostelry

Some nine and twenty in a company

Of sundry folk happening to fall

In fellowship, and they were pilgrimage all

That towards Canterbury meant to ride.

Chapter Two
Middle English Literature (1066–1510)

The rooms and stables of the inn were wide;

They made us easy, all was of the best.

And shortly, when the sun had gone to rest,

By speaking to them all upon the trip

I was admitted to their fellowship

And promised to rise early and take the way

To Canterbury, as you heard me say.

But none the less, while I have time and space,

Before my story take a further pace,

It seems a reasonable thing to say

What their condition was, the full array[8]

Each of them, as it appeared to me.

According to profession and degree[9]

And what apparel they were riding in;

And at a Knight I therefore will begin.

Notes

1. **Zephyrus:** the Latin word for Zephre, the west wind personified.

2. **Ram:** the first sign of the Zodiac, an imaginary belt in the heavens. The Zodiac has 12 signs. The sun is supposed to enter the Ram on March the 21st and leave it on April the 20th.

3. **stranger strands:** foreign shores.

4. **sundry:** diverse, different.

5. **wend:** go.

6. **the holy blissful martyr:** referring to Thomas Becket, who, upon being Archbishop of Canterbury, resisted the efforts of Henry II to deprive the Church courts of part of their power and was murdered by the King's men. Thomas was later considered a martyr and worshiped as a saint. His tomb at Canterbury became one of the most famous shrines in England. T. S. Eliot wrote a play about him, named *Murder in the Cathedral.*

7. **The Tabard:** an inn at Southwark, a suburb of London, where the pilgrims met on their way to Canterbury.

8. **the full array:** the whole outfit, dress and appearance.

9. **degree:** social rank.

Chapter Three
Literature of Renaissance and Reformation (1510–1620)

3.1 Historical Background

At the end of the 1400s, the world changed. Two key dates can mark the beginning of modern times. In 1485, the Wars of the Roses came to an end, and following the invention of printing, William Caxton issued the first imaginative book to be published in England—Sir Thomas Mallory's retelling of the Arthurian legends as *Le Morte d'Arthur*. In 1492, Christopher Columbus's voyage to the America opened European eyes to the existence of the New World, which both geographical and spiritual, is the key to the Renaissance, the "rebirth" of learning and culture, which reached the peak in Italy in the early sixteenth century and in Britain during the reign of Queen Elizabeth I from 1558 to 1603.

England emerged from the Wars of the Roses with a new dynasty in power, the Tudors. The greatest of the Tudor monarchs was Henry VIII, whose needs for the annulment of his first marriage in order to father a son and heir to the line brought him into direct conflict with Catholic Church, and with Pope Clement VII in particular. In reaction to the Catholic Church's rulings against remarriage, Henry took a decisive step which was to influence every aspect of English life and culture from that time onwards. He ended the rule of the Catholic Church in England, closed (and largely destroyed) the monasteries, which had for centuries been the depositors of learning, history, and culture, and established himself as both the head of Church and the head of State.

The importance of this move, known as the Reformation, is huge. In a very short period of time, centuries of religious faith, attitudes and beliefs were replaced by a new way of thinking. Now, for example, the King as "Defender of the Faith", was the closest human being to God—a role previously given to the Pope in Rome. Now, England became Protestant, and the nation's political and religious identity had to be redefined. Protestantism, which had originated with Martin Luther's *95 Theses* (1517), became the official national religion. All the Catholic tenets were questioned. It was the most radical revolution in beliefs ever to affect the nation.

After the Reformation, the relationship between man and God, and consequently the place of man in the world, had to be re-examined. The humanist thinking of the Dutch philosopher Erasmus had a great influence on generations of writers whose works placed man at the center of the universe. Neo-Platonic Philosophy, from the great age of classical Greece, became dominant in the Renaissance. Its ideal of the harmony of the universe, and the perfectibility of mankind, formulated before the birth of Christianity, opened up the humanist ways of thinking.

At the same time, there occurred the growth of modern science, mathematics, and astronomy. In the fourth decade of the sixteenth century, Copernicus replaced Aristotle's system with the sun, rather than the earth, at the center of the universe. In anatomy, Harvey discovered the circulation of the blood (1628). There was a similar explosion from the start of the seventeenth century in the discovery, development and use of clocks, telescopes, thermometers, compasses, microscopes—all instruments designed to measure and investigate more closely the visible and invisible world.

Politically, it was an unsettled time. Although Henry's daughter Elizabeth I reigned for some forty-five years, there were constant threats, plots and potential rebellions against her. Protestant extremists (Puritans) were a constant presence: Many people left the country for religious reasons, in order to set up the first colony in Virginia and Pennsylvania, the beginnings of another New World. Catholic dissent (the Counter-Reformation) reached its most noted expression in Guy Fawkes's Gunpowder plot of November 5, 1605, still remembered on that day every year. And Elizabeth's one-time favourite, the Earl of Essex, led a plot against his monarch which considerably unsettled the political climate of the end of the century. However, Elizabeth's reign did give the nation some sense of stability, and a considerable sense of national and religious triumph when, in 1588, the Spanish Armada, the fleet of the Catholic King Philip of Spain, was defeated. England had sovereignty over the seas, and her seamen plundered the gold of the Spanish Empire to make their own Queen the richest and most powerful monarch on the world. With this growth in wealth and political importance of the nation, London developed in size and importance as the nation's capital, and from the foundation of the first public theater in London, the stage became the forum of debate, spectacle, and entertainment. It was the place where the writer took his work to an audience which might include the Queen herself and the lowliest of the subjects. Hand in hand with the growth in theatrical expression went the growth of Modern English as a national language.

3.2 Literary Features

Literature before the Renaissance had frequently offered ideal patterns for living which were dominated by the echoes of the church, but after the Reformation the search for individual expression and meaning took over. Institutions were questioned and re-evaluated, often while being praised at the same time. Renaissance writing explored the geography of the human soul, redefining its relationship with authority, history, science and the future. This involved experimentation with form and genre, and an enormous variety of linguistic and literary innovations in a short period of time.

Reason, rather than religion, was the driving force in this search for rules to govern human behavior in the Renaissance period. The power mystique of religion had been overthrown in one bold stroke: Where the marvelous no longer held sway, real life had to provide explanations. Man, and the use he makes of his power, capabilities, and free will, are thus the subject matter of Renaissance literature, from the early sonnets modeled on Petrarch to the English epic which closes the period, *Paradise Lost*.

The Reformation gave cultural, philosophical, and ideological impetus to English Renaissance writing. The writers in the century following the Reformation had to explore and redefine all the concerns of humanity. In a world where old assumptions were no longer valid, where scientific discoveries questioned age-old hypotheses, and where man rather than God was the central interest, it was the writers who reflected and attempted to respond to the disintegration of former certainties. For it is when the universe is out of control that it is at its most frightening and its most stimulating time. There would never again be such an atmosphere of creative tension in the country. What were created were a language, a literature, and a national and international identity.

The literature of the English Renaissance contains some of the greatest names in all world literature: Shakespeare, Marlowe, Webster, and Johnson among the dramatists; Sidney, Spenser, Donne, and Milton among the poets; Bacon, More, Nash, Raleigh, Browne, and Hooker in prose; at the center of them all is the *Authorized Version of the Bible*, published in 1611.

3.3 Renaissance Poetry

The literary form most commonly associated with the sixteenth century is the sonnet. The sonnet is a poem of fourteen lines, which in its Petrarchan form divides into an eight-line unit and a six-line unit: The "octave" develops one thought, and there is then a change of direction in the "sestet". The form was widely used by Italian poets in the late Middle Ages, usually for love poems. Wyatt and the Earl of Surrey introduced the convention into England in the early sixteenth century; the form flourished, its popularity reaching a peak in the 1590s, with sequences—a series of poems, usually dwelling on various aspects of one love affair—by Sir Philip Sidney, Samuel Daniel, Thomas Lodge, Michael Drayton and Edward Spenser. The most celebrated sequence is by Shakespeare. The central theme of the great sonnet sequences is usually the constant assertion of control, of order, but that control is always being undermined, challenged or doubted.

Though the sonnet is the form that is most typical of the Renaissance period, it is, of course, not the only form poets employed. Edmund Spenser's epic *The Faerie Queene* is regarded as the greatest poem ever since Chaucer's *The Canterbury Tales*.

3.3.1 Sir Phillip Sydney (1554–1586)

The major sonnet sequences of the Renaissance, for the most part, were written by men whose lives were conducted on the public stage, as soldiers and politicians. A key figure is Sir Philip Sidney. Sidney's sonnet sequence, *Astrophel and Stella* published in 1591, was instrumental in inspiring the numerous other sonnet sequences of the 1590s, including Shakespeare's. It consists of 108 sonnets and 11 songs, which diversify the sequence. The sonnets describe the development of the unrequited love of a star-lover (Greek: astrophel) for a distant star (Latin: Stella). The difference between the two classical tongues from which the names of the lovers are derived itself suggests the irreconcilable nature of the relationship. Stella is the ungiving beloved and the generous inspiration of poetry, the object of the poem and the provoker of it, and the dumb-founder of the giver of eloquence. However, she is also the star, "the only Planet of my light", who in Sonnet 68 seeks to quench the star-lover's "noble fire". Throughout the sequence, the "noble" concerns of a soldier and courtier intrude only to be frustrated by a woman who commands chivalric service and who exercises sometimes whimsical authority over those who willingly give her service. This sonnet sequence is typical of the love poems of the Renaissance, in which a male poet addresses a female subject; essentially, he strives to bring her under his control. But the woman remains free and elusive (hence the need to return to her in sonnet after sonnet). The issue of control and the fragility, perhaps impossibility, of control is thus always well to the fore in a love poem. It is this troubling problem that connects to larger social and political questions outside the text.

3.3.2 Edmund Spenser (1552–1599)

Edmund Spenser, the great poet of the Renaissance, started his literary career in 1569 with the translation of a number of texts, including sonnets by Petrarch. *Shepheardes Calendar*, a pastoral poem, looking back to a lost golden age, followed in 1579; significantly, it includes a panegyric to Elizabeth I, the queen of Shepherds. In 1595, he published *Amoretti*, a sonnet sequence, and *Epithalamion*, a poem celebrating Spenser's marriage to Elizabeth Boyle at Cork, in Ireland, in 1594. Then he wrote some other works such as *Colin Clouts Come Home Again*, another pastoral poem, and *A View of the Present State of Ireland*, a prose dialogue. His crowning achievement, however, was *The Faerie Queene*.

Spenser's influence on English poetry has been immense. He has been justly called "the poet's poet". Men of the most diverse gifts have admired and imitated him. He is the inventor of one of the most individual and romantic styles in literature, the chief marks of which are the meter and the vocabulary. The Spenserian stanza of nine lines, intricately rhymed and ending with an Alexandrine, was revived by Thomson and others in the eighteenth century, and has since been imitated by many great poets. Byron and Shelley both used it, each subduing its character to his own genius. But the spirit of the stanza has been more finely recaptured by two poets who were more akin in temperament to its inventor—by Keats in *The Eve of St. Agnes*, and by Tennyson at the beginning of *The Lotus-Eaters*.

Spenser, more than any other writer, is the founder of the "great diction". His practice of preserving old words has been of great service to the English poets. He also enjoys the rare distinction of having added words of his own coining to the English language. His masterpiece *The Faerie Queene* has won him a place not only in the admiration of poets but in the memory of the English people.

The Faerie Queene was intended not only to look back to a golden age of pastoral harmony but also to celebrate the court of Elizabeth, through drawing a parallel with King Arthur's legendary court. The poem absorbs and reflects a vast range of myth, legend, superstition and magic, and explores both history and contemporary politics.

The Faerie Queene is Elizabeth, seen abstractly as Glory, and appearing in various guises. In a deliberate echo of the Arthurian legends, twelve of her knights undertake a series of adventures each encountering threats to their honour and integrity, but outwitting, repelling or fighting off all such threats. The work is highly symbolic and allusive, and is inevitably episodic in its effects. "A Gentle Knight", with a red cross on his breast, is on a quest. He is Saint George, the symbolic saint of England. He had seen Gloriana (the Faerie Queene) in a vision, and would go in search of her.

> Upon a great adventure he was bond,
> That greatest Gloriana to him gave,
> That greatest Glorious Queene of Faerie Land,
> To winne him worship, and her grace to have;
> Which of all earthly things he most did crave;
> And ever as he rode, his heart did earne,
> To prove his puissance in battle brave,
> Upon his foe, and his new force to learne;
> Upon his foe, a Dragon horrible and stearne.
>
> (*The Faerie Queene*)

The knight's adventures in trying to find her would form the poem's story. The Faerie Queene has an annual twelve-day feast, on each day of which one of her courtiers leaves the court to set right a wrong. Each journey would involve a different virtue and the hero would be involved in each, while still seeking Gloriana. Thus perfection of the virtues, and the affirmation of truth are expressed through the adventures of the queen's Knights: Truth, Temperance, Chastity, Friendship, Justice and Courtesy, each representing the respective theme of the six completed books.

Spenser makes a radical attempt to relocate and reintroduce the epic form for England and the Elizabethan age by inventing the Spenserian stanza for his poem. The epic, as in *Beowulf*, celebrates the achievements of heroes or heroines of history and myth, affirming nation and values. The consistent use of the Spenserian stanza creates an interesting effect; the poem can flirt with danger, but repeatedly everything is made safe, in effect embraced in and subdued by the untroubled repetition of this soothing stanza pattern. Essentially, the Faerie Queene, aided by her loyal knights, can cope with and subdue every challenge, every hint of insurrection and every sign of danger. There is even a kind of magic about the way in which the court can maintain such a good order. This indicates that Elizabeth I, supported by numerous agents and servants of the crown, all dedicated to supporting her authority, sought to unite the country through the force of her personality and even more through the projection of an image of herself as semi-divine.

3.4 Renaissance Prose

The age of Elizabeth seems to have despised the pedestrian merits of the earlier prose. Something more brilliant was wanted. It was not enough to supply one's readers with information; they must be astonished by wit. For some time, prose-writers had been trying to make their style more sparking, when in 1579 a book appeared which seemed to do this with splendid success. This was the *Euphues* of John Lyly. The book was important not for its subject matter, but for its flowery style. It is a prose romance, but scarcely a novel. The story is of no great interest and the dialogue is far removed from real life. The characters in it are perpetually making long speeches in a style which was supposed to be the perfection of eloquence. Alliteration and antithesis are its chief ornaments. Another feature of the book is a display of obscure learning and a great parade of authorities.

Before long, Lyly's book came to be regarded as a type of all that is unnatural in literary style, and "Euphuistic" is now a name generally applied to writers of the time who thought more of eloquence than of simplicity. Most of the earlier Elizabethans affected some sort of verbal dexterity and some ingenious playing with words, which recalled the features of Lyly's style. Among them are Sir Philip Sidney, whose pastoral romance *Arcadia* exhibited a narrative sophistication much courtly Elizabethan prose fiction aspired to; Thomas Nashe, who is credited by some as having "invented" modern narrative, particularly with *The Unfortunate Traveller* (1564); Robert Greene, whose romances *The Triumph of Time* (1588) and *Menaphon* (1589) greatly influenced the developing art of story-telling in prose.

The period also saw a growth in travel writing, with the most exotic and imaginative texts heiring to the tradition established by the earlier appearance of Thomas More's *Utopia* (1516). *Utopia* sits strangely in the history of English literature—not only because More wrote it in Latin when a new confidence in the English language was evident in the strength of vernacular prose writing during the sixteenth century, but because it was the first, and for a good while the most significant entry of Greek thought of human intellect and human capabilities into an Englishman's writing. "Utopia", the name of an imaginary perfect state, is derived from the Greek and means "no place"; Hythlodaeus, the character who tells us those about Utopia, means "nonsense-peddler". The book, initially set in the semi-autonomous cities of the Netherlands, speculates about a form of government alien to most other European states of the early sixteenth century. The island which Hythlodaeus describes is a loosely decentralized Kingdom ruled by a shadowy, elected monarch who governs with the consent of a council of the great and good. Personal property, money, and vice have been effectively abolished and the root-causes of crime, ambition, and political conflict have been eliminated. It has several religions, all of them officially tolerated, and all of them dominated by the principle of a benevolent Supreme Being. Its priesthood, which includes some women, is limited in numbers because it is open only to the exceptionally pious, which means there are very few. It is a proto-welfare state in which the old are honoured and the young are taught to be conformist and respectful; dress is uniform and meals are served in communal canteens. It is a place which has abolished original sin, the prospect of redemption, and the idea of history. Nothing changes because its ideology insists that it has fulfilled all human aspirations.

Critics debate how far More's Utopia is a model for a real society or a satire on the contemporary—"anyone who committed a really shameful crime is forced to go about with gold rings on his ears and fingers". In either case, *Utopia* is an account of a journey which had enormous influence on subsequent fiction—*Robinson Crusoe* (1719), *Gulliver's Travels*, *Brave New World* (1932), *Nineteen Eighty-four* (1949), and *Lord of the Flies* (1954), to name a few—as well as on the strange mixture of fact and fantasy in Renaissance travel writing such as Hakluyt's *A Discourse Concerning the Western Planting* (1564) which, together with his other publications, helped shape and encourage the expanding role of English exploration and colonization.

Chapter Three
Literature of Renaissance and Reformation (1510–1620)

3.5 Renaissance Drama

The most important effect of Tudor Reformation on contemporary writing was in many ways the result of its increasingly secular, as opposed to devotional, emphasis. The stress on the secular is particularly evident in the prolific development of vernacular drama during the sixteenth century. The move is in part due to the work of the "university wits": Christopher Marlowe, Robert Greene, George Peeler, Thomas Nashe and Thomas Lodge, the generation educated at Oxford and Cambridge universities who used their poetry to make theater, breathed new life in classical model and brought a new audience to the issues and conflicts which the stage could dramatize.

The earliest plays of the period, in the 1550s and 1560s, established comedy and tragedy as the types of drama. Both were derived from Latin sources. The medieval miracle and mystery plays, and the kind of court "interludes" played for the monarch, also contributed to the development of Renaissance drama, whose broad humor, use of ballad, poetry, dance and music, tendency towards allegory and symbolism flowed from the native English source. Thus, although drama went through rapid changes in the period, its historical credentials were rich and varied as indeed were its range and impact. It was an age when the need for a social demonstration of an English nationalism and Protestantism climaxed in the public arena of a diverse and energetic theater. This was the golden age of English drama.

Ralph Roister Doister (1552) by Nicholas Udall and *Gorboduc* (its alternative title *The Tragedy of Ferrex and Porrox*) by Thomas Norton and Thomas Sackville are generally taken to be the first comedy and tragedy respectively. *Grammer Gurton's Needle* (1566, the author unknown) introduced a farcical element within a local domestic scenario more closely related to the daily life of the audience. What emerges in these first plays, as opposed to many direct translations from the classics, is the essential Englishness of the characters and settings, despite continuing adherence to classical models in the works of some major playwrights. *Gorboduc*, for instance, replaced the awkward distancing of the characters speaking in rhymed verse with its blank verse which became the standard form of Elizabethan and Jacobean drama.

With the appearance of these new plays, fixed theaters were established in London and while most, like the Globe, were open to the sky, a small number were completely enclosed. Alongside the development of theaters came the growth of acting culture. Plays had generally been performed by amateurs—often men from craft guilds. Towards the end of the sixteenth century, there developed companies of actors usually under the patronage of a powerful or wealthy individual. These companies encouraged playwrights to write drama which relied on ensemble playing rather than the more static set pieces associated with the classical tradition. They employed boys to play the parts of women and contributed to the development of individual performers.

The evolution of theater buildings and companies was to some degree paralleled by the rapid development of a newly expressive blank-verse tragedy. The key figures in the evolution were Thomas Kyd (1558–1594) and his close associate Christopher Marlowe. Kyd's *The Spanish Tragedy*, or, *Hieronimo Is Mad Again* (1582–1592), proved amongst the most popular and influential of all the plays of the period. It introduced a new kind of central character: an obsessive, brooding, mistrustful and alienated plotter, and it set a pattern from which a line of dramatic explorations of the theme of revenge developed. Prominent in this line of "revenge" plays are Marston's *The Malcontent* of 1604, Middleton's *The Revenger's Tragedy* of 1607, and above all, Shakespeare's *Hamlet* (1601). What particularly established the reputation of *The Spanish Tragedy* was its intermixture of dense plotting, intense action, swiftly moving dialogue, and long rhetorically shaped speeches.

Christopher Marlowe (1564–1593)

Christopher Marlowe, the first great dramatist of the Renaissance period, was born in 1564, the same year as Shakespeare. The son of a shoemaker, he was educated at King's School in Canterbury and then Corpus Christi College, Cambridge, gaining his BA degree in 1584, and then his MA in 1589. This was the traditional route for a career in teaching, the church or the law, but Marlowe turned to writing plays, producing no fewer than seven tragedies as well as the narrative poem *Hero and Leander* (1598). He died violently in 1593, in a brawl in a tavern, receiving a dagger wound above the eye, in some way connected with his homosexuality. Marlowe's plays explore the boundaries of the new world and the risks that mankind will run in the quest for power, knowledge, and love. His plays are full of spectacular action, bloodshed, and passion, to match his language of calculated exaggeration coupled with a great control of metrical pace and inventive poetic effect. All these help to determine the often startling and disconcerting quality of Marlowe's dramatic verse, verse that brought English iambic pentameter to its first maturity.

Marlowe's first great theatrical success is *Tamburlaine the Great* (1587). The play is in two parts. Part I tells the story of a Scythian shepherd chieftain (Tamburlaine) who overthrows the King of the Persians and then overcomes the Turkish emperor before going on to capture Damascus from the Sultan of Egypt. Essentially the action of the play consists of a series of conquests of the most powerful armies on earth; Tamburlaine's unbounded ambition and cruelty carry all before him. The only feeling Tamburlaine seems to show is for Zenocrate, the captive daughter of the Sultan, whom he marries. In Part II, Tamburlaine continues his conquests as far as Babylon and is only finally defeated by death. In terms of plot, the play offers little more than a sequence of brutal victories by Tamburlaine over weak rulers who do not deserve to keep power. Where interest lies, and why the play made a great impact on the Elizabethans are in Marlowe's mightily blank-verse lines that express Tamburliane's restless ambition.

As is the case with all Marlowe's heroes, Tamburlaine can be seen as a figure of Renaissance man overthrowing the old order of religion and law in order to achieve his full human potential. Closely connected with this is the idea of the overreacher: Marlowe's heroes aspire to a kind of godhead, craving divine power, but overreach themselves. Such a pattern gives the plays a tragic structure of rise and fall, and also fits in with the epic nature of Marlowe's plotting, which adds incident to incident, rather than exploring one situation in detail. This, however, is less true of *Doctor Faustus* (1592), Marlowe's most famous play.

Doctor Faustus tells the story of a man who sold his soul to the Devil for twenty-four years of power, knowledge and pleasure. At the start of the play, Faustus, tired of traditional learning and science, turns to magic, calls up the devil Mephistopheles and makes a contract with him. In return for his soul, Faustus will be given whatever he desires. The central section of the play shows Faustus enjoying his power, but not gaining the kind of knowledge of heaven and hell that he thirsts for. As time runs out—the bargain is for no more than twenty-four years—and his eternal damnation approaches, Faustus hovers between despair and belief. The play consequently seems to teach a moral lesson in the fashion of the earlier morality plays, but also questions the limits placed on human knowledge by an apparently vengeful God. The doubleness of the play is evident both in its form, which employs Good and Bad Angles to dramatize the division in Faustus's conscience, and its language, most famously in Faustus's final soliloquy:

> Oh, Faustus,
> Now hast thou but one bare hour to live,
> And then thou must be damn'd perpetually.
> Stand still, you ever-moving spheres of heaven,
> That time may cease and midnight never come!
> Fair nature's eye, rise, rise again, and make
> Perpetual day. Or let this hour be but
> A year, a month, a week, a natural day,
> That Faustus may repent and save his soul.
> Leute, leutecurrite noctis equi
> (O slowly, slowly, horses of the night)
> The stars move still, time runs, the clock will strike.
> The devil will come, and Faustus must be damn'd,
> O, I'll leap up to my God; who pulls me down?
> See, see, where Christ's blood streams in the firmament,
> One drop would save my soul, half a drop. Ah, my Christ!
>
> (*Doctor Faustus*)

Here Faustus both clings to his cleverness by quoting an amorous line from Ovid (run slowly, slowly, horses of the night) and desperately attempts to reverse his old dismissal of the scheme of salvation and to claim Christ for his own. Yet still, neither will his arrogance admit true repentance nor will his intellect fully accept service to the God he has so spectacularly rejected.

Marlowe's other significant works are *The Jew of Malta* and *Edward II* (1590). The former is another story of an overreacher who glories in the kind of illicit manipulation and fails by his miscalculation, and the latter examines sexual choice and preference in relation to the question of authority, power, and love, thus making Marlowe one of the first major writers to affirm a clearly homosexual sensibility.

Throughout Marlowe's plays, there is a sense of new world being explored, where human knowledge aspires to new heights, but also a sense of limits and boundaries. In that

Chapter Three
Literature of Renaissance and Reformation (1510–1620)

combination of elements, Marlowe's plays reflect the changing world of the early modern world. What Marlowe's plays particularly illustrate is the force of language itself in shaping and altering the world, as he questions the fixed hierarchies of the old and opens up new perspectives. At the same time, however, his plays acknowledge the continuing power of the established regime: Faustus is damned, Tamburlaine dies, and Edward II is tortured to death for permitting his homosexuality to conflict with the role that he is expected to play as the King. In the stress they place on death and violence, Marlowe's plays expose the fear that helped maintain the old order in power despite the subversive forces that were raised against it.

3.6 William Shakespeare (1564–1616)

1. Life and Career

William Shakespeare was born in Stratford-upon-Avon, a small but important market town, on April 23, 1564, the third of a family of eight children. His father was a well-to-do merchant and leading citizen in the town who had repeatedly served as a member of the town council and had held almost all the important town offices at one time or another. Shakespeare got married to Anne Hathaway when he was a little more than eighteen, and his wife, a yeoman's daughter, eight years his senior. They had three children, Susanna, Hamnett, and Judith. Shakespeare left Stratford for London in about 1585. He perhaps began his connection with the theater as a horse-holder, and before long became an actor, and a refurbisher of old plays to one of several London companies. But by 1592, his success was such that a contemporary, Robert Greene, one of the best known of the university men, wrote to his colleagues jealously denouncing the upstart crow, beautified with our feature. In 1593, appeared his first work, the remarkable *Venus and Adonis* (1590), and the next year the rather less remarkable *Lucrece*. He was connected soon with diverse theaters, became a shareholder in them and by 1597 could buy a good house, new place at Stratford, where he afterwards enlarged his property. He died on April 23, 1616.

Shakespeare's dramatic career extended from about 1590 to 1613. In the space of those twenty-three years he passed through early phase of artistic development. He began as an immature young man, with some knowledge of the theater and little power to interpret life, and scarcely any literary style. Within four years he was producing masterpieces, foil of poetry and passion. Two years more, he reached maturity. Henceforth, his work, through changing year by year, shows that close grasp of life which belongs to a man at the height of his powers. Altogether, Shakespeare wrote 37 plays, 154 sonnets, and a comparatively small number of longer poems. He wrote all these while working with his theater company and frequently performing with them. In terms of dramatic creation, his literary career can be divided into three periods: the early period of comedies and histories, the middle period of tragedies, and the late period of tragic-comedies.

The starting point of Shakespeare's writing career was English history. Shakespeare's principal history plays deal with a line of English monarchy from Richard II through to the defeat of Richard III by Henry VII, the first Tudor monarch. The period covered is the century up to 1485, the last thirty years of which were dominated by the Wars of the Roses. They explored divisions, depositions, usurpations, and civil wars, but they also bolstered the corruption of the secure monarchic government propagated by officially approved apologists for the Tudor dynasty. Besides the glorification of the nation and its past, Shakespeare's histories also examine the qualities which make a man a hero, a leader, and a king. This is a process not of hero-worship, but of humanizing the hero. The king is brought close to his people. His virtues and faults are brought to life beyond the audience's eyes. Literature is no longer distant, no longer the preserve only of those who can read. It is familiar history enacted close to the real life of the people it concerns.

Henry VI is portrayed as weak, indecisive, in complete contrast to the heroic young Henry V. The audience can follow this prince in his progress from the rumbustious, carefree Prince Hal to the most mature, responsible hero who wins the battle of Agincourt, but who becomes tongue-tied when he tries to woo the princess of France. This balance between the role of king and the role of man becomes one of Shakespeare's main concerns. Richard III is portrayed as a complete villain. But, as a theatrical character, this villain becomes a fascinating hero. Like Marlowe's heroes, he overreaches himself, and his fall becomes a moral lesson in the single-minded pursuit of power. This idea that the King, the nearest man to God, could be evil, and a negative influence on the nation, was a new and dangerous idea in the political context of England in the 1590s. It raises the frightening possibility that the people might want or, indeed, have the right to remove and replace their ruler. This idea comes to the fore not only in his histories such as *Richard III* (1591), but in his tragedies like

Chapter Three
Literature of Renaissance and Reformation (1510–1620)

Hamlet, *Macbeth* (1606) and *King Lear* (1605).

Shakespeare wrote ten historical plays, consisting of two sequences [the three parts of *Henry VI* (1623) and *Richard III*; *Richard II* (1597), the two parts of *Henry IV* (1597–1598) and *Henry V* (1598–1599)], and the isolated *King John* and *Henry VIII*.

Henry IV (Part 1 and Part 2) is Shakespeare's most important historical play. The subject of Part 1 is the rebellion of the Percys, assisted by Douglas and in concert with Mortimer and Glendower; its defeat by the King and Prince Hal, the Prince of Wales, at Shrewsbury (1403). Falstaff (one of Shakespeare's well-known clowns) first appears in this play. The Prince of Wales associates with him and his boon companions, Poins, Bardolph, and Pero, in their riotous life. Poins and the prince contrive that the others shall set on some travellers at Gadshill and rob them, and be robbed in their turn by themselves. The plot succeeds, and leads to Falstaff's well-known fabrication to explain the loss of the booty, and his exposure. At the battle of Shrewsbury, Prince Hal kills Hotspur in a heroic single combat, and then discovers Falstaff feigning death, whom he mourns with the words, "I could have better spar'd a better man."

Part 2 deals with the rebellion of Archbishop Scroop, Mowbray, and Hastings; while in the comic under-plot, the story of Falstaff's doings is continued, with those of the Prince, Pistol, Poins, Mistress Quickly, and Doll Tearsheet. Falstaff, summoned to the army for the repression of the rebellion, falls in with Justices Shallow and Silence in the course of his recruiting, makes a butt of them, and extracts £1,000 from the former. Henry IV dies, reconciled to his son, and Falstaff hastens from Gloucestershire to London to greet the newly crowned who rejects him in the speech beginning "I know thee not, old man. Fall to thy prayers", banishing him from his presence but allowing him "competence of life".

Henry V opens with the newly ascended Henry astonishing clergy and courtiers by his piety and statecraft (cf. Prince Hal). The archbishop of Canterbury demonstrates, in the long "Salic Law" speech, Henry's claim to the throne of France, and the Dauphin's jesting gift of tennis balls gives him an immediate pretext for invasion. Henry unmasks the three traitors, Scrope, Grey, and Cambridge, and sets out for France; he besieges and captures Harfleur, and achieves a resounding victory at Agincourt (1415), a battle for which he prepares his soldiers in the "Crispin Crispian" speech. Comic relief is provided by the old tavern companions of Falstaff who have fallen on hard times, and by some of Henry's soldiers, especially the pedantic but courageous Welsh captain Fluellen. The new, patriotic, comic characters symbolically defeat the old when Fluellen compels the braggart Pistol to eat a leek. The last act is given to Henry's wooing of Katherine of France.

2. Comedies

Shakespeare's period of great comedies begins with *The Merchant of Venice* (1596–1597), written in about 1597. He had already produced *All's Well That Ends Well* (1604–1605) and *The Taming of the Shrew* (1590–1600), and he had degraded Falstaff from a great comic figure into buffoon in *The Merry Wives of Windsor* (1602), written, it is said, at the request of Queen Elizabeth I, who desired to see "the fat knight in love". None of these three plays deserves to rank with *The Merchant of Venice*, or with the works which immediately followed it: *Much Ado About Nothing* (1598–1599), *As You Like It* (1598–1600), and *Twelfth Night* (1600–1602). These plays have certain features in common, and it seems natural to group them together as "romantic comedies".

A light atmosphere of unreality hovers over these plays. Shakespeare makes us laugh and sigh over the follies of mischances of men, but it is not his design that we should be deeply stirred. We are never quite in the real world, though we are never far away from it. The plot is often ludicrously improbable. A wooer wins a bride by choosing from a number of caskets marked with different inscriptions; a merchant borrows a sum of money on the security of a pound of his own flesh; a lady is driven from her uncle, and wanders off into a forest, accompanied by her cousin, in disguise. By a series of almost imperceptible touches, the playwright dispels much of our disbelief, and as the web of circumstance becomes more and more entangled, an old legend or a romantic intrigue affects us with half the seriousness of real life. The fanciful events take place in scenes as fanciful. Therefore, we can see the cheerful disclaimer of any serious intention in Shakespeare's comedies is something of a trap. In creating these lighthearted fantasies, Shakespeare seems to have a double purpose. On the one hand, certainly, he is insisting that art is art because it is not life, and that, as Touchstone said, "the truest poetry is the most feigning." On the other hand, Shakespeare knows that even his lightest comedies are images of life, and not least in suggesting the flimsiness, the insecurity, the evanescence of what we assume to be the firmer realities of our everyday lives. In emphasizing the insubstantiality of the plays, he hinds at the insubstantiality of our lives. It is not only art that can seem "an improbable fiction".

But the primary function of Shakespeare's comedies is to entertain the audience, to "take them out themselves", to perform the therapy of dissolving the cares of "this working day world" into "holiday foolery", and to use the words of *As You Like it*. Yet laughter alone is not enough to make the healing power of comedy work; laughter has to be generated within the action that moves the characters from discord, separation, and unhappiness to peace, unity, and concord. Most of the comedies begin with a strong scene of loss or enmity. In *As You Like It*, brother's hand is against brother; in *A Midsummer Night's Dream* (1600), Hermia is being forced to marry a man she hates. In some of the comedies, there is an escape from the initial unhappiness into a never-never land, a place of confusion, bewilderment, and transformation where difficulties eventually melt away. Other plays dispense with the symbolic change of location but this insists on confusion as an intervening state between misery and happiness. By presenting the movement of the characters from pain through confusion to pleasure, the plays manage to make their comment on the mystery of an uncontrollable and unpredictable future.

Shakespeare's comedies are usually connected with the pursuit of love. There is love between the sexes, love between members of a family, and love between friendship of the same sex. The quest in *The Comedy of Errors* (1623) is for the reintegration of a divided family. There are some striking hymns to friendship in his last plays, but the earlier comedies also contain many gestures indicating the strength and the rights of friendship, particularly in the figures of the two Antonios, one in *The Merchant of Venice* and the other in *Twelfth Night*, with their friendships for Bassanio and Sebastian. In *As You Like It*, the lovesick Rosalind, in the liberation of her disguise as a young man, mocks everything that lovers hold sacred—particularly the depth and the permanence of the emotions which seem all-in-all to them. But, resuming her own person, she can only say, "O coz, coz, coz... that thou didst know how many fathom deep I am in love!" Sexual love in the comedies is an irrational and inexplicable compulsion, as destructive as it is bountiful. In men in particular, desire is unstable and shifting. Women are more constant and true in their affection.

Much of the laughter of the comedies lies within the temporary transformations of the characters. New identities are acquired by disguise or are foisted on to a character by the spell of an inefficient Puck or mistakes in recognition. Great gifts can come from the grafting of these new identities, as Sebastian found when he was swept off to church to marry Olivia.

But not all are so lucky. In *The Taming of the Shrew*, Petruchio's psychological warfare makes life a nightmare for Katherina, and while in *Twelfth Night*, Sebastian is marveling at his new existence. Malvolio is in despair, fooled into believing he is loved by Olivia, then locked away and taunted as a madman. The good and bad deceptions help us to see that the abounding insecurity of personality in the comedies is not too far distant from the insecurity of the characters of tragedy who suddenly find that the ground they stand on has begun to shift beneath their feet. If there is a lesson in the comedies apart from the lesson that laughter is a great blessing, it is a lesson teaching us that the self which always seeks its completeness through love of others is an unfixed, indefinite, and wandering thing. The comedies suggest that we are all very tentative as persons, ready enough to try to alter the lives of others but with precious little control over ourselves or our destinies.

The structure of a Shakespearean comedy is a harmony of seemingly incompatible voices. *A Midsummer Night's Dream* is famous for its polyphonic construction. Scene by scene the different elements are introduced: the seas, the Athenian court, the young lovers, the stage-struck workingmen, and the fairy creatures of the forest. In *As You Like It*, the ponderous satire of the non-joiner Jacques chimes with and clarifies the wittier tones of Rosalind and Touchstone. Every play is a complex pattern of contrasts. The playwright's task is to keep us from attending too much to the darker elements. If there is a villain in the piece, our thoughts are not allowed to dwell on his villainy. In *Much Ado About Nothing*, the crime of Don John and Borachio even contributes to the general harmony, for it is the means of bringing the love between Beatrice and Benedick to a head. Tragedy is often in the air, but it is held in suspense by the equilibrium of forces.

In *The Merchant of Venice*, Bassanio, a noble but poor Venetian, asks his friend Antonio, a rich merchant, for 3,000 ducats to enable him to prosecute fittingly his suit of the rich heiress Portia at Belmont. Antonio, whose money is all employed in foreign ventures, undertakes to borrow the sum from Shylock, a Jewish usurer, whom he has been wont to upbraid for his extortions. Shylock consents to lend the money against a bond by which, if the sum is not repaid on the appointed day, Antonio shall forfeit a pound of flesh. By her father's will, Portia is to marry that suitor who selects of three caskets (one of gold, one of silver, one of lead) that which contains her portrait. Bassanio makes the right choice—the leaden casket—and is wedded to Portia and his friend Gratiano to her maid Nerissa. News comes that Antonio's ships have been wrecked, that the debt has not been repaid when due, and that Shylock claims his pound of flesh. The matter is brought before the duke. Portia disguises herself as an advocate, Balthazar, and Nerissa as her clerk, and they come to the court to defend Antonio, unknown to their husbands. Failing in her appeal to Shylock for mercy, Portia admits the validity of his claim, but warns him that his life is forfeit if he spills one drop of blood, since his bond gives him right to nothing beyond the flesh. Pursuing her advantage, she argues that Shylock's life is forfeit for having conspired against the life of a Venetian citizen. The duke grants Shylock his life, but gives half his wealth to Antonio, half to the State. Antonio surrenders his claim if Shylock will turn Christian and make over his property on his death to his daughter Jessica, who has run away and married a Christian and been disinherited, to which Shylock agrees. Portia and Nerissa ask as rewards from Bassanio and Gratiano the rings that their wives have given them, which they have promised never to part with. Reluctantly they give them up, and are taken to task accordingly on their returning home. The play ends with news of the safe arrival of Antonio's ships.

Through the clash between Antonio and Shylock, the play shows the conflict between friendship, love, greed and cruelty. In it, Shakespeare praises the friendship between Antonio and Bassanio, the love between Bassanio and Portia, idealizes Portia as a heroine of beauty, wit, and loyalty, and exposes Shylock's greed and cruelty. Many people today tend to regard the play as a satire of the Christian's hypocrisy and love, their cunning ways of pursuing worldliness and their unreasoning prejudice against Jews.

Twelfth Night (or *What You Will*) is the story that Sebastian and Viola, twin brother and sister and closely resembling one another, are separated during a shipwreck off the coast of Illyria. Viola, brought to shore in a boat, disguises herself as a youth, Cesario, and takes service as page with Duke Orsino, who is in love with the lady Olivia. She rejects the duke's suit and will not meet him. Orsino makes a confidant of Cesario, and sends her to plead his cause on Olivia, much to the distress of Cesario who has fallen in love with Orsino. Olivia in turn falls in love with Cesario. Sebastian and Antonio, captain of the ship that has rescued Sebastian, now arrive in Illyria. Cesario, challenged to a duel by Sir Andrew Aguecheek, a rejected suitor of Olivia, is rescued from her predicament by Antonio, who takes her for Sebastian. Olivia, coming upon the true Sebastian, mistakes him for Cesario, invites him to her house, and marries him out of hand. Orsino comes to visit Olivia. Antonio, brought before him, claims

Cesario as the youth he rescued from the sea while Olivia claims Cesario as her husband. The duke, deeply wounded, is bidding farewell to Olivia and the "dissembling cub" Cesario, when the arrival of the true Sebastian clears up the confusion. The duke, having lost Olivia and becoming conscious of the love that Viola has betrayed, turns his affection to her, and they are married.

Much of the play's comedy comes from the sub-plot dealing with the members of Olivia's household: Sir Toby Belch, her uncle; Sir Andrew Aguecheek, his friend; Malvolio, her pompous steward; Maria, her waiting-gentlewoman, and her clown Feste. Exasperated by Malvolio's officiousness, the other members of the household make him believe that Olivia is in love with him and that he must return her affection. In courting her, he behaves so outrageously that he is imprisoned as a madman. Olivia has him released and the joke against him is explained, but he is not amused by it, threatening, "I'll be revenged on the whole pack of you".

The play's gentle melancholy and lyrical atmosphere are captured in Feste's beautiful song "Come away, come away, death".

In *A Midsummer Night's Dream*, Hermia, ordered by her father Egeus to marry Demetrius, refuses, because she loves Lysander, while Demetrius has formerly professed love for her friend Helena, and Helena loves Demetrius. Under the law of Athens, Theseus, the duke, gives Hermia four days in which to obey her father or else she must suffer death or enter a nunnery. Hermia and Lysander agree to leave Athens secretly in order to be married where the Athenian law cannot pursue them, and to meet in a wood a few miles from the city. Hermia tells Helena of the project and the latter tells Demetrius. Demetrius pursues Hermia to the wood, and Helena follows Demetrius, so that all four are that night in the wood. This wood is the favourite haunt of the fairies.

Oberon and Titania, the King and the Queen of the fairies, have quarrelled, because Titania refuses to give up to him a little changeling boy for a page. Oberon tells Puck, a mischievous sprite, to fetch him a certain magic flower, of which he will press the juice on the eyes of Titania while she sleeps, so that she may fall in love with what she first sees when she wakes. Overhearing Demetrius in the wood reproaching Helena for following him, and desirous to reconcile them, Oberon orders Puck to place some of the love-juice on Demetrius's eyes, so that Helena shall be near him when he does it. Puck, mistaking Lysander for Demetrius, applies the charm to him, and as Helena is the first person Lysander sees, he at once woos her, enraging her because she thinks she is being made a jest of. Oberon, discovering Puck's mistake, now places some of the juice on Demetrius's eyes; he on waking also first sees Helena, so that both Lysander and Demetrius are now wooing her. The ladies begin to abuse one another and the men go off to fight for Helena.

Meanwhile Oberon has placed the love-juice on Titania's eyelids, who wakes to find Bottom the weaver near her, wearing an ass's head (Bottom and a company of Athenian tradesmen are in the wood to rehearse a play for the duke's wedding, and Puck has put an ass's head on Bottom); Titania at once becomes enamored of him, and toys with his "amiable cheeks" and "fair large ears". Oberon, finding them together, reproaches Titania for bestowing her love on an ass, and again demands the changeling boy, whom she in her confusion surrenders; whereupon Oberon releases her from the charm, Puck at Oberon's orders throws a thick fog about the human lovers, and brings them all together, unknown to one another, and they fall asleep. He applies a remedy to their eyes, so that when they awake they return to their former lovers. Theseus and Egeus appear on the scene, the runaways are forgiven, and the couples get married. The play ends with the "play" of "Pyramus and Thisbe", comically acted by Bottom and his fellow tradesmen, to grace these nuptials and those of Theseus and Hippolyta.

3. Tragedies

Shakespeare's greatest tragedies were written between 1601 and 1609. The first of the series is *Julius Caesar* (1599–1601). The tragedies differ from the plays which precede them in that the atmosphere of make-believe which hangs over the comedies is dispelled and we look down upon the real world of men. In each tragedy, the action revolves round matters of deep and lasting importance, especially the contemporary political concerns. *Hamlet*, a play directing intense light on the recesses of personality, is all the same a play about the state of Denmark, its government and its relation with neighbouring states. *King Lear* has the political stability of England at its center. *Macbeth* is concerned with rebellion, civil war, foreign invasion, and usurpation.

Thematically, Shakespeare's tragedies fall into several groups. We might begin with revenge, a major issue in his greatest play *Hamlet*, and a much inferior one *Titus Andronicus*. To Shakespeare, the nerve-center of the revenge play is not the thrill of vindictiveness but the trauma of trying to obtain justice in an unjust and indifferent society. This is true in *Hamlet*.

To Hamlet, totally alienated from Danish society, the voice of the Ghost asking for revenge gives meaning to a life that has lost all meaning. His conception of his mission extends beyond killing Claudius to cleansing of Denmark, and includes what was specifically forbidden by the Ghost, the moral rescue of his mother. Disabling doubts about the authenticity of the Ghost, and about the value of any act (in the "To be or not to be" soliloquy), alternate with the exultation of conviction, and the impulsiveness of the sword-thrust that killed the wrong man, Polonius. So Hamlet becomes the object of a counter-revenge, Laertes seeking requital for the murder of his father. By the last act of the play, Hamlet is utterly convinced of the rightness of his cause and the necessity of killing Claudius, whom he describes as a cancer in society. But it is too late; Laertes wounds him fatally before he at last kills the King. The Denmark that he had sought to preserve from the odious Claudius passes into the hands of the foreigner Fortinbras. Hamlet ends in both victory and failure.

Another theme in the tragedies is love, which is the inspiration of four plays: *Romeo and Juliet* (1595), *Troilus and Cressida* (1609), *Othello*, and *Antony and Cleopatra* (1607). In each of the plays, everything is staked upon a love relationship which to a greater or lesser extent is unpalatable to society; in each play, the love fails to abide and ends disastrously.

Romeo and Juliet is Shakespeare's love tragedy of youth. To Juliet, a girl of fourteen, hedged around by nurse and parents and a family feud, comes the liberation of first love. The poet moves forward by a simple mechanism of ironic reversals which are responsible for the tragic outcome. Romeo's love for a Capulet leads to his killing Juliet's cousin; the Friar's good offices for the lovers lead to the tragic mistiming at the tomb. Yet the young lovers are not victim of coincidence and bad luck, but of the feudal society governed by their elders and betters. "Catharsis" there is in *Romeo and Juliet* in our feeling that the lovers, completing their union in death as they could not complete it in life, are at least safe, and in our feeling that such love as theirs, passionate and sexual though it was, was a dedication to a higher scale of values than obtained in the violent commerce of the worldly society they lived in.

This must surely be the case in *Othello* too. To the wealthy citizens of Venice, epitomized in Desdemona's father, Othello is a totally undesirable match; it is against "all rules of native" for her to fall in love with a black man. Yet she knows him, approves him and loves him. For Othello, her love, after a career of soldiering, is a miracle of happiness. But Iago was born to oppose happiness. The strength of the love between Othello and Desdemona is an offence to him. He cannot corrupt Desdemona, but he can corrupt Othello into misconceiving her very goodness. So comes the painful scene in which Iago begins his work, crumbling Othello's confidence in his wife's chastity and fidelity and stirring up that unappeasable jealousy which ends in his killing a totally innocent woman. Iago's attack is a manifestation of evil that almost cannot be withstood. At any rate, Desdemona's dedication of herself is cruelly betrayed.

Besides the tragic heroes' commitment to revenge and to love, there is another type of commitment to a political violence, and this brings together two very different plays in which the hero assassinates the ruler of the state: *Julius Caesar* and *Macbeth*.

In *Macbeth*, the hero aims at the heart of existing society, intending to change that society by killing the governor. Macbeth and his wife share in a guilty fantasy of becoming the King and the Queen of Scotland. He is a hardened loyal soldier, capable of the bloody suppression of rebels, who is a prey to these strange imaginings, which seem to torment him as much as they give him pleasure. When the weird sisters on the heath hail him as the future King, they have pierced to the secret life of his thoughts. Tempted by the prophecy of the witches and taunted by his wife, Macbeth turns his vivid dream of majesty into reality by murdering the King, Duncan. He is in a state of horror before, during, and after the murder. The man whose very experience was made doubly alive by the workings of a powerful imagination now finds only deadness in both imagination and reality.

Shakespeare's tragedies are also concerned with displacement, such as the conflict between the generations in a terrible warfare in *King Lear*. King Lear proposes to divide his kingdom among his three daughters and retire from a long life of ruling, looking forward in particular to finding rest in the "kind nursery" of his beloved Cordelia. The play shows us the painful process of the collapse of the hero's world, and of the self that fitted that world, and the equally painful process of learning a new identity. In some other tragedies, especially *Antony and Cleopatra,* the tussle of older person to hold on and assert his right to exist is fused with the movement of history. New epochs are coming into being, brashly ousting a more cultivated and humane but incompetent past.

Hamlet (or *Prince of Denmark*) tells the story that Old Hamlet, the King of Denmark, is recently dead, and his brother Claudius has assumed the throne and married his widow Gertrude. Young Hamlet, returning from university at Wittenberg, learns from the ghost of his father that Claudius has murdered him by pouring poison into his ear, and is commanded to avenge the murder without injuring Gertrude. Hamlet warns his friend Horatio and the guard (who have also seen the apparition) that he intends to feign madness, and swears them to secrecy. Immediately after his famous speech of deliberation beginning "To be, or not to be", he repudiates Ophelia, whom he has loved, while spied on by Claudius and by Ophelia's father Polonius. He welcomes a troupe of visiting players, and arranges a performance of a play ("the Mousetrap") about fratricide, which Claudius breaks off in apparently guilty and fearful fury, when the player Lucianus appears to murder his uncle by pouring poison into his ear. Hamlet refrains from killing Claudius while he is at prayer, but stabs through the arras in his mother's bedroom, killing the old counselor Polonius, before reprimanding his mother for her affection for Claudius. Claudius sends Hamlet to England with sealed orders that he should be killed on arrival. Hamlet outwits him, however, returning to Denmark, having arranged the death of his old friends Rosencrantz and Guildenstern, who were his uncle's agents. During Hamlet's absence Ophelia has gone mad with grief from Hamlet's rejection of her and her father's death, and is found drowned. Her brother Laertes returns from France intent on avenging his sister's death. Hamlet and Laertes meet in the graveyard where Ophelia is to be buried, and fight in her grave. Claudius arranges a fencing match between Hamlet and Laertes, giving the latter a poisoned foil; an exchange of weapons results in the deaths of both combatants, not before Gertrude has drunk a poisoned cup intended for her son, and the dying Hamlet has succeeded in killing Claudius. Fortinbras, prince of Norway, whose resolute military heroism has been alluded to throughout the play, appears fresh from wars with Poland and gives Hamlet a military funeral.

The first act of *Othello* is set in Venice. Desdemona, the daughter of Brabantio, a Venetian senator, has secretly married Othello, a Moor in the service of the state. Accused before the duke and senators of having stolen Brabantio's daughter, Othello explains and justifies his conduct, and is asked by the Senate to lead the Venetian forces against the Turks who are about to attack Cyprus.

In the middle of a storm which disperses the Turkish fleet, Othello lands on Cyprus with Desdemona, Cassio, a young Florence, who helped him court his wife and whom he has now promoted to be his lieutenant, and Iago, an old soldier, bitterly resentful of being passed over for promotion, who now plans his revenge. Iago uses Roderigo, "a gull'd Gentleman" in love with Desdemona, to fight with Cassio after he has got him drunk, so that Othello deprives him of his new rank. He then persuades Cassio to ask Desdemona to plead in his favour with Othello, which she warmly does. At the same time, he suggests to Othello that Cassio is, and has been, Desdemona's lover, finally arranging through his wife Emilia, who is Desdemona's waiting-woman, and that Othello should see Cassio in possession of a handkerchief which he has given to his bride. Othello is taken in by Iago's promptings and in frenzied jealousy smothers Desdemona in her bed. Iago sets Roderigo to murder Cassio, but when Roderigo fails to do this, Iago kills him and Emilia as well, after she has proved Desdemona's innocence to Othello. Emilia's evidence and letters found on Roderigo prove Iago's guilt; he is arrested, and Othello, having tried to stab him, kills himself.

In *King Lear*, Lear, the King of Britain, a petulant and unwise old man, has three daughters: Goneril, wife of the duke of Albany; Regan, wife of the duke of Cornwall; Cordelia, for whom the King of France and duke of Burgundy are suitors. Intending to divide his kingdom among his daughters according to their affection for him, he bids them say who loves him most. Goneril and Regan make profession of extreme affection, and each receives one-third of the kingdom. Cordelia, self-willed and disgusted with their hollow flattery, says she loves him according to her duty, neither more nor less. Infuriated with this reply, Lear divides her portion between her other daughters, with the condition that himself with 100 knights shall be maintained by each daughter in turn. Burgundy withdraws his suit for Cordelia, and the King of France accepts her without dowry. The earl of Kent, taking her part, is banished. Goneril and Regan reveal their heartless character by grudging their father the maintenance that he had stipulated for, and finally turning him out of doors in a storm. The earl of Gloucester shows pity for the old King, and is suspected of complicity with the French, who have landed in England. His eyes are put out by Cornwall, who receives a death-wound in the affray. Gloucester's son Edgar, who has been traduced to his father by his bastard brother Edmund, takes the disguise of a lunatic beggar, and tends his father till the latter's death. Lear, whom rage and ill treatment have deprived of his wits, is conveyed to Dover by the faithful Kent in disguise, where Cordelia receives him. Meanwhile, Goneril and Regan have both turned their affections to Edmund. Embittered by this rivalry, Goneril poisons Regan, and takes her own life. The English forces under Edmund and Albany defeat the French, and Lear and Cordelia are imprisoned; by Edmund's order Cordelia is hanged, and Lear dies from grief. The treachery of Edmund is proved by his brother Edgar. Albany, who has not abetted Goneril in her cruel treatment of Lear, takes over the kingdom.

Macbeth tells the story that Macbeth and Banquo, generals of Duncan, the King of Scotland, returning from a victorious campaign against rebels, encounter three weird sisters, or witches, upon a heath, who prophesy that Macbeth shall be the thane of Cawdor, and the King hereafter, and that Banquo shall beget kings though he is none. Immediately afterwards comes the news that the King had created Macbeth thane of Cawdor. Stimulated by the prophecy, and spurred on by Lady Macbeth, Macbeth murders Duncan, who is on a visit to his castle. Duncan's sons, Malcolm and Donalbain, escape, and Macbeth assumes the crown. To defeat the prophecy of the witches regarding Banquo, he orders the murder of Banquo and his son Fleance, but the latter escapes. Haunted by the ghost of Banquo, Macbeth consults the weird sisters, and is told to beware of Macduff, the thane of Fife; that none born of woman has power to harm Macbeth, and that he will never be vanquished till Birnam wood shall come to Dunsinane. Learning that Macduff has joined Malcolm, who is gathering an army in England, he surprises the castle of Macduff and causes Lady Macduff and her children to be slaughtered. Lady Macbeth goes mad and dies. The army of Malcolm and Macduff attacks Macbeth; passing through Birnam wood, every man cuts a bough and under these "heavy screen" marches on Dunsinane. Macduff who was "from his mother's womb/ Untimely ripp'd", kills Macbeth. Malcolm is hailed as the King of Scotland.

4. Tragic-comedies

Shakespeare's final plays move against the tide of most Jacobean theater, which was concentrating on blood tragedy or social comedy. After the tragedies of *Coriolanus* (1623) and *Antony and Cleopatra*, and the sheer misanthropy of *Timon of Athens* (1607–1608), there is a change of tone, a new optimism. Prose writing about voyages across the sea and faraway places has created a vogue for romances. His late plays—*Pericles* (1609), *The Winter's Tale* (1623), *Cymbeline* (1623), and *The Tempest* (1623)—have been variously described as pastorals, romances, and even tragic-comedies. They all end in harmony, and use the passage of time (usually a whole generation) to heal the disharmony with which the plays open. They echo the structure of the masque form which was then popular at court: anti-masque or negative elements being defeated by positive elements, and a final harmony achieved. A "brave new world", as Miranda describes it in *The Tempest* (the best of the late plays), is created out of the turbulence of the old.

Chapter Three
Literature of Renaissance and Reformation (1510-1620)

In *The Tempest*, Prospero's domination of the native Caliban has been interpreted by some critics as having overtones of colonialism, which reflects the period's interest in voyages and in the new colonial experiments in Virginia and elsewhere. This is the beginning of a theme which will grow considerably in importance in literature at the end of the century and on to the international recognition of colonial voices in literature in modern times. *The Tempest* is Shakespeare's farewell to his art.

5. Sonnets

If Shakespeare had not become the best-known dramatist in English, he would still be remembered as a great poet. His longer poems, such as *Venus and Adonis* and *The Rape of Lucrece* (1594), are classically inspired narratives. *Venus and Adonis*, in "sesta rima", is one of Shakespeare's most immediately popular works.

His sonnets, written in the mid-1590s, use the Elizabethan or Shakespearian form—rhyming *ababcdcdefefgg*—rather than the Petrarchan form. They are poems of love and of time; of love outlasting time, and poetry outlasting all. They examine the masculine/feminine elements in all humanity and in all love relationships. Power, as in the plays, is another major concern of the sonnets. The power of the beloved to command is a microcosm of all power. The suffering of a lover is a symbol of all suffering.

Shakespeare's 154 sonnets have generally been recognized as falling into three distinct groups. The first 126 are addressed to a "fair youth"; the next 26 refer to a new association with the "Dark lady"; the last two give a new twist to the erotic theme by playing fancifully with stories of Cupid and the loss of his (phallic) "brand". In the later poems, the ambiguous relationship between the narrator, the young man, and the dark lady takes on the nature of an emotional triangle in which the narrator is not only between "Two loves... of comfort and despair" but also between the love for the young man and the love for the woman who appears to have seduced him.

Indeed, ambiguity is at the heart of Shakespeare's sonnets. Whether the "I" loves or is loved by a man or a woman:

> Two loves I have, of comfort and despair,
> which like two spirits do suggest me still;
> The better angel is a man right fair,

The worsen spirit a woman coloured ill...

(Sonnet 144)

Whether, in the 1590s, he considers himself a success or a failure, together with the constant preoccupation with time and transience, all serving to underline the lack of certainty in the poems. "I" very often presents himself as rejected, some kind of outcast:

When in disgrace with Fortune and men's eyes,
I all alone beweep my outcast state,
And trouble deaf heaven with my bootless cries.
And look upon myself, and curse my fate...

(Sonnet 29)

Shakespeare's ambiguity anticipates the "negative capability" of John Keats.

6. Characters

Shakespeare's themes are frequently the great abstract, universal themes, seen both at the social level and at the individual level: ambition, power, love, death, and so on. The theater permitted him to create characters who embody the themes directly, and who speak to the audience in language that is recognizably the same language as they speak. From kings to ordinary soldiers, from young lovers to old bawds, Shakespeare's characters speak modern English. The language of Shakespeare is the first and lasting affirmation of the great changes that took place in the sixteenth century, leaving the Middle English of Chaucer far behind. In many ways, the language has changed less in the 400 years since Shakespeare wrote than it did in the 150 years before he wrote.

Many of Shakespeare's characters have become so well-known that they have almost taken on a life of their own. Queen Elizabeth's own favourite was Falstaff and it was at her command that a comedy, *The Merry Wives of Windsor*, was created around this jovial, cynical, humorous, fat, pleasure-loving adventurer who represents the large number of feudal retainers suddenly thrown on their own resources by the dissolution of feudal households under the Tudors. Romeo and Juliet are the embodiment of young love which triumphs over everything, even death; Othello and Desdemona are the perfect union of warrior and virgin (the classical Mars and Diana), whose union is ruined by the devil-figure, Iago; Shylock is almost the traditional stage Jew (avaricious and sadistic money lender), but as human as any other character, as he says,

> Hath not a Jew eyes? Hath not a Jew hands, organs, dimensions, senses,
> Affections, passions, fed with the same food, hurt with the same weapons,
> Subject to the same diseases, healed by the same means, warmed and
> Cooled by the same winter and summer, as a Christian is? If you pick us,
> Do we not bleed? If you tickle us, do we not laugh? If you poison us,
> Do we not die? And if you wrong us, shall we not revenge?
> If we are like you in the rest, we will resemble you in that.
>
> (*The Merchant of Venice*)

Shakespeare's women are just as much forceful modern Renaissance characters as his men—from Adriana in *The Comedy of Errors*, through Katherina in *The Taming of the Shrew*, to the determined Helena in *All's Well That Ends Well*. They demonstrate strength and assertiveness, as well as femininity. But it is usually an untraditional kind of femininity.

In fact, many of the female characters question the presumptions of a patriarchal society, even though they might yield to it by the end of the play. It is often the female characters who lead and "tame" the man—in the gender switching comedies *As You Like It* and *Twelfth Night*. It is Rosalind and Viola who, temporarily dressed as men, bring Orlando and Orsino respectively to the fullest realization of their own masculine potential.

In *Othello*, Emilia asserts to Desdemona, "But I think it is their husbands' fault if wives do fall." There is a questioning of male/female roles here, as in so much of Shakespeare's writing. Shakespeare gives us mothers (Volumnia in *Coriolanus*, Gertrude in *Hamlet*, Queen Margaret in *Richard II*, the countess in *All's Well That Ends Well*), young lovers, such as Juliet, Ophelia and Miranda, and strong decisive women who might well take on conventionally masculine roles and qualities, such as Portia and Lady Macbeth. These women characters are studied by many major Shakespearian critics as if they were real people. This has been widely regarded as testimony to the timeless universality of their preoccupations, desires, fears, and basic humanity. Although the concerns are Renaissance and Western Europe, they strike a chord in many other cultures and times.

The character and the play of *Hamlet* are central to any discussion of Shakespeare's works. Hamlet has been described as melancholic and neurotic, as having an Oedipus complex, as being a failure and indecisive, as well as being a hero, and a perfect Renaissance prince. These judgments serve perhaps only to show how many interpretations of one character may be put forward. "To be or not to be" is the center of Hamlet's questioning. Reasons not to go on living outnumber reasons for living. But he goes on living, until he completes his revenge for his father's murder and becomes "most royal", the true "Prince of Denmark", in many ways the perfection of Renaissance man.

Hamlet's progress is a "struggle of becoming"—of coming to terms with life, and learning to accept it, with all its drawbacks and challenges. He discusses the problems he faces directly with the audience in a series of seven soliloquies—of which "to be or not to be" is the fourth and central one. These seven steps, from the zero-point of a desire not to live, to complete awareness and acceptance (as he says, "the readiness is all"), give a structure to the play, making the progress all the more tragic, as Hamlet reaches his aim, the perfection of his life, only to die:

> ... we defy augury: there is a special providence in the fall of a sparrow. If it be now, 'its not to come; if it be not to come, it will be now; if it be not now, yet it will come—the readiness is all, since no man owes of aught he leaves, what isn't to leave betimes?

> (*Hamlet*)

The play can thus be seen as a universal image of life and of the necessity of individual choice and action. No matter how tortured or successful a life will be, the end is death, and, to quote Hamlet's final words, "the rest is silence."

7. Style

All Shakespeare's plays have come down to us in a standard form: five acts. In each act, he scatters metaphors profusely; instant abstract ideas are changed into images; it is a series of paintings which are unfolded in his mind; picture on picture, image on image, he is forever copying the strange and splendid visions which are engendered one after another, and are heaped up within his works. In accordance with his metaphors are vehement passion and frenzied expressions: mingled contrast, tremendous exaggerations, apostrophes and exclamations. "What have I done?" the queen asks Hamlet, he answers:

Such an act that blurs the grace and blush of modesty,
Calls virtue hypocrite, takes off the rose
From the fair forehead of an innocent love,
And set a blister there, makes marriage-vows
As false as dicers' oaths: O, such a deed
As from the body of contraction plucks
The very soul, and sweet religion makes
A rhapsody of words: Heaven's face doth grow;
Yea, this solidity and compound mass,
With thristful visage, as against the doom,
Is thought-sick at the act.

(*Hamlet*)

It is the style of phraseology. The metaphors are all exaggerated, and the ideas all verge on the absurd. All is transformed and disfigured by the whirlwind of passion. The contagion of the crime, which he denounces, has marred all nature. He no longer sees anything in the world but corruption and lying. Inanimate things are sucked into this whirlpool of grief. The sky's red tint at sunset and the pallid darkness spread by night over the landscape become the blush and the pallor or shame, and the wretched man who speaks and weeps sees the whole world totter with him in the dimness of despair. It is this kind of style that largely accounts for Shakespeare's greatness.

3.7 Reading

Sonnet 75

By Edmund Spenser

One day I wrote her name upon the strand,
But came the waves and washed it away:
Agayne[1] I wrote it with a second hand,
But came the tyde, and made my paynes his pray[2].
"Vayne man," said she, "that doest in vaine assay[3],
A mortal thing so to immortalise;

For I my selve shall lyke to this decay,

And eek my name bee wyped out lykewyse."[4]

"Not so," quod[5] I, "let baser things devise[6]

To dy in dust, but you shall live by fame:

My verse your vertues rare shall eternise,

And in the heavens wryte your glorious name:

Where whenas[7] death shall all the world subdew[8],

Our love shall live, and later life renew."

Notes

1. **Agayne:** again.

2. **made my paynes his pray:** made my pains his prey, washed away my hard work.

3. **assay:** attempt.

4. **And eek my name bee wyped out lykewyse:** And also my name be wiped out likewise.

5. **quod:** said.

6. **devise:** contrive.

7. **whenas:** while.

8. **subdew:** subdue.

Sonnet 18

By William Shakespeare

Shall I compare thee to a summer's day?

Thou art more lovely and more temperate:

Rough winds do shake the darling buds of May,

And summer's lease[1] hath all too short a date:

Sometime too hot the eye of heaven shines,

And often is his gold complexion[2] dimmed,

And every fair from fair sometime declines,

By chance, or nature's changing course untrimmed:[3]

But thy eternal summer shall not fade,

Nor lose possession of that fair thou ow'st,

Nor shall death brag thou wander'st in his shade,

When in eternal lines to time thou grow'st,

So long as men can breathe, or eyes can see,

So long lives this, and this gives life to thee.

Notes

1. **lease:** time, duration.

2. **his gold complexion:** the sun's gold face.

3. **By chance, or nature's changing course untrimmed:** cut short, destroyed by chance (fate).

Hamlet
ACT III, Scene I

By William Shakespeare

Ham. To be, or not to be[1]—that is the question:

Whether 'tis nobler in the mind to suffer

The slings and arrows[2] of outrageous fortune

Or to take arms against a sea of troubles,

And by opposing end them[3]. To die, to sleep—

No more—and by a sleep to say we end

The heartache, and the thousand natural shocks

That flesh is heir to[4]. 'Tis a consummation[5]

Devoutly to be wish'd. To die; to sleep.

To sleep, perchance[6] to dream: ay, there's the rub[7]!

For in that sleep of death what dreams may come

When we have shuffled off this moral coil[8],

Must give us pause[9]. There's the respect

That makes calamity of so long life.

For who would bear the whips and scorns of time[10]

Th' oppressor's wrong, the proud man's contumely[11]

The pangs of disprized love, the law's delay,

The insolence of office,[12] and the spurns

That patient merit of th' unworthy takes[13]

When he himself might his quietus[14] make

With a bare bodkin[15]?

Who would these fardels[16] bear,

To grunt and sweat under a weary life,

But that the dread of something after death,

The undiscover'd country, from whose bourn[17]

No traveller returns, puzzles the will,

And makes us rather bear those ills we have

Than fly to others that we know not of?

Thus conscience[18] does make cowards of us all,

And thus the native hue of resolution

Is sicklied o'er with the pale cast of thought[19]

And enterprises of great pitch and moment[20]

With this regard their currents turn awry[21]

And lose the name of action. —Soft you now!

The fair Ophelia! Nymph, in thy orisons

Be all my sins remembered.

Notes

1. **To be, or not to be:** to live on this world or to die; to suffer or to take action.

2. **slings and arrows:** attacks.

3. **by opposing end them:** end them by opposing.

4. **heir to:** certain to receive.

5. **consummation:** completion of one's life.

6. **perchance:** perhaps; maybe.

7. **the rub:** "rub" is a technical term in the game of bowls for any obstacle which diverts the bowl from its course. Here it refers to difficulties.

8. **this moral coil:** the turmoil of morality.

9. **give us pause:** make us hesitate.

10. **the whips and scorns of time:** the suffering of the world.

11. **contumely:** contempt.

12. **The insolence of office:** the contempt held by the people of high rank.

13. **That patient merit of th'unworthy takes:** the people of the worth endure at the hands of unworthy.

14. **quietus:** the final settlement of an account.

15. **bare bodkin:** mere dagger.

16. **fardels:** burdens.

17. **bourn:** boundary.

18. **conscience:** consciousness.

19. **thought:** anxiety.

20. **pitch and moment:** significance and importance.

21. **their currents turn awry:** turn away from their original purpose.

Chapter Four
Literature of Revolution and Restoration (1620–1690)

4.1 Historical Background

The politics and the literature of the seventeenth century are characterized by the contrast between the extravagant courtly theater of the masque and the determined refugees from James's religious policies who were to establish Plymouth Plantation. The masque celebrated an ideal monarch whose merits could be studied, like the Bible, as the book of all perfection; the narrow Bible-centered Puritanism of the Pilgrims demanded a rejection of a cornerstone of James's idea of kingship, an integrated union of the English state with the English church through the person of the King himself and the bishops appointed by him.

James's son, the successor to the throne as Charles I in 1625, was the first English monarch to have been born into the Church of England; he also proved to be its stoutest, and most extreme, defender. Charles's attempt to extend its ecclesiastical order and its liturgy to his northern kingdom of Scotland began the long-drawn-out challenge to his authority which ended in his trial and execution and in the abolition of "the kingly office" itself by the English Parliament, known as the Bourgeois Revolution.

In March, 1649, the Parliament led by Oliver Cromwell abolished the monarchy and the House of Lords. In May of the same year, the House of Commons affirmed that England should henceforward be ruled as a Commonwealth and free state by the supreme authority of this nation, the representatives of the people in Parliament. Once the King and his cause had been disposed of, power remained with the effective brokers of Parliament, and the commanders of the army, most of them gentlemen landowners. Oliver Cromwell was proclaimed Lord Protector in December, 1653. He made his impatience with truculent Parliament and with extra-parliamentary opposition to his rule perfectly plain. Despite the widespread, free and public debate about the nature of sovereignty and the potential of sustained constitutional development, the Cromwellian Commonwealth did not prove to be willing builders of a new social order either at home or abroad.

In 1660, Charles II returned to England from France following the end of Oliver

Cromwell's Commonwealth and the reestablishment of the monarchy. With the restoration of the King, there came a change in cultural direction. The returning court was heavily influenced by French fashion and ideas, especially by a more secular view of the world. Restoration replaced the power of the monarchy with the power of a parliamentary system which was to develop into two parties—Whigs and Tories—with most of the executive power in the hands of the Prime Minister. Both parties benefited from a system which encouraged social stability rather than opposition.

4.2 Literary Features

In thoughts, the Restoration replaced the probing, exploring, risk-taking intellectual values of the Renaissance. It relied on reason and on facts rather than on speculation. So in the decades between 1660 and 1700, the basis was set for the growth of a new kind of society, which was Protestant, middle class, and unthreatened by any repetition of the huge and traumatic upheavals of the first part of the seventeenth century. It is symptomatic that the overthrow of James II in 1688 was called the "Glorious" or "Bloodless" Revolution.

The beliefs and behavior of the Restoration reflect the theories of society put forward by Thomas Hobbes in *The Leviathan* (1651). Like many texts of the time, it is an allegory. The Leviathan is the Commonwealth, in which the individual is the absolute subject of state control, represented by the monarch. Man—motivated by self-interest—is acquisitive and lacks codes of behavior. Hence the necessity for a strong controlling state to keep discord is at bay. Self-interest and stability become the keynotes in British society after 1660, the voice of the new middle-class bourgeoisie making itself heard more and more in the expression of values, ideals and ethics.

After the upheavals of the Commonwealth, there was a strong affirmation of religion and a return to traditional beliefs. In such a context, Milton's *Paradise Lost* (1667) was read not as a Renaissance text about free will and freedom, but as a commentary on God's supremacy. It was read in order to confirm an image of God as the period demanded God should be. Questioning of religious values was not part of the age; once Protestant supremacy had been established after 1688, religious dissent was stifled. *Paradise Lost* took on the authority of a quasi-religious text—an imaginative representation of the beliefs contained in the *Authorized Version of the Bible* and the *Book of Common Prayer.* Besides

Paradise Lost, another fundamental text for the time was John Bunyan's allegorical *The Pilgrim's Progress* (1678).

4.3 Seventeenth-Century Prose

There is an established history of prose writing in the seventeenth century; this traces a movement from texts such as Francis Bacon's *Essays* (1597), Robert Burton's *The Anatomy of Melancholy* (1611), Izaak Walton's *The Compleat Anger* (1653) and Thomas Browne's *Hydriotaphia* (or *Urn Burial*, 1658) to stylistically far plainer texts at the end of the century. John Bunyan's *The Pilgrim's Progress* is one text that illustrates the new plainness in writing. Its manner is at a far remove from the fullness of rhetorical expression that characterizes works earlier in the century. Bunyan, with his Puritan convictions, concentrates upon a single example, his hero, Christian, on his journey through life. It is a work that seems to foreshadow the development of the novel in the early eighteenth century as Bunyan dwells on the individual and the importance of personal experience.

The texts which are amongst the most interesting of the seventeenth century prose are those with a political dimension. Milton in *The Reason of Church Government* (1642), for example, challenged the established church, and in the same year, after his wife deserted him to return to her Royalist relations, wrote a number of pamphlets defending divorce on the grounds of incompatibility. His *Areopagitica*, published in 1644, is a plea for freedom of the press. As with all Milton's prose works, it challenges established beliefs and practices.

Yet some of the most powerful new voices in prose are from religious groups and sects. A remarkable figure in this context is Anna Trapnel who, in January, 1654, fell into a trance. Her prophecies in the trance were published in verse as *The Cry of a Stone*. Also in 1654, her *Report and Plea* appeared which is an account of how she was called to Cornwall to preach and her arrest and interrogation there on a charge of witchcraft. Among the religious prose also stands out the *Authorized Version of the Bible*, the single most influential work of English prose.

4.3.1 Francis Bacon (1561–1626)

Bacon was born a commoner and died Baron of Verulam, Viscount St. Albans. Educated to the law which occupied him for over forty years, he became the first philosopher of

Chapter Four
Literature of Revolution and Restoration (1620–1690)

industrial science. He was also the first great English prose writer. It is he who perfected the essay form in English on the French model of Montaigne.

Bacon's range of interest was vast. He wrote on aspects of law, science, history, government, politics, ethics, religion and colonialism, as well as gardens, parents, children and health. The key work for appreciating the width of his interest is his *Essays*, originally published in 1597, and enlarged twice before his death. These little compositions, often no more than a page in length, are very compact and allusive. Ben Johnson once made a remark on Bacon's eloquence: "His hearers could not cough, or look aside from him, without loss." At first sight, many of the essays seem little more than a mosaic of maxims and quotations, but by degrees one comes to see how intensely expressive they are of their author's personality. The knotty sentences, the countless allusions, and the abrupt transitions from thought to thought are, in their totality, the mirror of a wonderful mind. They transmit the essence of their author's nature, and are, indeed, something like prose sonnets—the private record in the most finished form of their author's experience and wisdom. In his famous essay *Of Studies*, the amount of perennial wisdom has been compressed into a few words:

> Read not to contradict and confute; nor to believe and take for granted; nor to find talk and discourse; but to weigh and consider. Some books are to be tasted, others to be swallowed, and some few to be chewed and digested...
>
> Reading maketh a full man; conference a ready man; and writing an exact man: and therefore, if a man write little, he had need have a great memory; if he confer little, he had need have a present wit; and if he read little, he had need have much cunning, to seem to know that he doth not. Histories make men wise; poems witty; the mathematics subtle; natural philosophy deep; moral, grave; logic and rhetoric, able to contend.
>
> *(Of Studies)*

In Bacon, the intellect was paramount, and it is therefore in matters of general speculation that his wisdom shines brightest. On topics of ordinary life, he often naively reveals his nature, as in his essay *Of Marriage*, he remarks: "he that hath wife and children hath give hostages to fortune." Bacon's passion for self-advancement makes him master of worldly wisdom.

However, it is his passion for knowledge that makes Bacon so magnificent a figure. His dreams of advancing the sciences are partially set forth in his *The Advancement of Learning* (1617), which is at once a masterpiece of prose and one of the finest records of intellectual aspiration in existence. The concise style of *Essays* has given place to a simpler and freer manner.

The Advancement of Learning attempted to draw a distinction between two kinds of Truth, a theological Truth "drawn from the word and oracles of God" and determined by faith, and a scientific Truth based on the light of nature and reason. Both, he freely conceded, possessed an equal intellectual validity. Throughout his work, Bacon is a great classifier, a forthright proponent of the innovative power of human reason, and a firm believer in a "perpetual renovation" of knowledge. The theories of *The Advancement of Learning* were later reworked and expanded in its Latin version, *De Augmentic Scientiarum of 1623*, but both works should properly be seen as preliminaries to the larger overarching argument of "true directions concerning the interpretation of nature" contained in *Novum Organum* (the "New Instrument" by which human understanding would be advanced). *Novum Organum* argues in Latin for a new method of scientific thinking, free of the prejudices of the past and the received affectations of the present. It marks a decisive rejection of the old ways of syllogistic deduction and a defense of the inductive investigation of nature.

Authorized Version of the Bible, which appeared in 1611, shortly after King James's accession, is the crowning achievement of the Reformation in English literature, signaling the final victory of English, not Latin, prose as the medium for the affirmation of Anglicanism. The beauty of the translation is due to the devotion of learned and pious men, to whom the task of rendering the word of God into the language of the people stirred the deepest religious feelings. The work was commissioned by King James I and carried out by three groups of scholars, sitting at Oxford, at Cambridge, and at Westminster. They had before them the versions of their predecessors of the sixteenth century, and these they accepted as the foundation of their work. When *Authorized Version of the Bible* was complete, it soon surpassed all previous translations, and immediately began its task of moulding the lives, the thoughts and the speech of millions of English people.

Authorized Version of the Bible, the affirmation of Protestant England and a celebration of its freedom from Rome is usually regarded as the single most influential work in the English language. It is a repository rich in poetry as well as parable, so that its cadences

Chapter Four
Literature of Revolution and Restoration (1620–1690)

have not only been heard in church confirming the religious direction of the nation. But its language has contributed immensely to English cultural identity through the innumerable writers who for almost four centuries have echoed its phrasing.

4.3.2 John Bunyan (1628–1688)

Bunyan was the son of a tinsmith of Elstow near Bedford, and had fought in the Parliamentarian wars. He read the Bible diligently, and became a well-known preacher. At the Restoration, the laws against unlicensed preaching were enforced, and Bunyan spent most of his life between 1661 and 1672 in prison. He is said to have written *The Pilgrim's Progress* during another term of imprisonment in 1675. The book was published in 1678, and has never ceased to be widely read.

In one sense, *The Pilgrim's Progress* is a book of religious confession; in another, it is a work of fiction. In representing life under the similitude of a pilgrimage, Bunyan was following the ancient formal pattern of the allegory and used the words of the Bible. Of his other books, *Grace Abounding* (1666), with its details of vivid autobiography and deep self-searching, *The Life and Death of Mr. Badman* (1680), a work of warning to the godless, executed in a spirit of sober realism, and *The Holy War* (1682), a record of the siege of "Mansoul" by the forces of evil, are the most remarkable. But none of these can equal *The Pilgrim's Progress* either in literary art or in universality of interest.

The Pilgrim's Progress begins as a dream in which the narrator tells us he "saw a man clothed with rags, standing in a certain place, with his face from his own house, a book in his hand and a great burden upon his back. I looked, and saw him open the book and read therein; as he read, he wept and trembled; not being able longer to contain, he broke out with a lamentable cry, saying 'what shall I do'". The name is Christian, the pilgrim; his book is the Bible; the burden on his back is the weight of worldly cares and concerns.

Aroused to the evils of the world in which he lives, Christian attempts to convince his wife, children and neighbours of the dangers that the world will be destroyed on the last day, and to enlist their companionship in his search for salvation, but they are in love of the world. So he decides to start out alone, but at the last minute a friend, Pliable, is soon impressed by the strength of his conviction and he offers to go with him. They soon stumble and fall into the slough of Despond, at which Pliable is discouraged and turns back. Christian bravely struggles on but is persuaded to turn off from the right path by Mr. Worldly Wiseman who assures him that a Mr. Legality nearby can show him a much easier way to get rid of his burden. With the help of Mr. Evangelist, he eventually gets back to the main road, and is overtaken by a neighbour, Faithful, who has set out later but has made better progress. The two continue together through many adventures, including the great struggle with Apollyon, ruler of the world, who claims them as his subjects and refuses their allegiance to God.

After many other experiences, they try to pass through Vanity Fair where both are arrested as foreign agitators. Brought to trial before a Lord of the fair, Judge Hate-Good, Faithful is condemned and tortured to death. Christian, however, escapes and continues on his way, assisted by a new friend, Hopeful, who has been converted by Faithful's martyrdom.

They hold to the high road despite many difficulties and dangers but finally, then feet being weary and the road growing hourly much harder and rockier, they are tempted to take a by-path through a pleasant meadow which seems to follow the same good route. It soon diverges, however, and they are warned barely in time by the fate of Mr. Vain-confidence who, rushing ahead, falls into a deep pit and is dashed into pieces.

Unable to win back to the right road before nightfall, they are captured by Giant Despair and thrown into the dungeon of Doubting Castle. Here they are almost driven to suicide, but again escape and go on their way, posting a warning to help other pilgrims avoid their mistakes. At last they reach the Celestial City, which they enter to enjoy eternal life in the fellowship of the blessed.

The great literary interest of *The Pilgrim's Progress*, the most important forerunner of the English novel, lies in its rich variety of concrete situations, living characters and vital experiences. The profound psychological insight with which many of the minor characters as well as the hero himself who is realized are truly extraordinary, and what is more amazing is the rapidity of the narrative and the specific allegory it maintains throughout. Its central symbol of life as a pilgrimage and man as a pilgrim gives the story much of its emotional power and universality.

4.4 Seventeenth-Century Drama

The distinction between tragedy and comedy, in writers other than Shakespeare,

Chapter Four
Literature of Revolution and Restoration (1620–1690)

becomes more and more distinct during the first twenty-five years of the seventeenth century. The world of Jacobean tragedy is a dark world of corruption, perversion, blood and passion. The world of comedy is more localized, based on the city of London and its people, with their obsessions, and above all, with money and sex. The major figures in Jacobean drama (Shakespeare aside) are Ben Jonson (1572–1637), Thomas Middleton, John Webster, Thomas Dekker, Francis Beaumont and John Fletcher. Among their famous works (Jonson's aside) are Fletcher's *The Maid's Tragedy* (1610, in collaboration with Beaumont), Middleton's *A Game at Chess* (1624), and Webster's *The White Devil* (1612).

In 1642, the Long Parliament put an end to theatrical performances because of puritans' strong opposition to the theatrical activity. The closure of the theaters brought to an end the greatest period of English drama.

After the Restoration, the theaters were reopened. The lifting of the ban led to an explosion of dramatic writing, but of a different kind from the drama of Shakespeare and his successors. Restoration tragedy is "heroic" tragedy, showing a hero choosing between love and honour, and being set in faraway places associated with romance, such as Canada or Venice. They usually generate wonder rather than offering any real intellectual probing of issues. *All for Love* (1678) by John Dryden is a good example of the type. This play takes the story of Shakespeare's *Antony and Cleopatra* but makes a distinct and new play, in an elaborately formal and neoclassical style. It respects the formal unities of time, place and action, and concentrates on the final hours in the lives of the hero and heroine, rather than presenting the huge political, historical and passionate panorama which Shakespeare's drama had enacted.

The central dramatists of this period are Etherege, Wycherley, Congreve, and Aphra Behn, the first major woman dramatist in England. Restoration comedies are sometimes referred to as comedies of manners, debating the manners and morals of fashionable society. They are town comedies, laughing at the expense of fops and country squires. The dominant theme is sexual intrigue. But sometimes, as in Wycherley's *The Country Wife* (1675), the tone is bawdy, cynical and voyeuristic. In *The Country Wife*, the hero, Homer, pretends to be impotent in order to gain free access to women's bedroom. His name alludes not only to giving married men horns, in other words cuckolding them, but is also a homophonic pun on the word "honour", a euphemism for chastity. The puns implicit in Homer's name sum up the action of the play and its exposure of sexual hypocrisy.

The climatic work of all Restoration comedy is William Congreve's *The Way of the World* (1700). It is again concerned with honour and sexual betrayal. At the center of the play's satire is Lady Wishfort, an old woman susceptible to the charms of both young and old men.

Ben Jonson

Jonson was born in London, the son of a clergyman, and educated at Westminster school, where he acquired Jonson: the first great English theorist and practitioner of neoclassicism, the first really direct, learned, deliberate, and single-hearted heir of antiquity, a good knowledge of the classics. At first, Jonson worked as a bricklayer, but subsequently, after military service in Flanders, became an actor and playwright. In 1596, he was involved in a deal with a fellow actor whom he killed, but managed to escape hanging. His influence on English literature is great. Jonson was the first unofficial poet laureate, being given a pension by James I in 1616. In the same year, he published his collected *Works*, raising drama to the status of other literary texts. In addition to plays, he wrote poetry, and (after his death) his prose work *Timber* or *Discoveries*, which discusses poetic and dramatic principles, was published in 1640. Jonson is also known for his influence over younger writers (the "sons" or "tribe" of Ben, including the poets Thomas Carew and Robert Herrick). In everything he wrote, Jonson is likely to strike us as deeply conservative and get also remarkably innovative.

Jonson's first major play was *Everyman in His Humor* (1598). By humor Jonson meant the governing passions of human beings, such as greed, lust and ambitions, passions which he exaggerates for the purpose of satire. In Jonson's plays, set in the expanding economy of London and among its merchant class, avarice is nearly always the ruling passion that dominates, but folly, too, is found everywhere. At the center of *Everyman in His Humor* is the deceitful servant Brainworm who exploits the jealousy of the merchant Kitely and the credulity of his wife. Other figures include a cowardly boasting soldier, Bobadill. Kitely suspects that his brother-in-law Wellbred and his friends have sexual designs on his wife and on his sister Bridget. Brainworm tricks all the parties into meeting at the house of a water bearer where confusion and misunderstanding reign until Justice Clement restores order. The play is a characteristic piece by Jonson, combining satire, knock-about farce and a kind of surreal comedy in which, for a while, the world is dominated by ruling passions that threaten

Chapter Four
Literature of Revolution and Restoration (1620–1690)

to reduce everything to chaos.

On the surface, Jonson's works seem to be a comic world that is informed in a very simple way by recognition of humankind's propensity for foolishness. Underlying the plays, however, is a darker premise that people are greedy, lustful and liars, and that society is governed by vice rather than by virtue. It is this that makes Jonson a conservative classical playwright. He is an advocate of the tradition and traditional behavior, and against the kind of radical change that was taking place, especially in London. What Jonson favours is the restraint associated with ancient, and especially Roman, civilization. This is evident in the form of his plays, particularly his tragedies, such as *Sejanus* (1603), which conform to the classical unities of time, place, and action, restricting what can be shown so that it corresponds with what is possible. Jonson distrusts fancy and imagination, but he delights in the mad behavior of those on stage, as he manipulates everything towards impossible situations only to resolve them at the last moment.

This is evident in his great comic dramas, *Volpone* (1615), *The Alchemist* (1610) and *Bartholomew Fair* (1614), which exploit to the full the idea of people driven by humors. In *Volpone*, Volpone (the "fox") pretends to be near death. His would-be heirs and friends visit him, hoping to gain from his will. Meanwhile, his servant Mosca (the "fly") extracts costly gifts from them by suggesting that each is to be the sole heir. But Volpone overreaches himself. He leaves everything to Mosca and pretends to die. But Mosca then blackmails him. In the end, Volpone goes before the court to confess all and is punished by being cast in irons, while Mosca is sent to the galleys. In addition to the main plot, there is a subplot involving the foolish Sir Politic Would-be, an English traveller mocked for his absurd schemes and only brought to his senses when his friend pretends to have him arrested for treason. The play satirizes the greedy folly of humankind, as does *The Alchemist*. Here the plot turns upon the desires of the characters for instant wealth based on the pseudo-scientific hope that base metal can be turned into gold.

What strikes us about Jonson's plays as well as their caustic satire is their sheer ingenuity, as if Jonson delights in showing off his skill in a masterly exhibition of plotting and timing. Such a delight in artifice and elaboration, so evident in his comedies, presents us with a clue to the other aspect of his dramatic achievement: the masque. The masque became an important theatrical form during the reigns of James I and Charles I. It was a court entertainment, performed for the King and others of the court on special occasions. Masques were spectacular entertainments combining verse, music, dancing, disguises and visual effects. They were performed indoors, often by professionals, while the masquers were played by members of the court. The latter remained silent, and only the actors spoke, thus preserving court decorum by separating ladies and gentlemen from common players. A masque nearly always ended with dancing, with spectators and the courtly masquers involved, but not the actors. The plot was usually symbolic, with virtue triumphing over vice. This is the case in Milton's *Comus* (1634) where the lady resists the sexual temptations of the god Comus and preserves her virginity. *Comus*, however, has little of the spectacle that normally accompanies the masque and so could also be described as a pastoral drama. Comus disguised himself as a shepherd, and so did the Lady's brothers in their attempt to rescue her.

It was Jonson who established the masque as a definite form. He liked to add an anti-masque at the beginning, a burlesque or parody of the main masque. This fits in with the pattern of Jonson's comic writing, in that the purpose of the anti-masque was satiric while the main masque was educative and moral. For example, *The Masque of Queens* (1609) opens with a grotesque dance of witches before these are banished by the entrance of the queens of the title, parts taken by Queen Anne, the wife of James I, and her ladies. They represent the moral virtues as opposed to the witches who stand for the world of evil.

4.5 Seventeenth-Century Poetry

In the early years of the seventeenth century, Spenser, as the greatest non-dramatic poet of the sixteenth century, continued to be an influence. Then another great poet as ambitious as Spenser appeared. It was John Milton. Milton, however, has to be seen as rather detached from the poetic fashion of his day, whereas Donne both typifies and distastes the fashion. The so-called metaphysical poets of the 1630s–1660s—George Herbert, Richard Crashaw, Henry Vaughan, and Andrew Marvell—all worked in a manner initiated by Donne. Ben Jonson, on the other hand, favoured a more restrained form of social poetry. Among those who fell under his influence were the "Cavalier" poets: Richard Lovelace, Sir John Suckling and Thomas Carew, as well as Robert Herrick and Edmound Waller, each of them singing the praise of the monarchy. Jonson would also prove a major influence on the neo-classical approach of John Dryden, the writer who, specifically in his satirical poems, seems to

Chapter Four
Literature of Revolution and Restoration (1620–1690)

embody the spirit of the Restoration period.

An overview of the century's poetry creates an impression of coherent change and development, whereas more accurate impression is of variety and confusion. Indeed, in poem after poem, there is an emphasis on the perplexity nature of life, a stance that is substantiated by the use of rhetorical devices such as paradox and antithesis, conceit and hyperbole. These rhetorical devices convey a sense of the complex and contradictory nature of experience.

For Your Information

The Metaphysical Poets

The metaphysical poets refer to a group of religious poets in the first half of the seventeenth century whose works were characterized by their wit, imaginative picturing, compression, often cryptic expression, play of paradoxes and juxtapositions of metaphors. The use of the term "metaphysical" in this context was first given critical currency by the eighteenth century critic, Samuel Johnson, and it sprang from Johnson's distaste for the far-fetched or strained "conceits" (witty and ingenious ideas) in which Donne's poetry abounds. Now the term is only a label, which is used to refer to the modern impact of Donne and his followers' writing. After three centuries of neglect and distain, the metaphysical poets have come to be very highly regarded and have been influential in recent British poetry and criticism. They used contemporary scientific discoveries and theories, the topical debates on humanism, faith, and eternity, colloquial speech-based rhythms, and innovative verse forms to examine the relationship between the individual, his God, and the universe. Their "conceits" metaphors and images, paradoxes and intellectual complexity make the poems a constant challenge to the reader. John Donne (1572–1631) and George Herbert are the most significant of these poets.

4.5.1 John Donne (1572–1631)

John Donne, the poet who does so much to mould the impression of the first half of the seventeenth century, was born into a Catholic family in 1572. In 1592, he entered Lincohn's Inn, to train as a lawyer, and in 1596, he joined a naval expedition against Spain.

On his return, he became private secretary to Thomas Egerton, Lord Keeper of the Great Seal, and was briefly the Member of Parliament for Brackley, but a clandestine marriage to a relative of Egerton's led to the termination of his employment. It was in this decade that Donne wrote most of his love poems. Then his attention, both in poetry and prose, began to turn more and more towards religious concerns, and in 1610, he published his most notable prose work, *Pseudo-Martre*, which argued that English Catholics should agree to the Oath of Supremacy and swear allegiance to James I. It was around this time that Donne wrote his "holy sonnets", poems which reflect a dark sense of despair. In 1615, he took orders in the Church of England and was made a royal chaplain by James I. In 1621, he was appointed Dean of St. Paul's, a position he held until his death in 1631. In this final decade, he continued to write, especially sermons. His *Satires*, *Elegies*, *Paradoxes and Problems*, and some poems in his songs and sonnets are regarded as the greatest collection of lyric poems in English literature.

From his poems, we can see Donne was breaking away from the ways of writing of the sixteenth century. The typical poets of the sixteenth century for the most part worked within conventional lyric forms, whereas Donne and many other seventeenth-century poets favoured the orthodox and personalized lyric forms. Donne did write sonnets, but he wrote them in a changed form, which enabled Donne to move from the sonneteers' conventional sense of an idealized love to a sense of love as a mysterious and untidy complex of physical desire and spiritual impulse. Donne's originality in his love poems can be seen in his *The Sun Rising*:

> Busy old fool, unruly sun,
> Why dost thou thus,
> Through windows, and through curtains call on us?
>
> (*The Sun Rising*)

Here Donne chides the sun for disturbing him and his partner in bed in the morning. The sun has no business disturbing them, since lovers are subject to no laws or duties but their own:

> Love, all alike, no season knows, nor clime,
> Nor hours, days, months, which are the rays of time.
>
> (*The Sun Rising*)

Chapter Four
Literature of Revolution and Restoration (1620–1690)

The lovers form a unit outside time, and outside the world, in one sense, above it. One of the great insights of Donne's new attitude to love is that a love relationship constitutes an experience knowable only by the two people involved in it. Other people's judgments are of no relevance, indeed anything else pales into insignificance compared to the value that the lovers have in each other's eyes:

> She is all states, and all princes, I,
> Nothing else is.
>
> (*The Sun Rising*)

In the *Paradoxes*, Donne developed a very individual line in turning the lovers into saint-figures. In *A Valediction: Of the Book*, the lovers' love letters are to be used by future historians to write for "love's clergy", an authentic record of love, where "love's divines" will preserve all human knowledge. No less original was the opposed procedure, the cynical rejection of love. In this mode, constancy is mocked as being pointless or impossible both in women ("swear/Nowhere/Lives a woman true and fair") and in men ("I can love both fair and brown... / I can love any, so she be not true.").

Donne's originality is specially reflected in the concept of the "conceit". A conceit is a far-fetched metaphor in which a very unlikely connection between two things is established. Donne employs them extensively in his poetry, as when, in *A Valediction: Forbidding Mourning*, he describes lovers' souls as being like the two legs of a pair of compasses. A sense of strain seems to be intended. One way of thinking about conceits is to see them as the final expression of a medieval view of life, in which every aspect of experience is linked as part of a comprehensive religious pattern inexistence. And this leads us to what is perhaps the central paradox of Donne's poetry: He is the most original writer of this generation (inventing a great range of stanza forms), but he is also a traditional writer who would like to recover an old form of all-inclusiveness. He might have become a Dean in the Anglican Church, but a Catholic impulse towards the all-embracing vision survives in Donne's poetry.

This is the clearest in his religious poems, where he searches for truth and is disturbed both by doubt and by the distractions of daily life. In *Riding Westward*, for example, the poet is travelling towards the west, but is conscious that, in doing so, he has turned his back on the east and, by implication, Christ:

> There I should see a sun, by rising, set,
> And by that setting endless day beget;
> But that Christ on this cross did rise and fall,
> Sin had eternally benighted all.

(Riding Westward)

Such a stance between religious and secular aspects sets the tone for much of the seventeenth century.

4.5.2 John Dryden (1631–1700)

John Dryden was the leading poet of the Restoration in which the most prominent subject of poetry is political and religious infighting. He was at the center of all the greatest debates of his time: the end of the Commonwealth, the return of the monarch, the political and religious upheavals of the 1680s, and the specifically literary questions of neo-classicism opposed to more modern trends. He was appointed Poet Laureate by Charles II in 1668, but lost this position in 1688 on the overthrow of James II. Dryden had become Catholic in 1685, and his allegorical poem *The Hind and the Panther* (1687) discusses the complex issues of religion and politics in an attempt to reconcile bitterly opposed factions.

The first thing that needs to be established about Dryden is that he is a very impersonal poet; there is nothing in his works about his private feelings or state of mind. On the contrary, he is consistently and, as far as poetry is concerned, almost exclusively a commentator on matters of public concern. This is apparent in *Absalom and Achitophel* (1681), a verse satire (the popular form of poetry of Dryden's time) dealing with the political crisis of the late years of the reign of Charles II. Charles II has no son, and his heir, his brother James, a Catholic, was feared by many. The Whigs, led by Shaftesbury, attempted to exclude James from the throne, substituting Charles's illegitimate son, the Duke of Monmouth. Dryden, using a biblical story with certain parallels, attempted to influence the public against the Whigs, presenting them as anarchic enemies of God's anointed king. Dryden's political satire, together with his criticism, had an enormous influence on shaping neo-classical literature in the eighteenth century. Alexander Pope, in particular, as a verse satirist writing almost exclusively in heroic couplets, is the direct heir of Dryden.

After 1688, Dryden returned to the theater, which had given much of his early success in tragedy, tragic-comedy, and comedy, as well as adaptations of Shakespeare. His best play is *All for Love*, a tragedy about the eternal rivalry of war and love. In addition, Dryden is an important figure in the history of prose writing, helping to establish what might be regarded as the modern style of prose, with its closeness to speech and an emphasis on plainness and clarity. His most shapely critical manifesto is *Of Dramatic Poesie, An Essay* (1668). It takes the form of a conversation among four characters in which the assertion of one is answered by the response of another; each character is allotted a formal speech, one defend ancient drama, another the modern; one proclaim the virtues of French practice, another the English. There is a good deal of name-dropping and, latterly, of weighing the respective merits of Jonson, Fletcher, and Shakespeare. Jonson stands throughout as a touchstone of theatrical "regularity", while the more "natural" Shakespeare is approvingly allowed the rank of an English Homer or "Father of Our Dramatic Poets".

Dryden was an innovator, leading the move from heroic couplets to blank verse in drama. He experimented with verse forms throughout his writing life until *Fables Ancient and Modern* (1700), which brings together critical, translated, and original works, in a fitting conclusion, to varied career.

4.6 John Milton (1608–1674)

1. Life and Career

John Milton was one of the chief figures of the Renaissance, and today, is regarded by most critics as the greatest of English non-dramatic poets. Milton was a Londoner by birth, and was born in Bread Street on December 9, 1608. His father, a money-scrivener, resembled his son in combining puritan sympathies in religion with strong literary and artistic tastes. He was sent first to St. Paul's School, where he became an excellent classical scholar and an adept at versification, and then to Christ's College, Cambridge, where his personal beauty and correct moral character were observed, but where his insubordinate and unaccommodating temper seems to have got him into trouble with the authorities. He was once rusticated, but took his degrees in due time, becoming M.A. in 1632, at the end of the usual seven years. His father had bought a property at Horton in Buckinghamshire, and there Milton remained in unmolested and unprofessional study for six years, during which he produced most of his early verses. Then he left England in 1638 for a tour abroad, and spent the great part of two years chiefly in Italy. When he came home, he settled in Aldersgate Street, and, having the full Renaissance interest in education, acted as schoolmaster or tutor to his nephews and others.

During the twenty years of civil commotion, he wrote, except a few sonnets, no poetry, but was fertile in controversial prose. He married Mary Powell from a good Cavalier family in 1643, but the marriage was extremely ill assorted, and in a few weeks his wife left him and went to her parents. Milton constructed this desertion into a reason for divorce, and argued this point out in several tracts, which naturally caused a good deal of scandal. She returned in 1645 and died in 1652, leaving him three daughters. Meanwhile his tract-writing, not devoted to purely political matters, and especially the defense of the execution of the King, procured him the post, under the Commonwealth, of secretary of Foreign Tongues, that is to say, for diplomatic correspondence in Latin. He lost his eyesight in the same year in which his first wife died, and he married a second in 1656, but she, "the Tate espoused saint" of his sonnet, died also in 1658. At the Restoration, he hid himself but was not molested. He married a third time in 1665, this time more successfully in comfort and permanence. The publication of great epics followed at no long intervals, and he died in November, 1674, and was buried at St. Gile's, Cripplegate.

Milton's literary career, as has been seen, falls under three unusually well marked periods: the first including all the early poems up to *Lycidas*; the second fertile in prose, but yielding no poetry except most of the sonnets; the third giving the two *Paradises and Samson Agonistes*.

2. Early Poems

Milton's early poems include *L'Allegro* and *Il Penseroso* (both 1631), two masques (*Arcades*, 1633, and *Comus*), and an elegy (*Lycidas*, 1637).

L'Allegro and *Il Penseroso* are companion pieces advocating contrasting styles of life, the carefree and the studious. This pair of poems juxtaposes the cheerful and the thoughtful man, the one rejoicing in mirth, dance, pastoral landscape, feasting, and comedy and the other in melancholy, contemplative withdrawal, study, tragedy, and a solitary existence. While notionally opposed, as in the dispute tradition, the two are really complementary, dividing all legitimate pleasures into the public or private spheres. It is worthwhile to note that in these early poems Milton displayed his wonderful science of versification in the handling of the octosyllable, and his complete command of whatever expression he needs.

Comus is a masque, written for a family reunion at Ludlow Castle. The story is simple. A travelling lady, separated from her two brothers, was captured and tempted by Comus and his crew of revelers, and finally relieved through the intervention of an Attendant Spirit. In the poem, Milton presents the evil world of Comus, offspring of Bacchus and Circe, who haunts an "ominous wood". He lures travellers into drinking a magic potion that turns them into monsters who abandon their friends and "roll with pleasure in the sensual sty". Comus has many of the stock attributes of the tempter figure: specious reasoning ("Tis only daylight that makes sin"), a debased eloquence that can deceive the unwary, and a degraded conception of the human body as made only for sexual pleasure. Yet the lady, assailed by Comus, rejects his "false rules" and specious arguments with no difficulty. Nature's abundance is meant for those who live according to her sober laws, while his bestial indulgence is set below "the sage/and serious doctrine of virginity". *Comus* embodies the ethic of *Areopagitica*, that praise of God's providence, who "pours out before us even to a profuseness all desirable things, and gives us minds" that can choose temperance and justice.

Lycidas is one of the most-quoted elegies in English, moving from its commemoration of his Cambridge University friend, Edward King, to reflections on the writer's own mortality and ambitions, finishing in the remarkable optimism of a renewal, with the words:

> Weep no more, woeful shepherds, weep no more.
> For Lycidas, your sorrow, is not dead
>
> (*Lycidas*)

Like all Milton's works, *Lycidas* has been interpreted specifically Christian. But his beliefs go beyond any single doctrine, as can be seen from the wide range of political and social pamphlets he wrote between 1640 and 1660.

3. Prose

As a prose polemicist, John Milton produced at least eighteen major prose works defending the various causes he chose to espouse. In the early 1640s, he produced five pamphlets attacking both the idea and the supposed enormities of English episcopacy, the first being "Of Reformation Touching Church Discipline" (1641). Between 1643 and 1645, he published four tracts in favour of divorce, stemming from the unhappiness of his own marriage. In "The Doctrine and Discipline of Divorce" (1643), he draws extensively on arguments from history, theology, and the Scripture and he skirts round Christ's own explicit condemnation of divorce by flourishing a series of novel and convenient theological ideas, such as "Unmeet consorts" making for a kind of chaos which stands against God's order in Creation. In 1644, he offered his great defense of "free" speech, *Areopagitica*, as a means of countering the licensing ordinance of a predominantly Presbyterian Parliament. Following the execution of Charles I in 1649, he wrote "Defense for English People", arguing in both English and Latin for the propriety of bringing a tyrant to account. In 1660, shortly before the restoration of the monarchy, he proposed in "The Ready and Easy Way to Establish a Free Commonwealth", the establishment of a "Grand Counsel of ablest men chosen by the people" as a means of safeguarding the unsteady republic.

The greatest and most lastingly persuasive one of Milton's pamphlets, *Areopagitica*, argues for a far broader constitutional liberty. In his defense of free speech, Milton deploys a range of resources greater than that of any other prose-writer of his age, from inspiring metaphors to coarse abuse. In place of restrictive censorship, which would mean "a perpetual childhood of prescription", Milton appeals to God's gift of reason to man "to be his own chooser", for "reason is but choosing". Human beings are responsible for their actions, as are nations. The intellectual ferment in contemporary England would stagnate if knowledge were to be subject to strict controls like broadcloth or woolpacks. The condition of all intellectual progress is "liberty, the nurse of all great wits", the free exchange of ideas. The final sentence sums up Milton's argument memorably: "Give me the liberty to know, to utter, and to argue freely, according to conscience, above all liberties." The strength of utterance of this work, its grasp of colloquial English style coupled with resonant rhetorical appeals, makes it outstanding in Milton's prose.

4. Late Poems

The Restoration placed Milton's life in some danger, for though he was no "regicide", his polished writings and his whole career put his republicanism beyond doubt. His remaining years were passed in obscurity and devoted to the composition of three great poems, on which his fame largely rests. The three poems take their subject matter from the

Chapter Four
Literature of Revolution and Restoration (1620–1690)

sacred history and the early chronicles of Britain, and are written exclusively in blank verse.

Paradise Lost is an epic poem in twelve books on the fact of Man. The authority for the plot is the short account in the *Book of Genesis of the Temptation and Expulsion of Adam and Eve*. The story is as follows:

The fallen angels are discerned lying in a fiery gulf into which they have been flung after their rebellion against the Almighty. The first to stir out of their trance are Satan and Beelzebub. Summoned by their leader, the rest arouse themselves and seek footing on firm land. Through the skill of Mukaber, an immense palace is built, in which the rebel angels assemble to hold a debate and council of war. Several places are proposed, but the advice of Beelzebub, to make war on God's new world inhabited by man, wins universal favour, and it only remains to settle who shall set out in search of the earth. Satan himself undertakes the exploit, and passing to the borders of Hell comes face to face with two terrific beings, Sin and Death. Meantime, the Almighty in Heaven perceives the intention of Man's Foe, and though knowing the future, sends down an Angel to protect his creatures. The Garden of Paradise, in the midst of Eden, is now described, and a dialogue takes place between the first parents of Men. In the meanwhile, Satan, having made his way up from Hell, and through the vast intervening mass called Chaos, has discovered the earth and set foot in a mountain in the near neighbourhood of Eden. Overhearing the words that pass between Adam and Eve, he learns that one tree in the Garden they have been forbidden to eat. A messenger from Heaven now arrives, the Archangel Raphael, whose mission is to instruct Adam on the late Rebellion in Heaven and the creation of the world, and above all to fortify him in his obedience to the laws of God. Raphael departs, and Adam, having set forth to the duties of the day—for even Paradise needs its husbandman—Eve is left alone. Now is the Devil's chance. Assuming the fair form of a winged serpent, he summons up all his powers of flattery, awakens Eve's curiosity, and finally prevails upon her to perform the forbidden act. Adam, returning, is startled to find the change in Eve, but he is also induced to eat the fruit. The consequences of their sin now fall upon them. Angry words arise, and they seek to hide themselves from the face of God. A swift retribution lights on the fallen angels, for, just as Satan arrives in triumph to tell them the happy news, they are all transformed into hissing serpents. The doom of their sin also falls upon Adam and Eve, and the curses of the fall are pronounced upon them. But their expulsion is delayed while another messenger from heaven, this time the stern Archangel Michael, comes to show Adam the future of a world into which, through his act, Sin and Death have entered. When Adam beholds the consequences of his sin prolonged through generations, the plagues, sickness and wars that visit mankind, he is overcome by despair and begs for death; but bidden by the Angel to look further still, he sees the birth of the Son of Man and Redeemer of the world. To Eve, who is asleep, the same consolation is conveyed in a dream. And so the parents of man take leave of their Paradise.

A number of features stand out in the poem. Everything, as one might expect in an epic, is on a grand scale: The story encompasses the battle among Heaven, Earth and Hell, looking at the history of the world from the Creation to the final Flood which will destroy everything. Crucially, it is Milton's language that established the poem's stature. Part of this involves Milton's use of epic similes and allusions drawn from earlier writers, including Homer and Virgil, which lend the poem resonance and richness. But the poem also calls upon dramatic devices, such as the use of soliloquy, and visual spectacle, so that the reader is constantly surprised by new perspectives and new sights. We can see that Milton draws upon the whole tradition of Renaissance art, in which the visual interacts with the verbal to create a complex impression. Such complexity is seen again in the way the poem combines classical learning with religious faith, so that behind the poem lie the force of Christian humanism, and the belief that classical teaching and Christianity were complementary.

What makes *Paradise Lost* such a powerful poem, however, is precisely the way in which the Biblical past is pulled into the present in an intriguing way. Running through the poem are the key political questions of freedom and choice. These begin in Book I when the fallen angels debate what to do next. From the perspective of Satan and his followers, rebellion against God was inevitable. Heaven demanded obedience and servitude. The revolt may have failed, but it has left them their freedom. Freedom here may seem heroic, defiant and attractive, but it is clear that the fallen angels have also lost their former glory. In this way, the poem begins to construct an analogy with the rebellion of the God war and with Milton's own interrogation of established authority. That interrogation deepens in Book IX, with the fall of Adam and Eve. Milton does blame Eve for wanting to gain knowledge and equality with Adam, and blame Adam for taking the fruit and joining her in sin. Yet Milton knows that the Fall is also an act that leads to redemption by Christ, and that Adam and Eve act of their own free will. The final image of the poem is profoundly forward-looking, an image of gain through loss. As Adam and Eve go hand in hand out of Eden, the loss of Paradise is seen as the gain of a future for humanity on earth.

Paradise Regained (1671), following *Paradise Lost*, explores further the theme of temptation and fall: In this case, it is the tempting of Jesus by Satan to prove his godhead. Jesus refuses and refutes Satan's arguments. Initially the poem looks like a continuation of *Paradise Lost*, but it is a debate rather than a dramatic epic, as Milton teases out the implications of the contradiction of Christ's dual nature as man and God's son. As with *Paradise Lost*, Milton confronts fundamental questions in order to arrive at a more open sense of the relationship between the divine and the human.

Samson Agonistes (1671) is a blank verse tragedy. The hero, Samson, has been captured by the Philistines after being betrayed by his wife, Delilah; his hair, which gave him strength from God, has been cut off, and he has been blinded. In prison he is visited by a series of figures who tempt him in various ways. The tragedy ends, when, having recovered his strength and faith in God, he goes to the festival of the pagan god Dagon and pulls down the temple on his enemies. The play seems to echo Milton's life, but a larger framework is provided by the idea of spiritual crisis that marks all of Milton's writings. That crisis emerges from this historical moment of the Civil War, which seemed to promise change but which ended with the monarchy being restored. Looking for the reasons for such reversal, Milton turned to the past to see if God's plan still held good, or whether some new understanding of the relationship between religion and politics was needed. His works possibly mark the end of this Renaissance quest for such understanding.

5. Thoughts

As can be seen from the above, Milton wrote on a vast range of topics, from religion to politics, and from the divine to the human, but there is always one informing idea that the English people are special and elected, having been chosen by God to create a new state separate from the past and based on individual freedom and choice.

6. Style

Milton's great poems are all written in the special form of non-dramatic blank verse, which well suited his spacious description and his fiery and energetic narrative without the pressure of needing to find rhymes. But what makes Milton reach the climate of his powers as an artist is his words. His great merit is an almost unfailing command of what Matthew Arnold calls "the grand style".

Milton's skill in evoking the magic of words is certainly unequalled in literature. His vast knowledge often enables him to choose words more musical and more potently suggestive than those in common use. He does not need for many of his finest effects the thundering sound of learned words: The commonest monosyllables are, in his hands, often the most poetical. The simplest words are enough for the exquisite concluding line of the opening book in *Paradise Regained*, where Christ is left alone in the desert at nightfall:

> He added not; and Satan, bowing low
> His gray dissimulation, disappeared
> Into thin air diffused; for now began
> Night with her sullen wing to double-shade
> The desert, fowls in their clay nests were couched,
> And now wild beasts came forth the woods to roam.
>
> (*Paradise Regained*)

Milton's full power, however, is seen not so much in the details of his workmanship, as in the great resounding passages which succeed each other like billows of the sea. The unit of *Paradise Lost* is not the line, but the verse-paragraph. The first two books consist almost entirely of great passages, some of them a hundred lines or more in length. It is the memory of these verse paragraphs that stirs the reader to the highest admiration.

4.7 Reading

Of Studies

By Francis Bacon

STUDIES serve for delight, for ornament, and for ability. Their chief use for delight, is in privateness and retiring[1]; for ornament, is in discourse[2]; and for ability, is in the judgment, and disposition of business[3]. For expert[4] men can execute, and perhaps judge of particulars, one by one; but the general counsels, and the plots[5] and marshalling[6] of affairs, come best from those that are learned. To spend too much

Chapter Four
Literature of Revolution and Restoration (1620–1690)

time in studies is sloth; to use them too much for ornament, is affectation; to make judgment wholly by their rules, is the humor[7] of a scholar. They perfect nature, and are perfected by experience: for natural abilities are like natural plants, that need pruning[8], by study; and studies themselves, do give forth directions too much at large[9], except they be bounded in by experience. Crafty men contemn[10] studies, simple men[11] admire them, and wise men use them, for they teach not their own use[12]; but that is a wisdom without them, and above them, won by observation. Read not to contradict and confute; nor to believe and take for granted; nor to find talk and discourse; but to weigh and consider. Some books are to be tasted, others to be swallowed, and some few to be chewed and digested; that is, some books are to be read only in parts; others to be read, but not curiously[13]; and some few to be read wholly, and with diligence and attention. Some books also may be read by deputy, and extracts made of them by others; but that would[14] be only in the less important arguments, and the meaner sort of books, else distilled books are like common distilled waters, flashy things. Reading maketh a full man[15]; conference a ready man[16]; and writing an exact man. And therefore, if a man write little, he had need have[17] a great memory; if he confer little, he had need have a present wit[18]; and if he read little, he had need have much cunning, to seem to know, that he doth not. Histories make men wise; poets witty; the mathematics subtile[19]; natural philosophy deep; moral grave; logic and rhetoric able to contend. *Abeunt stadia in mores.*[20] Nay, there is no stond[21] or impediment in the wit, but may be wrought out by fit studies; like as diseases of the body, may have appropriate exercises. Bowling is good for the stone and reins[22]; shooting for the lungs and breast; gentle walking for the stomach; riding for the head; and the like. So if a man's wit be wandering, let him study the mathematics; for in demonstrations, if his wit be called away never[23] so little, he must begin again. If his wit be not apt to distinguish or find differences, let him study the schoolmen[24]; for they are *cymini sectores*[25]. If he be not apt to beat over matters[26] and to call up one thing to prove and illustrate another, let him study the lawyers' cases. So every defect of the mind, may have a special receipt[27].

Notes

1. **privateness and retiring:** private life and retreat.

2. **discourse:** conversation.

3. **disposition of business:** the administration and management of the affairs of the world.

4. **expert:** experienced.

5. **plots:** plans.

6. **marshalling:** arrangement.

7. **humor:** (archaic) temperament. Here it refers to peculiar character.

8. **pruning:** cultivation.

9. **too much at large:** too general and not to the point.

10. **contemn:** despise.

11. **simple men:** unlearned men.

12. **they teach not their own use:** Studies do not tell you how to use them.

13. **curiously:** carefully, attentively.

14. **would:** should.

15. **a full man:** a man with rich knowledge.

16. **a ready man:** a man who is quick in conversation.

17. **had need have:** ought to have.

18. **present wit:** ready mind.

19. **subtile:** subtle, able to make fine distinctions.

20. *Abeunt studia in mores* (Latin): Studies become ways of life.

21. **stond:** block, hindrance.

22. **stone and reins:** bladders and kidneys.

23. **never:** ever.

Chapter Four
Literature of Revolution and Restoration (1620–1690)

24. **the schoolmen:** medieval theologians.

25. **cymini sectores** (Latin): hair-spliters.

26. **beat over matters:** make thorough examinations of things.

27. **receipt:** recipe, cure.

The Flea

By John Donne

Mark but this flea, and mark in this,

How little that which thou deniest me[1] is;

It suck'd me first, and now sucks thee,

And in this flea our two bloods mingled be.

Thou know'st that this cannot be said

A sin, nor shame, nor loss of maidenhead;

Yet this enjoys before it woo,

And pamper'd[2] swells with one blood made of two;

And this, alas! is more than we would do.

O stay, three lives in one flea spare,

Where we almost, yea, more than married are.

This flea is you and I, and this

Our marriage bed, and marriage temple is.

Though parents grudge, and you, we're met,

And cloister'd in these living walls of jet.

Though use make you apt to kill me[3],

Let not to that self-murder added be,

And sacrilege, three sins in killing three.

Cruel and sudden, hast thou since

Purpled thy nail in blood of innocence?

Wherein could this flea guilty be,

Except in that drop which it suck'd from thee?

Yet thou triumph'st, and say'st that thou

Find'st not thy self nor me the weaker now.[4]

'Tis true; then learn how false fears be;

Just so much honour, when thou yield'st to me[5],

Will waste, as this flea's death took life from thee.[6]

Notes

1. **that which thou deniest me:** the blood which you refused to give me.

2. **pamper'd:** fed to excess.

3. **use make you apt to kill me:** habit makes you want to kill me (because I have taken your honour).

4. **Find'st not thy self nor me the weaker now:** finds neither you nor me become weaker because of the killing, meaning that the killing of the flea has done no harm to neither of us.

5. **when thou yield'st to me:** when you agree to my proposals of love.

6. **Just so much honour, … / Will waste, as this flea's death took life from thee:** The honour which you will lose is not any bigger than your loss of life at the death of the flea.

Paradise Lost

Book I

By John Milton

Of Man's first disobedience[1], and the Fruit

Of that Forbidden Tree, whose mortal taste

Brought Death into the World, and all our woe,

With loss of EDEN, till one greater Man[2]

Restore us, and regain the blissful Seat,

Sing Heavenly Muse[3], that on the secret top

Chapter Four
Literature of Revolution and Restoration (1620–1690)

Of OREB, or of SINAI[4] didst inspire

That Shepherd, who first taught the chosen Seed[5],

In the Beginning how the Heav'ns and Earth

Rose out of Chaos[6]: or if SION Hill[7]

Delight thee more, and STLOA'S Brook[8] that flow'd

Fast[9] by the Oracle of God[10], I thence

Invoke thy aid to my adventurous Song,

That with no middle flight intends to soar

Above th' AONIAN Mount,[11] while it pursues

Things unattempted yet in Prose or Rhime.

And chiefly Thou, O Spirit,[12] that dost prefer

Before all Temples th'upright heart and pure,[13]

Instruct me, for thou know'st[14]; Thou from the first

Wast present,[15] and with mighty wings outspread

Dove-like sat'st brooding on the vast Abyss

And mad'st it pregnant[16]: What in me is dark

Illumine, what is low raise and support[17];

That to the highth of this great Argument

I may assert[18] th'Eternal Providence[19],

And justify the ways of God to men[20].

Notes

1. **Man's first disobedience:** Adam and Eve's eating of the fruit from the Tree of Knowledge of good and evil, which is against the God's order.

2. **one greater Man:** Jesus Christ, son of God.

3. **Heavenly Muse:** Muse (the God of poetry) in heaven.

4. **OREB, SINAI:** the two places where Moses, "That shepherd" (in Line 8), heard the word of God and received the law.

5. **the chosen Seed:** the chosen people, i.e., the Israel.

6. **Chaos:** God created heaven and the earth and the whole world out of Chaos.

7. **SION Hill:** Zion or Jerusalem. It is worshiped as the Holy Hill.

8. **SILOA'S Brook:** in Jerusalem, near the Holy Temple.

9. **Fast:** close.

10. **the Oracle of God:** the holy temple of God.

11. **That with no middle flight intends to soar/Above th'AONIAN Mount:** The poet here means that he wants to write an epic greater than Homer's. In the time of Milton, it was believed that the earth consisted of three regions, among which the middle region leads to Heaven, while all gods and goddesses in the Greek mythology lived in Olympus, belonging to the middle air only. The God of poetry whom Homer begged to give him inspiration only lived on Aonian Mount, belonging to the middle air, too. Milton was determined to fly beyond the middle air and reach Heaven.

12. **Thou, O Spirit:** God. Here Milton means that his creation of this epic is just like God's creation of the universe.

13. **dost prefer/Before all Temples th'upright heart and pure:** (O Spirit) does prefer the uptight and pure heart to all temples.

14. **thou know'st:** you know all things.

15. **thou from the first/Wast present:** You were present ever since the remote antiquity.

16. **Dove-like sat'st brooding on the vast Abyss/And mad'st it pregnant:** The creation of the world as told in Genesis, the impregnation of Mary by the descending dove of the Holy Spirit, and the secondary creation of Milton's own great poem are here brought together. (Sat'st: sat; mad'st: made.)

17. **what is low raise and support:** raise and support what is low.

18. **assert:** take the part of.

19. **Providence:** beneficent and efficient concern.

20. **justify the ways of God to men:** show to human beings God's justice.

Chapter Four
Literature of Revolution and Restoration (1620–1690)

On His Blindness

By John Milton

When I consider how my light is spent,
Ere half my days, in this dark world and wide,
And that one talent which is death to hide
Lodged with me useless, though my soul more bent
To serve therewith my Maker, and present
My true account, lest He returning chide,
"Doth God exact day-labour, light denied?"
I fondly[1] ask; But patience, to prevent
That murmur[2], soon replies "God doth not need
Either man's work or his own gifts. Who best
Bear His mild yoke, they serve Him best.[3] His state
Is kingly: thousands at His bidding speed
And post o'er land and ocean without rest;
They also serve who only stand and wait."

Notes

1. **fondly:** foolishly.

2. **murmur:** complaint.

3. **Who best/Bear His mild yoke, they serve Him best:** They who best bear his mild yoke serve him best.

Chapter Five
The Eighteenth-Century Literature (1690–1780)

5.1 Historical Background

The eighteenth century is a century of change in England. The revolution of 1688 (or Glorious Revolution), which resulted in William III being declared the King, marked the introduction of constitutional monarchy and a new political and social order, Britain establishing political arrangements that reflected its emerging character as a dynamic trading economy. The new political order, characterized by parliamentary antagonism between the Whigs and Tories, is most clearly summed up in the figure of the Whig Prime Minister, Robert Walpole. For Walpole, the essence of politics was the pursuit of harmony within a propertied society; this means taking measures to encourage trade and, as far as possible, limiting the country's involvement in costly military disputes, while profiting from any wars, which did take place (the War of the Spanish Succession, 1701–1714, the Seven Years' War, 1756–1763, war against the Americans between 1775–1783, and protracted wars against revolutionary France which only finally came to an end in 1815. The results of the wars did lead to a growth in trade and a rapid expansion of the British Empire). The rise of Walpole reflected a significant shift in power from the monarch to parliament. The whole pattern of English life was being transformed.

With a new political order steadily emerging, there was a recurrent sense of crisis. This was particularly the case in the second half of the century. Up until about 1757, there was a kind of pact between George I and then George II and the Whigs. After 1787, however, things began to fall apart. In particular, towards the end of the eighteenth century, there was a far greater sense of confrontation between conservative and radical figures in politics. Essentially, the country was changing at a rate that outpaced the ability of political institutions to respond to and govern that sense of change. A large number of writers were trying to get hold of and to comprehend the process of change. It is the novel as a genre that illustrates this most clearly, as writers constructed new narratives for a new century, but we can also point to works such as John Gay's *The Beggars Opera* (1728), Oliver Goldsmith's *The Deserted Village* (1770), and the plays of Richard Sheridan, such as *The School for*

Chapter Five
The Eighteenth-Century Literature (1690–1780)

Scandal (1777). These works seem to confront the teeming variety of eighteenth-century life, but there are other works that seem more intent on summation and definition and explanation of the new age, such as Edward Gibbon's *The History of the Decline and Fall of Roman Empire* (1776–1788) and Samuel Johnson's *Dictionary of the English Language* (1755).

The eighteenth century saw the fast development of England as a nation. Abroad, a vast expansion of British colonies in North America, India, and the West Indies, and a continuous increase of colonial wealth and trade provided England with a market for which the small-scale hand production methods of the home industry were hardly adequate. This created not only a steady demand for British goods but also standardized goods. And at home in the country, Acts of Enclosure were putting more land into fewer privileged rich landowners and forcing thousands of small farmers and tenants off land to become wage earners in industrial towns. This coming-together of free labour from the home and free capital gathered or plundered from the colonies was the essence of the Industrial Revolution. So, towards the middle of the eighteenth century, England had become the first powerful capitalist country in the world. It had become the workshop of the world, her manufactured goods flooding foreign markets far and near.

Along with the fast economic development, the British bourgeois or middle class also grew rapidly. It was the major force of the Revolution and was mainly composed of city people: traders, merchants, manufacturers, and other adventurers such as slave traders and colonists. As the Industrial Revolution went on, more and more people joined the rank of this class. Marx once pointed out that the bourgeois class of the eighteenth-century England was a revolutionary class then and different from the feudal aristocratic class. They were people who had known poverty and hardship, and most of them had obtained their present social status through hard work. To work, to economize and to accumulate wealth constituted the whole meaning of life. This aspect of social life is best found in the realistic novels of the century.

The eighteenth century is also known as the Age of Enlightenment or the Age of Reason. The Enlightenment Movement was a progressive intellectual movement which flourished in France and swept through the whole Western Europe at the time. The movement was a furtherance of the Renaissance of the fifteenth and sixteenth centuries. Its purpose was to enlighten the whole world with the light of modern philosophical and artistic ideas. The enlighteners celebrated reason or rationality, equality and science. They held that rationality or reason should be the only, the final cause of any human thought and activities. They called for a reference to order, reason and rules. They believed that when reason served as the yardstick for the measurement of all human activities and relations, every superstition, injustice and oppression was to yield to "eternal truth" "eternal justice" and "eternal equality". The belief provided theory for the French Revolution of 1689 and the American War of Independence in 1776. At the same time, the enlighteners advocated universal education. They believed that human beings were limited, dualistic, imperfect, and yet capable of rationality and perfection through education. If the masses were well educated, they thought, there would be a great chance for a democratic and equal human society. As a matter of fact, literature at the time, heavily didactic and moralizing, became a very popular means of public education. Famous among the great enlighteners in England were those great writers like Alexander Pope, Joseph Addison and Sir Richard Steele (the two pioneers of familiar essays), Jonathan Swift, Daniel Defoe, Richard Brinsley Sheridan, Henry Fielding and Samuel Johnson.

5.2 Literary Features

The Enlightenment Movement brought about a revival of interest in the old classical works. This tendency is known as neoclassicism. According to the neoclassicists, all forms of literature were to be modeled after the classical works of the ancient Greek and Roman writers (Homer, Virgil, Horace, and Ovid) and those of contemporary French ones. They believed that the artistic ideals should be of order, logic, restrained emotion and accuracy, and the literature should be judged in terms of its service to humanity. This belief led them to seek proportion, unity, harmony and grace in literary expressions, in an effort to delight, instruct and correct human beings, primarily as social animals. Thus a polite, urbane, witty, and intellectual art developed.

Neoclassicists had some fixed laws and rules for almost every genre of literature. Prose should be precise, direct, smooth and flexible. Poetry should be lyrical, epical, didactic, satiric or dramatic, and each class should be guided by its own principles. Drama should be written in the Heroic Couplets (iambic pentameter rhymed in two lines); the three unities of time, space and action should be strictly observed; regularity in construction should be adhered to, and type characters rather than individuals should be represented. Neoclassicism overlaps with the label "the Augustan Age", which is applied to the period from approximately 1700 to 1745, the age of Anne. The original Augustan Age was the period of Virgil, Horace and Ovid under the Roman emperor Augustus (27 BC–AD 14). Writers such as Pope, Addison and Swift not only admired the Roman Augustans but also drew parallels between the two periods, imitating their literary forms, their emphasis on social concerns, and their ideals of moderations, decorum and urbanity.

In the last few decades of the eighteenth century, the neoclassical emphasis upon reason, intellect, wit and form was rebelled against or challenged by the sentimentalists, and was, in due time, gradually replaced by Romanticism. But it had a lasting wholesome influence upon English literature. The poetic techniques and certain classical graces such as order, good form, unified structure, clarity and conciseness of language developed in this period have become a permanent heritage.

5.3 Eighteenth-Century Poetry

The poetry of the eighteenth century can be classified with a completeness and convenience uncommon in literary periods. In the first division is the complete triumph of the classical or conventional, ideal at once exemplified and achieved in the work of Pope. This is followed by a rather longer period, in which the dominant poetry—the kind of verse admired and praised by almost all the vulgar—is imitation of Pope, tempered more or less by that of Dryden. But side by side with both these, there is a party of mostly unintentional revolt which first, as represented by Thomson, reverts to nature in observation; then, as presented by Gray, while not neglecting nature, changes all the sources of its literary inspiration, seeking them always further back and wider.

5.3.1 Alexander Pope (1688–1744)

Alexander Pope, the chief poet of Queen Anne's reign, was one of the greatest masters of poetic form and a considerable satirist. He was an invalid of small stature and delicate constitution. Born in 1688, the son of a Catholic linen-draper in London, his first major poem *Essay on Criticism* was published in 1711, and in the following year the first version of *The Rape of the Lock* appeared (it was expanded in 1744). Initially associated with the Whigs, by 1713, Pope was a member of Jonathan Swift's Tory literary coterie. *Windsor Forest* (1713), a pastoral poem celebrating the political order established under Queen Anne, confirmed his allegiance to the Tories. In 1720, Pope translated Homer's *Iliad* into heroic couplets. A translation of the *Odyssey* followed in 1721, together with an edition of *Shakespeare's Works* in 1725. *The Dunciad* (1728), another mock-epic poem, laments the prevalence of dullness in contemporary literary culture while subjecting it to scathing satire. Other significant works are *An Essay on Man* (1733–1740), and four *Moral Essays*, in 1731–1735. What we see in all these poems is a concern, echoed in Pope's commitment to classical literature, with values in public life, which finds an appropriate focus in verse satire.

The Rape of the Lock is the essence of the mock heroic. It makes a family quarrel, over a lock of hair, into the subject of a playful poem full of paradoxes and witty observations on the self-regarding world it depicts, as the stolen lock is transported to the heavens to become a new star. "Fair tresses man's imperial race in snare" makes Belinda's hair an attractive trap for all mankind—a linking of the trivial with the apparently serious, which is Pope's most frequent trick in puncturing his target's self-importance.

The Dunciad is Pope's best-known satire. It is again mock heroic in style, and, like Dryden's *Mac Flecknoe* some fifty years before, it is an attack on the author's literary rivals, critics, and enemies. Pope groups them together as the general enemy "Dulness", which gradually takes over the world, and reduces it to chaos and darkness:

> See now, what Dulness and her sons admire;
> See! What the charms, that smites the simple heart
> Not touch'd by Nature, and not reach'd by Art
>
> (*The Dunciad*)

Essay on Criticism is a didactic poem in heroic couplets. It begins with an exposition of the rules of taste and the authority to be attributed to the ancient writers on the subject. The laws by which a critic should be guided are then discussed, and instances are given of critics who have departed from them. The work is remarkable as having been written when Pope was only 21.

In style, Pope has no superior for condensing an idea into a couplet, and almost half his verses have the neatness and point which make an epigram. He disavows all claims to the discovery of new ideas, this not being the province of "wit" or poetry:

Chapter Five
The Eighteenth-Century Literature (1690–1780)

> True wit is Nature to advantage dressed,
> What oft was thought, but never so well expressed.
>
> *(Essay on Criticism)*

This combination of commonplace thought and perfection of technique has given a number of sayings to the English language.

> Who shall decide when doctors disagree?
>
> You were my guide, philosopher, and friend.
>
> Know then thyself, presume not God to scan;
> The proper study of mankind is man.
>
> Hope springs eternal in the human breast:
> Man never is, but always to be, blest.
>
> A little learning is a dangerous thing.
>
> *(Essay on Criticism)*

In thought, Pope is a conservative, who, deeply offended by the world he describes, wants a world that will stand still, but at the same time, displays a desire for confrontation and violence, for some form of final struggle with the forces of anarchy and change. This indicates how a writer is the product and reflection of all the contradictory forces of the period in which he or she is writing.

5.3.2 James Thomson (1700–1748)

James Thomson is the poet of *The Seasons* (1726–1730), the first eighteenth-century-work to offer a new view of nature, written largely in blank verse. Thomson's vision of nature as harsh, especially in winter, but bountiful, stresses the "pure pleasure of the rural life" with no denial of the pain these pleasures can involve. Celebration of nature is closely allied with a sense of desolation, of hard work and harsh landscapes, so the tone of *The Seasons* is far removed from the classical idyll. In "Winter" of *The Seasons*, Thomson sees the negative side of a "philosophic melancholy", which is very much of his own time:

> Now nature droops;

> Languish the living herbs with pale decay,
> And all the various family flowers
> Their sunny robes resign. The falling fruit,
> Through the still night, forsake the parent-bough.
> That, in the first grey glances of the dawn,
> Looks wild, and wonders at the wintry waste.
>
> ("Winter")

5.3.3 Thomas Gray (1716–1771)

Thomas Gray was perhaps the most significant poet of the mid-eighteenth-century England. His best-known poem *Elegy Written in a Country Churchyard* (1751) has often been associated with the earlier "Graveyard School" of poetry, such as Edward Young's *Night Thoughts* (1742–1745) and Robert Blair's *The Grave* (1743). These graveyard poets wrote melancholy and reflective works, often set in graveyards, on the theme of death and human mortality, creating an atmosphere of "delightful gloom".

Gray's *Elegy*, a realistic pastoral in four-line quatrains, stresses simple lives and their value in unadorned language, which met the mid-eighteenth century mood and became highly popular.

> Full many a gem of purest ray scene,
> The dark unfathomed caves of ocean bear:
> Full many a flower is born to blush unseen,
> And waste its sweetness on the desert air.
>
> (*Elegy*)

The greatness as well as the popularity of the *Elegy* consists in its universal appeal. The solemnity of evening, the simple pathos of human life and the moving associations of a village church set in a homely landscape of southern England are expressed with a perfection which makes them memorable forever.

Gray's other important works include *Ode on a Distant Prospect of Eton College* (a recall of lost innocence), *The Progress of Poesy* (celebration of the continuity of poetry), and *The Bard* (the discontinuity of poetry).

Chapter Five
The Eighteenth-Century Literature (1690–1780)

The true successors to Gray's poetry are Oliver Goldsmith's *The Deserted Village*, William Cowper's *The Task* (1785) and George Crabbe's narrative poems of rural life, such as *The Village* (1783) and *The Borough* (1810). These range from blank verse to heroic couplets and poetic "letters", in their search for a form that could document the real life of the rural poor. This was the time of the Agrarian Revolution, when many people were forced to move from the country to the newly industrialized cities in search of work. The resulting desolation is the subject of Goldsmith's poem, for example, which contrasts an idyllic past, of the "loveliest village of the plain", with the harsh reality of the peasant:

> How often have I blessed the coming day,
> When toil remitting lent its turn to play.
> And all the village train, from labour free,
> Led up thin sports beneath the spreading tree.
> While many a pastime circled in the shade,
> The young contending as the old surveyed;
> And many a gambol frolicked o'er the ground,
> And sleights of art and feats of strength went around.
>
> (*The Deserted Village*)

5.4 Eighteenth-Century Prose

The most striking features in the prose literature of the eighteenth century were clearness of style and a habit of generalization. It was an age in which philosophers abounded, for a great writer had, to all appearances, made philosophy easy. John Locke (1632–1704), the author of *An Essay Concerning Human Understanding* (1690), and the founder of an important school of English thought, wrote on the most abstract subjects in a style founded on the simplest and commonest words. His epistemology and his crucial rejection of innate ideas in favour of the notion of knowledge based on external sensation and internal reflection helped to determine the tendency in many eighteenth-century writers to describe the observable world rather than offer subjective interpretations of the working of the psyche. Locke's assessors, Berkeley and Hume, maintained the alliance between philosophy and literature, and thus helped to give metaphorical principles a place in the thoughts of ordinary educated men and women. The philosophical habit of generalization pervaded almost every region of thought. It was an age of Enlightenment and men turned their skill in analysis upon every subject, confident in their power to banish all mystery from the world. Many leaders of religion allied themselves with the movement, and studied to demonstrate the truths of Christianity by rational evidence. It was in the atmosphere of "enlightenment" that appeared the following group of great essayists: Swift, Steele, Addison, Gibbon, and Johnson.

5.4.1 Jonathan Swift (1667–1745)

In originality and intellectual power, Swift is by far the greatest writer of his time. To his contemporaries he is the formidable pamphleteer whose pen could endanger governments and discredit treaties. To children he has been seen as the author of one of the most entrancing of fairy stories. To the lover of literature he is the satirist whose irony and intellectual rage are like forces of nature—tragic in their destructive might, uplifting in their exhibition of irresponsible power.

A sense of the shifting social order in the early eighteenth century is apparent in the writings of Swift. Though born and educated in Dublin, Swift was fundamentally English. In the disturbed year of 1688, Swift crossed the Channel to England with many others, and for a time he was employed as secretary to Sir. William Temple, at whose house, Moor Park, Swift lived for many years. It was at Temple's house that Swift became famous to the world as "Stella", and wrote his first two important works, *A Tale of a Tub* and *The Battle of the Books*, both published in 1704.

A Tale of a Tub is a brilliant satirical narrative on the excesses of Catholics and Puritans as seen from the middle position of the Anglican Church. The story tells how a father left to each of his three sons, Peter, Martin and Jack, a magical coat that would last as long as the wearer needed it. The will enjoined that the coat should be kept intact, without addition or diminution of the three sons. Martin is the truest to his father's commands. But at first all three brothers compromise with the spirit of the world, trying to alter the coat according to the whims and fashion that they contortedly justify.

The Battle of the Books was a prose satire. Its occasion was a controversy between ancient and modern learning. The book was originated as a complement to Temple's defense

Chapter Five
The Eighteenth-Century Literature (1690–1780)

of classical literature as opposed to its modern vernacular rival. It is now chiefly rendered as having given rise to Swift's fable of the spider and the bee. The spider, who is the symbol of modern learning, does nothing but spins webs of sophistry from its own entrails, while the bee, who stands for the ancients, ranges far and wide over the fields, bringing back honey and wax, which provide men with the things they most need—sweetness and light.

Between 1705 and 1714, Swift played an active part in public affairs, and enjoyed political favour during the reign of Queen Anne when he was a prolific pamphleteer in the Tory cause. But when the Whigs came back into power in 1714, Swift left England for Ireland. For some years, he began to write on Irish matters, in particular denouncing the conduct of absentee English landlords. Significant works from the period include the *Drapier's Letters* (1724), a series of satiric pamphlets stemming from a public and popular indignation at English indifference to Ireland, and *A Modest Proposal* (1729), another satiric pamphlet, which, ironically, recommends cannibalism (or more accurately, the rearing of children by the poor for consumption by the rich) as the only solution to Ireland's economic problems. It is also in this period that Swift produced his most celebrated satirical work, *Gulliver's Travels* (1726), in which Lemuel Gulliver recounts journeys to imaginary locations. Swift, who wrote such a miscellaneous range of works, many of them outside the established literary genres (*Gulliver's Travels*, for example, cannot be described as a novel, even though it was influenced by Defoe's *Robinson Crusoe*), and who repeatedly adopted an elusive ironic stance, is one of the most difficult authors to pin down. Yet the very elusiveness of Swift makes him an apt commentator in the early eighteenth century.

Gulliver's Travels is both a romance and a satire. Swift's aim, in the first place, is to attack the real world as he knew it, by reducing men and their ways to ridiculous proportions. The narrative of *Gulliver's Travels* is divided into four books: *The Voyage to Lilliput*, *The Voyage to Brobdingnag*, *The Voyage to Laputa*, and *The Voyage to Houynhnms*. In Lilliput, while effortlessly admired and respected, Gulliver nonchalantly performs heroic exploits and insists on preserving a conquered people's liberty. In Brobdingnag, persecuted by pets and servants, he becomes a show-off eager to see a people's liberty crushed by cannon. In the first two books, the tiny and enormous people are clearly versions of the Englishmen of Swift's day. Their trivial disputes reflect the kind of political infighting between the Whigs and the Tories and the pointlessness of religious controversies between different denominations within Christianity that characterizes the early eighteenth century. The third book hits out at several directions: colonial power, pedantry, and abstract learning. In the flying island of Laputa, Gulliver is enabled to call up the great men of old, and discovers the deceptions of history. The Struldbrugs, a race endowed with immortality, turn out to be the most miserable of mankind. The fourth book presents us with beings which look like human but are loathsomely ape-like beasts (Yahoos), and beings which look like horses but which are endowed with human reason and civilization and offer the lure of a new ideal. The Houyhnhnms' perfect rationality is genuinely impressive, but they are also funny, with their neighing language and gawky equine politeness. Gulliver has never appeared so ludicrous on his earlier voyages as here, from the beginning when he is frisked by an enquiring hoof to the end when he signalizes his new adoption of perfect reason by loving the smell of English horses. Here Gulliver has to recognize sadly that the Yahoos (who are close to his own species) are inferior to the horses in their qualities.

5.4.2 Joseph Addison (1672–1719) and Sir Richard Steele (1672–1729)

Addison and Steele had in common an almost lifelong friendship and an interest in the theater. Between them they invented a new literary genre in their periodicals *The Tatler* and *The Spectator*.

The Tatler, founded by Richard Steele, ran from April 1709 to January 1711, to be followed by *The Spectator*, run by Steele with Addison from March 1711 until December 1712, and by Addison alone for several months in 1714. These were journals of coffee house gossip and ideas in London. *The Spectator* became the journal of a gentleman's club, led by the fictional, eccentric and lovable Sir Roger de Coverley. To center a periodical on sustained fictional characters became a pattern for later essayists such as Fielding.

The Spectator appeared six times a week, and it contained, besides general news, advertisements and other miscellaneous matters, an essay from one of a few regular contributors, among whom Addison was the most brilliant and inventive. These essays, accurately reflecting the spirit of their age, promote a type of gentleman: He believes in reason and control, values correct opinion higher than anarchic wit, and is less ready to call a spade a spade; he is civic-minded, moderate, Christian; he admires women for moral and supportive qualities rather than for drive, initiative or sex; he has noticed that they are badly educated and wishes to raise their standard of knowledge as well as behavior. Steele was susceptible to and fascinated by women, Addison more fastidious and critical. They have been at least sufficiently congratulated for improving the status of women. Both care deeply about minute points of social convention; both mix more than a touch of complacency with their humor. With them and all the others which contributed to those essays, a new kind of prose, direct, familiar, and flexible, came into being.

The reputation of *The Tatler* and *The Spectator* has eclipsed Defoe's *Review* (written single-handled, weekly from 1704–1713), a quiet achievement in its way but thoroughly political and historical rather than all-embracingly cultural.

5.4.3 Samuel Johnson (1709–1784)

Dr. Johnson became during his lifetime the very center of English literature and of a number of fertile literary groupings gathered by himself. Though an important poet of his day, today Johnson is mainly remembered for his *Dictionary of the English Language*, and as the first major critic in English.

Johnson's monumental *Dictionary of the English Language* was published in 1755; and the nine years of work it cost him bore immediate fruit, establishing him as the leading literary figure of his age. *The Dictionary* is more than just a set of definitions. It is a rich mine of quotations and references, and remains a valuable reference work to this day. Rather than fixing the language and its usages definitively, it is a starting point for the documentation, the constant enrichment, development and change in the English language. It is an ongoing process, with the *Oxford English Dictionary*, constantly documenting new coinages, new usages and new forms in the twenty-first century.

During his *Dictionary* years, Johnson wrote the *Rambler* (1750–1752). Though it follows *The Spectator* tradition, it differs from earlier essays in its steady maintenance of a non-frivolous tone. Johnson ponders religious and psychological processes such as self-delusion and procrastination; literary-critical matters such as biography, pastoral, and the new novel form; social and topical issues such as marriage, prostitution, and rural retirement. He is much concerned with the exceptional individual: outlets for talent, outcome of ambition.

Johnson's *Lives of the English Poets*, first published in 1779–1781, as *Prefaces, Biographical and Critical*, is dedicated to an ambitious collection of the poets' works. Here Johnson is combining personal biography, literary history, and analytical criticism. He maps a series of relationships: that of great writings, generally praised, with other works either worthy or unworthy of respect; that of the great writers' achievement with the unfulfilled aims and stalled aspirations of petty writers; that of books with their authors. The work remains a landmark in establishing criteria of taste, and in the documentation of literary history, which was to have a lasting influence on future generations of writers and critics.

James Boswell learned much from Johnson's practice. He gave himself the enormous task, after Johnson's death in 1784, of producing *Life of Johnson* (1791) (which is now held to be a model of biography; rich in detail and anecdote, a complete picture of the man and his times). Boswell's *Life of Johnson* carries on Johnson's own contribution to the growing art of biography, and consolidates Johnson's position as a major literary figure.

Johnson, as a poet, was Pope's chief successor. He carried on the tradition of the satire in his two poems *London* (1738) and *The Vanity of Human Wishes* (1749). Something in the somber and sincere nature of these two works, especially of the second, endears them to many readers, who can recognize beneath the pompous phrasing, the pulse of a human heart. When Johnson declaimed against the vanity of fame, of long life and of beauty, he expressed his profound belief that human pleasures are uncertain and unsatisfying. His verse rings truest in his lines on the vanity of literary ambition:

> When first the college rolls receive his name,
> The young enthusiast quits his ease for fame;
> Thro' all his veins the fever of renown
> Burns from the strong contagion of the gown;
> O'er Bodley's Dome his future labours spread
> And Bacon's Mansion trembles O'er his head;
> Are these thy views? Proceed, illustrious youth;
> And Virtue guard that to throne of Truth.
>
> (*The Vanity of Human Wishes*)

5.4.4 Edward Gibbon (1737–1794)

In the eighteenth century, with the growth of publishing and with the intellectual climate of the Enlightenment, there was a great demand for new historical writing. The greatest product of this was *The History of the Decline and Fall of the Roman Empire*, a massive six-

Chapter Five
The Eighteenth-Century Literature (1690-1780)

volume work published between 1776 and 1786, precisely between the American Revolution and the French Revolution. The content is important, as the author Edward Gibbon was examining not only the greatness of Rome, but the forces which brought about its decay. Gibbon's interpretation of history was controversial, but his accurate scholarship and engaging prose style have made *The History of the Decline and Fall of the Roman Empire* the most enduring work of history in English.

5.5 Eighteenth-Century Novel

The novel and fiction became the dominant form and genre in terms of readership in the eighteenth century, although for more than a century they would be considered "inferior" by critics.

The novel was not a sudden innovation at the end of the seventeenth century. Accounts of travels such as Sir Thomas More's *Utopia* and Thomas Nashe's *The Unfortunate Traveller*, essays, which often dealt in fiction, such as *The Talter* and *The Spectator*, and various prose narratives, primarily travels, biographies, and collection of letters, all paved the way for the eighteenth-century novels.

The novel as most people think of it today first appeared with the publication of Daniel Defoe's *Robinson Crusoe*. By the time Samuel Richardson's *Clarissa* (1747–1748), Henry Fielding's *Tom Jones* (1749) and Laurence Sterne's *Tristram Shandy* (1759–1767) had been published, the genre was not only well established but its distinctive features were also apparent.

The novel, emerging in the early eighteenth century when a new kind of commercial society was taking shape, by and large, reports upon the experiences of the new middle-class people, who had to work for a living. It serves for the middle-class audience as a mirror in which they can see, albeit with some exaggeration, the dilemmas of their own lives reflected. Such novels tend to be realistic and secular. Another thing that is worth noting here is that in many eighteenth-century novels, the story is of someone working their way in the world. The hero or heroine in a typical novel is not at ease with the established order, and sets out to create his or her own life. Then the eighteenth-century novel tends to be didactic. There is an ambiguous contrast between vicarious pleasure and excitement and the established morality.

5.5.1 Daniel Defoe (1660–1731)

Daniel Defoe, the first true master of the English novel, is one of the most prolific writers not only in his own time but in the entire history of English literature. Before he came to novel writing, Defoe had had the experience of writing essays, travels, didactic dialogues, political pamphlets and satirical verse, from all of which sprang his later great novels.

The novels of Daniel Defoe are fundamental to eighteenth-century ways of thinking. They range from the quasi-factual *A Journal of the Plague Year*, an almost journalistic (but fictional) account of London between 1664 and 1665 to *Robinson Crusoe*, one of the most enduring fables of Western culture. Each novel, written in a plain-written style, focuses on an individual's struggle for survival in a competitive world, and each has a certain topicality. *The Adventures of Captain Singleton* (1720) describes the career of a seafarer, initially possessed of "no sense of virtue or religion", who became both mutineer and private before discovering the virtues of religion, honest money, and marriage. *Colonel Jack* (1722) depicts Jack's struggles as a child pickpocket in the disorienting and claustrophobic slums of London. *Moll Flanders* (1722) and *The Fortunate Mistress*, better known as *Roxana* (1724), have the much-abused, belatedly penitent, entrepreneurial women characters. Beginning as a servant made pregnant by her employer's son, Moll then has to fend for herself even if this involves stealing and selling her body. By the end of the novel, she has adopted a pious religious tone as she looks back on the wicked life she has led, but here there is a telling sense of a huge gap between moral and religious platitudes and the conduct that is necessary for survival in a commercial society. Roxana declines from respectability, partly through the disgraceful treatment meted out to her by the men on whom she relies, and partly through her own, highly selfish, sense of self-preservation. These two novels include plenty of sexual incidents, and reflect Defoe's interest in redrawing the limits set to women's permissible activities in commercial and public life.

Robinson Crusoe differs from many of Defoe's earlier works in that it represents private moral zeal rather than a public plea for reform. Its emphasis is on spiritual rather than on political justice. Crusoe is "of good family" and because of his sound education he is "not bred to any trade". His decision to go to sea is an act of rebellion, determined on in defiance to both his mother and his father, and from it he traces his withdrawal from grace and embarkation on the slow, painful and redemptive journey back to a state of grace. Although

Chapter Five
The Eighteenth-Century Literature (1690-1780)

Crusoe's self-exploratory time on the island upon which he is shipwrecked, his cultivation of the land and of his soul, and his later imposition of his codes of belief and action on Friday, have frequently been interpreted as a fictional enactment of the processes of European colonization, his story has both a particular and a most universal application. When his island is "peopled" by Friday and by Friday's father and a Spanish sailor, Crusoe thinks of himself as a king with "an undoubted right of dominion", an "absolute lord and lawgiver". As such, however, he establishes a principle: a Liberty of Conscience which tolerates pagan, Protestant, and Catholic alike. More significantly, Crusoe's earlier heroism is that of the ordinary human will pitted against an alien environment; as far as he can, he brings his surroundings under his rational and practical control not as a proto-colonist but as a lonely exile. He records his experiences and his achievements meticulously, even repetitively, because he is logging the nature of his moral survival. He is the methodical diarist delighted both by his own resourcefulness and by his awareness that a benign God helps those who help themselves.

5.5.2 Samuel Richardson (1689–1761)

Richardson, the most significant novelist after Defoe, was born to a lower-middle-class couple and to limited schooling. He was apprenticed to a printer and flourished in that trade. Among the works he published in the late 1730s were books of moral advice and a version for the times of Aesop's *Fables*. The success of these led him to develop a series of "familiar letters" with their original aim being a manual of letter-writing, but these letters turned into a major epistolary novel, *Pamela*, published in 1740.

Pamela or *Virtue Rewarded* proved the most influential novel among those told in the form of letters. It concerns a servant girl, Pamela Andrews, whose fictional letters to her parents give a breathless, blow-by-blow accounts of how she resists her master's first advances, his bribes, his psychological pressures, and finally her own growing response to him; how once he has learned to appreciate and respect her nature; how he proposes marriage in earnest. The story does not end there: Richardson's didactic purpose requires Pamela to prove by her behavior in her married state that she is exceptional enough to deserve her exceptional promotion. The novel is a relatively simple moral fable for its audience, about how the ordinary person can thrive in the modern world. In it, Richardson indicates that a woman, without a career as a possibility, has to trade upon her physical attributes while resisting the notion of herself as a commodity.

Clarissa or *The History of a Young Lady* is Richardson's most epistolary novel and his masterpiece, which marks a major step forward. There are four major letter writers, and in *Pamela* almost all the letters come from the heroine alone. Unlike *Pamela*, *Clarissa* ends in tragedy. Clarissa, a beautiful young woman, is encouraged by her family to marry a rich neighbour, Solmes, but is also being pursued by a notorious rake called Lovelace. Clarissa eventually decides to run off with Lovelace. She is imprisoned in a brothel, where Lovelace drugs and rapes her. She escapes, and seems to be regaining a sense of her integrity and moral worth, but subsequently dies as she cannot come to terms with what she has experienced. At the end of the novel, Lovelace dies in a duel with Clarissa's cousin, Colonel Morden.

Clarissa demonstrates how authority and power are misused, both by parents and lovers. Although Clarissa is the victim of parental strictures, sibling rivalry, and the physical and spiritual abuse of her lover, she emerges as a model of discretion and conscience and she endures her slow martyrdom with patience and intelligence. She is the first great bourgeois heroine and the first female protestant saint of fiction. The characterization, with its unity of construction and psychological exploration of the secret places of the heart, makes the novel a great contribution to the development of the novel. Richardson's last novel, in which he attempts to draw the character of a perfect gentleman, is *Sir Charles Grandson* (1753–1754).

5.5.3 Henry Fielding (1707–1754)

Henry Fielding, the greatest English novelist in the eighteenth century, was born into a family that ranked among English gentry, and was well educated when he was young. He began his literary career in the theater and produced a large number of plays, neither very bad nor very good, of which *Tom Thumb*, a burlesque "tragedy of tragedies", is the best, and the only one which has kept any reputation. Fielding's flirtation with the theater came to an abrupt end in 1737 when his political satires *Paquin* and *The Historical Register for 1736* provoked Walpole's government into passing a Licensing Act which introduced official censorship and restricted London performances to two approved theaters.

Fielding learned much from his practical experience of the stage. His novels reveal a grasp of idiomatic speech and dialogue, a sound understanding of the patterning of incident and a relish for a well-established denouement. His delight in burlesque also influenced his

Chapter Five
The Eighteenth-Century Literature (1690–1780)

satires on *Pamela*, *Shamela* (1741) and *Joseph Andrews* (1742).

Unlike Richardson who was quite content with the sentimental view of things, and individual inward complexity, and who carefully guarded himself from the raw breath of the outer world, Fielding, on the other hand, knew life from firsthand experience of its gross and boisterous, as well as its polite and learned side, and insisted that people can be judged instantly on the basis of generally agreed social or moral truths about human nature. Where Richardson had sought to examine the inner life of his confessional correspondents, Fielding's narrator insisted that he must generalize and observe the evidence of external human characteristics. His moral preoccupation is not with a single class or with the individual ideal, but with the definition of a human norm. Fielding took the novel forward from Richardson's epistolary form to what he called "comic epics in prose". Fielding's ambition for prose romance is to take the wide range of character, incident, diction and influence from the epic and to remould this material according to comic rather than "serious" principles. This stress on comedy made for a further insistence on the place of the "ridiculous" in art. The true "ridiculous", he affirmed, had a single source in a human affectation which proceeds from either vanity or hypocrisy. Prose fiction could successfully adopt a moral stance without resorting to the cant of a novel such as *Pamela*, whose heroine's virtue of chastity as in Fielding's eyes becomes a valuable commodity to secure a husband. It could, moreover, endeavor to laugh away faults rather than to preach against them. All those feature Fielding's four great novels: *Joseph Andrews*, *Jonathan Wild the Great* (1743), *The History of Tom Jones, a Foundling* (1749), and *Amelia* (1752).

Joseph Andrews was intended as a parody on Richardson's *Pamela*, taking as his hero Joseph Andrews, Pamela's brother, whose adventures were to afford an amusing parallel to those of his sister. Joseph, in service of another branch of the Booby family, resisting the lures of his employer, is a bold but effective device for making fun of chastity (male) as a heavy moral issue. But after a few chapters, the novel rapidly transcends the parodic mood by experimenting with a new, neo-classical fictional form, humorous and ironic, with an omniscient narrative presence controlling the lives and destinies of his characters. The novel has, as its full title (*The Adventures of Joseph Andrews and His Friend, Mr. Abraham Adams*) suggests, two heroes, the innocent Joseph and his equally innocent Christian protector, Parson Adams. Adams is a man of learning and good sense but he is as entirely ignorant of the ways of this world as an infant just entered into it could possibly be. Joseph and Adams, cast out as wanderers, engage in an epic voyage of discovery during which they generally seem to encounter selfishness, villainy, and corruption. But the naughty world through which they pass is illuminated not simply by Adams's selfishness but also by the unexpected charity of the humble and meek. If the novel variously exposes hypocrisy, it also discovers simple honesty and ordinary generosity in the interstices of a corrupt society. It is a virtue that does not seek for a reward.

Jonathan Wild the Great is a story of a criminal. It further ramifies the novelist's experimental interest in the force of the ridiculous as an exposer of the hypocritical. It also reasserts the essentially social, as opposed to private, weight of his moral insistence. The narrative is shaped around a simple recurrent biographical formula: A "Great Man" brings "all manner of mischief on mankind", whereas a "good" man removes mischief; the "great" man exploits society, while the "good" man enhances it. In low life, as much as in high life, the "great" are heaped up as examples; thus, if the professional criminal and thief-taker Wild can be called "great", so a "great" man, such as the Prime Minister, Sir Robert Walpole, can be equated with a thief. So the satirical target is, as it was in Fielding's plays, the Prime Minister, who is "Newgate with the mask on". Wild's career of cheating, robbing, and vice leads him to Newgate, and a sentence of death. He faces it most unheroically, but emerges as a champion of hypocrisy and double-dealing—a devil-figure for the times. The steady, anti-heroic stance in the novel exerted a profound influence over Fielding's most dedicated nineteenth-century admirer, Thackeray.

Tom Jones, Fielding's masterpiece, starts with Tom being found as a baby by squire Allworthy. As he grows up, he falls in love with Allworthy's niece, Sophia Weston, but his relationship with Molly Seagrim, a gamekeeper's daughter, leads to his expulsion from the squire's house. He sets out for London, where he drifts into an affair with Lady Bellaston. After many complications, it is revealed that Tom is the son of Allworthy's sister, Bridget, and the rightful heir to the estate. He is now in a position to marry Sophia.

Tom Jones is Fielding's most meticulous response to the challenge of classical epic and his most considered comic redefinition of the role of the epic hero. That Tom and his "great nature" will be finally justified by the shape by the narrative is a basic assumption of the comedy; his journey towards justification is dependent on the very nature of the epic structure. The novel is divided into eighteen books, with three groups of six to tell Tom's life in different periods. The symmetry of the novels construction is not only a modern prose version of Homeric or Virgilian form but also a tidy neo-classical shape which can contain within it a whole series of comments on other eighteenth-century forms: the satire, the pastoral, the comedy, and the mock-heroic. It is a tour-de-force of patterning, an assertion of the ultimate tidiness and proportion of the universe, and a working-out of a representative human destiny. Tom remains resilient despite his misfortune; he makes mistakes; he is misjudged, and he is plotted against, but his triumph is viewed as a moral vindication.

Amelia is Fielding's most sombre novel. When it was published in 1752, Fielding announced that the book was "sincerely designed to promote the cause of virtue, and to expose some of the most glaring evils, as well public as private, which at present infest the country". *Amelia* is a novel of married life which dispenses with the epic journey of his earlier fiction. It traces the fraught and uncertain career of Captain Billy Booth and the frequent distress and isolation of his prudent, constant, lovely wife. It begins in a magistrate's court, descends to the squalid confinement of Newgate prison, and maintains an impression of the general oppressiveness and multiple temptations of London life. Only with the fortuitous final discovery that Amelia is an heiress does the couple manage to escape again to the purer pleasures and securities of country life. Despite its vivid depiction of urban tawdriness, its often-savage exposure of tricks and vulgarity, and its suggestion of psychological intensity, it cannot be compared to the other three novels in popularity.

5.5.4 Laurence Sterne (1713–1768)

Of the numerous successors of Richardson and Fielding, who either are psychological novelists following the model of Richardson or social and comic writers following the model of Fielding, there are two men of originality who struck out new paths for themselves. One is Laurence Sterne, and the other is Tobias Smollett.

Laurence Sterne is one of the strangest figures in English literature. His chief novel, *Tristram Shandy,* is as much the revelation of its witty and whimsical author as a picture of life. It professes to be the autobiography of Tristram, but from the outset there is disruption of the linear and progressive pattern that we might expect. The story starts before Tristram's birth, as he describes his own conception, and from that point on he finds it all but impossible to write a chapter without digressing. It actually takes the best past of three volumes before Tristram is born. Chapters are deliberately out of sequence. Sterne also employs tactics such as the use of a black page when a death occurs. The effect is a quite brilliant deconstruction of all the ways in which novels presume to arrange and interpret people's lives. But *Tristram Shandy* is also associated with the eighteenth-century cult of sensibility in which it focuses on delicate and sensitive emotions and their importance in contributing towards a civilized society. That is why Sterne sometimes is referred to as the leading figure of the sentimentalist school, which held that a powerful evocation of feeling or a shared compassion, made ultimately for a more humane society. Sterne wrote another novel, *A Sentimental Journey* (1768), a wonderfully curious parody of the conventional travel-book, and an episodic collection of sketches and interludes, selected so as to give an impression of artful randomness.

Sterne has been seen as the originator of what came in the twentieth century to be known as "stream of consciousness", by which the novel seems, first and foremost, to parody the developing conventions of the novel as a genre, pointing up the absurdities, contradictions, and impossibilities of relating time, space, reality, and relationships in a linear form. The plot of the novel in the early eighteenth century followed the natural order of things: beginning, middle, and end. Sterne was the first to employ these "not necessarily in that order". He also played with digressions, episodes going off at a tangent from the "main" line of the plot. Tristram Shandy is conceived right at the beginning, born in Volume III—but the story ends 4 years before this birth. In a famous use of graphological effect, Sterne's narrator, Tristram, displays the difficulty of keeping to one single line of his story.

5.5.5 Tobias Smollett (1721–1771)

Tobias Smollett was a Scotsman. His principal works are *Roderick Random* (1748), *Peregrine Pickle* (1751) and *The Expedition of Humphrey Clinker* (1771), novels that add an important extra dimension to our understanding of the eighteenth century.

Roderick Random is a series of episodes strung together on the life of the combative, often violent hero, who is also capable of generosity and affection. Roderick Random qualifies as a surgeon's mate but lacks money of the bribe that could secure him a commission in the navy. He is seized by a press-gang and forced into service as a common sailor, but becomes the surgeon's mate on the ship. Returning to England, he is shipwrecked and then robbed. Eventually, after a series of bizarre adventures, he meets up with a wealthy trader, Don Roderigo, who turns out to be his father. The novel shows Smollett's traditional stance in his use of the Picaresque, a loose form of narrative in which the hero wanders along falling into a miscellaneous mixture of traps and diversions, but offers an unblinking view of the brutality, inhumanity and rapaciousness of the eighteenth-century life, which is made more apparent in the volatility and violence of the language in the novel.

5.5.6 Oliver Goldsmith (1730–1774)

Oliver Goldsmith is a successful poet and comic dramatist as well as a novelist. He published his novel *The Vicar of Wakefield* in 1766, which became one of the most popular works of fiction in the English language. The novel is a kind of pastoral parable, an improbable fairy-tale of a vicar whose family is beset by misfortunes; but redemption and justice triumph in the end.

The story is told by the Revd. Dr. Primrose, the Vicar, kindly, charitable, and devoid of worldly wisdom. His wife Deborah is proud of her housekeeping and her six children, two girls, Olivia and Sophia, and four boys. The Vicar loses his independent fortune through the bankruptcy of a merchant. They move to a new living under the patronage of a certain Squire Thornhill. Thornhill, who is an unprincipled ruffian, seduces Olivia after a mock ceremony of marriage, and deserts her. She is discovered by her father and brought home, but his humble vicarage is destroyed by fire. He himself is thrown into prison for debt at the suit of Thornhill, and George Primrose, who challenges the latter to a duel to avenge his sister, is overpowered by ruffians and likewise sent to prison. The Vicar's second daughter, Sophia, is forcibly carried off in a post chaise by an unknown villain, and Olivia, who has been pining away since her desertion, is reported to the Vicar to be dead. All these are the misfortunes he bears with fortitude and resignation.

On their removal to their new vicarage, the Primrose family have made the acquaintance of a certain Mr. Burchell, who appears to be a broken-down gentleman, kind-hearted but somewhat eccentric. By good fortune he is now the means of rescuing Sophia. It thereupon appears that he is in reality the benevolent Sir William Thornhill, the squire's uncle. The squire's villainy is now exposed, and at last all ends happily. Sir William marries Sophia. Olivia is found not to be dead, and her marriage to the squire is shown to have been, contrary to his intentions, legal. The Vicar's fortune is restored to him, and George marries the young lady of his heart.

5.6 Eighteenth-Century Drama

In the first few decades of the eighteenth century, English drama went into critical decline, partly because the middle classes were turning to journals, newspapers and the developing new genre of fictional prose to find discussion, entertainment and reinforcement of their values and beliefs. Farce and musical plays became the regular entertainment, and only *The Beggar's Opera* (1728) by John Gay achieved lasting popular success. This so-called Newgate pastoral (an ironic description, since Newgate was London's principal prison, and frequently features in writing about the lower depths of London society of the time) explores the corrupt ways of the criminal underworld while subversively suggesting parallels between them and the shady maneuvres of politicians. Its political satire, together with that of Fielding's *The Historical Register for 1736*, brought about the Theaters Licensing Act of 1737, which did not altogether kill drama but did successfully stifle it. The history of the eighteenth-century theater became the history of actors rather than of plays, although most of the literary figures of the time did try writing for the theater at one time. Dr. Johnson's tragedy *Irene* ran for nine performances in 1749, for example, and Richard Steele, of *The Spectator* fame, left a heritage of sentimental comedy, which held the stage for more than sixty years after his death in 1729. Oliver Goldsmith and Richard Brinsley Sheridan were both Irishmen, the only two writers of theatrical comedy who managed to write lasting masterpieces which go against the prevailing trend of sentimentalism in the late eighteenth century.

5.6.1 Oliver Goldsmith (1730–1774)

Goldsmith's *She Stoops to Conquer* (1773) is seen as the successful reaction to the sentimental comedy originated by Steele. The comic premise is that the hero, Marlow, is shy with ladies of his own social level, but quite open with servants and barmaids. So the resourceful heroine, Miss Hardcastle "stoops" to an acceptable level to "conquer" him. The "stooping" is dramatically complicated by a succession of misunderstandings and social shortcomings.

5.6.2 Richard Brinsley Sheridan (1751–1816)

Richard Brinsley Sheridan is the most successful playwright of the eighteenth century. His plays, especially *The Rivals* (1775), *The School for Scandal*, and *The Critic* (1779), are generally regarded as important links between the masterpieces of Shakespeare and those of Bernard Shaw, and as true classics in English comedy. In his plays, morality is the constant theme. He is much concerned with the current moral issues and lashes harshly at the social vices of the day. In *The Rivals*, a comedy of manners, he is satirizing the traditional practice of the parents to arrange marriages for their children without considering the latter's opinion. *The School for Scandal* is a marvelously witty exposure of surfaces, of the affectations, petty hypocrisies, and peccadilloes which form the stuff of the "scandal".

Sheridan is a great artist. His plays are the product of a dramatic genius as well as of a well-versed theatrical man. Though his dramatic techniques are largely conventional, they are exploited to the best. His plots are well organized; his characters, either major or minor, are all sharply drawn, and his manipulation of such devices as disguise, mistaken identity and dramatic irony is masterly. Witty dialogues and neat and decent language also make a characteristic of his plays.

The School for Scandal presents London society as a hotbed of gossip and intrigue. It is Sheridan's most aphoristic and shapely play. The play contrasts two brothers, Joseph Surface, a sentimental and self-seeking hypocrite, and Charles, a virtuous and generous libertine. Charles is in love with Maria, the ward of Sir Peter Teazle, and his love is returned; Joseph is courting the same girl for her fortune, while at the same time dallying with Lady Teazle. Sir Peter, an old man who has married his young wife six months previously, is made wretched by her frivolity and the fashionable society he inhabits. This includes the scandal-mongers Sir Benjamin Backbite, Crabtree, Lady Sneerwell, and Mrs. Candour. Sir Oliver Surface, the rich uncle of Joseph and Charles, returns unexpectedly from India, and decides to test the characters of his nephews before revealing his identity. He visits Charles in the guise of a money-lender, Mr. Premium, and Charles cheerfully sells him the family portraits, but refuses to sell the portrait of Sir Oliver himself and thus unwittingly wins the old man's heart. Meanwhile Joseph receives a visit from Lady Teazle and attempts to seduce her. The sudden arrival of Sir Peter obliges Lady Teazle to hide behind a screen. The arrival of Charles sends Sir Peter in turn to hide. The conversation between Charles and Joseph proves to Sir Peter that his suspicions of Charles were unfounded. When Charles flings down the screen, he reveals Lady Teazle. Sir Oliver then enters in the character of a needy relative, begging for assistance. Joseph refuses, giving as his reason the avarice of his uncle,

Sir Oliver, and his characters now stand fully revealed. Charles is united to Maria, and Sir Peter and Lady Teazle are happily reconciled.

The play is a sharp satire on the moral degeneracy of the aristocratic-bourgeois society in the eighteenth-century England, on the various scandal-mongering among the idle rich, on the reckless life of extravagance and love intrigues in the high society and, above all, on the immorality and hypocrisy behind the mask of honourable living and high-sounding moral principles.

5.7 Reading

A Little Learning Is a Dangerous Thing

By Alexander Pope

A little learning is a dangerous thing;
Drink deep, or taste not the Pierian spring[1]:
There shallow draughts intoxicate the brain,
And drinking largely sobers us again.
Fired at first sight with what the Muse imparts,
In fearless youth we tempt[2] the heights of arts,
While from the bounded level of our mind
Short views we take, nor see the lengths behind;
But more advanced, behold with strange surprise
New distant scenes of endless science rise!
So pleased at first the towering Alps[3] we try,
Mount o'er the vales, and seem to tread the sky;
The eternal snows appear already past,
And the first clouds and mountains seem the last;
But, those attained, we tremble to survey
The growing labours of the lengthened way,
The increasing prospect tires our wandering eyes,
Hills peep o'er hills, and Alps on Alps arise!

Chapter Five
The Eighteenth-Century Literature (1690–1780)

Notes

1. **Pierian spring:** the Muses' spring. The water gives people inspiration.

2. **tempt:** attempt, try.

3. **Alps:** the highest mountain range in Europe, famous for its peaks and snows.

Tom Jones
Chapter VIII, Book Four

By Henry Fielding

Mr. Western had an estate in this parish; and as his house stood at little greater distance from this church than from his own, he very often came to Divine Service[1] here; and both he and the charming Sophia happened to be present at this time.

Sophia was much pleased with the beauty of the girl[2], whom she pitied for her simplicity in having dressed herself in that manner, as she saw the envy which it had occasioned[3] among her equals. She no sooner came home than she sent for the gamekeeper[4], and ordered him to bring his daughter to her, saying she would provide for her in the family, and might possibly place the girl about her own person, when her own maid, who was now going away, had left her.

Poor Seagrim was thunderstruck at this; for he was no stranger to the fault in the shape of his daughter. He answered, in a stammering voice, that he was afraid Molly would be too awkward to wait on her ladyship, as she had never been at service. "No matter for that," says Sophia, "she will soon improve. I am pleased with the girl, and am resolved to try her."

Black George now repaired to[5] his wife, on whose prudent counsel he depended to extricate him out of this dilemma; but when he came thither he found his house in some confusion. So great envy had this sack[6] occasioned, that when Mr. Allworthy and the other gentry were gone from church, the rage, which had hitherto been confined, burst into an uproar; and, having vented itself at first in opprobrious words, laughs, hisses, and gestures, betook itself at last to certain missile weapons[7]; which, though from their plastic nature they threatened neither the loss of life or a limb, were however sufficiently dreadful to a well-dressed lady. Molly had too much spirit to bear this treatment tamely. Having therefore—but hold, as we are diffident of our own abilities, let us here invite a superior power to our assistance.

Ye Muses, then, whoever ye are, who love to sing battles, and principally thou who didst recount the slaughter in those fields where Hudibras and Trulla fought, if thou went not starved with thy friend Butler, assist me on this great occasion.[8] All things are not in the power of all.[9]

As a vast herd of cows in a rich farmer's yard, if, while they are milked, they hear their calves at a distance, lamenting the robbery which is then committing, roar and bellow; so roared forth the Somersetshire mob[10] an hallaloo, made up of almost as many squalls, screams, and other different sounds as there were persons, or indeed passions among them: Some were inspired by rage, others alarmed by fear, and others had nothing in their heads but the love of fun; but chiefly Envy, the sister of Satan, and his constant companion, rushed among the crowd, and blew up the fury of the women; who no sooner came up to Molly than they pelted her with dirt and rubbish.

Molly, having endeavored in vain to make a handsome retreat, faced about; and laying hold of ragged Bess, who advanced in the front of the enemy, she at one blow felled her to the ground. The whole army of the enemy (though near a hundred in number), seeing the fate of their general, gave back many paces, and retired behind a new-dug grave; for the churchyard was the field of battle, where there was to be a funeral that very evening. Molly pursued her victory, and catching up a skull which lay on the side of the grave, discharged it with such fury, that having hit a tailor on the head, the two skulls sent equally forth a hollow sound at their meeting, and the tailor took presently measure of his length on the ground[11], where the skulls lay side by side, and it was doubtful which was the more valuable of the two. Molly then taking a thigh-bone in her hand, fell in among the flying ranks, and dealing her blows with great liberality on either side, overthrew the carcass of many a mighty hero and heroine.

Recount, O Muse, the names of those who fell on this fatal day. First, Jemmy Tweedie felt on his hinder head[12] the direful bone. Him the pleasant banks of sweetly-winding Stour[13] had nourished, where he first learnt the vocal art, with which, wandering up and down at wakes and fairs, he cheered the rural nymphs and swains,

Chapter Five
The Eighteenth-Century Literature (1690–1780)

when upon the green they interweaved the sprightly dance; while he himself stood fiddling and jumping to his own music. How little now avails his fiddle! He thumps the verdant floor with his carcass. Next, old Echepole, the sowgelder, received a blow in his forehead from our Amazonian heroine[14], and immediately fell to the ground. He was a swinging fat fellow, and fell with almost as much noise as a house. His tobacco-box dropped at the same time from his pocket, which Molly took up as lawful spoils. Then Kate of the Mill tumbled unfortunately over a tombstone, which catching hold of her ungartered stocking inverted the order of nature, and gave her heels the superiority to her head. Betty Pippin, with young Roger her lover, fell both to the ground; where, oh perverse fate! She salutes the earth, and he the sky.[15] Tom Freckle, the smith's son, was the next victim to her rage. He was an ingenious workman, and made excellent patterns; nay, the very pattern with which he was knocked down was his own workmanship. Had he been at that time singing psalms in the church, he would have avoided a broken head. Miss Crow, the daughter of a farmer; John Giddish, himself a farmer; Nan Slouch, Esther Codling, Will Spray, Tom Bennet; the three Misses Potter, whose father keeps the sign of the Red Lion; Betty Chambermaid, Jack Ostler, and many others of inferior note, lay rolling among the graves.

Not that the strenuous arm of Molly reached all these; for many of them in their flight overthrew each other.

But now Fortune, fearing she had acted out of character, and had inclined too long to the same side, especially as it was the right side, hastily turned about: for now Goody Brown—whom Zekiel Brown caressed in his arms; nor he alone, but half the parish besides; so famous was she in the fields of Venus[16], nor indeed less in those of Mars[17]. The trophies of both these her husband always bore about on his head and face; for if ever human head did by its horns display the amorous glories of a wife, Zekiel's did; nor did his well-scratched face less denote her talents (or rather talons) of a different kind.

No longer bore this Amazon the shameful flight of her party. She stopped short, and, calling aloud to all who fled, spoke as follows: "Ye Somersetshire men, or rather ye Somersetshire women, are ye not ashamed thus to fly from a single woman? But if no other will oppose her, I myself and Joan Top here will have the honour of the victory." Having thus said, she flew at Molly Seagrim, and easily wrenched the thigh-bone from her hand, at the same time clawing off her cap from her head. Then laying hold of the hair of Molly with her left hand, she attacked her so furiously in the face with the right, that the blood soon began to trickle from her nose. Molly was not idle this while. She soon removed the clout from the head of Goody Brown, and then fastening on her hair with one hand, with the other she caused another bloody stream to issue forth from the nostrils of the enemy.

When each of the combatants had borne off sufficient spoils of hair from the head of her antagonist, the next rage was against the garments. In this attack they exerted so much violence, that in a very few minutes they were both naked to the middle.

It is lucky for the women that the seat of fistycuff war[18] is not the same with them as among men; but though they may seem a little to deviate from their sex, when they go forth to battle, yet I have observed, they never so far forget, as to assail the bosoms of each other; where a few blows would be fatal to most of them. This, I know, some derive from their being of a more bloody inclination than the males. On which account they apply to the nose, as to the part whence blood may most easily be drawn; but this seems a far-fetched as well as ill-natured supposition.

Goody Brown had great advantage of Molly in this particular; for the former had indeed no breasts, her bosom (if it may be so called), as well in colour as in many other properties, exactly resembling an ancient piece of parchment, upon which any one might have drummed a considerable while without doing her any great damage.

Molly, beside her present unhappy condition, was differently formed in those parts, and might, perhaps, have tempted the envy of Brown to give her a fatal blow, had not the lucky arrival of Tom Jones at this instant put an immediate end to the bloody scene.

This accident was luckily owing to Mr. Square; for he, Master Blifil, and Jones, had mounted their horses, after church, to take the air, and had ridden about a quarter of a mile, when Square changing his mind (not idly, but for a reason which we shall unfold as soon as we have leisure), desired the young gentlemen to ride with him another way than they had at first purposed. This motion being complied with, brought them of necessity back again to the churchyard.

Master Blifil, who rode first, seeing such a mob assembled, and two women in the posture in which we left the combatants, stopt his horse to enquire what was the

Chapter Five
The Eighteenth-Century Literature (1690–1780)

matter. A country fellow, scratching his head, answered him: "I don't know, measter, un't I; an't please your honour, here hath been a vight[19], I think, between Goody Brown and Moll Seagrim."

"Who, who?" cries Tom; but without waiting for an answer, having discovered the features of his Molly through all the discomposure in which they now were, he hastily alighted, turned his horse loose, and, leaping over the wall, ran to her. She now, first bursting into tears, told him how barbarously she had been treated. Upon which, forgetting the sex of Goody Brown, or perhaps not knowing it in his rage—for, in reality, she had no feminine appearance but a petticoat, which he might not observe—he gave her a lash or two with his horsewhip; and then flying at the mob, who were all accused by Moll, he dealt his blows so profusely on all sides, that unless I would again invoke the Muse (which the good-natured reader may think a little too hard upon her, as she hath so lately been violently sweated), it would be impossible for me to recount the horse-whipping of that day.

Having scoured the whole coast of the enemy[20] as well as any of Homer's[21] heroes ever did, or as Don Quixote[22] or any knight-errant in the world could have done, he returned to Molly, whom he found in a condition which must give both me and my reader pain, was it to be described here. Tom raved like a madman, beat his breast, tore his hair, stamped on the ground, and vowed the utmost vengeance on all who had been concerned. He then pulled off his coat, and buttoned it round her, put his hat upon her head, wiped the blood from her face as well as he could with his handkerchief, and called out to the servant to ride as fast as possible for a side-saddle, or a pillion, that he might carry her safe home.

Master Blifil objected to the sending away the servant, as they had only one with them; but as Square seconded the order of Jones, he was obliged to comply.

The servant returned in a very short time with the pillion, and Molly, having collected her rags as well as she could, was placed behind him. In which manner she was carried home, Square, Blifil, and Jones attending.

Here Jones having received his coat, given her a sly kiss, and whispered her, that he would return in the evening, quitted his Molly, and rode on after his companions.

Notes

1. **Divine Service:** religious service held in the church of Mr. Allworthy's parish.

2. **the girl:** referring to Molly, daughter of George Seagrim, the gamekeeper.

3. **occasioned:** aroused.

4. **gamekeeper:** referring to George Seagrim.

5. **repaired to:** went to.

6. **sack:** the nightgown which Sophia had given to Molly.

7. **missile weapons:** things that can be thrown to hit people.

8. **Ye Muses, then, ... assist me on this great occasion:** You Muses, whoever you are, whoever love to sing of battles, and especially you who in the past had given an account of the fierce battle between Hudibras and Trulla, if you hadn't used up all your power in assistance to the work of your friend Butler, help me now in my account of the "great" fight between Molly and the villagers. Muses: Goddesses of poetry. Hudibras and Trulla: heroes in Samuel Butler's poem *Hudibras*.

9. **All things are not in the power of all:** Not everybody can do everything.

10. **Somersetshire mob:** the men and women who were gathered against Molly.

11. **took presently measure of his length on the ground:** immediately fell flat on the ground.

12. **hinder head:** back of the head.

13. **Stour:** a river.

14. **Amazonian heroine:** women in Amazon are said to be valiant fighters. Here it refers to Molly.

15. **She salutes the earth, and he the sky:** she fell down on her belly, and he fell down on his back.

16. **in the fields of Venus:** in conquering men. Venus: Goddess of love in Roman mythology.

17. **in those of Mars:** in fighting. Mars: God of war in Roman mythology.

Chapter Five
The Eighteenth-Century Literature (1690–1780)

18. **fistycuff war:** a fight in which the participants fight with the fists.

19. **vight:** fight.

20. **scoured the whole coast of the enemy:** completely defeated the enemy.

21. **Homer:** a great ancient Greek poet, author of famous epics *Iliad* and *Odyssey*.

22. **Don Quixote:** hero in a famous romance by Spanish writer Cervantes (1547–1616).

Chapter Six
The Literature of the Romantic Period (1780–1831)

6.1 Historical Background

The Romantic period began in 1798, which saw the publication of *Lyrical Ballads* (1798) by Wordsworth and Coleridge and ended in 1832, a year which saw the death of Sir Walter Scott and the enactment of Parliament of the First Reform Bill. These years link literary and political events. The Romantic period is an era in which a literary revolution took place alongside social and economic revolutions. So the Romantic period is also called "the Age of Revolution".

The period was one of rapid changes as the nation was transformed from an agricultural to an industrial one. The laws of a free market, developed by the economist Adam Smith in his book *Wealth of Nations* (1776), dominated people's lives. At the same time, power and wealth were gradually transformed from the landholding aristocracy to the large-scale employers of modern industrial communities. An old population of rural farm labourers became a new class of urban industrial concerns called the working class. Those workers were concentrated in cities and the new power of an increasingly large and restive mass began to make itself felt.

The Industrial Revolution created social changes, unrest and eventually turbulence. Deep-rooted traditions were rapidly overturned. Within a short period of time, the whole landscape of the country changed. In the countryside, the open fields and communally worked farms were "enclosed" by hedges and walls. The enclosure movement improved efficiency and enabled the increasing animal farming necessary to feed a rapidly expanding population; but fewer labourers were required to work the land, and that led to an exodus to the cities of large numbers of people seeking employment. Increasing mechanization both on the land and in the industrial factories meant higher levels of unemployment. Acute poverty followed. In the cities, smoking factory chimneys polluted the atmosphere; poor-quality houses were built in large numbers and quickly became slums. The mental landscape also changed. The country was divided into those rich who owned property or land and those

Chapter Six
The Literature of the Romantic Period (1780–1831)

poor who did not. A new world was born, which Benjamin Disraeli, who was both a novelist and prime minister of Britain under Queen Victoria, was later to identify as "Two Nations".

The Industrial Revolution paralleled revolution in the political order both at home and abroad. The American Declaration of Independence in 1776 struck an early blow for the principle of democratic freedom and self-government, but it was the early years of the French Revolution, with its slogan of "Equality, Liberty and Fraternity", which most influenced the intellectual climate in Britain.

Debate in Britain was, however, polarized between support for radical documents such as Tom Paine's *Rights of Man* (1791), in which he called for greater democracy in Britain, and Edmund Burke's more conservative *Reflections on the Revolution in France* (1790). Later in the 1790s, more measured ideas were contained in the writings of William Godwin, an important influence on the poets Wordsworth and Shelley, who advocated a gradual evolution towards the removal of poverty and the equal distribution of all wealth. Such a social philosophy caused much enthusiasm and intellectual excitement among many radical writers and more liberal politicians; but these ideas also represented a threat to the existing order. Positive use of the words "Jacobin" or "radical" was dangerous in the 1790s. "Jacobin", in particular, which derived from French, implied strong sympathy with ideals of absolute social equality.

However, as the French Revolution developed with Napoleon Bonaparte becoming emperor and then dictator of France, support of it in Britain declined. Then, in 1793, England went to war against France, and, after many years, finally defeated Napoleon at the Battle of Waterloo in 1815. The end of the war led to a decline in manufacturing output and to unemployment, as soldiers returned from war to a world in which the divisions between "two nations" were becoming sharper. In the immediate aftermath of the Napoleonic wars, the government and ruling classes adopted especially repressive measures. These culminated in the "Peterloo Massacre" of 1819, in which government troops charged a large group of workers who were meeting in Manchester to demand social and political reforms.

The period from 1820 to 1832 was a time of continuing unrest. The unrest took place against a background of the cycles of economic depression. The prevailing economic philosophy was that of laissez-faire, meaning "leave alone". The consequences were that the government did not intervene directly in economic affairs. It let the free market and private individual decisions control the course of events. During this time, the wealth of the country grew, but it was increasingly concentrated in the hands of the new manufacturing and merchant classes.

This new middle class wanted to see its increased economic power reflected in greater political power. A general alliance arose between working-class reformers, liberal Whig politicians and this new middle class, resulting in pressure on the Tory government for political reform. After many struggles, the first Reform Act was passed by Parliament in 1832. The bill extended voting rights to include a most representative proportion of the country. The immediate benefits were limited, but the bill was of great symbolic importance and a movement was started which would lead, decades later, to universal suffrage and greater democracy in the country.

6.2 Literary Features

The Romantic Age in literature is often contrasted with the classical or Augustan age, which preceded it. The comparison is valuable, for it is not simply two different attitudes to literature which are being compared but two different ways of seeing and experiencing life.

The classical temperament trusts reason, intellect, and the head. The Romantic temperament prefers feelings, intuition, and the heart; the classical writer looks outward to society, while Romantic writers look inward to their own soul and to the life of the imagination; the classical writer concentrates on what can be logically measured and rationally understood, while Romantic writers are attracted to the irrational, mystical and supernatural world; the classical writer is attracted to a social order in which everyone knows his place, while Romantic writers celebrate the freedom of nature and individual human experience. In fact, the writings of the Augustan age stress the way societies improve under careful regulation; Romantic literature is generally more critical of society and its injustices, questioning rather than affirming, and exploring rather than defining. In terms of their attitude to children, for the Augustan writer, the child is only important because he or she will develop into an adult, and so the child's savage instincts must be trained, making it civilized and sophisticated; for the Romantic writers, the child is holy and pure and its proximity to God will only be corrupted by civilization, and the child then is a source of natural and spontaneous feeling.

Chapter Six
The Literature of the Romantic Period (1780–1831)

The language and form of the literature of the two ages also show two different ways of seeing. The Augustans developed a formal and ordered way of writing characterized by the balance and symmetry of the heroic couplet in poetry and by an adherence to the conventions of a special poetic diction. The Romantics developed ways of writing which tried to capture the ebb and flow of individual experience in forms and language which were intended to be closer to everyday speech and more accessible to the general reader.

Of course, there are exceptions to such general contrasts. For example, the eighteenth-century writers such as Gray, Collin, and Cowper show a developing Romantic sensibility, and Romantic poets such as Byron are inspired by Augustan poetic models.

The Romantic period is seen today as a crucial time in history. It embodies many of the conflicts and ideological debates which are still at the heart of the modern world: political freedom and repression, individual and collective responsibility, masculine and feminine roles, and past, present, and future. It was a time when ideologies were in the melting-pot, when radicalism and tradition, change and stability, the old and the new, were just as vital as the more traditionally literary themes of innocence/experience, youth/age, country/city, man/nature, and language/expression. Many of these issues are as alive today as they were two hundred years ago.

6.3 Romantic Poetry

The most prevailing literary genre during the Romantic period is poetry. The publication of *Lyrical Ballads* is seen as a landmark in English poetry. The volume contains many of the best-known Romantic poems. The second edition in 1800 contained a preface in which Wordsworth discusses the theories of poetry which were to be so influential on many of his contemporaries. The preface represents a poetic manifesto which is very much in the spirit of the Romantic movement of the age. The movement towards greater freedom and democracy in political and social affairs is paralleled by poetry which sought to overturn the existing regime and establish a new, more "democratic" poetic order. To do this, the writers used "the real language of men" and got directly involved in political activities themselves. In general, Romantic poets fall into three groups: the older generation, the younger generation, and the Scottish poets.

> **For Your Information**
>
> **Poets of the Older Generation**
>
> The Romantic poets of the older generation include Blake, Wordsworth, Coleridge and Southey, who are generally regarded as passive romanticists, for they largely reflected the thinking of the classes ruined by the bourgeoisie, and by the way of protest against capitalist development turned to the past ("the merry old England") as their ideal.

6.3.1 William Blake (1757–1827)

William Blake was an engraver as well as a poet, who illustrated many of his poems. His life was spent in rebellion against the rationalism of the eighteenth century and he rejected, in particular, the formal restrictions of Augustan poetry, writing in a lyrical visionary style and developing, in the process, an individual view of the world. A characteristic feature was a tendency to see the world in terms of opposites. Blake wrote that "without contraries is no progression" (*The Marriage of Heaven and Hell*) and much of his poetry illustrates this. The major opposition reflected in his poetry is a contrast between the order of the eighteenth century and the sense of liberation felt in the 1790s as a new century approached.

Blake makes extensive use of symbolism in his poetry. Some of the symbols are straightforward: Innocence is symbolized by children, flowers, lambs, or particular seasons; oppression and rationalism are symbolized by urban, industrial landscapes, by machines, by those in authority, and by social institutions. Blake's best-known symbol is that of the tiger in his poem *The Tyger*. The tiger has been interpreted differently by successive generations but its basic meaning is the natural and creative energy of human life.

Images of childhood have a central place in Blake's poetry, as they do in the work of many Romantic poets. Blake's most famous collection of poetry, *Songs of Innocence and Experience*, published separately in 1789 (*Songs of Innocence*) and 1790 (*Songs of Experience*), together in 1794, abounds in images of children in a world in which people are exploited (A good example is his poem *The Chimney Sweeper*.). The child in Blake's poetry stands for the poet's dissatisfaction with society and for his belief in the power of uncorrupted feeling and imagination. Through the images of childhood, Blake dramatizes the conflict between nature and social order, and between natural innocence and the pressures of social experience.

In *Songs of Innocence and Experience*, several poems are written in pairs, contrasting the state of innocence, in which the world is unthreatening; there is no moral restriction, and God is trusted implicitly, and the state of experience, which reflects a fallen world of repression and religious hypocrisy. In them, Blake reveals a profound understanding of psychology and an ability to explore the spiritual side of human existence, both of which are remarkably modern.

Blake was also conscious of the effects on the individual of a rapidly developing industrial and commercial world. He saw the potential dangers of a mass society in which individuals were increasingly controlled by conventional system of organization. In his poem *London*, he refers to these systems as the result of "mind-forg'd manacles", and even the River Thames has been "chartered (given a royal charter to be used for commercial purpose)", expressing his fierce social indignation.

6.3.2 William Wordsworth (1770–1850)

William Wordsworth, the poet Laureate in succession to Southey, was the most accomplished and subtle poet of the Romantic period. His birth and early education in the mountainous northwestern countries of England which contain the Lake District gave him a particularly acute sensibility to wild nature and to the cooperative workings of humankind and nature. Wordsworth was initially enthusiastic about the French Revolution, and his early poetry is marked by protest against unnecessary or imposed suffering, injustice, incomprehension, and inhumanity. Then the rein of "Terror" in 1793 changed Wordsworth's radical view. And *Lyrical Ballads* marks his withdrawal from public and political life. In the last poem of *Lyrical Ballads*, *Tinterm Abbey*, Wordsworth offers a self-justifying explanation of his retreat from politics. Here it is the sensations of remembered natural scenery, "felt in the blood, and felt along the heart", that bring "tranquil restoration" to a once troubled soul, and the recall of the "still, sad music of humanity" that makes for a chastening and subduing of restlessness. The intensity of his expressed love of nature and its teachings seems to preclude other perceptions, particularly those related to the acute class division inherent in urban industrialization and in the related depopulation of the countryside. What Wordsworth elsewhere in his preface to *Lyrical Ballads* calls "emotion recollected in tranquility" is an emotion uniquely stimulated by nature and then related outwards, and variously applied or illustrated by moral and social incident. The understanding of society is essentially secondary to, and derivative from, the primary and essential experience of a natural world still largely undamaged by human mismanagement. To Wordsworth, nature is the teacher and the giver of an impulse from a vernal wood that may teach more than all the sages can.

Wordsworth's insistence on the morally educative influence of nature, and on the interrelationships of a love of nature and a love of humanity, pervades his autobiographical poem *The Prelude*. This poem, at epic length, draws upon Wordsworth's life, recollecting his childhood in the Lake District. As in the case in Wordsworth's shorter poems, the strength of *The Prelude* resides in the fact that, as well as conveying the mood of his childhood, Wordsworth moves on to examine the manner in which ways of thinking and seeing are changed in the light of the dawn of the French Revolution, specifically the new privileging of the individual such as emphasis on the formation of the individual sensibility having since become a major characteristic of Western literature.

Like Blake, Wordsworth lays emphasis on the value of childhood experience. Throughout his poetic career, Wordsworth continued to regard the child as the single most important source of wisdom and truth. In his *Ode: Intimations of Immortality*, the child, as a symbol of all that is holy and good, is directly addressed:

> Thou best Philosopher, who yet dost keep
> Thy heritage, thou Eye among the blind,
> That, deaf and silent, read'st the eternal deep,
> Haunted forever by the eternal mind.
>
> *(Ode: Intimations of Immortality)*

The child is seen here as "father of the man". Although lines such as these do not strictly adhere to Wordsworth's poetic principles of simple and unadorned language, many of his poems do create a new poetic language. Wordsworth's language frequently moves towards the language of everyday speech and the lives of ordinary people. It breaks with the artificial diction of the previous century, creating a more open and democratic world of poetry. Wordsworth stated later in his life that he had aimed to show that men and women who do not wear fine clothes can feel deeply. In poems such as *The Old Cumberland Beggar* and *The Leech Gatherer*, Wordsworth gives detailed accounts of the lives of ordinary people—characters of a new social position not normally represented in Augustan poetry. He celebrates the spirit of man, living in harmony with his natural environment and away from the corrupt city.

6.3.3 Samuel Taylor Coleridge (1772–1834)

Coleridge's fame, as a great romantic poet, mainly lies in his joint venture *Lyrical Ballads* with Wordsworth. These two writers have a great deal in common, but there is also much that separates them. Both of them are great new poets who create a new kind of poetry, innovating in form, language and subject matter and creating a lasting influence on English poetry. Both turn to nature and write how imagination can perceive a sense of harmony in the natural scene. Besides, they show the same goal of making poetry closer to the rhythms and diction of everyday language. Their differences lie in that Wordsworth's poetry is concerned with the ordinary, everyday world and with the impact of memory on the present, while Coleridge's poetry frequently communicates a sense of the mysterious, supernatural and extraordinary world. Wordsworth stated that he wanted to explore everyday subjects and gave them a Romantic or supernatural colouring, and by contrast, Coleridge wanted to give the supernatural feeling of everyday reality.

Coleridge's most memorable contribution to *Lyrical Ballads* is his best-known poem *The Rime of the Ancient Mariner*. In the poem an old sailor or mariner narrates the terrible sequence of events which followed when he shot an albatross and was cursed. His ship is becalmed; he is subjected to nightmare visions and to a long period of suffering and his water supply runs out as a punishment for his deed. When the mariner blesses some sea-creatures, his offence against the power of nature is forgiven and he is able to return home, revitalized through his shared suffering. The whole poem, like many of Wordsworth's, is written in a form recalling that of a medieval ballad. In essence, it is a story of sin and penance as the mariner wanders the earth, unable to find rest in conventional religion. The wedding guest to whom he tells his story is wrapped in both wonder and fear, afraid of the uncanny figure and his strange narrative in which disturbing symbols mix with alarming characters such as Life-in-Death. Despite its framework of Catholic Christian faith and ritual, the mariner appears to discover a series of meanings concerning the interdependency of life, not merely the consequences of breaking taboos. His route back to the place from which he started requires suffering, but his pain is explored in the context of benevolence, and the truths he perceives stretch beyond mere religious formulas into an affirmation of universal harmony.

Coleridge's other visionary "Gothic" poems include *Christabel* and *Kubla Khan*. The former is in many ways a complement to *The Ancient Mariner*, not simply because it also echoes the style of old ballads, but because it appears to link the nature of Christabel's experience of the powers of life and death to that of the mariner. The poem is concerned with the penetration of Christabel's psyche by the daemonic force represented by Geraldine, but it also allows for a balancing contrast of two powerful aspects of nature, the sympathetic and the energetic, and for a symbolic investigation of what Coleridge later called "the terra incognita of our nature".

Kubla Khan presents an exotic landscape which has often been interpreted as symbolizing the movement of the creative imagination. The poem opens with a basic contrast between the River Alph, a potentially destructive force, and the pleasure-dome, a source of deep perception and understanding. The poem famously remains a "fragment" because it was reported that Coleridge had composed two to three hundred lines in a profound sleep, and, when he was writing it down after waking, he was interrupted by a visitor. The "Vision in a Dream" remains a riddle, a pattern of vivid definitions amid a general lack of definition, expressed with a rhythmic forward drive which suggests a mind taken over by a process of semi-automatic composition.

Not all of Coleridge's poems are so exotic. His "Conversation" poems, such as *Dejection*, *Frost at Midnight* and *This Lime-Tree Bower My Prison*, like many of Wordsworth's, are based on everyday observation. They reflect on universal issues such as the relationship between parents and children and are intimate and conversational in tone.

In addition to poetry, Coleridge also has a considerable reputation as a prose writer, in particular, as a philosopher and literary theorist. His most important critical work is *Biographia Literaria*, which is a loosely shaped, digressive series of meditations on poetry, poets and, above all, the nature of poetic imagination and literature. It has become one of the most influential works of criticism.

Chapter Six
The Literature of the Romantic Period (1780-1831)

> **For Your Information**
>
> ### The Scottish Poets
>
> Late eighteenth century Scotland experienced general prosperity under the union with England and the opening up of its trade with the English colonies. Edinburgh steadily won itself a position as a leading educational, intellectual, and artistic center of Europe. Coupled with this achievement were an often self-conscious redefinition of "Scottishness" and a revival of serious interest in the Scots vernacular and in Scots traditions. Burns's first published volume, *Poems, Chiefly in the Scottish Dialect* (1786) found a responsively enough local and national audience, attuned to the literary use of the vernacular by the pioneering work of the poet and editor of earlier verse, Allan Ramsay (1636–1758), and by the verse of Robert Ferguson (1750–1774). Another poet who wrote in the Scottish tradition is Walter Scott.

6.3.4 Robert Burns (1754–1796)

Robert Burns was born in Allowny, son of a tenant farmer. On the success of his first volume of poems, he spent some months in Edinburgh where he was praised and patronized as a "ploughmen poet". Thereafter he returned to farming in which he failed, and spent his last years as an excise officer in Dumfries. In terms of English literature, Burns may be seen as the greatest of the eighteenth-century "rustic" poets. But in essence, he was a Scottish poet.

Burns's poetry always remained close to its vital roots in the oral traditions of Scotland. His keen ear for Scots vocabulary, idiom, and rhythm enabled him to transform folk-song into poetry of his own. Many of his most circulated songs were set to old tunes, notably "Scots whahae" of 1793, and "O whistle an'I'll come to you, my lad" and "The Birks of Aberfeldy", both published in the volumes of *The Scots Musical Museum* (1787–1803). Burns's aspiration, as a distinctly national poet, emerges most fully in his dialect poems. His verse in "standard" English, even his musings in Scottish history and patriotism, is compared to his evocations of locality through the medium of local language. Much of his finest work is satirical or descriptive of the hardness of rural work, the uprightness of "honest poverty", and the raucousness of country amusements. His most savage satire is *Holy Willie's Prayer*, a dramatic monologue by a church officer in which the hypocrisy of the speaker and the vengefulness of his Calvinist religion are revealed. Burns's most celebrated long poem, the verse tale *Tam O'Shanter* (1791), in drolly ironic narrative manner, contrasts the vividly sketched, welcoming interior of an inn with the unfriendly terrors of Tam's frenzied escape from a witches' coven.

Burns is celebrated for his defense of freedom and the rights of the common man, and for his sympathetic observation of nature. It is typical of him that he should sympathize with the mouse whose nest he has destroyed ("To a Mouse"). The most distinguished of his poems in celebration of freedom is his cantata of love and liberty (published under the title *The Jolly Beggars* in 1799). This cantata draws on *The Beggar's Opera* and a whole tradition of vagabond literature. The ebullient songs celebrate not only liberty in the late eighteenth-century political sense, but also the freedom of the untrammeled life of the road.

6.3.5 Walter Scott (1771–1832)

Walter Scott has the same genius for folk poetry as his fellow countryman, Burns. Scott was of Border descent and spent much of childhood in Roxburghshire. He was a young lawyer in Edinburgh when he started to search out the Border ballads that he had heard in his youth. The result was *The Minstrelsy of the Scottish Border* (1802–1803), a collection of ballads.

Although Scott is now best known as a novelist, he first became famous with a poem, *The Lay of the Last Minstrel* (1805), which recounts the story of a family feud in the sixteenth century, repute with sorcery, alchemy, and metaphysical intervention. Scott's energetic, rushing meter, his varying line-length and wandering stress within the lines, and his highly effective introduction of shorter lyrics or songs into the narrative also mark three further long and involved verse tales: *Harmion: A Tale of Flodden Field* (1808), *The Lady of the Lake* (1810), and *Rokely* (1813).

For Your Information

Poets of the Younger Generation

A new way of looking at both the individual and the world at large is at the heart of the poetry of Byron, Shelley and Keats, three writers conventionally grouped together as the second generation of English Romantic poets, whose landscapes generally turned away from the dark, illiberal north of the older generation to the warmer and more generous climate of the Mediterranean.

6.3.6 George Gordon Byron (1788–1824)

George Gordon Byron was the most famous and popular poet in the Romantic era. Many readers, especially those in the nineteenth century, regarded Byron as the prototype of the Romantic poet, and many writers across the whole Europe were influenced by his approach.

1. Life and Career

Byron was the son of a dashing but spendthrift father and a Scottish heiress whom his father had married to restore his fortunes. At the age of ten, on the death of a great-uncle, he became Lord Byron and the owner of Newstead Abbey in Nottinghamshire. He was educated at Harrow and Cambridge. Byron was a handsome young man, though with a deformed foot of which he was acutely conscious. He had an aristocratic bearing, with a liking for action. In 1809, he published a satire on the current literary scene, *English Bards and Scottish Reviewers*. In the same year, at the age of twenty-one, he set out to travel abroad. He travelled to Portugal and Spain, and thence to Albania and Greece. In Greece, he started to write a poem, in Spenserian stanzas, in his travel. The first two cantos were published after his return to England under the title *Childe Harold's Pilgrimage* (1812), which was an immediate success, as Byron famously remarked "I awoke one morning and found myself famous". In 1815, he married, but was separated from his wife the following year, and left England amid rumors of an affair with his half-sister. He never returned. In 1817, from Italy, he published *Manfred*, a metaphysical verse drama, set in the Alps, which was plainly autobiographical. In 1818, Byron began what was to be his major work, *Don Juan*, which was unfinished in over sixteen cantos at his death.

2. Thoughts

Byron, with a particular hatred of hypocrisy and tyranny, was heavily involved with contemporary issues. Byron the libertarian and Byron the libertine readily assumed the public role of a commentator on his times because he both relished his fame and enjoyed the latter Romantic pose of being at odds with established society. As a lord, Byron held an unconventional liberal (Whig) view of society, supporting Catholic emancipation and defending the Luddites. His poetry is informed not by nature or by the contemplation of nature, but by public life and recent history, by British politics and by the feverish European nationalism stirred by the French Revolution. There is a consistent stress in his poems on the importance of independence, an ideal that connects with ideas of sincerity and natural spontaneity. In his poetic dramas *Manfred* and *Cain* (1821), for example, Byron reflects on the tension between the potentialities of the individual and the restraints of the world in which the individual lives. There is a desire to strike out a new path, surpassing conventional behavior and conventional morality, but at the same time the texts betray a sense of guilt, as well as nostalgia for the old orders. In this lonely, isolated stance, Byron's political dimension is also apparent in his masterpiece *Don Juan* which, as with his other works, articulates the language of liberty, but there are clearly complications when the hero is a sexual libertine. His evocative lines on "The Isles of Greece" in Canto II of *Don Juan* are a great hymn to the national freedom.

3. Style

Byron brought into English poetry a vast and valuable stock of new imagery, new properties, new scenery and decorations. He employed the verse-tale scheme of Scott with a novelty and intensity of apparent passion which made it quite a different thing. His lyrics, though never possessing the exquisiteness of those of Keats and Shelley, have force and fire, and not uncommonly great sweetness as well. His handling of the Spenserian stanza in *Childe Harold*, though it never attains to the dulcet dreaminess which is the true virtue of that form, has energy, picturesqueness, and a narrative motion very different from that of the original indeed, but for the purpose preferable. *Don Juan* was original, and is still practically almost unique, as a medley of observations on life, tinged with sarcastic innuendo. Indeed, satire features many of Byron's poetry. The tone of the poem is light-hearted and comic throughout, even when the subject matter is at its most serious, moving easily through black comedy and the pathos of tragedy. This is in part due to the *ottava rima* (eight lines and eleven syllables) rhyme scheme and partly due to the mixture of different styles, from the most formal poetic diction to the most informal colloquial and everyday English.

4. Byronic Hero

The heroes of Byron's long narrative poems were often imitated, and almost became literary fashion that has come to be known as the "Byronic Hero". His qualities were summed up by Macaulay: "a man proud, moody, cynical, with defiance on his brow, and misery in his heart, a scorner of his kind, implacable in revenge, yet capable of deep and strong affection." The character owes something to Milton's Satan, to the dauntless figures of contemporary German literature, and to the dark and discontented heroes of the Gothic novel. It has a delirious effect on the European public.

The Byronic hero appears for the first time in *Childe Harold's Pilgrimage*. The term "childe" is a medieval word for a young nobleman waiting to become a knight. The hero, Childe Harold, is often identified with Byron himself. He is a restless wanderer, alternating between despair and great energy and commitment to new, usually forbidden, experiences.

A more developed example of the Byronic hero comes in his dramatic poem *Manfred*. Manfred is a particularly passionate outcast and rebel whose typically Romantic heroism contrasts with the restraint and humility of the typical Augustan, Classical hero. Manfred's distain for ordinary humanity, his unidentified guilt, his sense of gloom and doom, make him, paradoxically, a deeply attractive, even erotic, figure. He seems to be beyond good and evil and to define his own moral codes. His unsatisfied quest makes him not so much a hero as an anti-hero, with literary descendants in characters such as Heathcliff in Emily Brontë's *Wuthering Heights* (1847).

Don Juan again features the Byronic hero, but what is particularly apparent here is Byron's good-humored ironic stance: He takes his hero seriously, but also treats him dismissively. Don Juan is gallant, charming, arid and reckless, and led by desire. His buoyancy and zest for experience and sensation makes him a little away from the breeding Byronic hero.

5. Major Works

Don Juan is an adventure poem as well as ongoing series of love stories. The story is about a young Spaniard named Don Juan, who has a love affair with an older and married woman. His pious mother, accordingly, sends him abroad to keep him from further indiscretions. He is shipwrecked, but survives. He finally comes to a Greek island, where he meets Haidee, the beautiful daughter of a pirate. When Haidee's father discovers that Juan and his daughter are in love, he has Juan put in chains and sent away. Haidee goes mad and dies. Juan is sold into slavery in Constantinople. His purchaser is a sultana who has fallen in love with Juan's manly beauty. The sultana becomes jealous and orders Juan's death. Juan manages to escape and joins the Russian army. His gallantry and handsomeness attract the favourable attention of Catherine the Great, who is notorious throughout Europe for her amorousness. Catherine sends Juan on a political mission to England, and thus ends the story.

The poem's essence is the restless, amorous adventures of Don Juan, but there are departures from the main plot line so that Byron, as narrator, can advance his own ideas on a range of subjects and can satirize many aspects of contemporary life and of his contemporaries. Byron himself insisted that *Don Juan* is a satire on abuses of the present state of society but, in several places, judgment is passed upon many of the institutions and values of Western society. But unlike Pope, whose satires are based on a vision of positive values, Byron had no moral policy, no sense of what should be to balance his angry knowledge of what should not. He is a moralist who has neither accepted nor thought out an ethic. His character of Don Juan is a constant seeker of meaning rather than one who already knows the moral bases for his actions. Yet, Byron is a true scourge of villainy.

Childe Harold's Pilgrimage is about a gloomy, passionate young wanderer who escapes from the society he dislikes and travels around the continent, questing for freedom. It teams with all kinds of recognizable features of Romantic poetry—the medieval, the outcast figure, love of nature, hatred of tyranny, preoccupation with the remote and savage, and so on. With his strong passion for liberty and his intense hatred for all tyrants, Baron shows his sympathy for the oppressed Portuguese under French occupation; he gives his strong support to the Spanish people fighting for their national independence; he laments over the fallen Greece, expressing his ardent wish that the suppressed Greek people should win their freedom; he glorifies the French Revolution and condemns the despotic Napoleon period; he appeals for the liberty of the oppressed nations, while exalting the great fighters for freedom in history.

6.3.7 Percy Bysshe Shelley (1792–1822)

Percy Bysshe Shelley, like Byron, is a writer whose life, as well as his verse, is the expression of his poetic nature. Like Byron, too, he was a rebel. He is the most politically radical of the Romantic party, and as such, the most optimistic, who consistently nurtures a belief that faithful adherence to ideal values will result in the transformation of human society.

1. Life and Career

Shelley was born in Sussex, the eldest son of Timothy Shelley, a member of Parliament and heir to a baronetcy. He was educated at Eton, where he was distinguished by his warm affections and his queer hobbies. As a young man, Shelley absorbed the political radicalism of William Godwin, author of *Political Justice* (1793). In 1810, he went up to Oxford University. Two terms later, he was expelled for refusing to satisfy the university's enquiries of withdrawing a pamphlet he had published entitled *The Necessity of Atheism*. He was eighteen then. He was fervently opposed to the tyranny of king, church, and family and he devoted his life to his vision of liberty.

In 1811, he made run-away marriage with Harriet, a 16-year-old girl, and established a life in which he attempted to put his ideas into practice. He wrote and campaigned on the radical issues of the day. In 1813, he published his first long poem, *Queen Mab*, a statement of his views, with forthright prose notes. In 1814, he abandoned Harriet and their two children and eloped with Mary, the daughter of William Godwin. Two years later, he published a volume of poems in which the title poem was *Alastor*, a dream-like allegory in which the poet-hero pursues a visionary beloved. In 1818, Shelley left England for Italy, and never returned. Like Byron, he left behind him a considerable reputation with his radical pamphleteering, his atheism and the suicide of Harriet.

In Italy, Shelley's poetic genius quickly ripened. His spirit had kinship with light and fire, and under the blue Italian skies he created poetry of nature expressive of his own imagination. Of all his nature poems, the greatest is *Ode to the West Wind*, where, in lines of impetuous speech, he likens his spirit to the wild force of approaching winter, which destroys that it may "quicken a new birth". Residence in Italy did not remove Shelley's interest in English politics. The occasion of his best-known political poem, *The Mask of Anarchy* (1819), was the receipt of the news of the Peterloo Massacre. Also in 1818, Shelley began his greatest work *Prometheus Unbound*. In 1822, Shelley was drowned in a storm off Spezzia in Italy. Besides the works mentioned above, Shelley's other important works include *The Revolt of Islam* (1817), *The Cenci* (1819), *Adonais* (1821), and *Julian and Maddalo* (1824), and his critical essay "A Defense of Poetry".

2. Thoughts

Like his friend Byron, Shelley had an equally low view of "public applause" and an equally distinct distaste for the British establishments, literary and political. Unlike Byron's, his work derives from a consistent ideology, one determined by a philosophical skepticism which questions its platonic roots as much as it steadily rejects Christian mythology and morality. Although Shelley's rejection of "revealed" religion and its dogmas remained a cardinal element in his thought, and though he systematically maintained his faith in the principle that every reflecting mind must allow that there is no proof of the existence of a Deity, his later work suggests both a steady qualification of arguments based purely on "reason" and a search for the source of the mysterious "power" that he acknowledged to be implicit in wild nature and in the inspiration of poetry. This complex and intellectually demanding aspiration is paralleled by Shelley's abiding interest in the politics of revolution and evolution and by the idea of a gradual and inevitable social awakening.

Shelley's political thought, informed as it is with experimental scientific theory and with the social ideas of his father-in-law Godwin, elucidates more than simply an opposition of liberty and tyranny; it explores future possibilities and not past defeats and, in attempting to adduce the nature of egalitarianism, it moves beyond the general disillusion resultant from the defeat of the ideals of the French Revolution. Shelley's radicalism, which led him with an almost adolescent enthusiasm to espouse a whole range of worthy causes from Irish nationalism to vegetarianism, was more than simply an instinctive rejection of the restrictive political, religious, and moral formulae of his aristocratic English background; it was at once the root and the fruit of his intellectual idealism. In fact, at the heart of Shelley's thinking is the idea that there is an eternal, rational order, a pattern for all our finest values: beauty, harmony, justice and love. Characteristically, his poems are cloudy and blurred, with images of indistinct, shadowy things, as he invokes an ideal that can be sensed but not described.

In terms of poetry, Shelley, like several of his contemporaries, believed that poetry could reform the world. Central to this belief is that the creative power of the imagination and the poetry quest for beauty and the eternal truths of beauty will show the way to a better society. According to Shelley, this makes poets "the unacknowledged legislators of the world". In his "A Defense of Poetry", Shelley wrote a poetic manifesto for these beliefs, making the poet a missionary, a prophet, a potential leader for a new society. The view of the creative artist as hero was later embraced by other writers in the Victorian and modern periods.

3. Style

Shelley shares with almost all the Romantic poets a skill in the brief lyric. But he is the

Chapter Six
The Literature of the Romantic Period (1780–1831)

most delicate and sensitive. He wrote many intense short lyrics which draw direct inspiration from nature and are written in controlled, sparse language:

> A window bird sat mourning for her love
> Upon a wintry bough;
> The frozen wind crept on above,
> The freezing stream below.
> There was no leaf upon the forest here,
> No flower upon the ground,
> And little motion in the air
> Except the mill wheel's sound.
>
> *(A Window Bird)*

Here the images from nature are employed to express inner feelings and states of mind. A sense of loss and emotional numbness is conveyed through the cold, the emptiness of the scene and the overall lack of movement.

However, Shelley is happier with more extensive verse forms which allow for his profusion of thoughts and images. *Alastor*, a study of the ill effects of solitude, is the best proportioned, and shows the nearest approach to what Shelley never in any long poem gave completely, a piece with a definite scheme definitely carried out in blank verse. *Prometheus Unbound* is a dream cast in dramatic form, but with hardly any action and consisting really of a series of the ineffable lyrics which Shelley alone would write. *The Witch of Atlas* (1820) is a similar dream, thrown into a form as narrated as the writer could manage. *Adonais*, a following of the Greek elegy, is a shrine for separate passages of incomparable beauty:

> Life, like a dome of many-coloured glass,
> Stains the white radiance of eternity.
>
> *(Adonais)*

And so his other long poems, and his short lyrics, are distinguished in different ways, but all are permeated by Shelley's special political enchantment, an enchantment of indefinite, but haunting suggestions of beauty, in thought sometimes and in sound and visual effect always.

4. Major Works

Alastor (or *The Spirit in Solitude*) is at once characteristic of Shelley's thoughts and a splendid piece of blank verse. The title of this work is taken from the Greek name of a demon, which drives its victim into desert places. Indefinite in outline, and often obscure, *Alastor* is really a piece of poetic autobiography. The poem describes the infinite aspirations of the idealist. The hero is a poet who has fed his youth on the loftiest speculations, and conceived unlimited ideas of goodness and beauty. In a dream he beholds "a veiled maid", whom at first he believes the realization of all that he has imagined. He yields at first to irresistible joy, but the unreality of the vision is soon forced upon him. He continues a wanderer and a solitary, consumed by his dream of the impossible, and shunning all human intercourse. There is no escape from his disillusionment but by death, and he dies amid wild Alpine scenery of fantastic terror and beauty. The poem may be read as a protest against an indulgence in solitude.

Prometheus Unbound, a lyrical drama, is generally regarded as Shelley's most successful long poem, in which Shelley employs the Greek myth of Prometheus, who appealed to Shelley because, having defied Zeus in bringing man the gift of fire, he represented a champion of mankind against a tyrannical god. According to the myth, Zeus punished Prometheus by chaining him to a rock in the Caucasus. It is with the chained and suffering Prometheus that Shelley's drama begins. Prometheus and Jupiter (Zeus) are in conflict. Prometheus undergoes ages of staunch endurance, refusing to bargain with Jupiter for his release. However, he is liberated from the tyrannical evil at last. The ideas behind the story are Platonic: Good overcomes evil in the long run because of the radiant attractiveness of good, and self-destructiveness of evil. Jupiter, the tyrant, is overthrown, as the original myth hinted, by his own progeny: Demogorgon, the son, representing "fate" or "time" (he calls it "Eternity"). The positive side of the overthrow of Jupiter is wrought by Asia, representing Love, the invisible power of good. The poem takes on a sublime lyricism as it celebrates Love:

> Child of Light! thy limbs are burning
> Through the vest which seems to hide them;
> As the radiant lines of morning
> Through the clouds ere they divide them;

> And this atmosphere divinest
> Shrouds thee wheresoe'er thou shinest.
>
> *(Prometheus Unbound)*

Such passages, where the sheer splendor of Platonic ideas is expressed, contrast with passages describing experience more nearly human, the sufferings imposed by the tyrant, and the paradisal freedom enjoyed after his defeat. Shelley projects his philosophy through ethereal characters and spiritualized landscapes; earth, ocean, and all nature share both the suffering and the triumph. The drama presents a magnificent vision of a universe on the side of good.

Julian and Maddalo can in many ways be taken as a central text of English Romanticism. It is described as "a conversation" and its couplets reflect a chatty and intimate tone. The two characters, Julian and Maddalo, clearly represent Shelley himself and Byron. Their conversation is naturalistic, rather than idealistic, and takes in the life and atmosphere the two characters observe as they ride on the sands or sail around Venice. The city, and in particular its lunatic asylum, take on a universal significance as the discussion ranges around free will, religion, progress, frustration, and love. It is an evocation of a wasteland. The lido inspires the phrase "I love all waste/And solitary places", aspiring to the boundless possibilities of the human soul, but the city and the asylum return the characters to real life, and the persons of the soul, ending the "conversation" in a silence which is astonishingly modern in its resonance, uncertainty and religious doubt.

Adonais, Shelley's elegiac tribute to the dead Keats, pursues the idea of the poet as hero, here triumphant even in the face of death and "awakened from the dream of life". Keats/Adonais is "one with Nature" and has become "transmitted effluence" which cannot die "so long as fire outlives the parent spark", the earth-bound survivor yearns, almost suicidally, for a part in the same life-transcending immortality.

6.3.8 John Keats (1795–1821)

1. Life and Career

John Keats, one of the few geniuses who died young, was as great a Romantic poet as Shelley. He was born into a family which ran an inn and stables in London. He went to school in Enfield, where he had a fair education. In 1811, he was apprenticed to a surgeon, and by no means neglected his profession for seven years. But his real interests were entirely literary, and, as he had some small means, he determined, about the year 1818, to abandon medicine and devote his life to poetry. He joined the liberal literary circle associated with Hunt. In 1817, he published a small volume of *Poems,* which did not display anything like his real powers. Next year followed the great, though still very immature and unequal, poem of *Endymion*, which was mocked by magazine reviewers. His health now began to fail, and consumption declared itself unmistakably. He had time, however, to publish, in 1820, a third volume, containing the three narratives: *Lamia*, *Hyperion* and *The Eve of St. Agnes*; the odes, and a few sonnets, which are Keats's enduring monument. Then, to escape the English winter, he made a voyage to Italy, and died at Rome in the care of his friend, the painter Severn in the February of 1821.

2. Thoughts

Besides a great poet, Keats was also a magnificent letter-writer, and in his letters we can trace his thoughts on life and poetry. Keats wrote, "We hate poetry that has too palpable a design upon us." By this he means that we distrust poetry which tries overtly to persuade or convert us to the poet's point of view. Poetry should be more indirect, communicating through the power of its images without the poet making his own presence too obvious. For this quality, Keats coined the term "Negative Capability", that is when man is capable of being in uncertainties, mysteries, doubts, without any irritable reaching after fact and reason... Out of this creative indolence, the imagination is the active quality: "What the imagination seizes as Beauty must be truth—whether it existed before or not." For Keats, it is a platonic article of faith:

> Beauty is truth, truth beauty, —that is all
> Ye know on earth, and all ye need to know.
>
> *(Ode on a Grecian Urn)*

Keats also wrote, "Do you not see how necessary a world of pains and troubles is to school an intelligent and make it a soul?" Here Keats shared with both Wordsworth and Coleridge the view that suffering is necessary for an understanding of the world and the great poetry grows from deep suffering and tragedy.

Chapter Six
The Literature of the Romantic Period (1780–1831)

From his poetic theories arises the major theme of Keats's poetry: the conflict between the everyday world and eternity, that is, the everyday world of suffering, death and decay, and the timeless beauty and lasting truth of poetry and the human imagination.

3. Style

In writing his long narrative poems, Keats developed a characteristic feature of the style of all his poems: lush, sensuous imagery, which supports precise descriptive detail. Keats, like Coleridge, was also attracted to exotic settings for his narratives. These include mythic classical backgrounds and medieval contexts of High Romance. Keats's admiration for the Middle Ages allows him to make particular use of the ballad form to explore aspects of the irrational, unconscious and supernatural world.

Keats is also a master of the couplet poetic form, Ode. At the same time, he develops a poetic language appropriate both to the form of the ode and the nature of his themes. Keats's language renders experience precisely; it captures the rhythm and movement of thoughts and feelings; it registers a full range of sense impressions. For example, in the following lines from *Ode to a Nightingale*, the poet asks for a drink of cool wine:

> O, for a draught of vintage! That hath been
> Cooled a long age in the deep-delved earth.
> Tasting of flora and the country green,
> Dance, and Provencal song, and sunburnt mirth!
>
> (*Ode to a Nightingale*)

The description is an example of synaesthesia—a feature which recurs frequently in Keats's poetry and in the poetry of others, such as the twentieth-century poets Wilfred Owen and Dylan Thomas, who were much influenced by Keats. Synaesthesia is a use of imagery and language choices which describe sensory impressions in terms of other senses. In the lines above, Keats manages to appeal to sight, colour, movement, sound, and heat almost simultaneously. For example, the movement of dancing and the sound of song are described as a taste. "Sunburnt mirth" describes the sight of sunburnt faces at the same time as we hear the same people laughing. Keats also created a rich poetic music. An example of his control of the rhythmic movement and syntax is the following lines from *Ode to Autumn*:

> Then in a wailful choir the small gnats mourn
> Among the river sallows, borne aloft
> Or sinking as the light wind lives or dies.
>
> (*Ode to Autumn*)

Here the rise and fall on the rhythm of the lines mark the fight of the gnats.

4. Major Works

Endymion is written in four books and is derived in style and structure from Greek legends and myth: the shepherd Endymion's love for the moon and his journey in search of her. The theme is the search of an ideal love and happiness beyond earthly possibility. The poem starts with an elevated utterance revealing Keats's deeper thoughts, "A thing of beauty is a joy for ever."

The Eve of St. Agnes is a narrative poem in Spenserian Stanzas. It is based on a folk superstition that if on St. Agnes' Eve young girls should observe certain ceremonies on going to bed they would "soft adorings from their loves receive/upon the honeyed middle of the night". It is the tale of a girl named Madeline who decides to observe this superstition. As she does so her lover arrives at the castle, and, with the help of old Angela, is hidden in her chamber. It is Porphyro's "stratagem" to make Madeline's dream come true. Madeline does dream of her lover, and at that moment Porphyro attempts to waken her. As she opens her eyes she experiences the abrupt juxtaposition of his pale figure and her dream of him. The disappointment is painful until it is dispersed as "Into her dream he melted...". Love is achieved, but it is not exempt from the conditions of ordinary life. The noise of sleet on the window wakens the lovers; "St. Agnes' moon hath set". Porphyro has entered a dream; Madeline now has to enter the waking world. The realities of that world are that he is in the enemy castle, and she is a "deceived thing". The poem is rescued from tragedy a second time by Porphyro's initiative.

> Awake! Arise, my love and fearless be!
> For o'er the southern moors have a home for thee.
>
> (*The Eve of St. Agnes*)

The lovers escape, and the reader is left feeling the preciousness of love won against such difficulties. The subject of the poem is absorption in love and beauty, and the problems these ideals meet in the real world. The poem is shaped around a series of intense contrasts, of cold and warmth, of dark and light, of harshness and softness, of noise and stillness, and above all, of cruelty and love, but it is ultimately as ambiguous and uncertain as the superstition on which its heroine sets new hopes.

5. Odes

The perfection of Keats's art is especially seen in his odes, of which, *To Psyche, To a Nightingale, On a Grecian Urn, To Autumn* and *On Melancholy* stand out above the rest, and are among the masterpieces of poetic art. *Ode to Psyche* has often been seen as an enactment of a ceremonial dedication of the soul—"as distinguished from an Intelligence"—and as a variation on the idea of the world as "the vale of soul-making". *Ode to a Nightingale* takes as its subject the vocal presence of a nightingale, and the contrast of the "full-throated ease" of its singing with the aching "numbness" of the human observer, the rapt and meditative poet. The ode progresses through a series of precisely delicate evocations of opposed moods and ways of seeing, some elated, some depressed, but each serving to return the narrator to his "sole self" and to his awareness of the temporary nature of the release from the unrelieved contemplation of temporal suffering which the bird's song has offered. The more succinct *Ode on Melancholy* opens with a rejection of traditional, and gloomy, aids to reflection and moves to an exploration of the interrelationship of the sensations of joy and sorrow. The perception of the transience of beauty which haunts the poem also informs the speculations derived from the contemplation of the two scenes which decorate an imagined Attic vase in *Ode on a Grecian Urn*, one showing bucolic lovers, the other a pagan sacrifice. Both scenes are frozen and silent, images taken out of time and remembered eternally only by the intervention of art. The Grecian Urn and the artistic carvings on it represent the permanence of art and celebrate the power of the artist to immortalize human activity, to make it permanent, preserving it against mortality and the passing of time. The beauty of art is seeing the real truth of existence. In the latest of the ode, *Ode to Autumn*, tensions, oppositions, and conflicting emotions are diminished amid a series of dense impressions of season whose beauty contains both fulfillment and incipient decay, both an intensification of life and an inevitable, but natural process of ageing and dying.

6.4 Romantic Essayists

It is natural that the essay, like every other form of imaginative literature, should be affected by the new spirit of the age. The Romantic essayists—De Quincey, Lamb, Leigh Hunt, Hazlitt and others—revolutionized the form of the essay and gave it a new literary impetus. Like the Romantic poets, the essayist rebelled against eighteenth-century conventions. They developed new styles and wrote on a wider range of topics. Instead of describing the leisure pursuits of the upper and middle classes, these essayists wrote about the lives of the clerks, chimney-sweepers and prize-fighters. Instead of an elaborate formal style, they developed looser, more subjective and impressionistic uses of language, giving each essay their own personal stamp. Like the Romantic poets, the essayists of the Romantic period put their own responses to experience at the very center of their work. So their prose is usually in a form of personal essays and autobiographies. Charles Lamb and William Hazlitt wrote a large number of letters and essays on a range of topics, literary and otherwise, and in the process established the importance of the literary form of critical essay which came to particular prominence in Coleridge's *Biographia Literaria* (1817).

6.4.1 Thomas De Quincey (1785–1859)

Thomas De Quincey is a rare example of a journalist whose essays remain classic of the genre. They have been influential ever since they were written, and some of them have never been surpassed in their psychological and imaginative acuity. "On the Knocking at the Gate in *Macbeth*" and "On Murder Considered as One of the Fine Arts" are among the most remarkable. He also writes widely on the nature of dreams, and anticipates modern psychological studies in relation to childhood experience and imaginative creation. His "Confessions of an English Opium Eater" is an autobiographical account of his opium addiction. In it, he penetrates the depths of his own subconscious world, describing the simultaneously nightmarish and ecstatic experience with great precision and lyrical intensity. Opium provided the Romantic writer with a starting point for a further journey of the imagination into extreme feelings and experiences. De Quincey is a very modern figure in many ways, not only in relation to the drug culture. He is a link between the Romantics, with his *Reflections of the Lake Poets*, dating from the mid-1830s, and the decadent modern sensibility of such figures as Baudelaire in France and Edger Allan Poe in America. From 1853 until his death in 1859, he was occupied in collecting his works under the title selections *Grave and Gay*.

6.4.2 William Hazlitt (1778–1870)

William Hazlitt is, with Coleridge, the foremost literary critic of the age. He used the popular forms for criticism: the lecture, the review, and the essay. His works on earlier writers, such as *An Essay on the Principles of Human Action* (1805) and *Characters of Shakespeare's Plays* (1817), are so extensive that it in some sense constitutes a critical history of English literature. Hazlitt is an equally sharp and original critic of his literary and political contemporaries in the essays published as *The Spirit of the Age* in 1825. In this attempt to examine aspects of the Zeitgeist of a period that Hazlitt himself sees as "an age of talkers and not of doers", he deals with twenty-five prominent politicians, thinkers, and writers. He praises, discriminates and, when the occasion suits, damns with an aphorism or an image.

6.4.3 Charles Lamb (1775–1834)

Since Bacon's time, essays had usually discussed matters of some general interest or importance. Lamb and his friend Hazlitt were as capable as any men of serious writing, but they hated to appear as slaves of method. In their hands, the essay was drawn away as far as possible from the formal treatise with its clear headings and logical arrangement. Subjects were chosen, not as themes to be developed but as starting points for flights of imagination; the author was content to display the skill of his gyrations, without any thought for his orderly progress towards an anticipated conclusion. In a word, the essays of Lamb and Hazlitt are the intimate self-revelations of their authors.

Lamb's earlier works such as *Tales from Shakespeare* (1807), which he wrote with his sister Mary, his life-long companion and colleague, and his anthology *Specimens of English Dramatic Poets Who Lived About the Time of Shakespeare* (1808) showed Lamb's cogent appreciation of classic English drama and were well received. But it was with his two series of *Essays of Elia* published in 1823 and 1833 that Lamb achieved a real rapport with contemporary readers and a reputation. "Elia" (Lamb) writes of himself: "I am a bundle of prejudices made up of likings and dislikings—the veriest thrall to sympathies, apathies, and antipathies." It is because his "likings and dislikings" are so strong and because they are so genuinely intuitive, and not reasoned or intellectual, that his essays are so distinct a revelation of himself. The whole fabric of the essays is wrought out of impressions and memories, and the sentences follow each other by laws of association known only to the author himself. The vocabulary is a record of his wanderings among old books, and his very rhythms have an echo of the seventeenth century. That essays so individual should carry the reader with them and impose their author's own taste and experience upon him proves the depth of Lamb's humanity and the fineness of his literary taste. It is natural enough that a sketch so universal in its feeling as *Dream Children: A Reverie* should make an immediate appeal.

6.5 Romantic Novels

During the eighteenth century, the novel had evolved into a wide-ranging genre. In the forty or so years after the French Revolution in 1789, novelists brought new themes and new approaches to the novel, and in doing so, they raised it from the inferior level of critical esteem to the most significant, most popular, and most highly regarded genre of literary expression.

The intellectual climate of the time is reflected in the wide range of issues, themes, and settings which the novel was now beginning to encompass: High-class society contrasts with the primitive; national concerns with regional; male points of view with female; present with past, as more and more new subjects become the raw material for fiction.

William Godwin's *The Adventures of Caleb Williams* (1794), subtitled *Things as They Are*, is a novel of propaganda, but it contains elements of crime, detection, pursuit, and punishment which are remarkably innovative. It is one of the first novels to give a psychological portrait of character at the same time as illustrating conflicts of political ideals and beliefs.

The subtitle of *Hermsprong* (1796), by Robert Bage, *Man as He Is Not,* and the title of his *Man as He Is* (1792), echo Godwin's subtitle and show a similar concern to examine views and values in what can be seen as a more "truthful" realistic way. The "truth" in this case is found, as with much of Romantic poetry, in a return to nature. *Hermsprong* is the novel, which, more than any other, marks its hero a "natural" man—a primitive, brought up by American Indians without the constrictions of civilized religion, morality, and ethics.

Chapter Six
The Literature of the Romantic Period (1780–1831)

It thus becomes a satire on the values which Hermsprong finds in the civilized society to which he returns. Many views—for example, on social class and privilege, and on equality for women—are aired in ways which are critical of conventional English society. Equality, and rights for women, had been the subject of discussion among educated women for several decades. In 1792, these views reached their most noted expression in Mary Wollstonecraft's *A Vindication of the Rights of Women*, a work which was to have a lasting impact on future women thinkers and writers.

Other female novelists that were well received in the Romantic period were Jane Austen, Frances Burney (1752–1840), Clara Reeve (1729–1807), and Mary Shelly (1797–1851), the daughter of Mary Wollstonecraft and William Godwin and the wife of Percy Byshe Shelley. Frances Burney's novels, from *Evelina* (1778) through *Cecilia* (1782) to *Camilla* (1796), are novels of how a young woman grows up and develops as she enters and experiences the society of her day. Clara Reeve's *The Old English Baron* (1777) and Mary Shelly's *Frankenstein* (1818) featured the Gothic novel.

The Gothic novel is a form which concentrates on the fantastic, the macabre and the supernatural, with haunted castles, specters from the grave and wild landscapes. *The Castle of Otranto* (1764) by Horace Walpole (son of the Prime Minister Sir Robert Walpole) is the first of this kind. It is a story of medieval times, set in Southern Italy, with castles, vaults, ghosts, statues which come to life, appearances and disappearances, sudden violent death, forest caves, and the whole paraphernalia of horror. The Gothic novel's immediate widespread popularity can be seen in Matthew Lewis's *The Monk* (1796), Ann Radcliffe's *The Mysteries of Udolpho* (1794), and other works of this kind. The clichés of the Gothic were looking some worn out by the beginning of the nineteenth century, but the Gothic villain can be detected behind such characters as Mr. Rochester in *Jane Eyre* and Heathcliff in *Wuthering Heights*.

Frankenstein or *The Modern Prometheus* is an epistolary novel told through the letters of Walton, an English explorer in the Arctic. It relates the exploits of Frankenstein, an idealistic Genevan student of natural philosophy, who discovers the secret of imparting life to inanimate matter. He constructs the semblance of a human being and gives it life. The creature, endowed with supernatural strength and size and terrible in appearance, inspires loathing in whoever sees it. Lonely and miserable, it turns on its creator and murders his brother, his friend, his bride and eventually the creator. The tale has been regarded as the origin of modern science fiction, in which a nature essentially good is corrupted by ill treatment.

For a more mainstream thread of the English novel in the opening decades of the nineteenth century, we have to turn to Jane Austen and Sir Walter Scott.

6.5.1 Jane Austen (1775–1817)

Jane Austen is quite different from any novelist before her, and an important part of the difference is that for many years she was not consciously writing for publication. Female writers were not unusual before her, but soon she came to be regarded as the greatest woman writer of her time. Now Jane Austen has been established as one of the major novelists and the first woman writer in the English tradition who is unassailably in the first rank.

1. Life and Career

Jane Austen was the daughter of a clergyman in North Hampshire. She was well educated, but lived an uneventful life in the country towns, especially Bath, Southampton, and the village of Chawton close to Alton. Besides one sister she had six brothers, whose more active lives gave her some knowledge of the greater world. Two of her brothers, for instance, entered the navy, and to them are owed the sympathetic accounts of the navy in *Mansfield Park* (1814) and *Persuasion* (1818). Her family was on visiting terms with the gentry of Hampshire which supplied her with the parties and outings on which many scenes in her novels are based.

Jane Austen was writing before she was twelve years old. Her first attempts to get a work published, however, were unsuccessful, and she was thirty-five when *Sense and Sensibility* appeared in 1810. Thereafter she published *Pride and Prejudice* (1813), *Mansfield Park*, and *Emma* (1816). She died unmarried at the age of forty-two, leaving to appear posthumously *Persuasion* and the early *Northanger Abbey*.

2. Thoughts

Austen's work may seem to stand apart from the preoccupations of many of her literary contemporaries, but it remains very much of its time. It can be, in many significant ways, defined against current radical enthusiasms. The late eighteenth-century cultivation of sensibility and sentiment, and the new Romantic insistence on the propriety of passion are consistently countered in her novels by an ironic exposure of affection and by a steady affirmation of the virtues of restraint. Austen chose her own literary limitations, not simply because she held that three or four families in a country village were an ideal subject for the novel, but because her omissions were considered and deliberate. Her moral message is infused with an ideological insistence on the merits of good conduct, good manners, sound reason, and marriage as an admirable social institution. She never scorns love, but she balances its often disconcerting and disruptive nature with a firm advocacy of the complementary qualities of self-knowledge, self-discipline, and practicality. Her heroines can be as vivaciously intelligent as Elizabeth Bennet and as witty, egotistic, and independent as Emma Woodhouse, but both, like the essentially introspective Elinor Dashwood or the passive and self-effacing Fanny Price, are finally brought to mature judgment and, by proper extension, emotional fulfillment. The narrative line of *Sense and Sensibility*, which balances maturity against impulsiveness, also systematically undermines the attractions of superficial glamour and contrast conflicting value systems and ways of seeing. In *Northanger Abbey* (1798) and *Pride and Prejudice*, first impressions, illusions, and subjective opinions or prejudices give way to detachment, balance, reasonableness and, more painfully, to humiliating reassessment. Her cleverness, wit, or spontaneity, though admirable in themselves, are never allowed to triumph without being linked to some steadier moral assurance. All these indicate that what Jane Austen emphasizes is harmony in microcosm, the search for order in a world beset by chaos and threatened by war, by class division, or by such human fears as loneliness, uncertainty and failure.

3. Style

Austen was the first real artist to devote herself to the novel. Her style can be described as simple, suggestive and half-ironic. No author before Austen had attempted so successfully to apply the techniques of the novel to the acute observation of society in microcosm: "the little bit (two inches wide) of Ivory on which I work", as she wrote in her letters. Austen deliberately avoids effect, exaggeration and excess. Going against the trends of the novels of her time, she applies the microscope to human character and motivation, with no great didactic, moral, or satiric purpose, but with a gentle irony and perspicacity which make her novels unique, as representations of universal patterns of behavior, and as documentation of an aspect of the provincial society of her time. In writing novels with a realistic and ordinary setting about the reconciliation of the claims of the individual and of society, in which the concluding marriage is a symbol that that harmony has been reached, Jane Austen was in a tradition of the English novel which lasted throughout the nineteenth century to die out, if indeed it has, only in the modern world.

4. Major Works

Northanger Abbey is about a young girl named Catherine Morland, who has been brought up in a large happy family in the country and is introduced to the ways of wider society when she is invited by her neighbours, Mr. and Mrs. Allen, to accompany them to Bath. In Bath, she meets and becomes friends with Isabella Thorpe and her brother John, and with Eleanor Tilney and her bother Henry, with whom Catherine falls in love. Catherine's views of the world have been largely formed by reading romantic novels and when she is invited to stay at the Tilneys' home, Northanger Abbey, she indulges in melodramatic speculations about their father's ill treatment of his wife. She is brought down to earth by Henry's criticism of her unrealistic fantasies and by the news that her friend Isabella, who had been engaged to Catherine's brother James, has eloped with Captain Frederick Tilney, Eleanor and Henry's brother. After some difficulties with Henry's father, who discovers that Catherine is not heiress to a fortune as he had at first thought and who as a result abruptly sends her home from Northanger Abbey, Catherine and Henry are married "to begin perfect happiness at the respective ages of twenty-six and eighteen".

Northanger Abbey was the first of Jane Austen's novels. It gently satirizes the 1790s enthusiasm for the Gothic novel, by contrasting day-to-day life with the imaged horrors of Ann Radcliffe's *The Mysteries of Udolpho*, which have had a considerable effect on the impressionable heroine, Catherine. The author's distanced, slightly ironic observation of the heroine and of the love intrigues in fashionable Bath, displays the tone and the point of view which Austen was to refine in her later works, which are less obviously intended to ridicule and more concerned with acute depiction of character and interaction.

Sense and Sensibility is about two sisters, Elinor (standing for sense and self-control) and Marianne (standing for impulsiveness and sensibility) Dashwood. The unexpected death of Mr. Dashwood forces the sisters and their mother to live on a much reduced income

Chapter Six
The Literature of the Romantic Period (1780–1831)

because the family estate is left to the male line, to a son by their father's first marriage. They are persuaded to move from Norland, their home in Sussex, to a cottage on the estate of a cousin, Sir John Middleton, of Barton Park in Devonshire. Before they leave Norland, an attachment has formed between Elinor and Edward Ferrers, the brother of her sister-in-law and heir to a large estate. At Barton, Marianne meets and falls deeply in love with Willoughby, the cousin of a neighbour.

Both relationships encounter problems. Elinor discovers that Edward has been engaged for some years to Lucy Steele, an ambitious and unpleasant young woman. He feels bound to honour their engagement, though he no longer loves her. Willoughby abruptly disappears from Barton with no explanation and, when the sisters spend some time in London, fails to get in touch with Marianne in spite of her notes to him and in spite of the fact that many people, including Marianne herself had taken their engagement for granted. They then hear that he has married a rich heiress, and also that in the past he was responsible for seducing and then abandoning the close relation of Colonel Brandon, a neighbour at Barton Park who is in love with Marianne. The shock of Willoughby's behavior makes Marianne dangerously ill. However, things work out in favour of the sisters in the end. Lucy Steele elopes with Edward's younger brother, now the heir since Edward's mother disinherited him when she found out about his engagement to Lucy. This leaves Edward free to marry Elinor. And when Marianne recovers from her illness, she has realized her fault in being so infatuated with Willoughby and eventually marries her much older but loyal and respectable admirer Colonel Brandon.

Pride and Prejudice, Jane Austen's masterpiece, is about the Bennets, a family with five daughters whose irresponsible mother's only concern is to see them all well married. By the end of the novel, she has succeeded with the three eldest, Jane, Elizabeth and Lydia, though in Lydia's case disgrace is only narrowly avoided when the family manage to secure her marriage to the worthless Wickham, with whom she has eloped. Jane marries Mr. Bingley, a charming and rich young man whom she meets when he rents nearby Netherfield Park, and Elizabeth, the heroine of the novel, marries her proud and even richer friend Darcy, but not before Darcy has tried to remove Bingley from Jane's influence because he thinks the marriage would be beneath him. Elizabeth is already prejudiced against Darcy because he snubs her at a ball and because she believes he has behaved badly to Wickham, whose true character has not yet been revealed. When she discovers the way in which he has influenced Bingley, she spiritedly refuses his first offer of marriage. It gradually becomes clear, however, that, though proud, Darcy is not guilty of mistreating Wickham and when Wickham and Lydia elope, he pays Wickham's debts in order to secure their marriage. This, together with the experience of visiting Darcy's home, Pemberley, convinces Elizabeth that she loves him after all. Darcy and Bingley return to Netherfield, propose to the Bennet sisters and are accepted.

Persuasion has a heroine who is much older than those in Austen's other novels. Eight years before the novel begins, Anne Elliot was engaged to Frederick Wentworth, a young naval officer with uncertain prospects, and was persuaded to break off the engagement by Lady Russell, who saw the match as socially and financially risky and whose opinion Anne respected because she had been a close friend of her mother's before her death. Lady Russell was proved wrong: Captain Wentworth was highly successful and Anne never got over her feelings for him.

As the novel begins, Anne's extravagant and vain father, Sir Walter Elliot, is forced by financial problems to let their home, Kellynch Hall, to Admiral Croft, whose wife happens to be Captain Wentworth's sister. Sir Walter and his elder daughter Elizabeth move to Bath, together with Elizabeth's companion, Mrs. Clay, who is suspected of wanting to marry Sir Walter. Anne goes to stay with her younger sister and her husband, Mary and Charles Musgrove, who live close by at Uppercross, near Charles's parents and lively younger sisters, Henrietta and Louisa Musgrove. On a trip to Lyme Regis, Louisa is badly injured jumping off the sea wall, the Cobb, into Captain Wentworth's arms and he is impressed by Anne's prompt, levelheaded response to this crisis. Anne returns to Uppercross to look after the Musgrove children and Louisa stays with the Harvilles, naval friends of Captain Wentworth, until she recovers. There she becomes engaged to Captain Benwick, who when he first appears is still mourning the death of his first fiancée. Captain Wentworth is thus still free.

Anne and Lady Russell join Sir Walter in Bath where the Elliots are approached by their estranged cousin William Walter Elliot, the heir to Kellynch, who has been expected some years before to marry Elizabeth. He now shows interests in Anne but she mistrusts him and her suspicions are confirmed when she hears from Mrs. Smith, an old school friend and now a poor widow, of how he ruined herself and her husband. Mr. Elliot's attentions to Anne

Chapter Six
The Literature of the Romantic Period (1780–1831)

reawaken further Captain Wentworth's love for her, and he is convinced of her continuing affection when he overhears a conversation between Anne and Captain Harville in which she defends women's constancy in love. Anne and Captain Wentworth are finally united and William Elliot, with his plans thwarted, goes off to London with Mrs. Clay.

Emma is a novel focusing on the development and moral growth of its heroine. Emma lives with her father. Her governess leaves the household to marry a neighbour, Mr. Weston, and Emma, who relishes acting as a match-maker, makes a protégée of Harriet Smith, an illegitimate girl of no social standing. George Knightly, a friend of the family, disapproves of Emma's attempts to manipulate Harriet. Emma half-believes that she is in love with Mr. Weston's son by his first marriage, Frank Churchill, but eventually realizes that, without actively considering it, she has always assumed Knightly will marry her. This, together with the revelation that Frank is already engaged, forces Emma to examine her conduct and resolve to behave better. Knightly proposes to Emma, and is accepted. Emma matures: She changes from being vain, self-satisfied and insensitive to the needs of others. Essentially, she has fallen in line with, and come to accept the wisdom and value of the code of conduct for personal behavior that should operate in polite society.

Mansfield Park is Jane Austen's last novel. Sir Thomas Bertram of Mansfield Park, a stern but kind-hearted man, has two sons, Tom and Edmund, and two daughters, Maria and Julia. Fanny Price, Lady Bertram's niece, is brought to live with the family and she is befriended by Edmund, but his sisters Maria and Julia seek only to humiliate her. While Sir Thomas Bertram is off visiting his estates in the West Indies, Mansfield Park is visited by Henry and Mary Crawford from London. They tempt the sisters to throw off restraints, resulting in Maria entering into marriage with Mr. Rushworth, and then an adulterous elopement with Henry Crawford. Julia also elopes, while Edmund is tempted by Mary Crawford to give up the idea of becoming a clergyman. Edmund resists and finally marries Fanny. For all its tidiness, it is an uncomfortable ending to the novel in its perfunctoriness. There can be little doubt that the old way of life symbolized by Mansfield Park is under threat both from outside and inside, and the Bertram family clearly lacks any real moral energy to sustain this way of life and to defend it against the clever London socialites Henry and Mary Crawford. It is no accident that Austen alerts us to the real-world economics of Sir Thomas's plantation or to the equally real collapse of sexual restraint in his own home.

The forces of change are too powerful to be controlled.

6.5.2 Walter Scott (1771–1832)

Walter Scott was the most popular novelist of his day. Already established as a poet, in 1814 he started a second career as a historical novelist with the publication of *Waverley*. Scott is usually said to have created the historical novel. The most requirement of a historical novel is that it should be set in the past. Most of the Gothic novels are set in the past, but it is Scott that gives the novel tradition a sense of history. Scott's historical novels take in many periods, from the Jacobite rebellion of 1745 in *Waverley* to the twelfth-century crusades in *The Talisman* (1825), from the clash between Saxon and Norman in *Ivanhoe* (1819) to the time of Mary, Queen of Scots in *The Abbott* and on to the Porteous riots in Edinburgh in 1736 in *The Heart of Midlothian* (1818). *Ivanhoe* is, with *Rob Roy* (1817), the best known of Scott's novels, with Robin Hood and King Richard the Lionheart among its characters.

Scott's initial, highly successful, impulse to concern himself with Scottish affaires, and yet always to include the observation and experience of a pragmatic outsider (often an Englishman), links his first nine novels together as Waverley novels. The shape and theme of *Waverley*, which is concerned with the gradual, often unwitting, involvement of a commonsensical English gentleman in the Jacobite rising of 1714 and his exposure to the thrilling but alien culture of the Highland clans, are subtly repeated, with significant variation, in *Guy Mannering* (1815), *Old Morality* (1816), and *Rob Roy*. In these novels, Scott exposes his protagonists to conflicting ways of seeing, thinking and acting; his Scotland is variously divided by factions, and in each he suggests an evolutionary clash of opposites, the gradual convergence of which opens up a progressive future. The fissures of Scottish history are allowed to point the way to a present in which Scotland's fortunes are inexorably bound up with those of liberal, more homogeneous and shop-keeping England.

In 1820, with the publication of *Ivanhoe*, Scott's fiction took a fresh direction in moving abruptly away from Scotland and from recent, even remembered, history. *Ivanhoe*, together with *The Talisman* and *The Bethrothed* (1825), forms a continuous discourse, which questions the origins and usefulness of the medieval code of chivalry and military honour and distantly reflects on the survival of both into the age of the French Revolution.

Chapter Six
The Literature of the Romantic Period (1780–1831)

As a novelist, Scott's influence was immense: His creation of wide range of characters from all levels of society was immediately likened to Shakespeare's; the use of historical settings became a mainstay of Victorian and later fiction; his short stories helped initiate that form; his antiquarian researches and collections were a major contribution to the culture of Scotland.

6.6 Reading

The Sick Rose
By William Blake

O Rose, thou art sick!
The invisible worm
That flies in the night,
In the howling storm[1],
Has found out thy bed
Of crimson[2] joy:
And his dark secret love
Does thy life destroy.

Notes

1. **howling storm:** a rough and vigorous storm. This is an image frequently occurring in Blake's poems.
2. **crimson:** deep purplish-red. Notice the pun in this word here.

The Daffodils
By William Wordsworth

I wandered lonely as a cloud
That floats on high o'er vales and hills,
When all at once I saw a crowd,

A host, of golden daffodils;
Beside the lake, beneath the trees,
Fluttering and dancing in the breeze.

Continuous as the stars that shine
And twinkle on the milky way,
They stretched in never-ending line
Along the margin of a bay:
Ten thousand saw I at a glance,
Tossing their heads in sprightly dance.

The waves beside them danced; but they
Out-did the sparkling waves in glee:[1]
A poet could not but be gay,
In such a jocund company[2]:
I gazed—and gazed—but little thought
What wealth the show to me had brought:

For oft, when on my couch I lie
In vacant or in pensive mood,[3]
They flash upon that inward eye[4]
Which is the bliss of solitude;
And then my heart with pleasure fills,
And dances with the daffodils.

Notes

1. **Out-did the sparkling waves in glee:** They surpassed the bright waves with their cheerful dance.

2. **jocund company:** a happy companion.

3. **In vacant or in pensive mood:** in thoughtless or deeply thoughtful mood.

4. **inward eye:** heart.

Chapter Six
The Literature of the Romantic Period (1780–1831)

Pride and Prejudice
Chapter One
By Jane Austen

It is a truth universally acknowledged that a single man in possession of a good fortune must be in want of a wife.

However little known the feelings or views of such a man may be on his first entering a neighbourhood, this truth is so well fixed in the minds of the surrounding families, that he is considered as the rightful property of some one or other of their daughters.

"My dear Mr. Bennet," said his lady to him one day, "have you heard that Netherfield Park is let at last?"

Mr. Bennet replied that he had not.

"But it is," returned she; "for Mrs. Long has just been here, and she told me all about it."

Mr. Bennet made no answer.

"Do not you want to know who has taken it?" cried his wife impatiently.

"You want to tell me, and I have no objection to hearing it."

This was invitation enough.

"Why, my dear, you must know, Mrs. Long says that Netherfield is taken by a young man of large fortune from the north of England; that he came down on Monday in a chaise and four[1] to see the place, and was so much delighted with it that he agreed with Mr. Morris immediately; that he is to take possession before Michaelmas[2], and some of his servants are to be in the house by the end of next week."

"What is his name?"

"Bingley."

"Is he married or single?"

"Oh! single, my dear, to be sure! A single man of large fortune; four or five thousand a year. What a fine thing for our girls!"

"How so? How can it affect them?"

"My dear Mr. Bennet," replied his wife, "how can you be so tiresome! You must know that I am thinking of his marrying one of them."

"Is that his design in settling here?"

"Design? nonsense, how can you talk so! But it is very likely that he may fall in love with one of them, and therefore you must visit him as soon as he comes."

"I see no occasion for that. You and the girls may go, or you may send them by themselves, which perhaps will be still better; for, as you are as handsome as any of them, Mr. Bingley might like you the best of the party."

"My dear, you flatter me. I certainly have had my share of beauty, but I do not pretend to be any thing extraordinary now. When a woman has five grown up daughters, she ought to give over[3] thinking of her own beauty."

"In such cases, a woman has not often much beauty to think of."

"But, my dear, you must indeed go and see Mr. Bingley when he comes into the neighbourhood."

"It is more than I engage for[4], I assure you."

"But consider your daughters. Only think what an establishment it would be for one of them. Sir William and Lady Lucas are determined to go, merely on that account, for in general, you know they visit no new comers. Indeed you must go, for it will be impossible for us to visit him, if you do not."

"You are over-scrupulous, surely. I dare say Mr. Bingley will be very glad to see you; and I will send a few lines by you to assure him of my hearty consent to his marrying whichever he chooses of the girls; though I must throw in a good word for my little Lizzy[5]."

"I desire you will do no such thing. Lizzy is not a bit better than the others; and I am sure she is not half so handsome as Jane[6], nor half so good-humored as Lydia[7]. But you are always giving her the preference."

"They have none of them much to recommend them," replied he, "they are all silly and ignorant like other girls; but Lizzy has something more of quickness than her sisters."

"Mr. Bennet, how can you abuse your own children in such a way? You take delight in vexing me. You have no compassion on my poor nerves."

"You mistake me, my dear. I have a high respect for your nerves. They are my old friends. I have heard you mention them with consideration these twenty years at least."

Chapter Six
The Literature of the Romantic Period (1780–1831)

"Ah! you do not know what I suffer."

"But I hope you will get over it, and live to see many young men of four thousand a year come into the neighbourhood."

"It will be no use to us if twenty such should come, since you will not visit them."

"Depend upon it, my dear, that when there are twenty I will visit them all."

Mr. Bennet was so odd a mixture of quick parts[8], sarcastic humor, reserve, and caprice, that the experience of three and twenty years had been insufficient to make his wife understand his character. Her mind was less difficult to develop.[9] She was a woman of mean understanding, little information, and uncertain temper. When she was discontented, she fancied herself nervous. The business of her life was to get her daughters married; its solace was visiting and news.

Notes

1. **a chaise and four:** a lightweight carriage drawn by four horses.

2. **Michaelmas:** September 29, church festival in honour of the Archangel Michael.

3. **give over:** stop.

4. **It is more than I engage for:** I could not give my permission for this.

5. **Lizzy:** Mr. Bennet's second daughter.

6. **Jane:** Mr. Bennet's eldest daughter.

7. **Lydia:** Mr. Bennet's youngest daughter.

8. **quick parts:** wit.

9. **Her mind was less difficult to develop:** It was easier to understand her mind.

Don Juan
Canto III

By George Gordon Byron

THE ISLES OF GREECE[1]

The Isles of Greece, the Isles of Greece!

Where burning Sappho[2] loved and sung,

Where grew the arts of war and peace,

Where Delos[3] rose, and Phoebus[4] sprung!

Eternal summer gilds them yet,

But all, except their sun, is set.

The Scian[5] and the Teian[6] Muse[7]

The hero's harp[8], the lover's lute[9]

Have found the fame your shores refuse[10];

Their place of birth alone is mute

To sounds which echo further west

Than your sires'[11], 'Islands of the Blest.'[12]

The mountains look on Marathon[13]—

And Marathon looks on the sea;

And musing there an hour alone,

I dream'd that Greece might still be free;

For standing on the Persians' grave,

I could not deem myself a slave.

A king sate[14] on the rocky brow[15]

Which looks o'er sea-born Salamis;

And ships, by thousands, lay below,

And men in nations[16];—all were his!

He counted them at break of day—

And when the sun set where were they?

And where are they? and where art thou.

My country? On thy voiceless shore

The heroic lay is tuneless now—

The heroic bosom beats no more!

And must thy lyre, so long divine,

Degenerate into hands like mine?

Chapter Six
The Literature of the Romantic Period (1780–1831)

'Tis something, in the dearth of fame[17],
Though link'd among a fetter'd race,
To feel at least a patriot's shame,
Even as I sing, suffuse my face;
For what is left the poet here?
For Greeks a blush—for Greece a tear.[18]

Must we but weep o'er days more blest?
Must we but blush?—Our fathers bled.
Earth! render back from out thy breast
A remnant of our Spartan dead[19]!
Of the three hundred grant but three,
To make a new Thermopylae!

What, silent still? and silent all?
Ah! no;—the voices of the dead
Sound like a distant torrent's fall,
And answer, 'Let one living head,
But one arise—we come, we come!'
'Tis but the living who are dumb.

In vain—in vain: strike other chords;
Fill high the cup with Samian wine[20]!
Leave battles to the Turkish hordes,
And shed the blood of Scio's vine!
Hark! rising to the ignoble call—
How answers each bold Bacchanal[21]!

You have the Pyrrhic dance[22] as yet;
Where is the Pyrrhic phalanx[23] gone?
Of two such lessons, why forget
The nobler and the manlier one?
You have the letters Cadmus[24] gave—
Think ye[25] he meant them for a slave?

Fill high the bowl with Samian wine!
We will not think of themes like these!
It made Anacreon's song divine:
He served—but served Polycrates[26]—
A tyrant; but our masters then
Were still, at least, our countrymen.

The tyrant of the Chersonese
Was freedom's best and bravest friend;
That tyrant was Miltiades!
O that[27] the present hour would lend
Another despot of the kind!
Such chains as his were sure to bind.

Fill high the bowl with Samian wine!
On Suli's rock, and Parga's shore,
Exists the remnant of a line
Such as the Doric mothers[28] bore;
And there, perhaps, some seed is sown,
The Heracleidan[29] blood might own.

Trust not for freedom to the Franks[30]—
They have a king who buys and sells;
In native swords, and native ranks,
The only hope of courage dwells;
But Turkish force, and Latin fraud[31],
Would break your shield, however broad.

Fill high the bowl with Samian wine!
Our virgins dance beneath the shade—
I see their glorious black eyes shine;
But gazing on each glowing maid,
My own the burning tear-drop laves[32]
To think such breasts must suckle slaves

Chapter Six
The Literature of the Romantic Period (1780–1831)

Place me on Sunium's[33] marbled steep,
Where nothing, save the waves and I,
May hear our mutual murmurs sweep;
There, swan-like[34], let me sing and die:
A land of slaves shall ne'er be mine—
Dash down yon cup of Samian wine!

Notes

1. This selected material is a song sung by a singer. The versification of the song is different from the rest of the long poem. The song is composed of 16 stanzas, each stanza consisting of 6 lines of iambic tetrameter, with a rhyme scheme *ababcc*. The poem tries to call the Greek people to rise up against the invasion by the Turks and defend their national liberty by contrasting the glory of Greek history with the disgrace of the existing condition in Greece and insists that the pleasure-seeking life cannot solve any problem but only to make themselves slaves forever and their freedom lies only in their struggling instead of depending on some foreign countries.

2. **burning Sappho:** passionate Sappho. Sappho: a famous poetess in ancient Greece, well known for her love poems.

3. **Delos:** an island in the Aegean Sea, the birthplace of Apollo, god of the sun.

4. **Phoebus:** the Greek name for Apollo.

5. **Scian:** the birthplace of Homer.

6. **Teian:** the birthplace of Anacreon, an ancient Greek poet famous for his lyric singing in praise of wine and women.

7. **Muse:** a goddess of poetry. Here the word refers to Homer and Anacreon.

8. **The hero's harp:** It refers to Homer whose *Iliad* and *Odyssey* are about the adventures of heroes.

9. **the lover's lute:** It refers to Anacreon.

10. **the fame your shores refuse:** Greece does not honour Homer and Anacreon who are

Greek but are honoured in other countries.

11. **sires:** ancestors.

12. **Islands of the Blest:** islands in Greek mythology where the blessed people live after death.

13. **Marathon:** a plain to the northwest of Athens, where the Greeks defeated the invading Persians (490 BC).

14. **sate:** sat.

15. **rocky brow:** the edge of a cliff.

16. **men in nations:** In the Persian navy, there were many soldiers from different nations.

17. **in the dearth of fame:** in the age of shame and disgrace. dearth: in lack of.

18. **For Greeks a blush—for Greece a tear:** I blush at the thought of the Greek people being slaves and shed tears at the thought of Greece being invaded.

19. **Spartan dead:** It refers to the three hundred Spartans killed in the Battle of Themopylae, a mountainpass in Greece, fought between the Spartans and the Persian invaders in 480 B.C.

20. **Samian wine:** Samos is an island in the Aegean Sea, which is famous for its wine.

21. **Bacchanal:** worshipper of Bacchus, Roman god of wine.

22. **Pyrrhic dance:** a dance invented by Pyrrhic, the King of Epirus, an ancient Greek city.

23. **Pyrrhic phalanx:** a solid formation of heavily armed infantry invented by Pyrrhic, with which he defeated the Roman army in the third century, BC.

24. **Cadmus:** In Greek mythology, he was the founder of the city state of Thebes. It was believed he invented the Greek alphabet.

25. **ye:** you.

26. **Polycrates:** a despot of Samos during the invasion of Teos by the Persian army.

27. **O that:** I wish.

28. **Doric mothers:** brave Spartan mothers.

Chapter Six
The Literature of the Romantic Period (1780–1831)

29. **Heracleidan:** of Heracles, god of strength in Greek mythology. Spartans were supposed to be his descendents.

30. **Franks:** western European countries in general.

31. **Latin fraud:** tricks played by western European countries.

32. **laves:** washes.

33. **Sunium:** the temple of Athena, built in Sunium.

34. **swan-like:** It is supposed that the swan sings most beautifully when it is dying.

Chapter Seven
Victorian Literature (1832–1900)

7.1 Historical Background

The term "Victorian age" is often used to cover the whole of the nineteenth century. Queen Victoria came to the throne in 1837, at a time when the monarchy as an institution was not particularly popular. But as the success of the nation reached its peak and then began to decline, the monarch assumed a greater and greater symbolic importance. Victoria, widowed in 1861, became Empress of India, and by her death in 1901 had come to represent the nation in a way which only Queen Elizabeth I had done in the past.

A history of the Victorian age records a period of economic expansion and rapid change. When Queen Victoria came to the throne, the population of London was about two million inhabitants; at her death, the population had increased to 6.5 million. The growth of London and other major cities in Great Britain marked a final stage in the change from a way of life based on the land to a modern urban economy based on manufacturing, international trade and financial institutions.

Great Britain was one of the first countries of the world to industrialize, to establish markets and to reinvest the profits in further manufacturing developments. Britain became the center of the new philosophy of Free Trade, of new technology and of continuing industrial inventions. The country became the workshop of the world, and from the 1870s onwards had become the world's banker. In a period of a little more than sixty years of Queen Victoria's reign, the major invention of Steam Power was exploited for fast railways and ships, for printing presses, for industrial looms and for agricultural machinery. An efficient postal service was developed; the telephone invented and communications improved. The country of the United Kingdom, indeed the world as a whole, became a smaller place. The age was characterized by optimism and a sense that everything would continue to expand and improve. Beneath the public optimism and positivism, however, the nineteenth century was also a century of paradoxes and uncertainty.

The contrast between social unrest, with related moves towards change, and the

Chapter Seven
Victorian Literature (1832–1900)

affirmation of values and standards which are still referred to as "Victorian values", are an essential part of the paradox of the age. "Victorian compromise" is one way of seeing this dilemma. It implies a kind of double standard between national success and the exploitation of lower-class workers at home and of colonies overseas, a compromise between philanthropy and tolerance (the abolition of slavery, 1833; tolerance for Catholics, 1892) and repression (the conditions of the poor).

The literature of the time reflects these concerns from the very beginning. Benjamin Disraeli, who was later to become Prime Minister of Great Britain, gave one of the main "labels" of the Victorian age in his political novels. *The Two Nations*—i.e., *The Rich and the Poor*—was the subtitle of his novel *Sybil*, published in 1845. It underlines the fact that social concern and reform were sympathetic subjects for a novel many years before Disraeli himself actually implemented some of the reforms described. Thirty years after the battle of Waterloo, the working-class Chartist movement was still considered too radical and dangerous to be tolerated. This movement arose directly as a result of the First Reform Bill of 1832, which, although it extended the franchise and gave some people the right to vote, excluded the working classes by its insistence on property ownership. It was not until 1918 that universal suffrage, the first claim of the Chartists, was reached in Britain. Even then, it was not until 1928 that the vote was given to all adult women.

There was thus a movement throughout the Victorian period towards democracy, as there was in the rest of Europe. But where mainland Europe suffered revolutions and political upheavals (1848 came to be called the Year of Revolution), the British government kept a strong hold on power. Working-class movements, republican groups, trade unions and similar dissident expressions were contained as far as possible. In literature, however, such expressions flourished.

7.2 Literary Features

Victorian writers were the children of the new industrial age. Yet they were far from being in sympathy with its spirit. On the contrary, they were, for most of their time, in conscious revolt against it. Inevitably, however, they were all affected by the spirit of the age. It was an age of individualism, and they themselves were individualists. All were men and women of marked originality in outlook, character or style. In Macaulay, there was much of the energy and enterprise of the "self-made" man. Tennyson loved to sing the praises of sturdy independence. Ruskin felt himself a voice crying in the wilderness and gloried in it. In Dickens's books, there are, perhaps, more "originals" than in those of any other novelist in the world. The Brontë sisters pursued their lonely path in life with pride and endurance. Carlyle and Browning cultivated a manner full of eccentricity; Thackeray, though more regular in style than his contemporaries, loved to follow a haphazard path in the conduct of his stories, indulging in undaunted license of comment and digression.

7.3 Victorian Novel

Great as have been its achievements in poetry and history, and not small as they have been in literary criticism and the essay generally, the Victorian period, as a whole, is the age of the novel in the same sense that the Restoration is an age of drama and the Romantic period is an age of poetry. The Victorian fiction is first of all characterized by its richness and variety, which is well presented in these great writers: Dickens, the great novelist in the language; Thackeray, a brilliant satirist and realist; Charlotte and Emily Brontë, who wrote the most famous romances in English; George Eliot, whose work marks the highest point of an English realist tradition in which Trollope, Elizabeth Gaskell, and Gissing also figure; Meredith, the writer who extended the intellectual range of the novel through innovation and experiment; Hardy, a challenging and often controversial novelist in his own time, whose critical reputation has risen steadily in the present time; Stevenson, the leading figure in the late nineteenth-century revival of romance.

The greatest of the Victorian novel is not only qualitative—a matter of a galaxy of major talent—but also quantitative. For the work of a host of other writers, ranging from Wikie Collins to Rider Haggard, from Disraeli to George Moore and from Charles Kingsley to Mrs. Humphrey Ward, still lives in the sense that it is still read and is also the subject of closer critical attention today than at any time since its publication—particularly the work of women writers who have been reassessed by feminist critics and biographers, as well as by other scholars.

Thematically, Victorian novelists favour stories about middle-class life and ordinary domestic experience; the novels are then narrated in a tone of voice that clearly identifies the ruling social and moral principles of such a society. The novelists are simultaneously

Chapter Seven
Victorian Literature (1832–1900)

constructing and endorsing the middle-class values, and in doing so, they, to an extent, and not always consciously, are able to stand outside those values and see their own shortcomings.

Stylistically, the Victorian novel is generally discussed under a rubric such as "the rise of realism", since the period saw the consolidation of fictional technique in the "mainstream realist novel". The word "realism" in mid-Victorian criticism applies to a variety of literary categories. In terms of subject matter, for example, realism could mean simply the depiction of modern life. More specifically, and particularly later in the nineteenth century, realist novelists were those whose subject matter was offensive. Alternatively realism meant a type of minute description or simply the dull opposite of the imaginative in fiction. All these definitions are related to the writers' attempt to depict everyday things as they are actually and historically. In the eyes of many critics, the nineteenth century witnessed the function of realism in the work of Jane Austen and the best novelists of the Victorian period: Anthony Trollope, George Eliot, William Makepeace Thackeray and Charles Dickens.

But the Victorian period was equally marked by trends, tendencies, and schools that contested the dominance of realism. Among these sub-genres is the social-problem novel, in which conflicts between the classes, between master and man, or between male seducer and female victim, are dramatized. Benjamin Disraeli, Charles Kingsley, and Elizabeth Gaskell are the most persuasive representative of this genre. Then the religious fiction most directly addressed the burning issues of religious controversies. Sectarian strife or the challenge to orthodox belief of biblical criticism, materialist philosophy and science were also recurrent themes of leading writers from Dickens to Hardy, who adapted the stereotypes of the period's religious fiction, such as the thin, hypocritical dissenter and the female philanthropist of High church persuasion, to their own broader purposes. Many novelists such as Edward Butler Lytton and Harrison Ainsworth also rivaled historians like Carlyle and Macaulay, in the highly popular heroes or of its broadly progressive sweep towards an enlightened present. In either case, the Victorian historical novelist examines the past in order both to entertain and to teach his or her generation. It was not until the last quarter of the nineteenth century that the idea that fiction should embody some kind of moral teaching was seriously challenged by the comparatively amoral novel of ideas, which was generally described as romance or fantasy. This new sub-genre includes science fiction, detective story, ghost stories and utopian writing, all of which represent the escapist search for other worlds in ways which were to become increasingly popular in the twentieth century.

7.3.1 Charles Dickens (1812–1870)

1. Life and Career

The life of Charles Dickens can be seen to mirror the intellectual patterns of the Victorian age, in which he became the dominant figure. Dickens was born in 1812, his father being a clerk in Navy Pay-Office. The family, which was in financial difficulties during most of Dickens's boyhood, moved from place to place, and at length settled at Camden Town, in a mean, small tenement, with a wretched little back garden abutting on a squalid court. Dickens received little school-education at any time, and it ceased altogether when his father was arrested for debt and sent to Marshalsea Prison. Dickens was obliged to work in a blacking manufactory, where the coarseness of his companions nearly drove him to despair. After a time, however, he found work on the press. He learnt shorthand and became a reporter at seventeen. At the end of 1833, he began to contribute short articles to magazines, and *Sketches by Boz* was collected out of them and issued as a book early in 1836, while before the spring of that year was over Dickens began *The Pickwick Papers* and was married. He was ever afterwards a prosperous man as far as money was concerned, and *The Pickwick Papers* immediately made him famous. In 1838 came out his first "novel with a purpose", *Oliver Twist*, which was followed by *Nicholas Nickleby*, an unequal novel with some excellent scenes of grim humor and some feeble attempts at social satire. *The Old Curiosity Shop* (1840–1841) and *Barnaby Rudge* (1841) were his next two books, one a romance coloured largely by the popular sentimentality of the time, the other a historical novel on the Gordon Riots.

In 1842, Dickens visited America and on his return recorded his somewhat crude impressions in *American Notes* and *Martin Chuzzlewit*. About the same time he began his *Christmas Books*, a series which has done much to foster the genial spirit of Christmas time. For some time Dickens gave his energy to journalism, but a new novel, *Dombey and Son*, was finished in 1848, and it was followed by *David Copperfield*, commonly regarded as Dickens's greatest work, and, in any case notable for its large element of autobiography. *Bleak House* (1852–1853), the onslaught on the old Court of Chancery, is one of Dickens's most vigorous pieces of social criticism. *Hard Times* (1854) has an equally serious purpose.

Chapter Seven
Victorian Literature (1832–1900)

It is a grave study on the problems of capital and labour. *Little Dorrit* (1857) preserves its author's dismal memories of the Marshalsea Prison in some scenes of much truer pathos than the exaggerated descriptions of Little Nell and Paul Dombey. For the next few years, much of Dickens's energy was consumed in the public readings from his novels that he gave in England and America. The enthusiasm displayed by the audience was without bounds, but the readings were too exhausting for the performer, and probably shortened his life. His last four books are *A Tale of Two Cities* (1859), *Great Expectations* (1859), *Our Mutual Friend* (1864–1865), and the unfinished *Edwin Drood*, which was appearing when he died. Most of Dickens's novels came out in numbers with illustrations, a plan very popular in the middle of the century.

2. Thoughts

Influenced by Carlyle, Dickens learned, as did his literary contemporaries, to direct his fiction to a questioning of social priorities and inequalities, to a distrust of institutions, particularly defunct or malfunctioning ones, and to a pressing appeal for action and earnestness. He was prone to take up issues, and to campaign against what he saw as injustice or desuetude, using fiction as his vehicle. He was not alone in this in his own time, but his name continues to be popularly associated with good causes and with remedies for social abuses because his was quite the wittiest, the most persuasive, and the most influential voice. Dickens was faithful to the teaching, and to the general theological framework, of Christianity as a moral basis for his thought, his action and, above all, for his writing, nevertheless. A critical awareness that there was something deeply wrong with the society in which he lived sharpened the nature of his fiction and gave it its distinct political edge. Dickens's novels are multifarious, digressive and humorous. In an important way, they reflect the nature of Victorian urban society with all its conflicts and disharmonies, its eccentricities and its constrictions, its energy and its extraordinary fertility, both physical and intellectual. But the standard pattern in his novels is the basic conflict between money on the one hand, and love on the other. What this conflict usually reveals is that the people who have the greatest love for their fellow humans are also the ones who are most hurt by the world of money, simply because money is power. In his novels, the people who possess most money and most power seem incapable of love, whereas the people who are capable of love are very often both poor and powerless. This is a potentially gloomy vision of the world because it suggests that the good and the poor will always suffer at the hands of the bad and the rich. And yet, this gloomy view is counteracted by Dickens's comic way of dealing with his characters.

3. Style

Dickens's intensely funny early fiction, from *Sketches by Boz* to *Martin Chuzzlewit*, suggests the degree to which he was loosely but happily working in the literary tradition, which he inherited from Defoe, Fielding and Smollett. Significantly though, he was the artist of the new era, the Victorian writer best equipped to transform the eighteenth century novels into fluid, urban fiction of a new age. His early experiments have established him a writer with an acute ear for speech, and for aberrations of speech, and with an equally acute observation of gesture and habit, of London streets and London interiors, of spontaneity and of misery. Dickens's plots are rarely tight-knit. *Sketches by Boz* is essentially anecdotal and descriptive. If Dickens' novels have struck certain critics as vulgar, random, inconsistent, or simply as too prolix, it is because those are the leading characteristics of the age itself. Dickens took a popular art form, the comic novel, and gave it a distinctive wit, energy and variety. Comedy in Dickens's novels consists of laughing at characters trapped in difficult situations. People are commonly seen as types, illustrating particular human traits—traits such as greed or lust. As a result, these human weaknesses are exaggerated to comic proportions and emerge as funny. This kind of comedy is concerned to draw our attention to the absurdity of human affection and social pretensions, and also to the darker, irrational desires lurking just behind the social facade. Dickens is the artist of "many voices", but he is also, as T. S. Eliot recognized, an artist like Shakespeare who can with a phrase make a character as real as flesh and blood. His many voices are also the echoes of the contradictory and clamorous noises of the century.

4. Major Works

Oliver Twist concerns Oliver, an orphan child of the workhouse, who is apprenticed to an undertaker, but then runs away and encounters the Artful Dodger, an impudent young pickpocket, who introduces him to Fagin in the London slums. Fagin is the organizer of a set of young thieves, and an associate of Bill Sikes, a violent criminal, and Nancy, a prostitute. After a series of complications Nancy reveals that Fagin is being bribed, by the boy's half-brother Monks, to corrupt Oliver. Nancy's betrayal is discovered, and Sikes murders her. A hue and cry is raised; Sikes, trying to escape, accidentally hangs himself, and the rest of the gang are secured and Fagin executed. Monks confesses his desire to ruin Oliver for retaining the whole of his father's property, and dies in prison. Oliver is adopted by a benevolent Mr. Brownlow.

An obvious target of the novel was the New Poor Law of 1834, which confined paupers to workhouses. A deeper issue, however, lies behind the immediate issue of the Poor Law; this is the way in which Britain in the first half of the nineteenth century had to introduce new legislation and new mechanisms of social regulation in order to control an increasingly complex society. But the novel, like Dickens's other novels, in looking at the question of how to control an increasingly complex society, offers a vivid sense of the dangerous forces that threaten this society.

Hard Times tells the story that Thomas Gradgrind, a citizen of Coketown, a northern industrial city, is a misguided exponent of Utilitarianism, who believes in facts and statistics and brings up his children Louisa and Tom accordingly. He marries Louisa to Josia Bounderby, a manufacturer 30 years older than Louisa. Louisa consents partly due to the indifference and cynicism engendered by her father's treatment, partly due to a desire to help her brother, who is employed by Bounderby. James Harthouse, a young politician without heart or principles, taking advantage of her unhappy life with Bounderby, attempts to seduce her. The better side of her nature is awakened at this experience, and she flees for protection to her father, who in turn is awakened to the folly of his system. He shelters her from Bounderby and the couple is permanently separated. But Tom has robbed the bank of his employer, and although he contrives for a time to throw suspicion on a blameless artisan, Stephen Blackpool, is finally detected and hustled out of the country.

The novel contains a picture of the industrialized England which emphasizes the dehumanizing aspects of the industrialization: the philosophy of utilitarianism. Throughout the novel, the central conflict is located in the opposition between the world of money, affectation and self-interest and the world of love and a natural simplicity. Here Dickens is focusing on the corrupting power of money, and the way in which it can poison both the physical and emotional parts of people's lives.

Great Expectations tells the story of Philip, known as "Pip", an orphan brought up by his bad-tempered sister and her warm-hearted husband, Joe Gargery, the village blacksmith.

He is introduced to the house of Miss Havisham, a lady half-crazed by the dissertation of her lover on her bridal night, who, in a spirit of revenge, has brought up the girl Estella to use her beauty as a means of torturing men. Pip falls in love with Estella, and aspires to become a gentleman. Money and expectations of more wealth come to him from a mysterious source. He goes to London, and meanly abandons the devoted Joe Gargery. Misfortunes come upon him. His benefactor proves to be an escaped convict, Albel Magwitch, whom he, as a boy, had helped; his great expectations fade away and he is penniless. Estella marries his sulky enemy Bentley Drummle, by whom she is cruelly treated. Taught by adversity, Pip returns to Joe Gargery and honest labour, and is finally reunited to Estella who has also learned her lesson.

The novel is Dickens's most complicated one with the major theme that money actually obscures the expression of love.

Bleak House contains a vigorous satire on the abuses of the old court of Chancery, the delays and costs of which brought misery and ruin on its suitors. The major characters are Ada Clare and Richard Carstone, wards of their kind, elderly relative, John Jarndyce. The other major character is Esther Summerson, a young girl whose schooling was paid for by John Jarndyce, and who is now taken into his household as housekeeper and companion to Ada Clare. Richard and Clare fall in love and secretly marry. They marry secretly because Richard has become obsessed with the "Jarndyce and Jarndyce" suit, concerned with the distribution of an estate. Richard's health gradually declines because of his obsession with the suit. When a new will is discovered, and the suit finally settled, it is found that the whole estate has been swallowed up in legal costs. This is the final blow to Richard's failing health, and he dies.

Running parallel to this story is the narration of Esther. This is the story of Lady Dedlock, who is Esther's mother as the result of a youthful relationship with a captain Hawdon. Hawdon is supposed to have perished at sea, but is actually working as a scrivener. When Lady Dedlock sees his handwriting on a legal document, she realizes he is still alive and is thrown into some confusion. Hawdon dies shortly afterwards, and Lady Dedlock secretly visits his grave. She believes that the secret of her past is safe, but when it is uncovered by a law clerk, Guppy, Lady Dedlock is forced to make herself known to Esther. Later she becomes a murder suspect when her husband's solicitor Tulkinghorn is murdered. Learning that her husband has been told her secret by Inspector Bucket, who is investigating

Chapter Seven
Victorian Literature (1832–1900)

Tulkinghorn's murder, Lady Dedlock flies from the house in despair, and is found dead near Hawdon's grave. Meanwhile Esther has accepted a proposal of marriage from Jarndyce out of her devotion and gratitude to him. But Jarndyce, discovering that she really loves another man, Allan Woodcourt, surrenders her to him in an act of self-sacrifice, thus allowing them to marry.

Here Dickens is setting up a fairly straightforward contrast between a corrupt society represented by the Chancery suit and simple love and self-sacrifice represented by John Jarndyce and Esther. Love and self-sacrifice do triumph in the end, but at considerable human cost.

In *Dombey and Son*, when the story opens, Mr. Dombey, the rich, proud, frigid head of the shipping house of Dombey and Son, has just been presented with a son and heir, Paul, and his wife dies. The father's love and ambition are centered in the boy, a delicate, prematurely old child, who is sent to Dr. Blimber's school, under whose strenuous discipline he sickens and dies. Dombey neglects his devoted daughter Florence, and the estrangement is increased by the death of her brother. Walter Gay, a good-hearted youth in Dombey's employment, falls in love with her but is sent to the West Indies by Dombey, who disapproves of their relationship. He is shipwrecked and believed drowned. Dombey marries again a proud and penniless young widow, Edith Granger, but his arrogant treatment drives her into the arms of his villainous manager Carker, with whom she flies to France. They are pursued; Carker meets Dombey in a railway station, falls in front of a train, and is killed. The house of Dombey fails; Dombey has lost his fortune, his son, and his wife; Florence has been driven by ill treatment to fly from him, and has married Walter Gay, who has survived his shipwreck. Thoroughly humbled, Dombey lives in desolate solitude till Florence returns to him, and at last finds the way to his heart.

In this novel, the basic conflict between money and love at the center of Dickens' view is in plain evidence. Dombey, despite all his money, does not know how to love, and it is only after he has lost everything that he is able to return Florence's devoted affection. At the center of this is the theme, which binds the novel together: pride. It is Dombey's self-glorifying pride that causes suffering to Florence, and in another way to Paul, and it is the same pride that attracts to him the equally proud and worthless characters of Major Bagstock and James Carker, who eventually desert him.

Martin Chuzzlewit tells the story of Martin, the grandson of the irascible old Martin Chuzzlewit, a wealthy, elderly man who has become very suspicious of the selfish greed of members of his family. Young Martin, to spite his grandfather, gets himself apprenticed to another relative, the hypocritical Pecksniff. Learning of this, and seemingly taken in by Pecksniff's fawning, Martin's grandfather persuades Pecksniff to dismiss him. Young Martin determines to go to America with Mark Tapley, intent on making his fortune and returning to marry his grandfather's young guardian, Mary Graham. But while in America, he is duped by the fraudulent Eden Land Corporation, loses all his money, and nearly dies of fever. Returning to England, he discovers his grandfather has moved in with Pecksniff, who is now trying to bully Mary Graham into marrying him so that he will benefit from the old man's will. But old Martin has not been taken in by Pecksniff and has been living with him only to see at first hand the depths of Pecksniff's hypocrisy and meanness. Satisfied with the true nature of Pecksniff's character, the old man exposes him for what he is and unites the two young lovers, Mary and young Martin.

This novel examines a wide range of selfishness, self-centeredness, criminality, and exploitation, and allows for the title character's discovery that America contains as many shams, frauds, and delusions as does his native England.

The two cities of *A Tale of Two Cities* are Paris, in the time of the French Revolution, and London. Dr. Manette, a French physician, having been called in to attend a young peasant and his sister in circumstances that made him aware that the girl had been outrageously treated and the boy mortally wounded by the marquis de St. Évremonde and his brother, has been confined for 18 years in the Bastille to secure his silence. He has just been released, demented, when the story opens; he is brought to England, where he gradually recovers his sanity. Charles Darnay, who conceals under the name the fact that he is a nephew of the marquis, has left France and renounced his heritage from detestation of the cruel practices of the old French nobility; he falls in love with Lucie, Dr. Manette's daughter, and they are happily married. During the Terror he goes to Paris to try to save a faithful servant, who is accused of having served the emigrant nobility. He is arrested, condemned to death, and saved only at the last moment by Sydney Carton, a reckless wastrel of an English barrister, whose character is redeemed by his generous devotion to Lucie. Carton, who strikingly resembles Darnay in appearance, smuggles the latter out of prison, and takes his

Chapter Seven
Victorian Literature (1832–1900)

place on the scaffold.

The book gives a vivid picture (modeled on Carlyle's *The French Revolution*, 1837) of Paris at this period. It has Dickens's most carefully contracted plot, and, by means of its charged and very public historical setting, particularly successfully dramatizes personal dilemmas, divisions and commitments.

In *Pickwick Papers*, Mr. Samuel Pickwick, general chairman of the Pickwick club which he has founded, Messrs Tracy Tupman, Augustus Snodgrass, and Nathaniel Winkle, members of the club, constitute a corresponding society of the club to report to it their journeys and adventures, and observations of characters and manners. This is the basis on which the novel is constructed, and the club serves to link a series of detached incidents and changing characters, without elaborate plot. The entertaining adventures with which Mr. Pickwick and his associates meet are interspersed with incidental, moral and melodramatic stories. Mr. Pickwick's innocent and trusting nature repeatedly makes him the butt of comic adventures. In the book's most prolonged episode, he gives his landlady Mrs. Bardell the impression that he wishes to marry her, and so provokes a suit for breach of promise.

A Christmas Carol, the novella, is the first and most popular of Dickens's Christmas stories. On Christmas Eve, Scrooge, an old curmudgeon, receives a visit from the ghost of Marley, his late partner in business, and beholds a series of visions of the past, present, and future, including one of what his own death will be like unless he is quick to amend his ways. As a result of this, he wakes up on Christmas morning an altered man. He sends a turkey to his ill-used clerk Bob Cratchit, positively enjoys subscribing to Charismas charities, and generally behaves like the genial old fellow that he has become.

7.3.2 William Makepeace Thackeray (1811–1863)

1. Life and Career

Thacheray was born in Calcutta where his father worked. At the age of five, his father died, and his mother married again. He was sent home at Charterhouse. Then in 1829, he went to Trinity College, Cambridge, but took no degree. After leaving Cambridge, he travelled in Germany, and began to read for the bar. But the loss of a competent income, which he had inherited, made some more speedily remunerative occupation necessary, and he took to journalism for livelihood. He contributed to *Punch* and wrote some novels, such as *Catherine*, *The Great Hoggarty Diamond* and *Barry Lyndon*, which, however, didn't bring him fame. It was not until he was 37 that he brought out a really great work, *Vanity Fair* (1848). This was followed by *The History of Pendennis* (1850), *The History of Henry Esmond* (1852), and *The Newcomes* (1855). His last novels, *The Virginians* and *The Adventures of Philip*, show some falling-off in power, as Thackeray's mind was distracted by political ambitions. Like Dickens, Thackeray appeared on the public platform after he was famous, and his lectures on *The English Humorists of the Eighteenth Century* were an social event in London. He died in 1863 before he finished *Denis Daval*.

2. Thoughts

As a clear-sighted moralist and satirist who often adopts the tone and stance of the preacher, Thackeray's most famous text is Ecclesiastes 1.2 ("Vanity of vanities, saith the preacher, vanity of vanities; all is vanity"), which he quotes in the final paragraph of *Vanity Fair*. The vanity theme also recurs in the novels, which follow *Vanity Fair*. More central to Thackeray's vision, however, is his profound interest in the nature of the universal human lot, irrespective of time and place. His conviction that there is no new thing under the sun helps to explain both his lifelong interest in history and his impatience with Dickens's nagging concern with the specific social ills of his time. This conviction surfaces in a number of recurrent preoccupations in Thackeray's fiction. First, and most explicitly, there is his often world-weary sense that the plots of most individual lives are remarkable only in their predictability. For example, in the "Overture" chapter of *The Newcomes*, Thackeray answers his own question, "What stories are new?", with the answer, "All types of all characters march through all fables", but although "there may be nothing new under and including the sun", it "looks fresh every morning, and we rise with it to toil, hope, scheme, laugh, struggle, love, suffer, until the night comes and quiet". These words say as much about Thackeray as a writer as they do about us as readers. Thackeray dwells on the idea of the inexorable wheel of time, which brings all people to their deaths. He habitually emphasizes the universality of his theme by breaking into the narrative with authorial commentary or some kind of moral fable.

3. Style

Thackeray the novelist owes much to his training as an artist and journalist. Having mastered the art of the comic pen and pencil sketch, he went on to make his name as one of the leading writers of his day with the publication of *Vanity Fair*, a long novel of panoramic

Chapter Seven
Victorian Literature (1832–1900)

range which still retained the freshness of an improvised series of sketches. The subjects of his early work—ambition and the willful hero or heroine, class and snobbery, money, speculation and the marriage market—also recur later in his career, although they are treated more seriously as his satire broadens and deepens. Indeed, the sameness of much of his mature fiction, in which characters reappear and themes are reworked in several novels, reflects his sense of the universal qualities of the human condition.

Another kind of continuity in Thackeray's career is his commitment to the portrayal of the real rather than the ideal. He often restated his intention to portray the world as it really is. Early in his career he described the sordid realities of crime and rascality in Catherine and Barry Lyndon. In his major novels, he exposed the reality behind the social appearance or the wish-for ideal and thus reaffirms his sense of the ambivalence of human condition in a fallen world.

4. Major Works

Vanity Fair: A Novel Without a Hero, is a vast satirical panorama of a materialistic society. The story is set at the time of the Napoleonic wars, and gives a satirical picture of a worldly society, which Thackeray intended to be applied to his own times.

The story follows the fortunes of two sharply contrasted characters, Rebecca (Becky) Sharp, the penniless orphaned daughter of an artist and a French opera dancer, and Amelia Sedley, the sheltered child of a rich city merchant. The two girls have been educated at Miss Pinkerton's Academy. Becky, having failed to capture Amelia's elephantine brother Jos, becomes governess to the children of Sir Pitt Crawley, a coarse old man who bullies his fading second wife. Becky charms the Crawley family, and becomes a favourite of Miss Crawley, Sir Pitt's rich sister. When his wife dies Sir Pitt proposes to Becky, but she has to confess that she is already married to his younger son Rawdon. The young couple abruptly fall from favour with Miss Crawley, and have to live on Becky's wit.

Meanwhile Amelia's father has lost all his money and her engagement to George Osborne, the vain and shallow son of another city magnate, has been broken off in consequence. William Dobbin, George's awkward loyal friend, who is secretly in love with Amelia, persuades George to defy his father and go on with the marriage, and Mr. Osborne disinherits his son. George, Rawdon and Dobbin are all in the army, and Amelia and Becky accompany their husbands to Belgium, where Becky carries on an intrigue with George Osborne. George is killed at Waterloo, and Amelia, with her baby son Georgy, goes to live in poverty with her parents, while Becky and Rawdon manage to make a brilliant display in London society on "nothing a year". Amelia is finally forced by poverty to part with Georgy to his grandfather. Dobbin, despairing of ever winning Amelia's love, has spent ten years in India. Becky and Rawdon part, after Rawdon has discovered his wife in a compromising situation with Lord Steyne. Becky leads an increasingly disreputable life on the Continent. Rawdon, who has become governor of Coventry Island, dies of fever. Amelia steadfastly refuses to marry Dobbin, until Becky tells her of George Osborne's infidelity. Disillusioned, she marries Dobbin, but by then his love for her has lost much of its intensity.

The History of Henry Esmond, set in the reign of Queen Anne, is generally considered the finest Victoria example of historical fiction.

Henry Esmond, who narrates his own story, mainly in the third person, is supposed illegitimate son of the third Viscount Castlewood, who dies at the battle of the Boyne. Henry, a serious, lonely boy, continues to live at Castlewood House under the protection of the fourth viscount, his father's cousin, and his young wife Rachel. The couple has two children, Frank, the heir, and Beatrix, a beautiful, but willful girl. Henry is devoted to Lady Castlewood, who treats him with much kindness. The Castlewoods become estranged after Lady Castlewood catches smallpox, inadvertently brought to the household by Henry, and loses much of her beauty. The wicked Lord Mohun takes advantage of Castlewood's neglect of his wife to attempt to seduce her. There is a duel and Castlewood is killed. On his deathbed he reveals the fact that Henry is legitimate and the rightful heir. But Henry keeps silent for the sake of Lady Castlewood and her son. He is imprisoned for a year for having acted as Castlewood's second in the duel, for which Lady Castlewood bitterly reproaches him, and on his release joins the army and fights in the wars of the Spanish Succession. On a visit to England, he is reconciled to Lady Castlewood, who is secretly in love with him, and falls in love with Beatrix, now grown up. But Beatrix is too ambitious to consider a man who has no fortune or position in society. Henry goes back to the wars. The wayward Beatrix becomes engaged, first to Lord Ashburnham, then to the much older duke of Hamilton, who fights a duel with Lord Muhun, in which both are killed. Beatrix and her brother Frank, now the fifth viscount, are ardent Jacobites, and Esmond becomes involved with them in a

Chapter Seven
Victorian Literature (1832–1900)

plot to restore James Edward Stuart, the Old Pretender, to the throne on the death of Queen Anne. The plot fails because Beatrix is carrying on an intrigue with the Pretender, and at the moment when he should be in London he is at Castlewood. Esmond, disillusioned with Beatrix and the Jacobite cause, marries her mother Rachel and they emigrate to Virginia. The later history of the family in America and England is told in *The Virginians*.

Pendennis has strong autobiography elements. Arthur Pendennis is brought up by his widowed mother, who lives with his adopted daughter Laura Bell. His worldly uncle, Major Pendennis, saves him from an imprudent marriage to an actress, Miss Fotheringay, daughter of the tipsy Captain Costigan. Pen goes to Oxbridge, where he becomes idle and extravagant. Back at home he flirts with the shallow Blanche Amory, daughter of the second wife of Sir Francis Clavering, and dutifully proposes to Laura, who rejects him. In London, where he lodges with George Warrington, he starts to write for the *Pall Mall Gazette* and publishes a successful novel. He meets Blanche again and becomes attracted to a porter's daughter, Fanny Bolton. She nurses him when he is ill and his mother wrongly suspects her of being his mistress. Mother and son are reconciled before her sudden death. Major Pendennis uses his knowledge of family scandal to try to arrange a worldly marriage between Pen and Blanche. When Pen discovers the scandal that Blanche's father is alive and a criminal, he repudiates the arrangement but decides to honour his engagement. She, however, has transferred her affection to his friend Harry Fiker. Pen proposes to Laura, whom he has come to love, and she accepts him.

Another Pendennis reappears in Thackeray's fictions as the narrator of *The Newcomes* and *The Adventures of Philip*.

In *The Newcomes*, Colonel Thomas Newcome is a simple and honourable gentleman. His son Clive is in love with his cousin Ethel, daughter of the wealthy banker, Sir Brian Newcome. Their union is opposed by Ethel's relatives—notably her snobbish brother Barnes and her grandmother, the Countess of Kew—though she resists their pressure to marry her cousin, Lord Kew. Clive is maneuvred into marrying Rosey, daughter of the scheming Mrs. Mackenzie. When Colonel Newcome loses his fortune he is so bullied and reproached by Mrs. Mackenzie that he takes refuge in the Greyfriars almshouse, where he dies. Clive's fortunes are restored by the discovery of a will, and his wife's death leaves him free to marry Ethel.

> **For Your Information**
>
> **Women Novelists**
>
> After the flourishing of women's writing towards the end of the eighteenth century, the nineteenth century brought great popularity to many female writers. Equality was still some way as is shown by Marry Ann Evan's choice of pen name, George Eliot, when she began to write fiction. After Sir Walter Scott made the novel popular worldwide, it was, for two decades, seen largely as a man's genre. Women writers were expected to write the kinds of novel which George Eliot was to condemn in an essay as *Silly Novels by Lady Novelists*—the sub-genres of romance, fantasy and sensation. But several of the major figures of the Victorian novel are women, and the heroines they created began to throw off the victim's role that male authors had created. Jane Eyre's "Reader, I married him" close to the end of Charlotte Brontë's novel that bears the character's name, shows the reversal of roles and the decision-making capacities that the new generation of socially aware women could demonstrate.

7.3.3 The Brontë Sisters (1818–1848, 1820–1849)

The three sisters—Charlotte, Emily and Anne Brontë—opened up new possibilities for the form of English novel, and at the same time they provided a basis for which psychological exploration became a key component in the development of the genre of the novel. They also contributed much to the position of women at their time. They did much to alter the way in which women were viewed, demonstrating new social, psychological and emotional possibilities for women. Like George Eliot, however, they adopted pseudonyms (Curer, Ellis and Acton Bell) in order not to draw attention to the fact that they were women. Charlotte and Emily were both in many ways opposites of Jane Austen. They were distinctly romantic in temperament, exploring in their novels extremes of passion and violence. Although there are some features of Romanticism in Jane Austen's novels, her work is essentially Augustan in spirit. She prefers exploration of the individual within clear boundaries of decorum and restraint. *Jane Eyre*, Charlotte Brontë's first novel, was published in 1847 to considerable critical acclaim. Like Dickens' *David Copperfield*, it is a novel of growing up.

Chapter Seven
Victorian Literature (1832–1900)

The heroine, a penniless orphan, has been left to the care of her aunt Mrs. Reed. Harsh and unsympathetic treatment rouses her defiant spirit, and Mrs. Reed consigns her to Lowood Institution. There, consoled by the kindness of the superintendent Miss Temple, she spends some miserable years, eventually becoming a teacher. She then becomes a governess at Thornfield Hall to Adele, the illegitimate daughter of Mr. Rochester, a Byronic hero of grim aspect and sardonic temper. Rochester, despite Jane's plainness, is fascinated by her sharp wit and independence, and they fall in love. After much resistance she agrees to marry him, but on the eve of their wedding her wedding veil is rent by an intruder who is the next day revealed to be his mad Creole wife Bertha, confined to the upper regions of the Hall for years, whose unseen presence has long disturbed Jane. Despite Rochester's full confession, Jane flees. After nearly perishing on the moors, she is taken in and cared for by St. John Rivers and his sisters Mary and Diana. It emerges that they are her cousins, and that Jane has inherited money from an uncle. Under pressure from the dedicated Rivers, she nearly consents to marry him and share his missionary vocation in India, but is prevented by a telepathic appeal from Rochester. She returns to Thornfield Hall to find the building burned, and Rochester blinded and maimed from his attempt to save his wife from the flames. She marries him, and in the last chapter we learn that his sight is partially restored.

On one level, the novel is a rags-to-riches story. On another level it is a novel of love, mystery and passion, which poses profound moral and social questions. The good characters win, but only after they have suffered and been forced to examine their own conscience and to explore their moral selves. The plot is characterized by melodramatic incidents, but in each phase Jane grows in maturity and understanding. She becomes increasingly independent and self-reliant in her judgment. Like the heroine in Charlotte's another novel, *Villete* (1853), she is not strikingly beautiful but plain, and on the surface at least, reticent. However, she is passionate and afraid of her strong feelings. In the novel, Charlotte sends out a signal that ordinary women can experience deep love and begin to take responsibility for their own lives.

Wuthering Heights is Emily Brontë's only novel, also published in 1847. It is a novel of unique imaginative power. It contains a degree of emotional force and sophisticated narrative structure, not seen previously in the history of the English novel.

The story is narrated by Lockwood, temporary tenant of Thrushcross Grange, who has stumbled into the violent world of Wuthering Heights, the home of his landlord Heathcliff. The narration is taken up by the housekeeper, Nelly Dean, who has been a witness to the interlocked destinies of the original owners of the Heights, the Earnshaw family, and of the Grange, the Linton family. Events are set in motion by the arrival at the Heights of Heathcliff, picked up as a waif of unknown parentage in the street of Liverpool by the elder Earnshaw, who brings him home to rear as one of his own children. Bullied and humiliated after Earnshaw's death by his son Hindley, Heathcliff's passionate and ferocious nature finds its complement in Earnshaw's daughter Catherine. Their childhood collusions develop into an increasingly intense, though vexed, attachment, but Heathcliff, overhearing Catherine telling Nelly that she cannot marry him because it would degrade her, and failing to hear her declare her passion for him, leaves the house. He returns three years later, mysteriously enriched, to find Catherine married to the insignificant Edgar Linton. Heathcliff is welcomed by Hindley, by now widowed with a son, Hareton, and a hardened gambler. Heathcliff marries Edgar's sister Isabella and cruelly ill-treats her, hastens Catherine's death by his passion as she is about to give birth to a daughter, Cathy, and brings Hareton and Hindley under his power, brutalizing the latter in revenge of Hindley's treatment of himself as a child. Edgar Linton dies, after doing his best to prevent a friendship between Cathy and Heathcliff's son Linton. Heathcliff then lures Cathy to his house, and forces a marriage between her and young Linton in order to secure the Linton property. Young Linton, always sick, also dies; affection springs up between Cathy and the ignorant Hareton, whom she does her best to educate. Heathcliff's desire for revenge has now worn itself out, and he longs for his death that will reunite him with Catherine. At his death there is promise that the two contrasting worlds and moral orders represented by the Heights and the Grange will be united in the next generation, in the union of Cathy and Hareton.

The novel is cyclical in structure. It moves in a tragic circle from relative peace and harmony to violence, destruction and intense suffering, and finally back into peace and harmony again. It is a work of extreme contrasts set in the wild moorland of Yorkshire, which is appropriate to the wild passions it describes between the two main characters, Catherine and Heathcliff. Heathcliff is a man of dark and brooding passions, whose love for Catherine has no boundaries. At times, their love for each other is violent and destructive; at others, it appears to be a completely natural phenomenon. As Catherine says, my love for Heathcliff resembles the eternal rocks beneath: "a source of little visible delight, but necessary." The tragic outcome to the novel is inevitable, but the depths of their mutual feeling endure.

The third sister, Anne, wrote *The Tenant of Wildfell Hall* (1848), which has been overshadowed by Charlotte and Emily's more spectacular successes. It is, however, an important novel in its own right. In it, Anne depicts a bitterly unhappy marriage followed by the departure of the wife, Helen Huntingdon, and her search for new freedom. One critic wrote that the slamming of Helen's bedroom door against her husband reverberated throughout Victorian England.

7.3.4 George Eliot (1819–1880)

George Eliot is the most earnestly imperative and the most probably intelligent of the great mid-Victorian novelists. In her works, the English novel reached new depths of social and philosophical concern, and moral commitment. For some twentieth-century critics, Virginia Woolf and F. R. Leavis among them, her writings are seen as having brought the novel to new height of maturity. She shares with the greatest European writers of her century—Balzac, Flaubert, Dostoevsky, and Tolstoy—a concern for her characters' vulnerability and weakness in the face of "progress" and the moral imperatives of duty and humanity. Eliot's principal theme is egoism, and her standard plot is an educational one, in which the central character comes to understand that he or she has been self-absorbed, and starts to think about his or her social commitment.

The scope of Eliot's writing is considerable. From the early stories in *Scenes of Clerical Life* (1857–1858) to the massive *Middlemarch* (1871–1872), and *Daniel Deronda* (1876), she touches on many of the major issues of her day, such issues having not lost their pertinence over a century later: how a wife copes with a drunken husband ("Janet's Repentance" in *Scenes of Clerical Life*); what happens when an unmarried girl is accused of murdering her infant child (*Adam Bede*, 1859); how an orphan child brings humanity to a miserly social outcast (*Silas Marner*, 1861); how a sister and brother achieve reconciliation in the moment of tragedy after bankruptcy, moral compromise, and ostracism have separated them (*The Mill on the Floss*, 1860). These themes show Eliot's concern for the outsider in society, and her search for illustration illuminated the moral areas of experience, which more traditional Victorian thought would have tried to handle in absolute terms—black and white, wrong and right.

Besides a moralist, George Eliot is a realist. Her novels are largely set in the realistically presented location of the Midlands area of her childhood—Warwickshire—and her characters tend to be ordinary, unheroic people caught up in circumstances, which are greater than any individual. Her realism not only involves the close observation of ordinary life, but also involves a discourse that has in common with her readers. It is a discourse that is characterized by a shared understanding of the world and shared values. Eliot does very little in terms of actually describing her characters. Instead, she calls upon ideas, in particular, a shared apprehension that she can identify in her readers. Thus readers can easily understand all about her characters and can easily identify in them.

The Mill on the Floss tells the story that Maggie and Tom Tulliver are the children of the miller of Dorlcote Mill, an honest but unimaginative man, and his weak and foolish wife. Tom is a prosaic youth, narrow in imagination and intellect. In this oppressive environment Maggie's intelligence, scholarly competence and wider-ranging imagination become liabilities, especially in a woman. She turns to Philip Wakem, the deformed son of a lawyer in the nearby town of St. Ogg's, for intellectual and emotional companionship. Unfortunately lawyer Wakem is the object of Mr. Tulliver's suspicion and dislike, which is developed into hatred when Tulliver is made bankrupt as results of litigation in which Wakem is on the other side. Tom, loyal to his father, makes Maggie give up Philip's friendship. After Mr. Tulliver's death, Maggie visits St. Ogg's, where her cousin Lucy Deane is to marry the handsome and agreeable Stephen Guest. Stephen is attracted by Maggie, and she by him. A boating expedition on the river leads to Maggie's being immediately compromised; Stephen implores her to marry him, but she refuses. Her brother turns her out of the house, and the society of St. Ogg's ostracizes her. She and her mother take refuge with the loyal friend of her childhood, the packman Bob Jakins. In the last chapter, a great flood descends upon the town, and Maggie courageously rescues her brother from the mill. There is a moment of reconciliation before the boat overturns, and both are drowned.

The novel shows provincial English society, which, while it reinforces family values, serves to stifle aspiration and particularly its heroine's bid for personal liberation. Maggie is both an aspirer and a victim; she is blessed with a singularly happy childhood, but becomes disoriented when the stable world around her, and her assumptions about it, are gradually demolished. Experience brings only a limited wisdom, and the deluge of the novel's ending offers a resolution in the form of a catastrophe, which literally overwhelms its protagonist.

In *Silas Marner*, Silas Marner, a linen-weaver, driven out of a small religious community by a false charge of theft, takes refuge in the agricultural village of Raveloe. His only consolation in his loneliness is his growing pile of gold. This is stolen from his cottage by the squire's reprobate son Dunstan Cass, who disappears. Dunstan's elder brother Godfrey is in love with Nancy, but is secretly and unhappily married to a woman of low class in a neighbouring town. Meditating revenge for Godfrey's refusal to acknowledge her, this woman carries her child one New Year's Eve to Raveloe, intending to force her way into the Cass's house but dies in the snow. Her child, Eppie, who finds her way into Silas's cottage, is adopted by him. After many years the draining of a pond near Silas's door reveals the body of Dunstan with the gold. Moved by this revelation, Godfrey, now married to Nancy, acknowledges himself the father of Eppie and claims her, but neither she nor Silas wishes to be separated, and the novel concludes with her marriage to the worthy Aaron Wintthrop.

The story is spiced with rustic humor and forceful village characters. The novel is a moral fable, which explores a series of dense ethical, social, and spiritual dilemmas.

The scene in *Middlemarch* is laid in the provincial town of Middlemarch, Loamshire, during the years immediately preceding the first Reform Bill. It has a multiple plot, with several interlocking sets of characters. The opening section focuses on Dorothea Brooke, and shows how she comes to marry Edward Casaubon, a clergyman some thirty years her senior. As this story develops, a number of other strands are introduced. There is the story of Tertius Lydgate, a young doctor who newly arrives in this area, and his courtship of and marriage to Rosamond Vincy. Another couple who eventually marry are Mary Garth and Rosamond's brother, Fred Vincy, but in the early stages of the novel she refuses to marry him unless he mends his ways. For Dorothea, the reality of marriage to Casaubon is not at all what she has expected, although they come closer together when she learns that he is terminally ill. But Casaubon extracts a promise from her, that, after his death, she will continue with his futile scholarly work; moreover, he leaves a codicil to his will stating that Dorothea will be disinherited if she ever marries a young relative of Casaubon's, Will Ladislaw. Just as Dorothea's marriage has proved a disappointment, so has Lydyate's, whose wife, Rosamond, is extravagant and foolish. Dorothea finds Rosamond and Will Ladislaw together. This is a decisive moment for both women. Rosamond acts unselfishly for once, as she tells Dorothea that Dorothea herself is the woman Ladislaw loves, and, at the same point, Dorothea realizes her love for Ladislaw. This paves the way for their marriage.

Middlemarch is a novel that concerns itself with the ordinary dilemmas of life, with marriages, mainly unhappy marriages, and with people's working lives and their relationships with their neighbours. When characters are at odds with society, it is not so much a consequence of obvious ills in the world but a result of their own unrealistic expectations. The moral from the novel resides in the way that characters become less self-absorbed as the novel progresses; their egoism is cured by a sense of social obligation. Here we can see how Eliot acts as a kind of moral tutor to her audience, guiding them on the right kind of social reality.

7.3.5 Elizabeth Gaskell (1810–1865)

Elizabeth Gaskell is the greatest of the early Victorian social novelists. She is an active humanitarian and the message of several of her novels is the need for social reconciliation, for better understanding between employers and workers, between the respectable and the outcasts of society. In all of her novels—*Ruth* (1853), *North and South* (1854–1855), *Mary Barton* (1848), *Sylvia's Lovers* (1863) and *Wives and Daughters* (1864–1866)—there is the impulse towards social healing, an optimistic sense that society can heal its wounds and advance decisively. At the same time, Gaskell tries to seek a personal answer to a political problem, believing that a modification in the views on individuals can affect the whole nature of society. What is also apparent in Gaskell's novels is her belief that, in the end, everyone should share her vision of middle-class values: The workers are assumed to have the same long-term interests as their employers, if only they could see what is best for them. This is a form of ideological thinking that became prevalent in the Victorian period: a tyranny of the respectable norm. However, Gaskell is always aware of levels of contradiction. As with other novelists of her era, she might be actively involved in the creation of new middle-class values, but she is also skeptical about these values.

Gaskell is a keen observer of human behavior and speech, among both industrial workers in Manchester and farming and country-town communities, and a careful researcher of the background and technicalities of her novels. In a century rich in women writers, Mrs. Gaskell stands to the forefront in her sympathy for the deprived, her evocations of nature, her gentle humor and her attractive pace. Of note is her exceptionally direct

Chapter Seven
Victorian Literature (1832–1900)

development from loosely structured melodramatic writing to the urbanity and balanced form of her later work, particularly *Wives and Daughters*.

North and South is fundamentally about social reconciliation and overcoming hostility and division. It tells the story of Margaret Hale, who, when her father resigns his living as a clergyman in the south of England, accompanies him to Manchester. There she finds herself in conflict with a mill-owner, John Thornton, trying to persuade him to take a sympathetic view of his workers' problems. Eventually his attitude softens, and they marry at the end of the novel.

The dynamic of this novel is conciliatory: It wants to heal rifts and divisions within society, notably between employer and worker. But the novel also presents two distinct versions of middle-class ideology, and attempts to reconcile them. One version is a liberal vision of moral responsibility for the general well-being of society and a sense of obligation to the less fortunate; the other is that of business and profit. In uniting Margaret and Thornton, both sides learn from the other. The emphasis is conciliating and healing; as such, it is a novel with moral prospectus for society. And, in this respect, it matches a mood of the 1850s, that, with rising affluence, solutions can be found to the country's problems.

For *Mary Barton (A Tale of Manchester Life)*, Mrs. Gaskell took inspiration from Carlyle and Engels and their observations on working class life. The background of the story is Manchester in the "hungry forties" and the acute poverty of the unemployed mill-hands, when the Chartist movement was reaching its climax. Mary Barton is the daughter of an active and embittered worker and trade unionist, John Barton. She has attracted Henry Carson, son of one of the employers, and, flattered by his attentions and the hope of a grand marriage, has repulsed her faithful admirer Jem Wilson, a young engineering worker. A group of workmen, exasperated by the failure of the employers to consider their grievances, decide to kill young Carson, and the lot falls on Barton to do the deed. When Carson is shot dead, suspicion falls on Jem Wilson. Mary, by now realizing that it is Jem whom she loves, discovers that her father is the murderer. Jem is tried for his life, and is saved by Mary's frantic efforts to prove his innocence without betraying her father. John Barton confesses to the fiercely vindictive old father of Henry Carson, and wins his forgiveness as he dies.

The strengths of the novel lie not in its political analysis, or in its suggested resolution, but in its detailing, its observation and, above all, in the careful establishment of contrasted ways of living, working, and perceiving. What's more, the entirely working class cast of characters in this novel was then an innovation.

Sylvia's Lovers is one of the finest of provincial novels, indebted to the model provided by the Waverley novels. It explores the lives of humble people with a sympathetic and delicate power, which had rarely been seen before.

The scene is the whaling part of Monkshaven during the Napoleonic wars, and the plot hinges on the activities of the press-gangs whose seizure of Monkshaven men provokes bitter resentment. Sylvia's father, the farmer Daniel Robson, leads a mob attack on the press-gang's headquarters, and he is tried and hanged for this. Her lover, the harpooner Charley Kinraid, is carried off by the press-gang but sends her a message promising constancy and return by Sylvia's cousin, the pedantic, hard-working shopkeeper Philip Hepburn, who has long loved Sylvia. Philip yields to the temptation of concealing the message and Sylvia, believing Charley dead, and left in poverty after her father's execution, agrees to marry Philip years later. Charley returns and Philip's treachery is revealed to Sylvia, who swears never to forgive him. He flees from Monkshaven and enlists, but eventually returns, disfigured and beggared, and—recognized on his deathbed—dies in the arms of the now repentant Sylvia.

The novel is remarkable for its vivid reconstruction of life in the little town dominated by the whaling industry and at the farm where noisy, unreasonable Daniel Robson, his quiet, devoted wife, and their sturdy old servant Kester, combine to cherish the much-loved and lovely but hapless Sylvia.

Wives and Daughters, Gaskell's masterpiece, examines family relationships and social class from an amplified Trollopian perspective. It is made up of a series of interwoven stories, but it is also an ambitious, careful, and delicate psychological study of an often-fraught household and its social connection.

The novel centers on two families, the Gibsons and the Hamleys. Mr. Gibson, surgeon in the little country town of Hollingford, is a widower with one daughter, Molly. As she grows up, her father feels he ought to marry again for her sake. He marries a widow, Mrs. Kirkpatrick, formal governess in the family of Lord Cummor, the local magnate. Molly is made unhappy by her stepmother's shallow selfishness, but her lot is improved when her stepmother's daughter by her first marriage, Cynthia, joins the household. Cynthia is a fascinating beauty, more sincere than her mother, but with few moral principles.

The Hamleys are an ancient county family—the proud and hot-tempered Squire, his invalid wife, their elder son Osborne, who is handsome and clever, and a young son, Roger, sturdy, honest, and a late developer. Molly Gibson often stays with the Hamleys, and discovers that Osborne is secretly married to a French nursery-maid. Molly has begun to love and admire Roger, but he becomes engaged to Cynthia, and, being by now a successful scientist, goes on an expedition to Africa. Cynthia is in fact already secretly engaged to Peston, Lord Cummor's ill-bred agent, and she enlists Molly's help in extricating herself from this entanglement, thus compromising Molly's reputation. Osborne Hamley is bitterly estranged from his father, but when Osborne dies and the secret of his marriage is revealed, Squire Hamley, repenting his harshness, adopts Osborne's baby son. Cynthia throws over Roger Hamley and marries a man more suited to her, and when Roger returns he has realised that it is Molly whom he loves.

In this novel, the habits, loyalties, prejudices, petty snobberies, rumors, adjustments of a whole countryside hierarchy are displayed by Gaskell with minute and loving observation. Unlike some of Gaskell's earlier works, the novel is expertly constructed, convincing in all incidents and dialogues and peopled by fully realized characters.

7.3.6 George Meredith (1828–1909)

The work of George Meredith stands apart from most fictions of the nineteenth century. He did not follow any established tradition, nor did he found a school. His main teachers were not novelists, but philosophers and poets. His mind was highly selective. He confined himself principally to the upper classes of society, and his attitude towards life is that of the thinker and poet. Much of his own best writing, indeed, was in verse; *Love in the Valley*, and certain "sonnets" of the sequence *Modern Love*, are among the most beautiful poems of the age. In his novels, he cared little for incident or plot on their own account, but used them principally to illustrate the activity of the "Comic Spirit". Meredith loves to trace the calamities, which befall those who provoke Nature by obstinately running counter to her laws. A certain balance and sanity, a fine health of body and soul are, in his view, the means prescribed by Nature for the happiness of man. Many of his poems give expression to his "philosophy" of high courage and spiritual valour. The men and women of his novels are mostly persons of mental alertness and high animal spirits. It is the various infatuations of such people that give rise to the "comic" situations which it was his delight to study.

The Ordeal of Richard Feverel (1859), though one of Meredith's earliest books, is one of his best. Its main theme is the ill-advised upbringing of an only son by a well-meaning but too officious parent. *Evan Harrington* (1861) is much more conventional in its style, and the humorous situations which arise out of the social snobbery of the Harrington family have much of the ordinary Victorian flavour. Only in Meredith, there is a more conscious concentration on the comic issues. *Rhoda Fleming* (1865), *Sandra Belloni* (1864), *Harry Richmond* (1871), and *Beauchamp's Career* (1876), all have in a large measure the best qualities of Meredith's art. Intellectual brilliance, a ruthless exposure of social foibles, and an occasional poetic intensity of style are all in those books. The climax of his art was reached in *The Egoist* (1879), the most perfect illustration of what Meredith meant by "comedy".

The central character in *The Egoist*, the Egoist himself, is Sir Willoughby Patterne, rich and handsome, with a position in the county. Laetitia Dale, an intelligent young woman but past her first bloom, has loved him for many years. But the dashing Constantia Durham is a greater price, and she accepts his proposal. She soon discerns the true Sir Willoughby and elopes with Harry Oxford, an officer in the hussars, thus bringing Willoughby his first humiliation. Soon he discovers the qualities he requires in Clara Middleton, the daughter of an elderly scholar with a passion for wine. Clara becomes engaged to him but soon perceives his intention of directing and moulding her; her attempts to free herself from the entanglements of the engagement form the main theme of the book. Clara envies but cannot emulate Constantia, and Willoughby struggles frantically against an incredibly second jilting. Clara is meanwhile seeing more and more of Vermon Whitford, a poor and earnest young scholar, who lives at Patteme and is tutor to young Crossjay, son of a poor relation, an officer of the marines. The spirited Crossjay is finally the means of Clara's release, for he unintentionally overhears Willoughby proposing to Laetitia Dale, a proposal which she refuses. Willoughby finds himself trebly humiliated. In the end his persistence achieves the reluctant Laetitia, and Clara marries Vernon Whitford.

7.3.7 Wilkie Collins (1824–1889)

Wilkie Collins wrote many articles and short stories, but his reputation rests on his novels which began with *Antonia* (1850), a historical novel about the fall of Rome. With *Basil* (1852) he found his true métier as an expert in mystery, suspense, and crime. His finest work in this genre, *The Novel of Sensation*, was written in the 1860s, when he produced *The Woman in White* (1860, his masterpiece), *No Name* (1862), *Armadale* (1866), and *The Moonstone* (1868). *The Novel of Sensation* is a form of fiction that, like the realistic novel, focuses on ordinary middle-class life, but which includes extravagant and often horrible events. "Sensation" has two implications: The events are sensational, but they also affect the senses of the reader, instilling a spine-tingling fear. Collins's later novels are inferior in quality.

Collins wrote the first full-length detective story in English and set a mould for this genre which has lasted for well over a century. He excelled at constructing ingenious and meticulous plots, and made interesting experiments in narrative technique. Many of his novels contain vivid and sympathetic portraits of physically abnormal individuals—the blind, deaf, crippled, deformed, and obese.

The Woman in White is, for the most part, narrated by Walter Hartright, a young drawing-master. One evening in London, he encounters a woman dressed in white who is in deep distress. He later learns that she has escaped from an asylum. Hartright then takes up a position in a house in Cumberland, where he finds that Laura Fairlie bears an extraordinary resemblance to the woman in white, whose name is Anne Catherick. Hartright and Laura fall in love, but Laura has promised that she will marry Sir Percival Glyde. After their marriage, Glyde and Laura return to his family estate in Hampshire, accompanied by Glyde's friend Count Fosco. Glyde, desperate to get his hands on Laura's money, and Fosco then conspire to switch the identities of Laura and Anne Catherick; Anne dies of a heart attack and is buried as Laura, while Laura is dragged and placed in an asylum as Anne. With the help of her devoted half-sister, Marian Halcombe, she escapes, and they live quietly with Hartright, but they are determined to restore Laura's identity. Hartright discovers that Glyde has concealed his illegitimacy, but Glyde is killed in a fire. It is Fosco that Hartight then has to turn to in order to extract a written confession. Hartright and Laura are married. Fosco is forced to supply the information, which restores Laura to her identity, and is killed by a member of an Italian secret society which he has betrayed.

The novel appears nothing more than a highly contrived story. But in fact it deals with a whole range of issues that were of central concern in mid-Victorian Britain, such as its realism, its characters' reliance on the processes of law, and marriage, family and work—the core institutions upon which the Victorians established their lives.

7.3.8 Anthony Trollope (1815–1882)

Trollope was forty years old before he wrote a successful novel and most of his best works were published during the High Victorian period of the 1860s and 1870s. Concentrating almost exclusively on middle class and upper class circles, he explored the relationship between the individual and society, between private and public lives, between the personal and professional. Clergymen, politicians and doctors make decisions in their working lives, which reflect personal pressures upon them in their domestic lives. When men have to choose between women, and vice versa, the choice is often between love and money. In his treatment of these and other dilemmas, which are the very core of his novels, Trollope's conservatism is underpinned with a deep respect for established conventions and codes of conduct, English traditions of modesty, hard work and honesty, and with hostility towards rapid social change and personal ambition.

After early experiments he soon discovered the value of the multi-plot scheme in his novels, although he always admitted that character was more important to him than plot. In all but two of his novels he addresses the reader as an authorial narrator and often chats away about his own writing and contemporary literary treads. Trollope has a burning interest in the present which is revealed not only in the more obviously polemical novels, such as *The Warden* (1855) and *The Three Clerks* (1858), but also in the steady pressure of a general concern for contemporary issues and problems behind much of his narrative. Trollope combines his quiet realism with plots turning on dramatic events and comments interestingly on the critics' division of novelists into the sensational and the non-sensational.

As an admirer of Thackeray, Trollope took his cue from Thackeray's proposed example for sequences of novels which have later become known as the "Barchester" and the "Palliser" series. In the Barchester series lies the key to Trollope's success as a novelist and moralist. In the six Barchester novels, Trollope invented a small, almost closed community, the diocese of Barchester, with its own hierarchy, unwritten rules of conduct and store of shared history and experience: a microcosm in which the subtle shadings of a moral dilemma or small variations of behavior are magnified in relation to their settling. *The Walden* (1854), the beginning of the series, is a short study of how the ripples of a local scandal broaden

Chapter Seven
Victorian Literature (1832–1900)

into a national issue and how an upright man becomes a victim of circumstances beyond his control. Its sequel, *Barchester Towers* (1857), centers on the threat to the complacent security of the cathedral, Soptimus Harding, presented by the advent of a new Bishop, and, moreover, of the Bishop's Evangelical wife, Mrs. Proudie. It is one of Trollope's most successful comic observations of the political process at work, not on a national or a parliamentary scale, but as a series of ploys and maneuvres and as a clash of personalities. The upper cleric of those two novels figures prominently again in *The Last Chronicle of Beret* (1876), the novelist's personal favourite among his books and a conscious conclusion to the sequence. It suggests the effects of aging, death, and ill-founded suspicion on an established community. *Doctor Thorne* (1858), *Franley Parsonage* (1861), and *The Small House at Allington* (1862–1864) concentrate less on clerical politics and more on secular matchmaking and failures in love. All three move slowly and delicately, firmly rooted in genteel provinciality and in an England of rural backwaters and stable, traditional systems of value.

The Palliser series, loosely centered on the family connections of the Duke of Omnium, involve a more metropolitan consciousness and a cosmopolitan culture, and political affairs, such as reform of the franchise and the question of the secret ballot, are the running themes. But more central to Trollope's purpose is the examination of human frailties in the working of what he sees as the greatest of human institutions, the British Parliament. For Trollope's interest is in systems, classes and groupings and in the nature of community. *Can You Forgive Her?* (1864–1865) and *The Eustace Diamonds* (1871–1873) serve to justify Trollope's self-deprecating authorial ambition to relieve parliamentary concerns by putting in "love and intrigue, social incidents, with perhaps a dash of sport, for the sake of my readers". Both *Phineas Finn* (1867–1869) and *Phineas Redux* (1873–1874) concentrate on the advances and setbacks in the political career of an Irish Member of Parliament, an outsider to the British Establishment, but one who is variously the object of female flirtation and the victim of male jealousy and suspicion.

The real sharpness, and occasional disillusion, inherent in Trollope's vision of society and its corruption, are also evident in the complex ramifications of *The Way We Live Now* (1874–1875). This novel fits into no "series", but takes a broad, critical view of a nation caught up in deceit, decadence, and financial speculation. It is Trollope's most gloomy, pessimistic and disconcerting work, and his masterpiece. Augusus Melmotte is an apparently wealthy financier involved in a scheme to promote the central American railway. All are eager to help him and he has no trouble being elected to Parliament. The railway deal is a confidence trick, however, and Melmotte is exposed. He commits suicide. Meanwhile his daughter is betrayed and duped by the dissipated aristocrats who pursue her for her wealth. Everything in the novel is a sham, a deception, and built on nothing, with widespread corruption and profligacy. The novel, with its satiric picture of decadent society ruined by gambling and greed, seems to predict not simply the end of the Victorian era but the end of the Victorian realism of middle class progress and respectability.

7.3.9 Thomas Hardy (1840–1928)

1. Life and Career

Thomas Hardy was the most significant novelist in the last quarter of the nineteenth century. He grew up in Dorset and was trained as an architect; he spent some years as a young man on architecture, but was never at home there, and returned to his native county where he spent the rest of his long life. Hardy achieved fame with *Far from the Madding Crowd* (1874), and went on to produce a series of novels, including *The Return of the Native* (1878), *The Mayor of Casterbridge* (1886), *The Woodlanders* (1887), *Tess of the D'Urbervilles* (1891) and *Jude the Obscure* (1895). Prompted in part by the hostile reaction to the last of these novels, Hardy then turned exclusively to poetry, in which he achieved as much as in fiction.

2. Thoughts

Profoundly influenced by Greek tragedy and Aristotelian tragic theory, Hardy has developed a tragic vision of the world, and skeptical attitudes towards conventional morality. For Hardy, it is social regulations and conventions that ruin people's lives. The big picture in his novels therefore is of individual at odds with society. Unlike other Victorian novelists whose major characters usually achieve an accommodation with society, Hardy's main characters are rebels, but not willfully so; it is just that there is something in their nature that makes it difficult for them to fit in. They can see the advantages of conventional behavior, but simply do not seem able to conform. And on the whole, Hardy tends to side with those characters. He seems to recognize that the orderly ways of society can be at odds with an instinctive unruliness in human nature. Time after time Hardy shows us a kind of undisciplined wildness in human nature, and in many ways this resembles an undisciplined wildness in the whole of the natural world. This indiscipline of nature is seen most clearly in the weather in the novels, which is often presented as cruel and destructive. Hardy's novel, then, presents a wildness both in nature and in human nature which is set against the codes and order of society. At the center of a Hardy novel is the presentation of the experiences of one or more characters caught between their sense of how they should behave and their natural instincts that make them behave in a different way. This unruliness in human nature will be linked with a similar lack of discipline and restraint in nature generally.

This standard tension between society and nature interprets the particular scenes and details in Hardy's novels. For example, in the love relationship, which is often at the center of Hardy's novels, there is something in the nature of emotional feelings that runs counter to any idea of disciplined social behavior.

3. Style

Hardy is a regional novelist, whose imaginary world of "Wessex" covers a large area of the southern and western counties of England. His Wessex is not a romanticized landscape as in some of his critics' view. On the contrary, it is one of considerable social upheavals as settled communities face the disruption caused by the mechanization of agriculture in the late nineteenth century. His last novels embody these changes technically. Hardy focuses less on plot, but more on the lyrical revelation of character, using techniques of episodic structure; in this respect, though written at the end of the nineteenth century, his novels are frequently regarded as "modern" texts. He is one of the writers who best represent the transition from the nineteenth to the twentieth century.

As a poet, Hardy wrote formal poetry all his life. He kept alive the traditional forms of English poetry in the era of modernist innovation. Hardy is a realist in his poetry, not pursuing ideal worlds but soberly and ironically regarding everyday human dramas and hopes and fears. Hardy's craftsmanship is evident, though he was also given to clumsy diction and odd word formation. His poetry is engrained with a bleak, honest agnosticism that does not flinch from the grimmer sides of the human conduction.

4. Major Works

Far from the Madding Crowd is Hardy's early work, which shows his skepticism of conventional morality. Bathsheba Everdence inherits her father's farm and takes it over as its owner. She is loved by Gabriel Oak, who is just establishing himself as a sheep farmer. When his flock is destroyed in an accident, Gabriel finds employment on Bathsheba's farm. Another man in love with Bathsheba is a neighbouring farmer, Boldwood, but Bathsheba loves and marries a soldier, Sergeant Troy, who has deserted Fanny Robin, the mother of his child. After a few months of marriage Troy also deserts Bathsheba, making it appear that he has been drowned. Believing she is a widow, Bathsheba accepts a proposal from Boldwood only for Troy to reappear. Boldwood shoots him, and is arrested, and confined as criminally insane. The novel ends with marriage of Bathsheba and Gabriel and social renewal, but as in his other novels, Hardy places far more emphasis on the failure of relationships, the breakdown of marriages, and even divorce.

The story of *The Return of the Native* takes place on the somber Egdon Heath, a pagan place where people rarely go to church. Damon Wildeve, once an engineer but now a publican, dallies between the two women by whom he is loved—the gentle Thomasin Yeobright and the wild, capricious Eustacia Vye. Thomasin rejects her humble suitor Diggory Venn, a reddleman, and is eventually married to Wildeve, who takes her less for love than from a wish to hurt Eustacia. Thomasin's cousin Clym Yeobright, a diamond merchant in Paris, disgusted with the worthlessness of his occupation, returns to Egdon intending to become a schoolmaster in his native heath. He falls in love with Eustacia, and she in a brief infatuation marries him, hoping to induce him to return to Paris, thus escaping from Egdon, which she detests. But to her despair he will not return; his sight fails and he becomes a furze-cutter on the heath. She becomes the cause of estrangement between Clym and his beloved mother, and unintentionally causes the mother's death. This, together with the discovery that Eustacia's relationship with Wildeve has not ceased, leads to a violent scene between Clym and his wife, and ultimately to Eustacia's flight with Wildeve, in the course of which both are drowned. Clym, blaming himself for the death of his mother and his wife, becomes an itinerant preacher, and the widowed Thomasin marries Diggory Venn.

At the outset of the story, the untamed wildness of the heath is set against the order of society. The characters who live here are likely to be caught between the pull of society and that of nature, including their own nature. Hardy presents the human drama of the

Chapter Seven
Victorian Literature (1832–1900)

experiences of characters caught in this dilemma.

The Mayor of Casterbridge tells the story that Michael Henchard, a hay-trusser, gets drunk at a fair and sells his wife and child for five guineas to a sailor, Newson. When sober again he takes a solemn vow not to touch alcohol for twenty years. By his energy and acumen, he becomes rich, respected, and eventually the mayor of Casterbridge. After eighteen years his wife returns, supposing Newson dead, and is reunited with her husband. She brings with her her daughter Elizabeth-Jane, and Henchard is led to believe she is his child, whereas she is in fact Newson's. Through a combination of unhappy circumstances, troubles accumulate. Henchard quarrels with his capable young assistant Donald Farfrae; Mrs. Henchard dies and Henchard learns the truth about the girl; Farfrae marries Lucetta, whom Henchard has hoped to win. Soon Henchard's business is ruined. The story of the sale of his wife is revealed, and he takes again to heavy drinking. Farfrae now has Henchard's business, his house, and Lucetta, while Henchard works as a labourer in his yard. Eventually Farfrae becomes mayor. Henchard's stepdaughter is his only comfort, then Newson returns and claims her and after Lucetta's death Farfrae marries her. Henchard becomes lonelier and more desolate, and dies wretchedly in a hut on Egdon Heath.

Here is a strong character who by nature goes against the ways of society. For twenty-five years, Henchard disciplines himself and rises to the top of the social hierarchy as mayor. Then his world falls apart, partly through accidents of fate, such as his wife's returning, but also of his fiery nature, which seems at odds with the social role he has forced himself to play. Thus the conflict in the novel is between social discipline and natural indiscipline.

In *Tess of the D'Urbervilles* (*A Pure Woman*), Tess Durbeyfield is the daughter of a poor villager of Blackmoor Vale, whose head is turned by learning that he is descended from the ancient family of D'Urberville. Tess is cunningly seduced by Alec, a young man of means, whose parents, with doubtful right, bear the name of D'Urberville. Tess gives birth to a child, which dies. Later, while working as a dairymaid she becomes blissfully engaged to Angel Clare, a clergyman's son. On their wedding night she confesses to him the seduction by Alec, and Angel hypocritically abandons her. Misfortunes come upon her and her family, and accident throws her once more in the path of Alec D'Urberville. He has become an itinerant preacher, but his temporary religious conversion does not prevent him from persistently pursuing her. When her pathetic appeals to her husband, now in Brazil, remain unanswered, she is driven for the sake of her family to become the mistress of Alec. Clare, returning from Brazil and repenting of his harshness, finds her living with Alec in Sandbourne. Maddened by this second wrong that has been done her by Alec, Tess stabs and kills him to liberate herself. After a brief halcyon period of concealment with Clare in the New Forest, Tess is arrested at Stonehenge, tried, and hanged.

The publication of the novel created a violent sensation. Some reviewers were deeply impressed, but most considered the work immoral and extremely disagreeable. On the one hand, *Tess of the D' Urbervilles* is a deeply pessimistic novel, revealing how an intelligent and sensitive girl can be driven to death by a society which is narrow in morality and in spirit. On the other hand, Hardy presents a very physical, strongly visual sense of less and nature that strain against social convention. The tension between society and nature is reflected in the conflict between social attitudes which, in Angel's eyes, make Tess a fallen woman. Angel's social prejudices are stronger than his natural feelings. At the heart of the novel, therefore, there is a conflict between instinctive behavior and social dictates, which restrict behavior.

Jude the Obscure tells the story that Jude Fawley, a young man with a passion for learning, hopes that one day he might get into university. But he forgets his plans when Arabella Donn traps him into marriage. They are not suited to each other, however, and soon separate. Jude then turns to his studies again, but the university is not interested in the aspiration of this working class man. Jude at this point in his life meets his cousin, Sue Bridehead, and soon falls in love with her. Sue, however, marries a schoolmaster, Philloston, but this is another unsuccessful marriage and Sue flees from her husband. Sue and Jude start living together; they both obtain divorces but Sue is reluctant to marry Jude. They have two children and are joined by Jude's son Arabella. Disaster ensues: Jude's son, called "Old Father Time", murders the two younger children and then hangs himself. Sue, overwhelmed with feelings of guilt, returns to Philloston. Jude goes into decline, drifts into the company of Arabella again, and, in the end, dies.

Like Tess, Jude is an ambitious and articulate working class youth who finds it difficult to fit into the pattern of ordinary life and whose sensual nature cannot be accommodated by a rigid and inflexible social system. The novel has been seen by many as Hardy's most direct attack on Victorian chains of class consciousness and social convention.

Chapter Seven
Victorian Literature (1832–1900)

> **For Your Information**
>
> ### Late Victorian Novelists
>
> By the last twenty years of the nineteenth century, Britain's economic lead over all other nations was beginning to fade. And not only was there increasingly economic competition, there was also a growing sense of political, and even military, tension among European countries. In addition, at home there was a mounting awareness of social problems and class hostility. For much of the Victorian period, people could focus rather narrowly on their own domestic concerns in a secure environment, but by the end of the century this was becoming more difficult. As old convictions collapsed, many united behind the idea of the nation, but jingoistic rallying cries could not conceal the evidence of a more divided and anxious country.
>
> In the literature of the last twenty years of the nineteenth century were a number of writers trying to engage with these changes, whereas others seemed to seek a variety of forms of escape. The more engaged literature of this period was influenced to a substantial extent by the works of the French novelist Emile Zola. Zola is a "naturalist", a novelist who reports on life in an exhaustively researched manner, producing works that bear a degree of resemblance to a sociological report. One of his most celebrated novels in this mood is *Germinal*. Zola's works are informed by contemporary ideas about the influence of the environment and genetics; whereas most novels focus on the development and progress of an individual, Zola reports on an inevitable decline in people's lives. There is always a downward spiral of disease, alcoholism, poverty or madness. Zola's social thinking has an obsessive dimension, but the ideas in his novels overlap with widely held beliefs in the late nineteenth century, beliefs inspired to a large extent by the writings of Charles Darwin. Supporters of imperialism could claim that Britain's colonial successes confirmed the views of Darwin that the stronger race would defeat the weaker, and that this was an inexorable law of nature. Such social Darwinism, however, went hand in hand with fears about degeneration and with anxieties about the triumph of brute force. Consequently by the late nineteenth century, an interest in evolution, progress and reform went hand in hand with pessimistic fears about regression, atavism and decline.

7.3.10 George Gissing (1857–1903)

George Gissing was a naturalist writer in that he described everyday life in great detail. His novels provide evidence of late Victorian social pessimism. In novels such as *Workers in the Dawn* (1880) and *The Nether World* (1889), Gissing considers London working class life. Unlike Elizabeth Gaskell, who, when she deals with urban poverty, writes positively, with a conviction that class relations and individual lives can be improved, Gissing despairs, regarding many of the people he presents as little better than savages. In his best-known novel, *New Grub Street* (1891), his negative social vision connects with a sense of a culture that has been coarsened by commercialism; his hero is Edwin Reardon, a delicate novelist who cannot survive in the kind of vulgar environment where only the most crass or cynical taste succeeds. The impression in Gissing's novels is of a society that has lost direction because it has lost sight of traditional principles in politics, religion and morality. His fears focus most clearly, however, on the idea of the working class mob. It is an anxiety that he shares with many of his middle class contemporaries, an anxiety that the forces of darkness and irrationality are preparing to take over.

Gissing also wrote a substantial novel about single women. *The Old Women* (1893) deals with the wretched lives of the three Madden sisters. The least fortunate is Monica, the only one of the three to marry; her husband is neurotically jealous, and she dies in childbirth. Her sisters, Alice and Virginia, dedicate their lives to caring for the child.

7.3.11 George Moore (1852–1933)

George Moore was associated with various kinds of writing during his long career. After a period as an art student in Paris in the 1870s and early 1880s, he wrote *A Modern Love* (1883), a novel set in Bohemian artistic society; this was banned by the circulating libraries, and inspired Moore to fight censorship for the rest of his career. He wrote several plays, including *Martin Luther* (1879), one of the literary works in English to feature Luther as a tragic hero. The realistic novel *Esther Waters* made his name in 1894 as a scandalous novelist because of the frankness of its sexual content. Esther is a servant girl from a religious background, who is seduced and deserted by a fellow servant, William Latch. She is dismissed by her employer, and the novel then charts her life as a new mother. She is about to join a religious sect when Latch reappears. They marry and set up a public house in Soho, but his venture into book-making leads to ruin. He dies, leaving Esther destitute. The realism of the novel lies in its depiction of poverty, and in its settings, which include the world of racing establishment, a lying-in hospital and the workhouse. It takes the line of "seduction novels" on to a new level of social realism, and although its ending is less tragic than some, it caused a considerable scandal at a time when many novels were banned if they offended the tastes of the great circulating library.

Moore's earlier novel *Mike Fletcher* (1889) is of particular interest as the only decadent novel of the time, featuring a sensitive artistic hero whose suffering and sensibility dominate the whole tale. The modern novel as a chronicle of artistic sensibility is importantly anticipated in this neglected work, which can find a comparison only in Wilde's *The Picture of Dorian Gray* (1890–1891) as a novel of an aesthetic life lived for its own sake.

In his late work, Moore's Irish background comes more to the fore, and he is a major figure in the development of the short story in Ireland—*The Untilled Field* (1903) being a significant collection. His later novels, such as *The Brook Kerith* (1916), explore religious themes. Moore lived to become one of the grand old men of English theaters, and at the same time worked with years on plans for the Irish National Theater. His reputation has declined since his death, but several of his works are being rediscovered and reevaluated.

7.3.12 Samuel Butler (1835–1902)

Samuel Butler was another realistic novelist critical of the basis of Victorian society. His semi-autobiography novel *The Way of All Flesh* (1903) openly denounces Victorian family life with fathers as the moral center of society. Ernest Pontifex is tyrannized by his father. He is bullied into ordination as clergyman, even though he has lost his faith. In London he is cheated out of his inheritance and then imprisoned for six months for sexual assault. He marries one of his family's former servants, but she turns out to be a drunkard. Ernest is relieved to discover that her marriage to him was bigamous, and that he can become a happy recluse, free from all family and marital commitments. What is most obvious in the novel is that everything that is associated with a certain tradition in Victorian fiction is reversed: The family, marriage, a sound career and religion are all shown as having nothing to offer.

Erewhon (1872; the word "erewhon" is "nowhere" backwards) is Butler's another famous novel, which presents a utopian society. Like William Morris's *News from Nowhere* (1890–1891) and later Aldous Huxley's *Brave New World*, the form of a utopian novel, dating back to Sir Thomas More's *Utopia*, is used with a satirical aim. *Erewhon* is intended to satirize Victorian concepts of duty and religion. The narrator of the story (Higgs) crosses a range of mountains and comes upon the undiscovered country Erewhon. He is first thrown into gaol, where he is helped by his beautiful girl gaoler, Yram. On his release, he is lodged with Mr. Nosnibor (Robinson) and his family. In this society, morality is equated with health and beauty, and crime with illness. The Unborn selects their parents, who have to endure his selection. The Musical Banks produce a currency which is venerated but not used. The development of machinery, which at one stage threatened to usurp human supremacy, led to a civil war and is now forbidden. The country is ruled by so-called philosophers and prophets, whom Higgs sees to be merely faddists and fanatics. When he is threatened with prosecution for contracting measles, Higgs announces that he will visit the air-god and end the terrible drought; with Nosnibor's daughter Arowhena, he escapes in a balloon to England, where they marry.

7.3.13 William Morris (1834–1896)

William Morris was a fantasy novelist. Fantasy writing, set in other worlds or expressing other realities, became a popular phenomenon of the second half of the nineteenth century. Morris's *News from Nowhere* is a socialist utopian fantasy set far in the future, when all the contemporary ills of society (industrialism, government squalor, and even money) have been superseded after a bloody revolution, which takes place in 1952. Morris is, in effect, proposing an alternative society whose values are clearly the opposite of the actual values of the age. Morris's earlier work, *A Dream of John Ball* (1888), takes the genre back to 1381—John Ball being one of the leaders of the Peasants' Revolt—and the historical fantasy is a clear protest against exploitation. The book is intended to encourage a modern workers' revolt against the society and values of the 1880s.

News from Nowhere tells the story that the narrator falls asleep in the "shabby London suburb" of Chiswick, after an evening at the Socialist League spent discussing the Morrow of the Revolution, and wakes in the future, to find London and its surroundings transformed into a communist paradise where men and women are free, healthy, and equal, the countryside reclaimed from industrial squalor, and money, prisons, formal education, and central government abolished. At the close he fades back into the past, inspired by the vision of what he has seen and the need to work for its fulfillment.

Chapter Seven
Victorian Literature (1832–1900)

7.3.14 Robert Louise Stevenson (1850–1894)

Robert Louise Stevenson is a writer in many genres, from drama to travel writing, from fiction to verse. But his fame mainly rests on his fantasy writings. Stevenson made a cogent defense of fictional romance as a superior mode to the realistic novel that tried to capture "life" itself: "Life is monstrous, infinite, illogical, abrupt and poignant; a work of art, in comparison, is neat, finite, self-contained, rational, flowing and emasculate." But art could also improve on life by offering images of possibilities that for most people were unattainable in realistic terms. Stevenson's ideas of fiction as art were quite other than those of the aesthetes and decadents; he finds it best expressed in adventure stories, where human beings escape from the trivial contingencies of social life and are caught up in primitive and archetypal forms of action, such as "fighting, sailing, adventure, death or childbirth...". Stevenson is still enjoyed as a master of adventure fiction, such as *Treasure Island* (1883) and *Kidnapped* (1886), which appeal especially to young readers. In his most famous tale *The Strange Case of Dr. Jekyll and Mr. Hyde* (1886), he presents the archetypal image of the Doppelganger in the guise of a horror story. Stevenson's interest in evil and duality appears at great length in *The Master of Ballantrae* (1889), which is as much a novel as a romance, with complexity of form and considerable psychological insight.

In *Treasure Island*, The narrator is Jim Hawkins, whose mother keeps the Admiral Benbow Inn somewhere on the coast in the west of England in the eighteenth century. An old buccaneer takes up his quarters at the inn. He has in his chest information, in the shape of a manuscript map, as to whereabouts of Captain Flint's treasure. Of this his former confederates are determined to obtain possession, and a body of them, led by the sinister blind pirate Pew, makes a descent on the inn. But Jim Hawkins outwits them, secures them and delivers it to Squire Trelawney. The squire and his friend Dr. Livesey set off for Treasure Island in the schooner Hispaniola taking Jim with them. Some of the crew are the squire's faithful dependants, but the majority are old buccaneers recruited by Long John Silver. Their design to seize the ship and kill the squire's party is discovered by Jim, and after a series of thrilling fights and adventures is completely thwarted; the squire, with the help of the marooned pirate Ben Cunn, secures the treasure.

Doctor Jekyll and Mr. Hyde is the classic story of the other ego, personifying good and evil in one character. This dichotomy, essential to Calvinist thinking, runs through all

Stevenson's works, and can be seen to embody a part of the general Victorian crisis of identity—where good and bad cannot be easily delineated, and moral ambiguity, masks of social behavior covering up shocking secrets, and the disturbing psychological depths of the human character are revealed. Stevenson is a writer who reveals realism behind the social mirror.

Dr. Jekyll, a physician, discovers a drug by means of which he can create for himself a separate personality that absorbs all his evil instincts. This personality, repulsive in appearance, he assumes from time to time and calls Mr. Hyde, and in it he gives rein to his evil impulses. It gradually gains the greater ascendancy, and Hyde commits a horrible murder. Jekyll now finds himself from time to time involuntarily transformed to Hyde, while the drug loses its efficacy in restoring his original form and character. On the discovery and arrest, he takes his own life.

7.3.15 Henry James (1848–1916)

Henry James was an American by birth who preferred to live and write in England, and he now occupies a preeminent place in both English and American literature. Although much attached to English life and culture, James continued to think and feel like an American. His early novels such as *The Americans* (1877), *Daisy Miller* (1879) and *The Portrait of a Lady* (1881) focus on the adventures and misfortunes of American high society. James's theme, as is commonly recognized, is the collision of American innocence and European experience. But what is pervading his fiction is a strong sense of human loneliness and alienation. The earlier novels are written in the manner of a Bildungsroman (a growing-up novel) and in them he reveals considerable depths in understanding female psychology. In later novels such as *The Wings of the Dove* (1902) and *The Ambassadors* (1903), James's style is more subtle in order to render complexities of thought and feeling in the "stream of consciousness" of the main characters who are each in different ways "outsiders" in their society.

James was always deeply concerned with art, and how art both shapes and reflects life. From the short story *The Figure in the Carpet* (1895), which shows a concern with the mysteries and intricacies of a design, to his fine novel *The Golden Bowl* (1904), art, artifice and their role in human life are probed and evaluated.

James's language and syntax are carefully modulated—at the same time delicate and convoluted. His sentences and paragraphs can reach considerable length and complexity, but in doing so, they reflect the deep care and precision with which he worked to achieve the full expression of a highly refined consciousness.

The Portrait of a Lady tells the story which centers on Isabel Archer, the "Lady", an attractive American girl. Around her we have the placid old American banker, Mr. Touchett; his hard repellent wife; his ugly, invalid, wiry, charming son Ralph, whom England has thoroughly assimilated; the crude, brilliant, indomitably American journalist Henrietta Stackpole. Isabel refuses the offer of marriage of a typical English peer, the excellent Lord Warburton, and of a bulldog-like New Englander, Caspar Goodwood, to fall a victim, under the influence of the slightly sinister Madame Merle (another cosmopolitan American), to a worthless and spiteful dilettante, Gilbert Osmond, who marries her for her fortune and ruins her life; but to whom she remains loyal in spite of her realization of his vileness.

In *The Wings of the Dove*, the handsome and clever Kate Croy allows herself to be taken up by her rich aunt, Maud Lowder; she is as determined to feather her nest as she genuinely in love with Merton Densher, a journalist without financial prospects. While on a visit to New York, Densher meets Milly Theale, an orphaned, gentle girl who is immensely rich. Her wings are weighted with gold. Milly travels to Europe with her friend Susan Stringham, and in London she learns that she is gathered into Mrs. Lowder's circle. She is anxious to meet Densher again and is disturbed to learn, from a disapproving Mrs. Lowder, of his interest in Kate. While in London she learns that she is doomed and is advised by the sympathetic doctor Sir Luke Strett to seize whatever joy she can from life. She installs herself in a palazzo in Venice, and with their varying motives her friends gather around her. Kate and Densher become lovers. The predatory Kate persuades a reluctant Densher to make a show of love for Milly in the hope that, dying, she will provide for him—and for them. After Milly's death Densher does indeed discover that she has done so, but he finds himself unable to accept the money, and Kate. Their very success in the dreadful game has brought about the death of their relationship.

The Golden Bowl is about the story that the widowed American Adam Verver is in Europe with his daughter Maggie, who has all the innocent charm of so many of James's young American heroines. She is engaged to Amerigo, an impoverished Italian prince who must marry into money. The golden bowl first seen in a London curio shop is symbolic of the relationship between the main characters and of the world in which they move, whose perfect surface conceals a flaw.

Also in Europe is an old friend of Maggie's, Charlotte Stant, and Maggie is blindly ignorant of the fact that she and the prince are lovers. Maggie and Amerigo are married and have a son, but Maggie remains dependent for real intimacy on her father, and she and Amerigo grow increasingly apart. Maggie decides to find her father a wife and her choice falls on Charlotte. The affair with the prince continues and Adam Verver seems to Charlotte to be a convenient match. When Maggie finally comes into possession of the golden bowl, the flaw is revealed to her, and inadvertently, the truth about Amerigo and Charlotte. Fanny Ashingham (an older woman, aware of the truth from the beginning) deliberately breaks the bowl, and this marks the end of Maggie's "innocence". Abstaining from outcry and outrage, she takes the reins and maneuvres people and events. She realizes that to be a wife she must cease to be a daughter. Adam Verver and the unhappy Charlotte are banished forever to America, and the new Maggie will establish a real marriage with Amerigo.

7.3.16 Rudyard Kipling (1865–1936)

Rudyard Kipling was in 1907 the first English writer to receive the Nobel Prize. Yet he is seen more as a Victorian figure than a modern writer.

Many of Kipling's prose works are set not in England but in the countries of the British Empire. Born in India and intimately acquainted with the workings of Empire and colonialism, Kipling wrote about areas of experience new to literature—the psychological and moral problems of living among people who are subject to British rule but of a different culture. Kipling confirmed the importance and value of an Empire and the white man's responsibility to create a single rich civilization among diverse races, cultures, and creeds. His novels, such as *Plain Tales from the Hills* (1888) and *Kim* (1901), are usually read as children's stories. They reflect a significant understanding of the culture of the Indian subcontinent, but are often seen as representing the colonial sentimentality alone. Kipling's short stories often rise above this rather negative judgment. *The Jungle Book* (1894) is a vital text in establishing a colonial echo. This relates to the efforts of General Sir Robert Baden-Powell, a British hero of the Boer War (1899–1902), who founded the Boy Scout Movement and used Kipling's text to establish a basis of discipline for the Wulf-Cubs, an organization which brought together boys from the ages of 7 to 11, now known as Cub-Scouts. Avella, leader of the pack of wolves in Kipling's *The Jungle Book*, became a well-known name for many young boys in England, as leader of their quasi-military group of young associates. *The Jungle Book* has become well-known in England as an animated feature film from Disney studios.

Kim is generally considered Kipling's masterpiece. Kimball O'Hara, the orphaned son of a sergeant in an Irish regiment, spends his childhood as a vagabond in Lahore, until he meets an old lama from China and accompanies him in his travels. He falls into the hands of his father's old regiment, is adopted and is sent to school, resuming his wanderings in his holidays. Colonel Creighton of the Ethnological Survey remarks his aptitude for secret service (the Great Game), and on this he embarks under the directions of the native agent Hurree Babu. The book presents a vivid picture of India, its teeming populations, religions, and superstitions, and the life of the bazaars and the road.

7.4 Victorian Poetry

Victorian poetry is generally considered to be in the shadow of the popular genre of the novel: a reversal of the situation in the Romantic age. The main reason for this decline of poetry is perhaps that, unlike the Victorian novels which satisfactorily embody the life of the age, Victorian poetry tended to engage with some of the more marginal, extreme and unnerving dimensions of Victorian life. However, the poets of the time were numerous, and they included some people of talent and even of genius. Tennyson, Browning and Arnold were all born poets, and their work is the product of natural talents greatly improved by cultivation reaching a high degree of sophistication and showing a conscious care for style and form. The later generations of Victorian poets, Rosseti and Morris, who came first, Swinburne and Meredith, who followed shortly after, and the host of others who appeared in the later years of the century, possessed none of the stature of Tennyson and Browning. Swinburne, the greatest of the younger poets, though marvelous in the technique of verse, wanted the wide humanism of the earlier Victorians. Two characteristics mark Victorian poetry. The first is the great freedom in form and prosody, and the second is the sense poets felt that they had an immediate mission to utter a message.

7.4.1 Alfred Lord Tennyson (1809–1892)

Tennyson is the most influential and admired poet of the Victorian era. He passed his childhood at Somersby rectory in Lincolnshire, the home of his father, was educated at the Grammar School of Louth, and then went to Trinity College, Cambridge, where he obtained the scale of his productions, and published a volume, *Poems, Chiefly Lyrical*. Then he left Cambridge with the resolution to make poetry his profession, and in the retirement of Somersby he prepared his volume of 1832, a collection including among other pieces, *The Lady of Shallot*, *The Palace of Art*, *The Lotus Easters*, *The Dream of Fair Women*, and *The May Queen*. The book was enthusiastically received at Cambridge, but the world at large was indifferent and even hostile.

Tennyson was disappointed, but the blow was nothing to that which fell in the following year. His chief friend, Arthur Hallam, a steady and observant supporter of his art, died suddenly in Vienna. The grief of the bereavement first found expression in lines: "Break, break, break"; later in the brooding verse of *The Two Voices*; later still, when, the sorrow had at last spiritualized his whole view of life and the universe, in *In Memoriam* (1850, the year he was appointed Poet Laureate in succession to Wordsworth). Tennyson had to struggle through nine gloomy years of depression and silence before the success of his *Poems* (1842) gave his prospects a brighter look. The reviews were loud in their praise, and they recognized that Tennyson was not merely a gradual singer, but an interpreter of life. Most of the pieces, *Morte D'Arthur*, *St. Simeon Stylites*, *Ulysses* (1922), and *The Vision of Sin*, were new, but certain of the older poems, such as *The Lady of Shalott*, reappeared in an improved form. Then appeared *The Princess* (1847), *Idylls of the King* (1859), *In Memoriam*, *Maud* (1855), *Crossing the Bar* (1891), and *Silent Voices* (1892).

Tennyson owed much of his contemporary fame to the variety of his works. His verse was an instrument which could express every mood, from the airiness of a cradle song to the sonorous sorrow of a funeral ode. He could write for the many in the sentimental strains of *The May Queen* and for the few in the noble verse of *Ulysses*. He could express a national emotion with spirit and fire as in *The Change of the Light Bridge*; he could delight men of science by his minute observation, as in the lines of the dragonfly in *The Two Voices*; he could win the approval of philosophers by the profound experience of his elegiac and reflective verse. With this wide range, he had also a perfection of technique which made his English not only wonderfully expressive but also free from every offence of harshness and monotony.

Tennyson had all the qualities of a successful laureate, but he was also a poet whose original sense of beauty and fine talent for lyric give him a high place among the masters of English verse. Some of his short lyrics have a distinction of music and imagery which places them among the finest English songs.

Chapter Seven
Victorian Literature (1832-1900)

Tennyson's emotion is recollected in regret, rather than in Wordsworth's "tranquility". His sense of loss, doubt and anxiety gives his works a tone of melancholy.

The Princess: A Medley, Tennyson's first long poem, is his consummate expression of his mastery in blank verse. It is a deeply ambiguous and cautiously ambitious narrative poem, one which moves uncertainly from a present-day prologue to a story set in an undefined medieval past and which attempts to explore the pressing modern subject of women's higher education.

In Memoriam, composed of a large number of short pieces in the four-lined octosyllabic stanza rhymed *abba*, has been often put forward as Tennyson's greatest work. It is a tribute to Hallam as friend and mentor who evokes both an enervating grief and an elevating grasp of an idea of spiritual and physical evolution. A shifting and developing perception of Hallam as a mortal victim and an immortal spiritual pioneer runs through the poem, but Tennyson also points its long, steadily ramified argument with recurrent images, with visits to specific places, and with seasonal and calendar events which suggest the movement and measurement of time. What *In Memoriam* suggests is an almost totally disabling sense of loss and confusion. In it, Tennyson expresses the profound doubt his contemporaries felt about how to reconcile religion and science, God and nature, and possibly doubts about the entire domestic ideology they had constructed.

Maud, the title poem in *Maud, and Other Poems*, is one of the most inventive and distinctively original poems of the century. It is a love-poem which opens starkly with the words "I hate". It is through with violence, opprobrium, and failure. The exciting, various, and sometimes lurching rhythms manage to convey both an exalted passion and a sense of incipient breakdown, while the passages of lyrical imaging are countered by equally telling diatribes against social injustice and anguished accounts of mental distress. The narrator's painful and guilty dilemma is resolved in his final espousal of a war which destroys "the long, long canker of peace", "the blood-red blossom" of the thin red line.

Idylls of the King incorporates Tennyson's *Mort D'Arthur* from 1833 in a series of poems covering the whole tale of Arthur and Guinevere, through romance and chivalry, to adultery, denunciation, and the end of the kingdom, with the great sword Excalibur cast into the lake. The *Idylls* expresses something of Tennyson's own display at the opening future, with Arthur's court presented as a paradigm and its decay, due ultimately to sexual betrayal, as a guarded warning to modern idealists, libertarians and politicians alike.

7.4.2 Robert Browning (1812–1889)

Robert Browning lived a long, happy and uneventful life. He left school at 14, and received his education mainly in his father's large and electric library. After his marriage with Elizabeth Barrett, much of his time was passed in Italy. He was a man of vast knowledge, but his studies were unorthodox, and he loved the by-paths of learning. He had less practice than most writers in the elementary drill of expression, and it was natural that his first poems, being packed with thought and erudition, should be quite beyond the comprehension of the ordinary reader. Like that of Tennyson, the genius of Robert Browning was dramatic but not distinctively theatrical. Throughout his early career, however, he wrote for the stage, and his *Stradford* (1837) at least achieved a modest commercial success. It is in his four major collections of verse, *Dramatic Lyrics* (1837), *Dramatic Romances and Lyrics* (1845), *Men and Women* (1855), and *Dramatis Personae* (1864) that his energies found expression beyond the confines of the theater. Browning is generally at his most subtly fluent and concentrated writing in the form of the "dramatic monologue", a form in which a given speaker addresses a listener, a listener both implied by the poem and who is, by extension, the reader. Unlike in a soliloquy, the speaker is not alone or he tells the truth; Browning's characters do not necessarily articulate their minds or their natures, rather, they betray something. Character is suggested both by what is said, and by how it is said, by a reference, a turn of phrase, a rhythm, an image, or a reiteration.

Browning's dramatic monologues enable him to explore extreme and usually extremely morbid states of mind, plunging into the dark places of the human psyche. But his use of different characters and a range of different voices do not allow the reader to identify the speaker with Browning the author. The dramatic monologue acts as a kind of mask, which allows the writer to explore the human soul without the soul-searching being too directly personal, and which distances Browning from the more subjective style of a poet such as Shelley, who was a considerable formative influence on his writing.

Browning's monologues also reveal many contrasts in language and style with the poetry of Tennyson. Tennyson's poetry is in a tradition which includes Spenser, Milton, and Keats. Stylistically, they favour a polished poetic texture and smooth, harmonious patterns of sound. Browning draws on a different tradition which includes the soliloquies of Shakespeare,

Chapter Seven
Victorian Literature (1832–1900)

the poetry of John Donne, and later in the Victorian period, the sonnets of Gerard Manky Hopkins. Such poets use more colloquial language, draw on the more discordant sounds of spoken language, and employ contrasting stylistic tones which are often shocking and unpredictable, but serve to startle us into awareness of a world of everyday realities.

More than any other writer, Browning used his verse to go beneath the surface appearance given by his speakers. He examines "between the lines" a wide range of moral scruples and problems, characters and attitudes. He is the widest ranging of Victorian poets in his intellectual and cultural concerns. Browning's widely known poem is *My Last Duchess* (1842), and his greatest single success is *The Ring and the Book* (1867–1870).

My Last Duchess presents an imagined speaker, the Duke, who addresses the representative of the girl he hopes to marry. He inadvertently reveals himself as a tyrant who could not tolerate his first wife's independence; he is despotic, wishing to limit the freedom of another person. Here is a psychologically disturbed will to power that is at odds with the values of any kind of rational or liberal society. By the end of the poem, it becomes clear that the Duke's obsessive jealousy has destroyed the Duchess, but that, curiously, the jealousy still lingers together with his discipline of fear. Hovering somewhere between confessions and stream-of-consciousness, the poem takes us into the disturbed world of the mind, and away from the domestic and the comfortable concerns that are often the desired goal in Victorian literature.

The Ring and the Book employs the dramatic monologue in a multi-viewpoint historical reconstruction in blank verse, telling the story of a seventeenth-century Italian murder, examining relative "truth" "imagination", character and setting, in a "novel in verse" quite unlike any other.

The "Ring" of the title is a figure for the process by which the artist transmutes the "pure crude fact" of historical events into living forms; the "Book" is a collection of documents relating to the Italian trial of the murder. Browning found the volume on a market stall in Florence.

Pietro and Violante Comparini were a middle-aged childless couple living in Rome whose income could only be secured after Pietro's death if they had a child; Violante bought the child of a prostitute. This child, Pompilia, was eventually married to Count Guido Franceschini, an impoverished noble man from Arezzo. The marriage was unhappy, and the Comparini returned to Rome, where they sued Guido for the restoration of Pompilia's dowry on the grounds of her illegitimacy. Pompilia herself eventually fled from Arezzo in the company of a young priest, Giuseppe Caponsacchi. Guido pursued them and had them arrested on the outskirts of Rome; as a result, Caponsacchi was exiled to Civita Vecchis for three years, and Pompilia was sent to a convent while the lawsuits were decided. But then because she was pregnant, she was released into the custody of the Comparini. A fortnight after the birth of her child, Guido and four accomplices murdered her and her putative parents. They were arrested and sentenced to death.

7.4.3 Elizabeth Barrett Browning (1806–1861)

Elizabeth Barrett Browning was highly regarded as a poet on the strength of *Poems* (1849), and in the lifetime was more famous than her husband. An adventurous experimenter in form and style, she is now best remembered for her "novel in verse", *Aurora Leigh* (1857), the lifestory of a woman writer, which anticipates Virginia Woolf's *A Room of One's Own* in its strongly feminine affirmation of an independent viewpoint. Refusing the love of her cousin, who wishes her to renounce her writing and work on behalf of the poor, the heroine establishes herself as a poet in London. Later in Europe, she meets up with her cousin again and both confess their love. Though the story is simple, it actually played a central role in a debate about women, women's writing and sexual difference in the Victorian period. Whereas the Brontë question male values and examine the role of women in a middle-class society built around marriage and home, Barrett Browning, by questioning the exclusion of women from "true" poetry, confronts some very fundamental questions about gendered identity. *Aurora Leigh* explores the very language of Victorian verse, undermining the social codes that sought to restrict women's writing, and by extension women's ambitions, to the emotional, the domestic, and the slight. It seeks to reverse the assumption about gender that contributed so much to undermining the implicit assumptions of conventional writing and the conduct of conventional society.

As one of the earliest female writers, Elizabeth Browning's work records a constant search for poetic identity. As with Robert Browning, this search sometimes involved masks and disguises. For example, the causes of Italian nationalism enabled her to explore many contemporary social and moral issues; her *Sonnets from the Portuguese* (1850) is presented as a translation from Portuguese, but in fact records the stages of her love for Robert Browning.

Chapter Seven
Victorian Literature (1832–1900)

The following lines from one of the forty-four "Portuguese" sonnets show Elizabeth Barrett Browning to be, as Virginia Woolf described her, "the true daughter of her age":

> I love thee freely, as men strive for Lights;
> I love thee purely, as they turn from Praise,
> I love you with the passion put to use
> In my old griefs, and with my childhood's faith

(Sonnet 43)

7.4.4 Mathew Arnold (1822–1888)

Mathew Arnold was a great Victorian poet as well as a leading social critic. As a poet, he culminated in *Dover Beach* (1867), which brings together the major concerns of mid-Victorian writing. Set in a room overlooking the Straits of Dover, it describes love, faith, and desolation, bringing together classical and modern allusions, to conclude with a vision of the world more completely negative than any in the previous two centuries. Arnold begins with a version of a world of endless sadness:

> Listen! You hear the grating roar
> Of pebbles which the waves draw back, and fling
> At their return, up the high strand,
> Begin, and cease, and then begin again,
> With tremulous cadence show, and bring
> The eternal note of sadness in.

(Dover Beach)

And Arnold ends with a vision of bleak nothingness in which meaningless wars are fought for meaningless causes. Against such a background, human love has no purpose:

> And we are here as on a darkling plain
> Swept with confused alarms of struggle and flight,
> Where ignorant armies clash by night.

(Dover Beach)

It is a world, which has neither certitude, nor peace, nor help from pain.

This is the twentieth-century "wasteland", half a century before the First World War brought "no man's land" into the language. The vision of despair is the antithesis of the "high moral lesson" of mainstream of Victorianism, but it is a vision for which Tennyson, Dickens and others had amply prepared the ground. The reaction to despair might be the jingoism of Kipling, or the pessimism of Hardy and Conrad, or the positivist sense of duty of George Eliot, but the "eternal note of sadness" was now a part of Victorian literature.

Arnold was no pessimist, however: "Love, let us be true to one another" is the saving emotion in *Dover Beach*. But he was an acutely social observer. Like Trollope, he followed a professional career; he was a school's inspector for some 35 years, and became, like Dickens, an ardent campaigner for educational reform. His poems, from 1849, show concern about solitude and doubt, notably in *Empedocles on Etna* (1852) about its "dwindling faculty of joy".

Arnold's poetry, although imbued with the disillusionment of the mid-nineteenth century, has a wide range of theme, form and tone. *The Scholar—Gypsy* (1853) is a pastoral of the Oxford countryside which reached a wide readership with its observation of "the strange disease of modern life". *Sohrab and Rustum*, published in the same year, moves towards epic in its tale of a son's search for his father. But it is in *Balder Dead* (1858) that Arnold reaches the greatest heights in a long poem. It is a major poetic epic of the Victorian age, and is based on a Norse myth of the death of a god. It celebrates the ritual of passing on. With none of the elements of Tennyson, Arnold's hero Balder becomes a more human god, and his death is a reflection of the condition of mankind. With *Balder Dead*, the English epic is brought back to the human level of the end of *Paradise Lost*.

As a leading critic, Arnold's most famous work is *Culture and Anarchy* (1869), a collection of essays which contains his central arguments, and its importance lies in its difference from Carlyle, Mill, and the Victorian philosophers. Arnold starts from social observation rather than philosophical reflection, and stresses the importance of seeing "things as they really are". The work recommends culture as "the great help out of present difficulties". The title is itself significant: Arnold sees no central authority to control the drift of civilization towards anarchy, and so proposes culture as a source of value that will provide a direction in human affairs. The years after Darwin's affirmation of man's animal origins, Arnold's affirmation of culture as raising humanity above the level of Barbarians takes on a

Chapter Seven
Victorian Literature (1832–1900)

particular resonance. A new vision of what culture, art, and society mean will emerge as the century moves to its close.

> ... the world which seems
> To lie before us like a land of dreams
> So various, so beautiful so new,
> Hath really neither joy, nor love, nor light,
> Nor certitude, nor peace, nor help for pain.
>
> (*Dover Beach*)

For Your Information

The Pre-Raphaelite Poets

In the mid-nineteenth century, a new movement in art and literature was setting about a revolution against the ugliness of contemporary life. The Pre-Raphaelite Brotherhood—as they called themselves when their works first appeared at the Royal Academy—stressed their admiration for the Italian art of the period before the High Renaissance (which Raphael, who died in 1520, was taken as symbolizing). A mediaeval simplicity, a closeness to nature in representational clarity, and a deep moral seriousness of intent distinguish the Brotherhood, of whom the main figures were the painters John Millais and William Holman Hunt, and the brothers Dante Gabriel and William Michael Rossetti. The most distinguished poets associated with this movement are Algernon Charles Swinburne, William Morrise, Dante Gabriel Rossetti and his younger sister Christina Rossetti.

7.4.5 Algernon Charles Swinburne (1837–1909)

Algernon Charles Swinburne's poetry brings together many of the ideas of Pre-Raphaelites, with what Tennyson called a "wonderful rhythmic invention". But, more than any of the works of the Pre-Raphaelites, his writings shocked the Victorians, with their emphasis on sadism, sexual enchantment, and anti-Christian outlook. Swinburne's dominant theme is that of the sensual attack on conventional attitudes. Many of his poems were designed to scandalize and provoke. A prolific poet, using a wide range of forms from drama to ballad, Swinburne has a considerable influence on the generation of the 1890s. From the drama *Atalanta in Calydon* (1865) and *Poems and Ballads* (1866) to his second series of *Poems and Ballads*, Swinburne was the new original spirit in English poetry, a spirit of luscious sensuality which was both a moral and spiritual challenge to the echoes of the day. In his own life, Swinburne rebelled against established codes, rather in the manner of Shelley. In religion, he was a pagan, and in politics he wanted to see the overthrow of established governments. In poetry, his work confirms a collapse of conventional Victorian poetic standards. Now he is remembered for his masterful use of language, which projects a sensuality beyond ordinary images.

7.4.6 Dante Gabriel Rossetti (1828–1882)

Dante Gabriel Rossetti was first a painter and then a poet. His poetry is essentially decorative and descriptive. In some of his landscape poems (*A Half-Way Pause*, *Autumn Idleness*, or *The Woodspurge*, for example), he can colourfully suggest momentary experience and an intensity of vision, but the majority of his verses deal with his fascination with the female face and the female body. In his best-known poem *The Blessed Damozel*, Rossetti develops a fleshly but heavenly vision of a transfigured beloved from Dante's Beatrice, a figure who endlessly haunts his paintings. He idealizes women both sexually and spiritually, and with the exception of his strikingly earthy address to a woman of the streets in "Jenny", he distances them as objects of desire, even worship. In the sonnet sequence *The House of Life*, Rossetti yearns for the supreme and often elusive mistress.

7.4.7 Christina Rossetti (1830–1894)

Christina Rossetti was the most distinguished Pre-Raphaelite poet. Some of her early lyrics, like Tennysonian *Dream Land*, fit well into the narcotic world of the young Pre-Raphaelites (they were published in the PRB's short lived journal the *Germ*), but her real distinctiveness emerged in *Goblin Market and Other Poems* of 1862 and *The Prince Progress and Other Poems* of 1866. The longer narrative poems, like the title poems in these volumes, show considerable originality in their use of alliteration, assonance, and half rhyme, and in their odd combination of irregular meter and sing-song rhythms. *Goblin Market* is an extraordinary achievement accumulative in its images and sounds. It purports to be for children but explores, in an odd way, enclosed forms of female subjectivity. Lizzie and Laura are sisters. The goblins try to get the sisters to eat their mouth-watering fruit. Laura does so, paying for the fruit with a lock of hair, but then falls into decline when she cannot get more. Lizzie tries to buy fruit, but the goblins are angry that she will not eat it and pelt her with it. Laura is, however, able to lick the juices off Lizzie and so is saved by her sister's actions. The poem is at once a kind of fairy tale and erotic fable in which female desire is mixed with sisterly self-sacrifice. What is most remarkable about the poem, however, is the nature and power of the longing expressed, and the extent to which Rossetti gives voice to aspects of sexual needs and feelings that were silenced, excluded or denied by the Victorians at large in their public discourses:

> Hug me, kiss me, suck my juices
> Squeezed from goblin fruits for you,
> Goblin pulp and goblin dew
> Eat me, drink me, love me.
>
> *(Goblin Market)*

7.5 Victorian Critics and Historians

The prominent departments, apart from fiction, of English prose, during the last two-thirds of the nineteenth century, have been history and criticism, and, moreover, the two are connected closely. As a matter of fact, nearly all permanent historians of the time, Macaulay and Carlyle, for example, have been critics, even literary critics, while Ruskin, the most prominent critic, pure and simple, has paid constant attention to history. Whatever these writers are, historians or critics, they all win respect by their unremitting conscientiousness, their exemplary industry, and their breath of interests. They reveal a distinctively Victorian willingness to engage in moral and intellectual debate.

7.5.1 Thomas Carlyle (1795–1881)

The disconcertions and abnormalities of early Victorian Britain are nowhere more trenchantly examined than in the pamphlets, essays, letters, and books of its most noisy and effective critic, Carlyle, the son of a stone-mason living at Ecclefechan in Dumfriesshire. Carlyle was brought up in an atmosphere of stern Calvinism, and he soon learnt to look upon life as a battle to be fought with the weapons of industry, character and intellect. His early manhood was passed in teaching and miscellaneous writing; it was years before he found his true vocation. His essays, written in the regular reviewing style on the German authors of whom he had made a special study, were full of sound information and useful criticism. In 1833–1834 appeared his great original and characteristic book *Sartor Resartus*. In 1834, Carlyle settled in London and began to write histories, with the results of *The French Revolution*, *Oliver Cromwell's Letters and Speeches* (1845), and *Past and Present* (1843). Among these histories, Carlyle delivered a series of lectures, published later as a book entitled *Heroes and Hero-worship* (1841). Carlyle's most ambitious work, *The History of Frederick II of Prussia* (1858–1865), was not his greatest success. When he died in 1881, his greatness was recognized in America and Germany as well as in England.

Through a steady stream of his works, Carlyle emerged as the dominant social thinker of early Victorian England. He obliged his contemporaries to face the evident enough contradictions within their civilization and to attempt to make some sense of the disorder around them. The conflict he identified was not simply that of faith and doubt, of tradition and innovation, or of conservatism and reform, but of a gulf between the rich and the poor. National despair needed to be countered by social energy, the "Everlasting No" of the spiritual desert by the "Everlasting Yea" of determined action.

The variety, contradictions, and bluster of much of Carlyle's mature writing, and the aggressive inventiveness of his prose style, have tended to render him an unsympathetic figure to modern readers. Yet he remains crucial to the understanding of Victorian intellectual enterprise and energy. Carlyle was revered as both sage and prophet by his many disciples (Gaskell, Tennyson, Ruskin) and echoes of his voice can be heard in much of the literature of the first half of the century.

Sartor Resartus (*The Tailor Retailored*) is Carlyle's early ambition for a fiction which would speak "with a tongue of fire—sharp, sarcastic, apparently unfeeling" but which would nevertheless convey the central precepts of his philosophy: energy, earnestness, and duty. The work is a reflexive discourse molded around a learned study of the philosophy of clothes. It is made up of two undemarcated parts and of "multifarious sections and subdivisions" in which each part "overlaps, and indents and indeed quite runs through the other". The style in which it is written embodies this "labyrinthic combination" by intermixing German and English, by echoing earlier literature, and by playing games with meanings and with translations from one language to another. Like all Carlyle's styles, it works through a process of amalgamation and assimilation. Like Swift's *Battle of the Books* and Sterne's *Tristram Shandy*, *Sartor Resartus* looks uneasily forward to the experiments of James Joyce.

Sartor Resartus is more than simply game playing. It also carries a message which warned the world of the dangers of "sham" in all its forms and which contrasted the destructive force of the "Everlasting No" with the constructive imperative of the "Everlasting Yea", an imperative which solves all contradictions.

The French Revolution is Carlyle's central and most sustained achievement. The history opens with the death of Louis XV and with a scathing account of the deficiencies of French government, institutions, and culture under the "ancient regime" and it ends with Napoleon's bid for power as the Revolution declines into directionless anarchy. *The French Revolution* implicitly warns Victorian England of the nature, causes, and progress of civil disruption, but it also creates stylistic effects and presents carefully assembled, and highly individual, descriptions of characters and events which render it more than just obstreperous didacticism.

On Heroes, Hero-worship and the Heroic in History is made up of six lectures, in which Carlyle developed aspects of the thesis of *Sartor Resartus* by stressing that heroism manifested itself in a wide range of human activity and that the "hero" whether king or prophet, poet or philosopher, was a challenger of convention and of sham and a reformer of the defunct and the empty. More significantly, the lectures outlined an idea of history which profoundly influenced the work of Carlyle's English successors.

7.5.2 Thomas Babington Macaulay (1800–1859)

Macaulay was the most persuasive and influential Victorian advocate of gradual political evolution. Macaulay first made his reputation through the essays on literature, history, and politics published in the *Edinburgh Review* between 1844 and 1852. These essays reveal a probing mind, with clearly defined tastes and antipathies. Macaulay's strength lies in graphic description, in the massing of details, and in the rapid painting of bold background. The same qualities mark the five volumes of his monumental *History of England* published between 1848 and 1861.

The title of *History of England* has always been recognized as a misnomer, for Macaulay skims over medieval and Tudor history as a mere prelude to his real subject, the revolutions of the seventeenth century and, in particular, the origins and constitutional effects of the "Glorious Revolution" of 1688. Perhaps as a result of the impact of the Waverley novels, his volumes are as much concerned with the affairs of Scotland and Ireland as they are with England. As a narrative, *History of England* is compelling; its heroes and its villains are placed and defined and the larger life of the nation, working and creating beyond the court and the power of brokers, is steadily adumbrated. Macaulay's pellucid style, balancing long clausal sentences with punchy short ones and rhetorically inviting reader participation in the explicatory process, demands assent to his overarching argument, which insists that the history of England was "emphatically the history of progress... the history of a constant movement of the public mind, of a constant change in the institutions of a great society", powerfully served to reassure liberal Victorian England, and by extension, Scotland and Ireland, of the rightness of their historic evolution and of their constitutional singularity.

7.5.3 John Ruskin (1819–1900)

John Ruskin, one of the greatest masters of English prose, was also one of the most acute critics of his age. His most famous work, the five volumes of *Modern Painters* (1843–1860), forms one of the most suggestive works on aesthetics to be found anywhere, for Ruskin's love and understanding of the beautiful are almost unmatched. The vast learning and the range of literary references in *Modern Painters* still allow for substantial and carefully worked descriptive passages where Ruskin's wonderfully emotive mastery of a lucid style is most evident. When, in the early volumes of *Modern Painters*, he moved backward and forward in the history of landscape painting, and he also recognized the necessity of explaining the formation of clouds, the geological structure of marble and the massing of mountains; as an observer of plant, he was later to turn to an analysis of the "organic" forms of architecture (in his influential *The Seven Lamps of Architecture*, 1849); having formed a theory of good and bad building, he moved, in *The Stones of Venice* (1851–1853), to a commentary on how and why a particular historical society produced a style and how and why the style and the society declined. Like Carlyle, he saw modern instances in historical decline and fall and in the series of essays biblically entitled *Unto This Last* (1860–1862) asked social questions with a devastating directness. Despite this provocative forthrightness (which proved too strong for many middle-class stomachs), Ruskin's influence was pervasive, stretching from opening Victorian eyes to formerly unperceived beauty, to an awakening of both environmental and moral conscience. *Unto This Last* is followed by *Sesame and Lilies* (1865) and *The Crown of Wild Olive* (1866), which show Ruskin as a popular educator, clear in argument and skillful in illustration. They consist of lectures, of which one of the best, *Of Kings' Treasuries*, is an attempt to define the nature of good literature. Ruskin's last work, an autobiography called *Praterita*, opens with some interesting pages of reminiscence, but his powers were failing and he never finished the work before he died.

7.6 Victorian Drama

There is little to be said about drama in the Victorian period until its revival in the 1890s, when George Bernard Shaw's essay *The Quintessence of Ibsenism*, published in 1891 (the same year as Oscar Wilde's important *The Soul of Man Under Socialism*), gave the first great impetus to Ibsen's work, and to the concept of social controversial plays. The new flood of ideas—socialist, Fabian (Shaw's brand of socialism), and aesthetic—was leading to a re-evaluation of the role of artistic expression in helping to formulate public opinion.

7.6.1 Oscar Wilde (1854–1900)

Oscar Wilde was a Dubliner by both his class and his education. He was also the son of a romantically inclined mother who dabbled in sentimental nationalist verse. Having left Dublin to study at Oxford, he seemed thereafter to be the central figure in a fashionable metropolitan coterie of artists, writers, and wits. He also acted out the parts of a London socialite and of an amusingly provocative social critic. Wilde's homosexuality, both covertly and overtly expressed in what he wrote during the 1890s, might at first have seemed little more than a gesture to an imported French Decadence; after the terrible fall marked by his trial and imprisonment for homosexuality, the alienating bias of his art became manifest. The contrived style of much of his prose, the excessive elaboration of his poetry, and the aphoristic and paradoxical wit of his plays are all subversive. They do more than reject mid-Victorian values in life and art in the name of aestheticism; they defiantly provoke a response to difference.

Oscar Wilde was the most prominent figure of the Aesthetic Movement, whose insistence on "Art for Art's Sake" was just as much a search for new values as any philosophical or political movement. Aestheticism can be traced back to Keats' affirmation

"Beauty is truth, truth beauty", and then continued in Matthew Arnold's *Culture and Anarchy* and in the works of John Ruskin and Walter Pater. Wilde's aesthetic ideas are manifest in his essays, fiction, drama and poetry.

Wilde's essays suggest that he could be a perceptive critic. In his essays, he always questions institutions, moral imperatives, and social clichés. From the refined outrageous lectures he gave to Colorado miners in the early 1880s to the calculatedly annoying challenges to conventional literary morality publicly expressed during his first trial, Wilde employed his chosen role as an aesthetic and an iconoclast. His Platonic dialogue *The Decay of Lying* (1889) and the two parts of *The Critic as Artist* (1890) suggest something of the aphoristic dialogue of his later comedies. In these essays, Wilde derived his central arguments from awareness that art is far more than a mere imitation of nature. "A Truth in Art", he remarks in *The Truth of Masks* (1891), "is that whose contradictory is also true". In *The Decay of Lying*, there is also a recurrent pleasure in insisting that "the telling of beautiful untrue things is the proper aim of art". Wilde's longest and most provocating serious essay, *The Soul of Man Under Socialism*, does not argue primarily for a new social order or for a redistribution of property, but for a larger and expanding idea of freedom, a liberation from drudgery and the rule of machines.

As a novelist, Wilde's most important work is *The Picture of Dorian Gray*, which shows sharply Wilde's delight in provocation, and his exploration of alternative moral perspective. The novel's preface presents a series of attitudinizing aphorisms about art and literature which end with the bold statement: "All art is quite useless." The narrative that follows is a melodramatic, conveying the notion that art and morality are quite divorced. It is, nevertheless, a text driven by internal contradictions and qualifications. Aestheticism is both damned and dangerously upheld; hedonism both indulged and distained. *Dorian Gray* is a tragedy of sorts with the subtext of a morality play; its self-destructive, darkly sinning central character is at once a desperate suicide and a martyr.

As a playwright, Wilde's art has lasted far better in his comedies of manners, where the stagecraft is impeccable and the wit arresting. His greatest work for the theater, *The Importance of Being Earnest* (1899), transforms the inanities of fashionable social life into an inspired farce, a pure pastoral, where wit triumphs overreality. The story is as follows: John Worthing (Jack) and Algernon Moncrieff (Algy) are in pursuit respectively of

Gwendolen Fairfax (Algy's cousin) and Jack's ward, Cecily Cardew. Both young men lead double lives, in which Jack is known in town as Ernest, and while representing to his ward Cecily in the country, he has a wicked brother Ernest; Algy has created a fictitious character, the sickly Bunbury, whose ill health requires a visit whenever engagements in town (particularly those with his formidable aunt Lady Bracknell) render his absence desirable. After many confusions of identity, during which it transpires that Cecily's governess, Miss Prism, had once mislaid Jack as a baby in a handbag at Victoria Station, it is revealed that Jack and Algy are in fact brothers, and that Jack's name is indeed Ernest. All objections to both matches are thus overcome, and Gwendolen's addiction to the very name of "Ernest" is satisfied. As a whole, the play expresses a radical and thoroughly disconcerting vision of society. Wilde's other plays include *Lady Windermere's Fan* (1892), *A Woman of No Importance* (1893), and *An Ideal Husband* (1895). In *An Ideal Husband*, Wilde explores the mutual folly of husband and wife in pursuing belief in ideal partnership founded more conspicuously than most on the possession of property and high social status. By making the "ideal husband", an ambitiously successful politician, Wilde links his vision of the corrupt and corrupting institution of marriage with the more general legislative government of the State. In exposing the moral vacuum of the one, he infers the bankruptcy of the other.

7.6.2 George Bernard Shaw (1856–1950)

1. Life and Career

George Bernard Shaw had a long life span. He was not only the greatest dramatist in the late Victorian period, but also stood out as a modern dramatist in the early twentieth century. Like Wilde, Shaw was a Dubliner. He made a false start as a novelist before turning to drama, and he was an acute critic of music and theater. He was well known, too, as a political journalist and edited *Fabian Essays* (1889). Shaw was much influenced by Ibsen, and his book *The Quintessence of Ibsenism* explained Ibsen to English readers and upheld Ibsen's use of the drama as a force subverting accepted social attitudes. Shaw's early plays, *Philanderer* (1891) and *Mrs. Warren's Profession* (1891) were banned by the Lord Chamberlain's censorship. Of such official censorship Shaw complained in 1898 in the preface to the published version of the two plays, classifying them, together with *Widower's Houses* (1892), as what he called "unpleasant plays". His early plays also include *Arms and the Man* (1894), which sets out to subvert ideas of soldierly and masculine heroism in a fanciful Balkan setting; *Candida:*

A Mystery (1895) which turns Ibsen's *A Doll's House* inside down within the context of a Christian socialist household; *The Devil's Disciple* (1897), and *You Never Can Tell* (1899) which allows for the happy, liberating victory of a new generation over the old. During the early 1900s, Shaw began to write an alternative series of "pleasant" plays and became a dominant presence on the London stage, with such provocative but popular plays as *Man and Superman* (1903), *Major Barbara* (1907), and *Pygmalion* (1916).

2. Theme

Shaw's themes were the relations between men and women, husband and wife, and parents and children; the problems of conscience, character and disposition; the problems of individual and society; the conception of life as creative energy. Hence he presents the classic themes of drama, the clash within the individual mind, and the clash between individual characters, and between the individual and the customs, manners, religion, and politics of his time. His political plays express, in various forms of extravagance, the need for political philosophy. *The Apple Cart* is concerned with the absence of political education; *Too True to be Good* with the useless of political institutions without purpose; *On the Rocks* with lack of leadership; *The Millionaires* with how to choose leaders; *Geneva* with the challenge of false leadership and *Good King Charles's Golden Days* with how to decide upon who are fit to choose leaders. To Shaw, without a captain (a leader), the ship (society) will go on the rocks (*Heartbreak House*). Shaw's religious plays reveal his philosophical ideas, which were given practical expression in conscience and individual life. *The Showing-up of Blanco Posnet* (1909) shows how the sudden idea of a purpose beyond oneself interferes with a worthless man's life: A man who has "gone west" in both the literal and the moral sense discovers his real life to his own astonishment. *Androcles and the Lion* (1911-1912) is a picture of Christians thrown to the lions by the Romans for the sake of their faith, and of how simple faith saves them. The theme of *Saint Joan* (1923) is "it was never 'I say so', but 'God says so'".

3. Style

Shaw remains the most inventively unpredictable playwright in the English tradition. Shaw presupposes that history can be illuminating, that present can be vigorously reforming, and that the future will be exciting rather than exacting. His drama is not so much didactic as instructive; his arguments fuse elements of socialism, science, and philosophy; his dialogues can move easily, but disconcertingly, from broad comedy to anguish and declaration and back again to comedy; his protagonists have a vivid energy. His settings, like his preoccupation, are predominantly those of the England of the turn of the twentieth century, but he continues to surprise, to nag, and to provoke at the turn of the twenty first.

4. Major Works

Widower's Houses is Shaw's first play. It is designed to expose slum-landlordism and to show the manner in which the capitalist system perverts and corrupts human behavior and relationships.

Dr. Harry Trench, on a Rhine holiday, meets Blanche Sartorius, travelling with her wealthy father, and proposes marriage to her. Sartorius is willing to permit the match if Trench's family (including his aunt Lady Roxdale) agrees to accept her as an equal. All seems well until it is revealed in Act II that Sartorius is a slum landlord. Trench is horrified, refuses to accept Sartorius' money, suggests that he and Blanche should live on his £700 a year, and is even more horrified when Sartorius points out that this income is derived from a mortgage of Sartorius's property, and that he himself and his miserable rent collector Lickcheese are merely intermediaries: "You are the principal." Blanche, revealing a passionate and violent nature, rejects Trench for his hesitations. In Act III, Lickcheese himself now rich through dubious dealings in the property market, approaches Sartorius with an apparently philanthropic but in fact remunerative proposition, which involves Lady Roxdale as ground landlord and Trench as mortgagee. Trench, now considerably more cynical, accepts the deal, and he and Blanche are reunited.

Mrs. Warren's Profession boldly confronts two contemporary women's issues: the future professional careers of educated, would-be independent women, and the oldest profession, female prostitution. The arguments of the play suggest the propriety of both vocations, but its internal tensions derive from the juxtaposition of a liberated daughter, Vivie Warren, and her unashamed, brothel-keeping mother who sees "the only way a woman to provide for herself decently is for her to be good to some man that can afford to be good to her". The play was written, Shaw said: "... to draw attention to the truth that prostitution is caused, not by female depravity and male licentiousness, but simply by underpaying, undervaluing, and maltreating women so shamefully that the poorer of them are forced to resort to prostitution to keep body and soul together... Society, and not individual, is the villain of the piece."

Major Barbara explores the conflict and the ultimate mutual assent of a strong-willed father and his equally strong-minded daughter. It disturbed many of Shaw's socialist friends with its quizzical espousal of the idea of the future reconstruction of society by an energetic, highly motivated, and power-manipulating minority.

Pygmalion is a carefully worked study of the developing relationship between a "creator" and his "creation". It describes the transformation of a Cockney flower-seller, Eliza Doolittle, into a passable imitation of a duchess by the phonetician Professor Henry Higgins, who undertakes this task in order to win a bet and to prove his own points about English speech and the class system: He teaches her to speak standard English and introduces her successfully to social life, thus winning his bet, but she rebels against his dictatorial and thoughtless behavior, and "bolts" from his tyranny. The play ends with a truce between the two of them, as Higgins acknowledges that she has achieved freedom and independence, and emerged from his treatment as a "tower of strength: a consort battleship"; in his postscript, Shaw tells us that she marries the docile and devoted Freddy Eynsford Hill.

Pygmalion, in classical legend, was the King of Cyprus, who fell in love with his own sculpture: Aphrodite endowed the statue with life and transformed it into the flesh-and-blood of Galatea.

Heartbreak House is a picture of "cultured, leisured Europe before the War", ending with bombs falling, though nothing is said about bombs or war until they fall. It is an allegory of national affairs in the hands of governors who trust to chance without troubling to learn their business. Here Shaw is not only attacking idleness, but also attacking the cruelty, inhumanity, callous financial competition and political destructiveness engendered by the nineteenth century science and economics, with their doctrines of limited wealth and the struggle of existence.

7.7 Reading

A Tale of Two Cities
Chapter 1: The Period

By Charles Dickens

It was the best of times, it was the worst of times, it was the age of wisdom, it was the age of foolishness, it was the epoch of belief, it was the epoch of incredulity, it

Chapter Seven
Victorian Literature (1832–1900)

was the season of Light, it was the season of Darkness, it was the spring of hope, it was the winter of despair, we had everything before us, we had nothing before us, we were all going direct to Heaven, we were all going direct the other way—in short, the period was so far like the present period, that some of its noisiest authorities insisted on its being received, for good or for evil, in the superlative degree of comparison only.

There were a king with a large jaw and a queen with a plain face, on the throne of England[1]; there were a king with a large jaw and a queen with a fair face, on the throne of France[2]. In both countries it was clearer than crystal to the lords of the State preserves of loaves and fishes, that things in general were settled forever.

It was the year of Our Lord one thousand seven hundred and seventy-five. Spiritual revelations were conceded to England at that favoured period, as at this. Mrs. Southcott[3] had recently attained her five-and-twentieth blessed birthday, of whom a prophetic private in the Life Guards had heralded the sublime appearance by announcing that arrangements were made for the swallowing up of London and Westminster. Even the Cock-laneghost[4] had been laid only a round dozen of years, after rapping out its messages, as the spirits of this very year last past (supernaturally deficient in originality) rapped out theirs. Mere messages in the earthly order of events had lately come to the English Crown and People, from a congress of British subjects in America: which, strange to relate, have proved more important to the human race than any communications yet received through any of the chickens of the Cock-lane brood.

France, less favoured on the whole as to matters spiritual than her sister of the shield and trident, rolled with exceeding smoothness down hill, making paper money and spending it. Under the guidance of her Christian pastors, she entertained herself besides, with such humane achievements as sentencing a youth to have his hands cut off, his tongue torn out with pincers, and his body burned alive, because he had not kneeled down in the rain to do honour to a dirty procession of monks which passed within his view, at a distance of some fifty or sixty yards. It is likely enough that, rooted in the woods of France and Norway, there were growing trees, when that sufferer was put to death, already marked by the Woodman, Fate, to come down and be sawn into boards, to make a certain movable framework with a sack and a knife in it[5], terrible in history. It is likely enough that in the rough outhouses some old tillers of the heavy lands adjacent to Paris, there were sheltered from the weather that very day, rude carts, be spattered with rustic mire, snuffed about by pigs, and roosted in by poultry, which the Farmer, Death, had already set apart to be his tumbrils[6] of the Revolution. But that Woodman and that Farmer, though they work unceasingly, work silently, and no one heard them as they went about with muffled tread: the rather, for as much as to entertain any suspicion that they were awake, was to be atheistical and traitorous.

In England, there was scarcely an amount of order and protection to justify much national boasting. Daring burglaries by armed men, and highway robberies, took place in the capital itself every night; families were publicly cautioned not to go out of town without removing their furniture to upholsterers' warehouses for security; the highwayman in the dark was a City tradesman in the light, and, being recognized and challenged by his fellow-tradesman whom he stopped in his character of[7] "the Captain," gallantly shot him through the head and rode away; the mail was waylaid by seven robbers, and the guard shot three dead, and then got shot dead himself by the other four, "in consequence of the failure of his ammunition:" after which the mail was robbed in Peace; that magnificent potentate, the Lord Mayor of London, was made to stand and deliver on Turnham Green, by one highwayman, who despoiled the illustrious creature insight of all his retinue; prisoners in London goals fought battles with their turnkeys, and the majesty of the law fired blunderbusses in among them, loaded with rounds of shot and ball; thieves snipped off diamond crosses from the necks of noble lords at Court drawing-rooms; musketeers went into St. Giles's, to search for contraband[8] goods, and the mob fired on the musketeers, and the musketeers fired on the mob, and nobody thought any of these occurrences much out of the common way. In the midst of them, the hangman, ever busy and ever worse than useless, was in constant requisition; now, stringing up long rows of miscellaneous criminals; now, hanging a house-breaker on Saturday who had been taken on Tuesday; now, burning people in the hand at Newgate[9] by the dozen, and now burning pamphlets at the door of Westminster Hall; to-day, taking the life of an atrocious murderer, and to-morrow of a wretched pilferer who had robbed a farmer's boy of sixpence.

All these things, and a thousand like them, came to pass in and close upon the dear old year one thousand seven hundred and seventy-five. Environed by them, while the Woodman and the Farmer worked unheeded, those two of the large jaws, and those other two of the plain and the fair faces, trod with stir enough, and carried their

Chapter Seven
Victorian Literature (1832–1900)

divine rights with a high hand. Thus did the year one thousand seven hundred and seventy-five conduct their Greatnesses, and myriads of small creatures—the creatures of this chronicle among the rest—along the roads that lay before them.

Notes

1. **the throne of England:** referring to King George III (1760–1820) and his Queen.

2. **the throne of France:** refering to King Louis XVI (1774–1793) and his consort.

3. **Mrs. Southcott:** a fanatic of religion, who claimed to be the pregnant woman in the *Revelation*, and thus had some followers.

4. **Cock-laneghost:** the incident of "ghost" at Cock-lane in London in 1762, which was in fact the house-owner's daughter knocking at the door.

5. **movable framework with a sack and a knife in it:** guillotine.

6. **tumbrils:** prison van.

7. **in his character of:** in his capacity of.

8. **contraband:** smuggled.

9. **Newgate:** a prison.

My Last Duchess

By Robert Browning

That's my last Duchess painted on the wall,
Looking as if she were alive. I call
That piece a wonder, now: Frà Pandolf's hands
Worked busily a day, and there she stands.
Will't please you sit and look at her? I said
"Frà Pandolf" by design, for never read
Strangers like you that pictured countenance,
The depth and passion of its earnest glance,
But to myself they turned (since none puts by

The curtain I have drawn for you, but I)

And seemed as they would ask me, if they durst,

How such a glance came there; so, not the first

Are you to turn and ask thus. Sir, 't was not

Her husband's presence only, called that spot

Of joy into the Duchess' cheek: perhaps

Frà Pandolf chanced to say, "Her mantle laps

Over my lady's wrist too much," or "Paint

Must never hope to reproduce the faint

Half-flush that dies along her throat:" such stuff

Was courtesy, she thought, and cause enough

For calling up that spot of joy. She had

A heart—how shall I say?—too soon made glad,

Too easily impressed; she liked whate'er

She looked on, and her looks went everywhere.

Sir, 't was all one! my favour[1] at her breast,

The dropping of the daylight in the West,

The bough of cherries some officious fool

Broke in the orchard for her, the white mule

She rode with round the terrace—all and each

Would draw from her alike the approving speech,

Or blush, at least. She thanked men—good! but thanked

Somehow—I know not how—as if she ranked

my gift of a nine-hundred-years-old name

With anybody's gift. Who'd stoop to blame

This sort of trifling? Even had you skill

In speech—(which I have not)—to make your will

Quite clear to such an one, and say, "Just this

Or that in you disgusts me; here you miss,

Or there exceed the mark[2]"—and if she let

Herself be lessoned so, nor plainly set

Her wits to yours, forsooth, and made excuse,

Chapter Seven
Victorian Literature (1832–1900)

—E'en then would be some stooping; and I choose
Never to stoop. Oh, sir, she smiled, no doubt,
Whene'er I passed her; but who passed without
Much the same smile? This grew; I have commands;
Then all smiles stopped together. There she stands
As if alive. Will 't please you rise? We'll meet
The company below then. I repeat,
The Count your master's known munificence
Is ample warrant that no just pretence
Of mine for dowry will be disallowed;
Though his fair daughter's self, as I avowed
At starting, is my object. Nay, we'll go
Together down, sir. Notice Neptune[3], though,
Taming a sea-horse, thought a rarity,
Which Claus of Innsbruck cast in bronze for me!

Notes

1. **my favour:** my love-gift.

2. **exceed the mark:** in terms of archery, overshoot the target.

3. **Neptune:** the Roman god of the sea, whose chariot is often shown pulled by sea-horses.

Crossing the Bar[1]

By Alfred Tennyson

Sunset and evening star[2]
And one clear call for me!
And may there be no moaning of the bar,
When I put out to sea[3].

But such a tide[4] as moving seems asleep,
Too full for sound and foam,

When that which drew from out the boundless deep[5]
Turns again home.

Twilight and evening bell,[6]
And after that the dark!
And may there be no sadness of farewell,
When I embark;

For though from out our bourne[7] of Time and Place
The flood[8] may bear me far,
I hope to see my Pilot[9] face to face
When I have crossed the bar.

Notes

1. This poem was written in the later years of Tennyson's life. We can feel his fearlessness towards death, his faith in God and an afterlife. Bar: a bank of sand or stones under the water as in a river. "Crossing the Bar" means leaving this world and entering the next world.

2. **Sunset and evening star:** images of the end of life.

3. **sea:** the symbol of life.

4. **tide:** the symbol of life.

5. **deep:** the symbol of life.

6. **Twilight and evening bell:** images of the end of life.

7. **bourne:** boundary.

8. **flood:** the symbol of life.

9. **Pilot:** Here it refers to God.

Chapter Eight
The Twentieth-Century Literature (1900–1945)

8.1 Historical Background

By the end of the nineteenth century, the pre-industrial economy and the way of life had almost disappeared. In 1911, nearly 70 percent of the country's 45 million inhabitants lived in urban areas. The sense of "local" community was being lost: A greater anonymity of the individual in the urban context was a result. Society became more fragmented and individual identities more fluid.

The British Empire, which had expanded under Queen Victoria and in 1900 had reached 13 million square miles, also began to disintegrate. The colonies began to rebel against British imperialism one after another. Liberal beliefs in the gradual transition to a better world began to be questioned. The mass destruction of the First World War led many towards more extreme affiliations, and both Fascism and Marxism held attractions for many intellectuals and workers, particularly during the 1930s.

A strong social ethic, continued from the Victorian times of Dickens and Disraeli, began increasingly to influence the political character of the country and its institutions. After the Gladstone Parliament of 1880–1885, the aristocracy and upper classes exerted less influence and the state began to organize itself more in the interests of majority community needs. Institutions became more democratic. The Socialist Party grew as Liberalism declined. In 1928, universal suffrage for women was obtained, paradoxically during a time when growing economic depression and slum appeared to lend increasing weight to Marxist analyses of the inevitable failure of capitalist economic systems.

Culturally too, increasing access to literacy, and to education in general, led to profound changes in the reading public. The Education Act of 1870 made elementary education compulsory for everyone from the ages of 5 to 13. This led to the rapid expansion of a largely unsophisticated literary public, the rise of the popular press, and the mass production of "popular" literature for a semi-literate "low-brow" readership. Thus the avant-garde era in writing began. The twenty years following Queen Victoria's death (1901) saw Joseph

Conrad establish his reputation as a novelist, and the climb to fame of popular novelists such as Arnold Bennett and H. G. Wells. D. H. Lawrence published his first novel, *The White Peacock* (1911) and went on to write, among other works, *Sons and Lovers* (1913), *The Rainbow* (1915) and *Women in Love* (1921). Henry James was still writing, his novels moving into a new and more complex phase at the start of the century, and E. M. Forster published four novels—*Where Angels Fear to Tread* (1905), *The Longest Journey* (1907), *A Room with a View* (1908) and *Howards End* (1910)—in the space of a few years, followed by a period of literary silence before *A Passage to India* (1924). George Bernard Shaw was at the height of his powers as a dramatist, and T. S. Eliot, Ezra Pound and James Joyce all started to publish at this time. Perhaps most intriguingly, the Irish poet W. B. Yeats, who had made his name in the 1890s, developed a new mature voice around the time of the 1916, Easter Rising against British rule in Ireland. Other writers who stand out in the first half of the twentieth century are the novelist Virginia Woolf, the poet W. H. Auden, and the dramatists John Millington Synge, Sean O'Casey and William Somerest Maugham.

8.2 Literary Features

The First World War changed fundamentally the way in which people thought and wrote. Before 1914, English literature and ideas were in many ways still harking back to the nineteenth century. After 1918, "Modern" began to define the twentieth century. Modernism is one of the key words of the first part of the century. Among its influences were the psychological works of Sigmund Freud and the anthropological writings of Sir James Frazer, author of *The Golden Bough* (1890–1915), a huge work which brought together cultural and social manifestations from the universe of cultures. Modernism is essentially post-Darwinian: It is a search to explain mankind's place in the modern world, where religion, social stability and ethics are all called into question. This resulted in a fashion for experimentation. The workings of the unconscious mind became an important subject, and all traditional forms began to lose their place. What emerged focused on stream of consciousness, images in poetry (rather than description or narration), a new use of universal myth, and a sense of fragmentation both of individuality and of such concepts as space and time.

Against Modernism it was said it produced chaotic and difficult writing, which moved beyond the capacity of many readers and became elitist. Indeed, it is true that readers need a background awareness of psychology, anthropology, history and aesthetics to master some of the literature of the early years of Modernism. T. S. Eliot even finished footnotes to help the reader with his *The Waste Land* (1922). But all through what might be termed the period of Modernism, there are writers who kept working away in more traditional modes. Often these writers enjoyed greater popular success than the experimenters, but it is largely the innovators who are seen to have defined the new tastes of the times. Figures like John Galsworthy and Arnold Bennet in the novel tend now to be consigned to history as relics of Victorianism, rather than being read as contemporaries of Woolf, Joyce and Eliot. What is significant is that both kinds of writing could flourish at the same time.

8.3 Modern Poetry

The poetry of this period covers a vast number of writers who offer very different responses to the chaos of a world torn apart by the war. To begin with, there is the Georgian poetry during the early years of the rein of King George V (1910–1936). A great many of the most significant poets of the time—including Rupert Brooke, A. E. Housman, Walter de la Mare, John Masefield, Edward Thomas, Robert Grave and D. H. Lawrence—were published in the series *Georgian Poetry* (five volumes between 1912 and 1922). Their poetry is very traditional, celebrating the order of rural England. It is in sharp contrast with the poetry that follows—the War poetry of Wilfred Owen and Siegfried Sassoon and the Modernist poetry of T. S. Eliot and Ezra Pound. Where the Georgians create a sense of simple harmony and order, the poets that follow insistently offer us a sense of a world without links or coherence. What separates the poets is the cataclysmic shock of the First World War. The sense of shock is registered in the often bitter, grimly ironic verse of the trenches, with its use of dream and nightmare imagery, and, above all, its language of violence and slaughter, a language that just copes with the desperate world it depicts. And yet, at the same time, the War poetry is also marked by the echoes of order, for example, in the use of half rhyme and in references to love. There is, then, an intense awareness of disorder in War poetry, but also a recollection of, and clinging on to, the idea of order.

By contrast, all order has gone in the Modernist poetry, such as that of Pound and Eliot. The modernist poets seem to be writing in a language without grammar or syntax, and a language without rhyme or rhythm. The baffling experience of Eliot's poetry in particular conveys a sense of people alienated from each other and living broken, fragmented lives in a world without values. It is not simply that poetry seems to be in revolt against rational forms of verse, but rather, that it seems to register the extent to which language itself is in crisis as it confronts a world in decay which has no longer any role for poetry. Greatly influenced by the ideas of imagism and symbolism, the modernist poetry refuses to give us access to a tangible, solid world but instead draws attention to itself, as if there is no longer any meaning to be found in the world.

With the poetry of the 1930s, there is a shift away from this position with the political poetry of W. H. Auden, Stephen Spender, Louise MacNeice and G. Day Lewis. This poetry, with Auden the leading figure, is noticeably different from the poetry of the 1920s represented by Eliot. Eliot's poetry explores a private condition; Auden's poetry explores a more public situation. Eliot is searching primarily for spiritual solutions; Auden is stressing that private worlds cannot be separated from social and political contexts. Eliot uses form and language to embody the confusions and complexities of individual identity in the modern world; Auden uses form and language to communicate a more social perspective on the modern world. As a result, Eliot's is often obscure and difficult, while Auden's is more accessible and more popular. However, both Auden and Eliot share the same poetic quest for a meaning to life amidst images of a contemporary world which fail to form a coherent whole.

8.3.1 Thomas Hardy (1840–1928)

Few poets better convey the uneasy transition from Victorianism to Modernism than Thomas Hardy. His novels, written between 1870 and 1895, made him not only the recorder of his distinctive region of "Wessex", but the explorer of the transition of lives and minds from the age of traditional values and religious certainties to the age of godlessness. After the hostile reception of his tragic and bitter novel *Jude the Obscure*, he devoted himself largely to poetry and poetic drama until his death in 1928. In 1898, he published his *Wessex Poems*. Hardy's poems are largely traditional in theme, form, and structure, and show a continuity with the Wordsworthian art of recording the impact of ordinary daily events on an individual and sensitive mind. Yet behind Hardy's verse, the unease is plain. The familiar world is progressively growing darker, more unfamiliar and the drama of existence is lived in an uncertain, fated, and godless age.

Chapter Eight
The Twentieth-Century Literature (1900–1945)

Hardy was a prolific poet, author of some 900 poems with an extensive range of feelings and attitudes. Some of the poems are gently ironic; some are strongly felt love poems; some are written in a mordantly comic light verse. Others lament the brevity and fragility of human life; some are bleak and darkly pessimistic. The perspective constantly shifts from ordinary simple events and feelings to a more cosmic awareness. In *During Wind and Rain* (1917), a sudden sense of death and impermanence pervades pastoral moments of domestic happiness. Hardy's preoccupation with death results in a macabre humor, as in *Are You Digging on My Grave*, but it would also extend to the tragic sensibility of his verse drama *The Dynasts* (1904–1908), which is preoccupied with the power of fate.

Hardy's most famous poem, *The Darkling Thrash*, written on the last day of the old 19th century, shows his uncertainty about what the future holds. The poem ends in suspension, caught between hope and pessimism. Other poems, like *The Oxen*, carry the same mood, a sense of being suspended between a secure community and a world of isolation and uncertainty. Hardy looks back to the nineteenth century for security and forward to the twentieth century "in the gloom". The same attempt at balance is evident in his choice of poetic language. He does not reject completely the poetic voice of the Victorians, but adopts dialect words, colloquialisms, specialized terms, and the vernacular note in his verse.

8.3.2 William Butler Yeats (1865–1939)

Yeats had a literary career that extends from the 1880s to the outbreak of the Second World War (1939–1945). Born in Dublin, Yeats spent his early years between London and Sligo, his mother's home county in northwest Ireland. He studied art for a while, but by the 1890s he was deeply involved both with editing and writing poetry and also with the founding of the Irish National Theater at the Abbey Theater in Dublin. Yeats was manager of the theater, but also wrote plays for it, the most successful being *Cathleen ni Houlihan* (1902). Throughout his career, Yeats continued to write plays, which, like his poems, drew upon myths, folklore, the occult and contemporary Irish politics. The most significant period for his poetry began in 1919 with the publication of *The Wild Swans*, and then *Michael Robartes and the Dancer* (1921), *The Tower* (1928), and *The Winding Stair* (1933), poetry characterized by its symbolism and its sparse yet rich style. Yeats was central to the revival of Irish literature, beginning with his early poetry in *The Wandering of Oisin and Other Poems*, followed by collections such as *The Countess Kathleen and Other Legends and*

Lyrics (1892), *The Land of Heart's Desire* (1894) and *The Wind Among the Reeds* (1899), as well as prose works, studies of Irish culture and essays. The result is an enormous body of work, and a body of work that changes as the world changes. There are three main stages to Yeats's development as a poet. The first phase is characterized by a mixture of Romanticism, nationalized idealism, Irish mythology and mysticism. A good impression of Yeats of the early stage is provided by *The Lake Isle of Innisfree*, where he writes about how he longs to escape from the city to Innisfree.

> I will arise and go now, and go to Innisfree,
> And a small cabin build there, of clay and wattles made:
> Nine bean-rows will I have there, a hive for the honeybee,
> And live alone in the bee-loud glade.
>
> (*The Lake Isle of Innisfree*)

There is an implicit contrast here between the complications of the everyday world and the simplicity of Innisfree, where everything seems idyllic and harmonious.

The second main phase of Yeats's poetic career was dominated by his commitment to Irish nationalism, and it was Irish nationalism that first sent Yeats in search of a consistently simpler, popular, and more accessible style. As Yeats became more and more involved in public nationalist issues, his poetry became more public and concerned with the politics of the modern Irish state. In one of his most famous poems, *Easter 1916*, Yeats describes the Easter Rising of 1916 in which Irish nationalist launched a heroic but unsuccessful revolt against the British government. A number of the rebels were executed. The callous and unfeeling treatment of the uprising moved Yeats to deep anger and bitterness. Yeats recognized, however, that the causes of violence, disorder, and repression were complex and had to be confronted and understood. For example, his poem *The Second Coming* (1921) is a chilling vision of impending death and dissolution. It contains the famous lines:

> Things fall apart; the center cannot hold;
> Mere anarchy is loosed upon the world...
>
> (*The Second Coming*)

But the dissolution is part of a cycle of history which also guarantees order, joy and beauty. There are gaiety and celebration in Yeats's poetry in these years as well as terror and fear of anarchy. The refrain of *Easter 1916* is that "A terrible beauty is born". Terror and beauty are contraries, yet recognition of the essentially cyclical nature of life and of history helped Yeats to resolve many of the contraries and paradoxes he experienced. It is not surprising, therefore, that Yeats's poetry at this time contains many images of winding staircases, gyres, spinning-tops, and spirals.

Yeats developed an elaborate symbolic system which was private to him, in certain particulars drawn from traditions of esoteric thought which almost compensated for a lost religion. But his greatness as a poet lies in communicating both precisely and evocatively to readers who may know nothing of his sources. In *Sailing to Byzantium* (from *The Tower*), the concern is with the new Ireland, and its future; the poet "returns" to the holy city of Byzantium as a symbol of artistic/creative perfection. The concern with the passing of time, a major concern in many Modernist writers, becomes clear in the poem's last line, which speaks "Of what is past, or passing, or to come".

In the final phase of his career, Yeats reconciled elements from both his earlier periods, fusing them into a mature lyricism. His poetry of this phase is less public and more personal. He developed his theories of contraries and of progression, which could result from reconciling them, but he also wrote about the eternity of art, producing in the process many memorable poems, which explore contrasts between physical and spiritual dimensions to life, between sensuality and rationality, and between turbulence and calm.

8.3.3 Thomas Stearns Eliot (1888–1965)

Eliot was an American poet, playwright and critic, who lived in England from 1915. His first volume of poems, *Prufrock and Other Observations* (1917), was followed by *Poems* (1919) and *The Waste Land*. *Poems 1909–1925* (1925) and *Collected Poems* (1936) reveal a developing religious tendency, and impression that is consolidated in *Four Quartets* (1943). His plays include *Murder in the Cathedral* (1935) and *The Cocktail Party* (1950). His most notable critical work is *The Sacred Wood* (1920), which sets out his views in the poetic tradition. Eliot became a British subject in 1927, and was awarded the Nobel Prize for Literature in 1948.

Eliot shared the modern view that the world is chaotic and its life is futile and fragmentary. Most of his poetry concerns various aspects of the frustration and enfeeblement of individual characters caught in a world of monotonous repetition, and a world of aimless circling about, without end or purpose, and the quest for order and discipline became Eliot's major theme, which led him towards conservatism and to religion for salvation. In 1927, Eliot conversed to the Church of England and announced that he was a royalist in politics, a classicist in literature, and Anglo-Catholic in religion. His poetry moved from the secular to the ascetic, and from pessimism to religious faith. Most of his verse dramas and later poetry deal with religious themes.

Eliot's work is characterized by several principal qualities, which can be summarized as: first, his particular sense of the age he lived in (waste land); second, his conviction that poetry, although using the poet's emotions as its starting point, becomes impersonalized by the tradition in which the poet works; third, his use of quotations from and allusions to other poets' work for reference, parody, irony, and a sense of continuing intertextual communication and community; fourth, his shocking, bewildering and discordant urban images. As a whole, Eliot is formally experimental and innovative, and intellectually complex and philosophical.

The Love Song of J. Alfred Prufrock is Eliot's earlier poem, in which Eliot first demonstrates an almost total break with the conventions of Romantic poetry. He applies to poetry a technique similar to that of the stream of consciousness, giving fragments of the thoughts passing through the mind of the lonely Mr. Prufrock. This poem, as Pound rightly saw, has established modern poetry in English. It is ironic, discontinuous, imagistic, frequently dissonant, and yet overall intensely musical and memorable. The "character" of J. Alfred Prufrock himself—though he is not so much a character as a floating consciousness—has become the social archetype of not-so-young man who is fastidious, timorous, and yet also relentlessly observant and self-aware.

The Waste Land depicts a cultural and spiritual wasteland, a land populated by people who are, physically and emotionally, living a kind of death in the midst of their everyday lives:

> A crowd flowed over London Bridge, so many
> I had not thought death has undone so many
>
> (*The Waste Land*)

Chapter Eight
The Twentieth-Century Literature (1900-1945)

The poem consists of five sections, *The Burial of the Dead*, *A Game of Chess*, *The Fire Sermon*, *Death by Water*, and *What the Thunder Said*, together with Eliot's own *Notes* which explain his many varied and multicultural allusions, quotations, and half-quotations (from Webster, Dante, Verlaine, Kyd, etc.), and express a general indebtedness to the Grail legend and to the vegetation ceremonies in Frazer's *The Golden Bough*. The poem was rapidly acclaimed as a statement of the post-war sense of depression and futility; it was seriously praised by I. A. Richards as "a perfect emotive description of a state of mind which is probably inevitable for a while to all meditative people" (*Science and Poetry*, 1926), and less seriously but significantly chanted as a kind of protest against the older generation by the undergraduates of the day. Complex, erudite, cryptic, satiric, spiritually earnest, and occasionally lyrical, it became one of the most recognizable landmarks of modernism, an original voice speaking through many echoes and parodies of echoes. Eliot himself remarked that the poem could be seen not so much as an important bit of social criticism, but as the relief of a personal and wholly insignificant grouse against life; it is just a piece of rhythmical grumbling.

Four Quartets comprises four parts: *Burnt Norton*, *East Coker*, *The Boy Salvages*, and *Little Gidding*, all of which appeared previously in other volumes.

The four quartets represent the four seasons and the four elements; the imagery of the first centers on a Cotswold garden; that of the second round a Somerset village; the third mingles the landscape of Missouri and New England, the landscapes of Eliot's youth; the fourth uses as a symbol of Little Gidding. But all are concerned with time past and time present, with the wartime London of the blitz as well as the England of Julian of Norwich and Sir T. S. Eliot. These were the first of Eliot's poems to reach a wide public and they succeeded in communicating in modern idiom the fundamentals of Christian faith and experiences.

8.3.4 Edward Thomas (1871-1917)

Thomas is one of the representatives of the Georgian poetry. His poetry celebrates the beauty and richness of England. *Adlestrop* is one example. Adlestrop is a small village in Gloucestershire. The poem recalls how Thomas's train stopped there briefly one afternoon:

> What I saw
> Was Adlestrop—only the name
> And willows, willow-herb, and grass,
> And meadowsweet, and haycocks dry
>
> *(Adlestrop)*

This is, essentially, rural poetry, celebrating a certain vision of rural England as an unspoiled paradise. But there is also a chilling emptiness in the poem: There is no one on the platform, and no one comes to the train. Behind the poem, then, lies a sense of impending death, but this in the end serves only to intensify the stress on the value of the rural idyll of England.

Edward Thomas is sometimes regarded as a war poet. The war poem known by its first line, *As the Team's Head-Brass*, observes a ploughman and his team at work. Sporadic conversation develops between the ploughman and the narrator concerning the war and the consequent dearth of rural labour, but readers are made aware of their disjunctions. Conversation is interrupted each time the ploughman returns to his furrow and the war, somewhere over a horizon, suggests other, more drastic, breakings and severances:

> "From here?" "Yes." "Many lost?" "Yes, a good few."
> Only two teams work on the farm this year.
> One of my mates is dead. The second day
> In France they killed him. It was back in March,
> The very night of the blizzard, too. Now if
> He had stayed here we should have moved the tree.
> "And I should not have sat here. Everything
> Would have been different. For it would have been
> Another world." ...
>
> *(As the Team's Head-Brass)*

Thomas's sense of the encroachments of war in this poem is related to his evocations elsewhere of a transient and disappearing England, an England through which the poet passes, as in *Adlestrop*, merely as a traveller.

Chapter Eight
The Twentieth-Century Literature (1900–1945)

Thomas's poems which deal directly with the Western Front treat death as the ultimate disrupter and destroyer of the deadly often violent cooperation of man and nature. A poem *A Private* notes the strangely abrupt distinction between a former ploughman, now lying dead in France, and his old habit of sleeping under English bushes when drunk. A very different address to death is suggested by *Lights Out* where the military command of the title is translated into a journey through a dark wood "where all must lose". The unnatural silence of the wood imposes a sense of loss, a loss not simply of direction but ultimately of the violated self.

8.3.5 Wilfred Owen (1893–1918)

Wilfred Owen, the major poet of the First World War, began writing poetry in the manner of Keats, but his poetry underwent stylistic changes as he toughened and tightened his language under the pressure of traumatic front-line experience of war. One of his most bitterly ironic poems, *Dulce et Decorum Est* (meaning it is sweet and honourable to die for one's country) describes the horrors of a gas attack while commenting ironically on the limits of patriotism. Owen came to see it instead as a duty to warn of the horrors of war and to ask why political rulers allowed such mass destruction to continue for so long. He also questioned the necessity of war, stressed the common humanity of both sides in war and linked the futility of the deaths of individual soldiers to the cosmic indifference of a world from which God was conspicuously absent. The following lines from the poem *Futility* underline this stance:

> Was it for this the clay grew tall?
> O what made fatuous sunbeams toil
> To break earth's sleep at all.
>
> *(Futility)*

This plays ironically on the link between the clays of the earth and the biblical meaning of clay (the human body). The introduction of religious connotations here reinforces the poem's sense of spiritual emptiness.

One of Owen's technical qualities is also illustrated in these lines. Owen's innovative use of half-rhyme (e.g. tall/toil) is a pervasive feature of his poetry. Whereas full rhyme would underscore a sense of pattern and completeness, the use of half-rhyme reinforces a sense of things not fitting and being incomplete. It is an aspect of poetic form which is highly appropriate for the tone and subject matter of much of Owen's poetry, and for the bleak landscape which is the background to this poetry. Owen also concentrated on the immediate sound effects of his poems. The result is lines which reproduce the sounds of war:

> What passing-bells for those who die as cattle?
> Only the monstrous anger of the guns,
> Only the stuttering rifles' rapid rattle
> Can patter out their hasty orisons.
>
> *(Anthem for Doomed Youth)*

8.3.6 Wystan Hugh Auden (1907–1973)

Auden, the most significant poet of the 1930s, was associated with a group of writers who were committed to a Marxist social vision and were called the Auden Group. Auden's poems from the 1930s deal directly with specific social and international crisis. It is always a characteristic of a significant work of literature that it will reflect the fears and anxieties of the period of its production, and this is sharply apparent in Auden, who deals with a world that seems worryingly ready to embrace fascism and just as willing to abandon consideration for the individual. This can be seen in a poem such as *Spain 1937*, where he can accurately be described as the voice of his generation:

> The stars are dead; the animals will not look:
> We are left alone with our day, and the time is short
> and history to be defeated
> May say Alas but cannot help or pardon.
>
> *(Spain 1937)*

A vivid sense of the political tensions of the 1930s is also apparent in Auden's *Consider*.

> Consider this and in our time
> As the hawk sees it or the helmeted airman.
>
> *(Consider)*

Here the poet stresses the present, asking us to consider "this", something which is contemporary and "in our time", and inviting us to see more clearly what is taking place before our own eyes from a great height, like a hawk or an airman who can consider events clinically and objectively. The "helmeted airman", may refer to the airman in a battle helmet; his place is likely to be a warplane; his action is threatening the coming decade. One of the tasks of the poet is to warn us to consider our times and be prepared for appropriate action.

The most important members of the Auden Group were Louis MacNeice, C. Day Lewis and Stephen Spender. Their poetry is diverse and there is again a focus on social themes and on a use of clear, ordinary language and popular forms.

Auden's chief poetry includes *Poems* (1930), which established him as the strongest voices of his generation, *The Orators* (1932), *Nones* (1951), and *City Without Walls* (1970).

8.4 Modern Drama

The period from the end of the nineteenth century up to the Second World War was a great age for the drama. There is a substantial tradition of major dramatists from Ibsen, Chekhov and Shaw through to Synge, O'Casey, Coward, and Priestley. There are also a great many of the successful novelists and poets of the time trying their hands at writing for the theater: Lawrence, Eliot, Yeats, Maughham, et al.

A good point at which to start the modern drama is with Shaw's *Arms and Man*. Hero, Bluntschli, a mercenary fighting in a war, evades capture by hiding in the bedroom of Raima. As the plot unfolds, Bluntschli overturns all Raima's illusions about love and heroism. A light, comic play, it ends with her marriage. What makes Shaw's play modern is its debunking of conventional attitudes and beliefs. In terms of content, Shaw breaks the frame of traditional values. The same thing happens at the formal level: Shaw takes the neat format of the well-made play (in which the central interest is the plot), but subverts its tidy structure, introducing a sense of life's confusing complexity. Something very similar happens in plays such as Synge's *The Playboy of the Western World* (1907) and O'Casey's *Juno and the Paycock* (1924). Their traditional ideas and ideals are undermined by comedy. What marks such plays off as modern is, first, their undermining of conventional social myths, beliefs and convictions, and, second, the innovative form of such plays, the writers breaking up the neat pattern of the well-made play.

8.4.1 John Millington Synge (1871–1909)

Like Shaw, Wilde and Yeats, Synge was an Irishman. His plays, written in the brief period between 1903 and the writer's death in 1909, create their singular effects through a language which struck its first Dublin audience as "strange". Synge, like his associate Yeats, also sought to minimize conventional action, but his stress fell less on ritual than on distinctive ways of speaking which echo the rhythms of the English of Western Ireland. Yeats's observation that Synge's English "blurs definition, clear edges and everything that comes from the will" is particularly apposite to *Riders to the Sea* (1904), a short "poetic" play which suggests the perennial failure of those who work with and on the sea. Character and action are subsumed in something approaching a choric flow which, through a series of reiterated similes, expresses a submissive fatalism. In *The Tinker's Wedding* (1903–1907), *The Well of the Saints* (1905), and his masterpiece *The Playboy of the Western World*, Synge perfected a distinctively Irish comic form, one far removed from English Victorian convention. The plays reject the "joyless and pallid words" which Synge regarded as symptomatic of the modern realism of Zola and Ibsen, and they turn instead to the example of the London comedies of the seventeenth century, and transform an essentially slick, urban dialogue into something both more lilting and wilder.

The Playboy of the Western World tells the story that Christy Mahon, "a slight young man, very tired and frightened", arrives at a village in Mayo. He gives out that he is a fugitive from justice, who has killed his bullying father, splitting him to the chine with a single blow. His character as a dare-devil gives him a great advantage with the women (notably Pegeen Mike and Widow Quin). But admiration gives place to angry contempt when the father himself arrives in pursuit of the fugitive, who has merely given him a crack on the head and run away. The implication that Irish peasants would condone a murder and the frankness of some of the language caused outrage and riots when the play was first performed. This play is Synge's best-known effort to fuse the language of ordinary people with a dramatic rhetoric of his own making. The remote Mayo coastline, on which the play is set, serves to confine an isolated rural community, one that is disturbed by the arrival of the fugitive, a supposed patricide. Words, and the illusion words created, dominate the action. Christy Mahon's prestige depends not upon a fulfilled deed but on his recounting of a deed which failed to succeed; his final departure with his trice "resurrected" father is accompanied by a final, triumphant act of myth-making in which he declares that he goes away "like a gallant captain with his heathen slave".

8.4.2 Sean O'Casey (1880–1964)

Sean O'Casey was the last of the major early twentieth-century Irish playwrights to be associated with the Abbey Theater in Dublin. A poor protestant Dubliner by birth, he wrote about what he knew best—the sounds, the rhetoric, the prejudices, the frustrations, and the manners of tenement dwellers of the slums of the Irish capital. Unlike his Abbey predecessors (Yeats, Lady Augusta Gregory, Edward Martyn, and Synge), he was not prepared to romanticize Ireland or to finalize about either its pastor or its bloody present. Nor was he inclined to "poeticize" the vigorously rhythmical language of the Dublin poor. His three best plays are dealing realistically with the rhetoric and dangers of the Irish patriotism, and are characterized by their author as tragedies. *The Shadow of a Gunman* (1923) is set in a back room in "Hilljoy" Square at the time of the "Black and Tan" repression in 1920. The action of *Juno and the Paycock* also takes place in a single room in a two-room tenancy, though the period has moved forward to the time of the Irish Civil War in 1922. *The Plough and the Stars* describes the prelude to the eruption of the Easter Rising and the disjunctions of the Rising itself in 1916. Its action takes place in and around the Clitheroes' rooms in a fine old Georgian house struggling for its life against the assaults of time, and the more savage assaults of its tenants.

O'Casey moved to England in 1926; his alienation from Ireland was confirmed by a rift with Yeats and the Abbey Theater over its rejection of *The Silver Tassie* (1928), an experimental anti-war play about an injured footballer, which introduced the symbolic Expressionist techniques employed in his later works. These include *Within the Gates* (1933), *Red Roses for Me* (1942), *Cock-a-Doodle Dandy* (1949) and *The Bishop's Bonfire* (1950). None of these later plays managed to recall the tense, unsentimental energy of his Abbey plays.

8.4.3 Noël Coward (1899–1973)

Noël Coward was the most representative English dramatist of the inter-war period. His work contrasts vividly with that of O'Casey. Coward combined the talents of the actor, composer, librettist, playwright, and poseur and his long career allowed each aspect a more than ample expression. After uncertain theatrical beginnings in the immediately post-war years, he achieved fame in 1924 with *The Vortex*, a high-flown exploration of the condition of a drug-addict tormented by his slovenly mother's adulteries, and the equally melodramatic *The Rat Trap*, a study of the miserable marriage of a playwright and his novelist-wife. More characteristic of his talent were his comedies *Fallen Angels* (1925), *Hay Fever* (1925), *Private Lives* (1933). *Hay Fever*, in which absurdity meets incomprehension, exposes both the eccentric, self-centered rudeness of the Bliss family and the bafflement of their conservative quests. *Private Lives* is about two disastrous interconnected second marriages. Coward's patriotic work *Cavalcade* (1931) traces the fortunes and opinions of the Marryot family in twenty-one short scenes covering the years 1899–1930. His last great success *Blithe Spirit* (1941) offered an essential escape from the preoccupations of the "Home Front" in the Second World War, though it included, through the ethereal presence of Elvira and the spiritual interference of Madame Arcati, the reassurance to families parted by the war that death did not necessarily mark the end of a relationship. Coward also published volumes of verse, short stories, a novel (*Pomp and Circumstance*, 1960) and two volumes of autobiography.

8.4.4 John Boynton Priestley (1894–1984)

Priestley, like Coward, was one of the most familiar and popular figures in the realm of propagandist entertainment during the Second World War. He established his reputation as a novelist with *The Good Companions* (1929) and *Angel Pavement* (1930). The first, an account of the vagaries of the life of a travelling theatrical troupe, was successfully dramatized in 1931. It opened the floodgates to Priestley's career as a dramatist in his own right, a career which ultimately included more than forty plays. His stance as a no-nonsense populist and professional Yorkshireman, so self-consciously cultivated in his wartime radio broadcasts (published under the titles *Britain Speaks* and *All England Listened*), belied his genuine sophistications and dedications as an artist and critic. His best-remembered and most revived plays, *Time and Conways* (1937), *When We Are Married* (1938), and the mystery *An Inspector Calls* (1947), show a mastery of the conventional "well-made" form and a tolerant spotting with human folly. The two comedies in particular tend to reinforce the virtues of common sense and stolidity rather than to challenge preconceptions as to the nature of society or the role of the theater.

Chapter Eight
The Twentieth-Century Literature (1900–1945)

8.4.5 William Somerset Maugham (1874–1965)

Maugham is a novelist as well as a playwright. His first novel *Liza of Lambeth* (1897) drew on his experiences of slums and Cockney life as an obstetric clerk. He achieved fame with the production of *Lady Frederick* (1907), a comedy of marriage and money. In 1908, he had four plays running simultaneously in London. Maugham's best-known novel is a thinly disguised autobiography, *Of Human Bandage* (1915), which describes Philip Carey's lonely boyhood and his subsequent adventures. Of his short stories, the best-known is *Rain*, which relates the conflict between a life-affirming American prostitute, Sadie Thompson, and a repressed Scottish missionary, Davidson. It ends with Davidson's suicide. It is characteristic of Maugham's work in its remarkable and economical evocation of the atmosphere of hot, wet, tropical Samoa, and its neat twist of plot; it was staged successfully and it has been filmed three times.

Among Maugham's plays should be mentioned *Our Betters* (1917), a satire on title-hunting Americans; *The Circle* (1921); *East of Suez* (1922); *The Constant Wife* (1926); *For Services Rendered* (1932), an anti-war play. Maugham's plays are largely treatments of middle class attitude to love and money.

8.5 Modern Novels

For many critics, the years 1900–1945 are the highest point in the development of the English novel, a time when not only the greatest twentieth-century novels but also the greatest novels in the English language were written. Many commentators stress, in particular, the technical and aesthetic advances which occurred during this period and it was indeed a time of extensive formal innovation and experimentation. Yet it would be inaccurate to suggest that the novel of the period was one of total change. Many writers continued the tradition of the nineteenth century without making a radical departure from the main themes or from the main forms that sustained that tradition. Thus modern novelists can be divided into those who continue within a broad tradition of realism and those who experiment far more with the form of the novel. Writers such as John Galsworthy, Arnold Bennett, H. G. Wells, E. M. Foster and Graham Greene are essentially realists. They are less intrusive than the nineteenth century realists, presenting a credible picture in which we are not particularly aware of the narrator's presence. They deal with social, personal and ethical problems and offer us an entertaining yet at the same time instructive look at how people cope with life in the twentieth century. The outstanding figure within this tradition is D. H. Lawrence, whose novels conform to the usual pattern of presenting characters at odds with society but Lawrence goes much further than other writers in a romantic quest for an alternative way of life. He feels that there must be a new way in which people can relate to each other; however, his best novels, *The Rainbow* and *Women in Love*, are committed to exploring fresh areas of experience. Writing in an emotional style that suits his subject matter, he never forgets that his characters are bound by all the demands of ordinary existence.

The other major novelists of the time all employ the same basic pattern of individuals in conflict with society or their families, but the most noticeable feature of many great novels of the period is the extraordinary degree of formal experiment and innovation. This begins with the works of Joseph Conrad and Henry James. Conrad often uses a dramatized narrator, Marlow, and sometimes disrupts the time sequence of events. James's late novels, such as *The Wing of Dove*, repeat the story he had been writing for years of innocent young women coming in contact with a corrupt society, but become more and more elaborate, with extremely long sentences where it is impossible to trace the line of thought.

The reason for such innovations was the disappearance of shared values and shared beliefs. George Eliot writes confidently, as if she and her readers could share a view of the world, but at the end of the nineteenth century this confidence disappeared. A new awareness of individual psychology came into existence at this time. It began to be realized that everyone has a unique perception of the world.

Such changes in thinking have two overlapping consequences for the novel. There is far more emphasis on the mind of the individual, something that is most apparent in the technique of stream of consciousness: a new way of writing that reflects a new view of the human mind. The other consequence is that many of the great novels of the time advertise their own fictionality. In the works of such writers as Joyce and Woolf, there is thus a mixture of the exploration of characters' minds and a war of writing that draws attention to itself. Whereas the realistic novelist presumes to read the world, the experiment in fiction instead draws attention to the ways in which fiction tries to structure experience, for reality is always beyond the grasp of the text. In doing so, the experimental fiction does indirectly offer us a new view of the world.

8.5.1 John Galsworthy (1867–1933)

John Galsworthy has cultivated the drama, the short story and the novel with eminent success. He is one of the closest observers of manners and loves to watch the varying shadows which the changing years cast on the surface of life. His chosen religion is that in which he was born and bred—the upper-middle class; alike in his plays and novels, the faults which arise from worldly success—narrowness of outlook, hardness of heart, and the like—are the mainspring of the action. Mr. Galsworthy had been publishing some eight or nine years before he wrote *The Man of Property* (1906), now the first novel of *The Forsyte Saga*, his trilogy and masterpiece. Galsworthy began his playwriting career with *The Silver Box* (1906), a play about theft in which the power of money is shown as shielding the rich from penalties to which the poor are liable. In it, the manners of modern life in a well-to-do household, a very poor one, and a London police court are drawn with fine observation and occasional saturnine humor. Galsworthy achieved another success in *Strife* (1909), a somber tragedy on an industrial dispute.

The Forsyte Saga is a sequence of three novels, containing the stories, *The Man of Property*, *In Chancery* (1920), and *To Let* (1921, with two interludes, *Indian Summer of a Forsyte*, 1918, and *Awakening*, 1920). The trilogy traces the fortunes of three generations of the Forsyte family.

Soames Forsyte, a successful solicitor, the nephew of old Jolyon, lives in London surrounded by his prosperous old uncles and their families. He marries the penniless Irene and builds a country house for her, Robin Hill; when she falls in love with its architect, Bosinney, Soames asserts his rights over his property and rapes her. Bosinney is killed in a street accident and Irene returns to Soames. *In Chancery* describes the growing love of young Jolyon, Soames's cousin, for Irene; Irene's divorce from Soames and her happy marriage with Jolyon, and the birth of their son Jon. Meanwhile Soames marries Annette Lamotte and they have a daughter, Fleur. In *To Let*, Fleur and Jon fall in love; Jon's father feels compelled to reveal the past of Irene and Soames, and the agonized Jon, in spite of Fleur's Forsyte determination, rejects her. She marries Michael Mont, the heir to a baronetcy, and when young Jolyon dies, Irene leaves to join Jon in America. The desolate Soames learns that his wife is having an affair with a Belgian, and discovers that Irene's house, Robin Hill, is empty and to let.

The Man of Property is the best of the three, in which Galsworthy sets out to satirize the Victorian upper middle class, whom he sees as reducing everything to property values, including life itself. The whole saga is concerned with class-consciousness, and class conflict, a pressing theme in a period that might as well be on the brink of a social revolution.

8.5.2 Herbert George Wells (1866–1946)

H. G. Wells has great powers of imaginative creation. He combines the gifts of the novelist and the teacher. He has that stimulating gift of the teacher—the power to be always annexing new province of knowledge. Mr. Wells is the mirror of the changeable, inquiring age, and yet the future has always been much his sphere as the present. Nothing daunts him, however remote. Wells's influence is due largely to his vast mass of acquired information, and the confident dexterity with which he displays it. Force and cleverness are the two great qualities of his style.

Wells wrote more than a hundred books and pamphlets in his fifty-year career, including over forty novels. He is nowadays better known for his early science fiction works (*The Time Machine*, 1895; *The Invisible Man*, 1897; *The War of the Worlds*, 1898), and is important as a reforming writer who expresses a socialist-liberal vision of the future. Wells wanted to destroy all the inequalities and inconsistencies associated with the Victorian era, particularly the economic and social privileges granted to only a few. He believed that the advances of science could create a rational, and more enlightened society, indeed a new world order. In his scientific novels, he creates worlds in which the old certainties and fixed order of the world disappear: Man can travel to the moon; we can move backwards and forwards in time; we can be attacked by people from Mars; human size can be increased indefinitely; we can sleep for two hundred years and wake up in a strange scientific future.

Wells's English social fiction contrasts starkly with his fantasies though even here science and men of science have leading roles. Wells based his social novels on sober reality. He knew the drabness, the deprivations, and the humor of a lower middle class life, and he had always loved to observe the various ways of speech among the illiterate and half-educated. For example, *Love and Mr. Lewisham* (1900) tells the story of a struggling teacher; *Kipps* (1905) is that of an aspiring draper's assistant; *The History of Mr. Polly* (1910) recounts the adventures of an inefficient shopkeeper who liberates himself by burning down his own shop and bolting for freedom, which he discovers as man of all-work at the Potwell

Inn. Wells's best social novel is *Tono Bungay* (1909). The novel features George Ponderevo, who becomes a salesman for a quack medicine, and who is later involved in aviation, and then in the search for "quap", a radioactive material that might revive his family's fortunes. Invention is an issue in the novel, but it is essentially a story about decay: The collapse of the house of Ponderevo foreshadows the forthcoming collapse of Europe. Wells presents a vulgar, commercial society, bent on its own destruction.

8.5.3 Arnold Bennett (1867–1931)

Bennett's novels are set in "The Five Towns", the area in the English Midlands known as the Potteries and which has been the center for the manufacture of chinaware. Bennett's novels—he was influenced by the French naturalists—give a detailed picture of people confined in difficult and drab conditions. His best-known novels are *Anna of the Five Towns* (1902), *The Old Wives' Tale* (1908) and *Clayhanger* (1910), holding out little hope that the conditions in which people live can be changed. What remains is a well-documented portrayal of ordinary people caught in the grip of oppressive social conditions, but displaying great dignity and humanity in their struggles to survive.

The Old Wives' Tale is a long chronicle of the lives of two sisters, Constance and Sophia Baines, daughters of a draper of Bursley from their ardent girlhood, through disillusionment, to death. The drab life of the draper's shop, and its trivial incidents, are made interesting and important. Constance, a staid and sensible young woman, marries the superficially insignificant Samuel Povey, the chief assistant in the shop, and spends all her life in Bursley. The more passionate and imaginative Sophia elopes with Gerald Scales, a commercial traveller who has come into a fortune. He is an unprincipled blackguard, has to be forced to marry her, carries her to Paris, where she is exposed to indignities, and finally deserts her. She struggles to success as a lodging-house keeper in Paris, where she lives through the siege of 1870. The sisters are reunited, and spend their last years together in Bursley.

8.5.4 Edward Morgan Forster (1879–1970)

E. M. Forster published six novels, which are exclusively concerned with Edwardian middle class perceptions and imperceptions. In his novels, he intermixes a sharp, observant, and sometimes bitter social comedy with didactic narrative insistence on the virtues of tolerance and human decency. Contrasts are central to Forster's novels. In *Where Angels*

Fear to Tread and *A Room with a View*, he contrasts refined English gentility and sensuous Italian vitality. *Howards End* explores contrasts in relationships. In his last and best work *A Passage to India*, Forster contrasts British culture and a foreign tradition that has qualities missing in the British way of life. In *Maurice* (1919), a novel about homosexual love, emerges the conflict between the author's private world and the codes of behavior expected during the times in which he lived. Forster's *The Longest Journey*, like some of his other works, deals with the legacy of Victorian middle class liberalism.

Where Angels Fear to Tread is a tragedy describing the consequences of the marriage of Lilia Herriton, an impulsive young widow, to the son of an Italian dentist, Gino Carelia. Lilia dies in childbirth; Philip Herriton is dispatched by her ex-mother-in-law to rescue the baby, but falls under the spell of Italy, as Caroline Abbott, Lilia's chaperone, has fallen under the spell of Gino. The baby is killed in a characteristic Forsterian "muddle" and the two English characters return home empty-handed.

Howards End deals with personal relationships and conflicting values. The heart of the novel is Forster's attempt to explore the relationship between two realities. The Wilcox family represents material values and the effective management of the outer life; the Schlegels represent the inner life and the importance of spiritual values.

The Schlegel sisters, Margaret and Helen, and their brother Tibby, care about civilized living, music, literature, and conversation. The Wilcoxes, Henry and his children Charles, Paul, and Evie, are concerned with the business side of life and distrust emotions and imagination. Helen Schlegel is drawn to the Wilcox family, falls briefly in and out of love with Paul Wilcox, and thereafter reacts away from them. Margaret is stimulated by the very differences of their way of life. She marries Henry Wilcox, to the consternation of both families. Her marriage cracks but does not break. In the end, torn between her sister and her husband, she succeeds in bridging the mistrust that divides them. Howards End, where the story begins and ends, is the house that belonged to Henry Wilcox's first wife, and is a symbol of human dignity and endurance.

A Room with a View is essentially a love story, but one shaped around reiterated contrasts between, on the one hand, English emotional repression and, on the other, the freedom of the spirit, suggested by the music of Beethoven, and the freedoms allowed to the passions by the far more "civilized" Italians.

Chapter Eight
The Twentieth-Century Literature (1900–1945)

The novel opens in an English pensione in Florence with a confrontation between Lucy Honey, church's chaperone Miss Bartlett and the up-start Mr. Emerson and his son George; the two men offer to exchange rooms, in order to give the ladies a room with a view, a favour which they reluctantly accept. The novel describes the inmates of the Pensione Bertolini, among them the clergyman Mr. Beebe and the "original" lady novelist Miss Lavish and their reactions to Italy and to one another. Lucy is disturbed first by witnessing a street murder, and then by an impulsive embrace from George Emerson during an excursion to Fiesole. Miss Bartlett removes her charge from these dangers, and the two return to Surrey, where Lucy becomes engaged to a cultured dilettante, Cecil Vyse, whom Mr. Beebe, who has reappeared as the local vicar, ominously describes as "an ideal bachelor". The Bertolini cast continues to reassemble as the Emersons take a villa in the neighbourhood. Lucy comes to realize that she loves George, but it takes her some time to extricate herself from what she describes as "the muddle". The second half of the drama is played against a sharply and intimately observed background of tennis and tea parties and amateur piano recitals; it ends in the Pensione Bertolini, with George and Lucy on their honeymoon.

A Passage to India is told in three parts, *Mosque*, *Caves*, and *Temple*, and concerns Aziz, a young Muslim doctor, whose friendliness and enthusiasm for the British turn to bitterness and disillusionment when his pride is injured. A sympathy springs between him and the elderly Mrs. Moore, who has come to visit her son, the City Magistrate. Accompanying her is Adela Quested, young, earnest, and charmless, who longs to know the "real" India and tries to disregard the taboos and snobberies of the British circle. Aziz organizes an expedition for the visitors to the famous Caves of Marabar, where an unforeseen development plunges him into disgrace and rouses deep antagonism between the two races. Adela accuses him of insulting her in the Caves, and he is committed to prison and stands trial. Adela withdraws her charge, but Aziz turns furiously away from the British towards a Hindu-Muslim entente. In the third part of the book he has moved to a post in a native state, and is bringing up his family in peace, writing poetry and reading Persian. He is visited by his friend Mr. Fielding, the former Principal of the Government College, an intelligent, hard-bitten man. They discuss the future of India, and Aziz prophesies that only when the British are driven out can he and Fielding really be friends.

The novel offers a distinctly less generous and complacent picture of the Raj and its

British servants than had Kipling. The British form an elite, cut off by their ill-founded sense of racial, social, and cultural superiority from the multiple significance of the native civilizations of India, while maintaining the class-distinctions and petty snobberies of "home". Throughout the story connections fail, doomed by race, class, colonialism and religion.

8.5.5 Joseph Conrad (1857–1924)

1. Life and Career

Joseph Conrad was born of Polish parents in the Russian-dominated Ukraine. From an early age he longed to go to sea and in 1874 he went to Marseilles, embarked on a French vessel, and began the career as a sailor which was to supply so much material for his writings. In 1886, he became a British subject and a master mariner and in 1894, he settled in England and devoted himself to writing. He published his first novel at the age of 38, writing in English, his third language.

Almayer's Folly (1895) was followed by *An Outcast of the Islands* (1896), *The Nigger of the "Narcissus"* (1897), and *Lord Jim* (1900). The sea continued to supply the setting for most of his novels and short stories. In 1904 appeared the novel *Nostromo*, which explores one of Conrad's chief preoccupations—man's vulnerability and corruptibility. In his short story *Heart of Darkness* (1902), Conrad had carried this issue to a terrifying conclusion. *The Secret Agent* (1907) and *Under Western Eyes* (1911) are both novels with political themes, the latter set in Switzerland and Russia and centered on the tragedy of the student Razumov, caught up in the treachery and violence of revolution. Conrad's works were at first ill received by critics and public alike, and it was the novel *Chance* (1913) that brought him his first financial success. His other major works include *Typhoon* (1902), *The Mirror of the Sea* (1906), *The Rescue* (1920), and *The Rover* (1923). By the time of his death, Conrad was well established in the literary world as one of the leading Modernists.

2. Thought

Conrad's themes merely develop, broaden and open up in the larger world beyond the confined, masculine world of the ship. In the late sea-story, *The Secret Sharer* (1909), the narrator speaks disarmingly of the "great security of the sea as compared with the unrest of the land" and of a shipboard life which presents "no disquieting problem". The statement seems ironic as the narrative develops with the accounts of typhoons and tempests, of marine

Chapter Eight
The Twentieth-Century Literature (1900–1945)

disaster, and shipwrecks. Nevertheless, there is a sense in which Conrad's descriptions of ship life suggest a relatively ordered society which is, by its very nature, prepared to face the challenges of an external and impersonal hostility. The ship also contains a small hierarchical society in which individual decision and responsibility take on the moral force of paramount virtue. In the sea-stories "disquieting problems", frightful and utterly devastating as they may prove to be, do at least seem to find some kind of resolution, albeit a singularly fragile resolution.

Conrad's tales are also concerned with the nature and effects of European imperialism, both economic and colonial. Unlike Kipling, Conrad deals not with the multiple confrontations of India, but with the intrusion and interference of Europeans in the Pacific, in the East Indies, in South America, and in Africa. His colonizers are drawn from a variety of national backgrounds, and most of them disreputable, uncomprehending, intolerant, and exploitative. The title character in *Lord Jim* may have proved himself a successful colonial agent and have earned himself the title "lord" from his grateful subjects, but his organizing virtues are seen as countered by the lasting memory of the corruption of his predecessors and by the deception and ruthless of European piracy of Gentleman Brown. In Conrad's works such as *An Outpost Progress* and *Nostromo*, colonialism generally emerges as both brutal and brutalizing, alienating native and settler alike, and imperialism is initially expounded as a variety of brutish idealism.

Having been born unwilling subject of the Russian Tsar, and having accepted exile from nationalistic politics and his native language, Conrad steadily explores and interrelates themes of alienation and dislocation, which make him the first major modern writer of the twentieth century. In the works of novelists before Conrad, there is always a sense that a community used to exist, and that people used to belong to a place and to a family, but in Conrad there is a new, and far more extreme, sense of dislocated individuals in an unrelentingly cruel world. His heroes, as in the case with Jim, might have a place of origin and a family, but there is never any sense of their roots or connections offering them any strength or help. In his most explicitly political novels *Nostromo*, *The Secret Agent*, and *Under Western Eyes*, Conrad depicts human isolation, the conflict between different parts of one's personality and external fate as well as the difficulties of human communication. Conrad writes with a deep pessimism, reminiscent of Thomas Hardy.

3. Style

In order to present an instable, frail world without any shared set of moral values, Conrad develops the techniques of multiple points of view. A hero like Lord Jim is not judged directly by Conrad but his behavior is seen from different narrative viewpoints, including the viewpoint of a narrator, Marlow, who provides a commentary on the action. Conrad's narrative technique is also characterized by a skillful use of breaks in time-sequence, which prevents a reader from adopting too simplistic an interpretation of events. Conrad has been called an Impressionist, and the movement of the stories, of the images and emotions, is portrayed through each character's private vision of reality.

4. Major Works

Lord Jim tells the story that Jim is chief mate on board the *Patna*, an ill-manned ship carrying a party of pilgrims in Eastern waters. He is young, idealistic, and a dreamer of heroic deeds. When the Patna threatens to sink and the cowardly officers escape in the few lifeboats, Jim despises them, but dazed by the horror of the moment he joins them. The Patna does not sink and the pilgrims are rescued. What happens to Jim thereafter is related by an observer, Marlow. Jim, alone among the crew, remains to face the court of enquiry. Condemned by the court, he tries to disappear. Through Marlow's intervention, Jim is sent to a remote trading station in Patusan. His efforts create order and well-being in a previously chaotic community and he wins the respect and affection of the people for whom he becomes Tuan—or Lord Jim. When Gentleman Brown and his gang of thieves come to plunder, the village Jim begs the chiefs to spare them, pledging his own life against their departure. But Brown behaves treacherously and a massacre takes place. Jim feels he has only one course of action; rejecting the idea of flight he delivers himself up to Chief Doramin whose son was a victim of the massacre. Doramin shoots him and Jim willingly accepts this honourable death.

Nostromo is often considered to be Conrad's masterpiece. It is concerned with silver, insurrection, and external interference in an unstable South American republic. Its restless narrative suggests uncertain heroism, a tottering social order, and a corruption which is both imported and exportable.

In the imaginary South American country Costaguana, Charles Gould runs a silver mine of national importance in the province of Sulaco. He is married to Emilia, a woman of charm and intelligence, whose arrival has been of great benefit to the local people. In a time of political unrest and revolution, when the silver from the mine is in danger of being seized by the rebel forces, Gould becomes obsessed with the idea of saving it. He enlists the help of Decoud, the cynical, Paris-influenced journalist and of an older man, Dr. Monygham, and together they appeal to Nostromo, an Italian sailor, now a hero to all. With great daring, Decoud and Nostromo sail off to a nearby island where they bury the treasure. Decoud is left alone to quad the silver on the deserted island; he loses his mind and, after shooting himself, drowns, his body weighted with silver. The common assumption is that the silver was lost at sea and the temptation proves too much for Nostromo, who decides to steal it. His old friend Viola is appointed lighthouse keeper on the island and, unwittingly, guard for the silver. Nostromo trifles with Vola's two infatuated daughters, grows rich as he gradually pilfers the silver, and is finally shot when mistaken for an intruder. Mortally wounded, he sends for Emilia, and confesses his crime in the hope of absolution, but dies without revealing the whereabouts of the treasure.

Heart of Darkness contrasts Western civilization in Europe with what civilization has done to Africa. The theme of darkness leads to the figure of Kurts, the central character, a portrait of how the commercial and material exploitation of colonial lands can make men morally hollow, and create a permanent nightmare in the soul. Kurts's conduct of cannibalism also suggests that there might be something rotten at the very heart of civilization; indeed, it is possible that the very idea of civilized people and a civilized society might be nothing more than an anachronistic myth.

8.5.6 David Herbert Lawrence (1885–1930)

1. Life and Career

D. H. Lawrence was born at Eastwood, Nottinghamshire, one of five children of a miner and an ex-school teacher. He grew up in considerable poverty and his ill-suited parents quarreled continually. At 15 Lawrence was forced to give up his education and take a job for a short time as a clerk. He then became a pupil teacher, and subsequently took up a scholarship at Nottingham University College to study for a teacher's certificate.

His first novel, *The White Peacock* was followed by *The Trespasser* (1912). After the death of his mother he became seriously ill and gave up teaching. *Sons and Lovers* is a faithful account of these early years. In 1912 he met Frieda Weekley, wife of his old professor at Nottingham; she was six years older than Lawrence and mother of three children. They fell in love and eloped to Germany; their life together was passionate and stormy. His next novel, *The Rainbow*, was seized by the police and declared obscene; his frankness about sex, and his use of four-letter words, was to keep him in constant trouble with the law. In 1917 he published a volume of poems, *Look! We Have Come Through!* And in 1919 he and Frieda left for Italy. He had finished his novel *Women in Love* in 1916 but was unable to find a publisher until 1920 in New York. In the same year *The Lost Girl* won the James Tait Black Memorial Prize. *Aaron's Rod* (1922), which shows the influence of Nietzsche, followed and the same year he began his serious travels to Ceylon, America, Australia (where he wrote *Kangaroo*, 1923), and Mexico, where he began *The Plumed Serpent* (1926). While on a visit to Old Mexico, he was told that he was in an advanced state of tuberculosis. With his wife he returned to Italy where he finished *Lady Chatterley's Lover* (1928). Lawrence is also famous for his short stories and poems.

2. Thought

Lawrence is a moralist, believing that modern man is in danger of losing his ability to experience the quality of life. He hates art that keeps its distance from humanity and wants literature to enlarge and extend human sympathy, to make people more fully alive to themselves and each other. Many of his novels explore human individuality and all that might hinder or fulfill that essential individuality. At the heart of individual fulfillment is a proper basis for marital relationship. To Lawrence, complex honesty between lovers will lead to great self-knowledge, deeper fulfillment, and a stronger will to live. What is vital to this positive outlook is the theme of freedom from sexual inhibition.

Thus tension in sexual feeling is a recurring theme in Lawrence's fiction. Lawrence sees sexual love as a driving force in human relationships which can be both creative and destructive: Sexual love can be destructive if it is too mechanical or based on rationality or reason; if it is created on an instinctive level, it will be positive and can help individuals achieve a wholeness of personality through their love for each other. He describes relationships with uncompromising originality and genuinely seeks ways of reconciling tensions and contrasts. Above all, Lawrence is concerned to find ways of describing the deepest experiences of his characters. He once wrote that the human personality was like an iceberg, with its major part under the surface. His art attempts to capture the submerged parts of the self and to develop form and techniques in the novel which render those intense experiences.

3. Style

Lawrence explores human relationships with psychological precision and with poetic feeling. He combines a detailed realism with poetic symbolism in ways which makes us believe in his characters at the same time as we understand the most deeply buried aspects of their selves. Although technically more innovative and experimental, Lawrence's novels owe much to the nineteenth century tradition of realism developed by George Eliot, in which a central task of the novelist was to depict the formation and development of an individual character. However, as a novelist who is concerned to represent the innermost thoughts and feelings of his characters, the story or plot line of novels becomes less important than the shifts in feeling and the stream of consciousness of his characters. While probing this deeply into the recesses of his characters' psychology, Lawrence externalizes their relationships with the outside world, particularly the world of nature.

Stream of consciousness is a term used to refer to particular techniques of presentation which a number of Modernist novelists developed. It refers to the flow of impressions, perceptions and thoughts which stream unbidden through our minds. These impressions can be stimulated by something that happens to us or by subconscious impulses; the stream of consciousness can be illogical and random. We can be aware of various impressions in no particular order; past memories may intermingle with present actions or thoughts of the future; saying something to a friend may be quite different from the thoughts or impressions passing through the mind at the same time; sounds, smells, and sights are all registered and may stimulate unpredictable feeling. For many modern novelists, it becomes a central task to find a way of recording this kind of subjective "flow" in the language and form of the novel.

4. Major Works

Sons and Lovers is a closely autobiographical novel set in the Nottinghamshire coal mining village of Bestwood. Walter Morel has married a sensitive and high-minded woman better educated than him. She begins to shrink from his lack of fine feeling and drunkenness. Morel, baffled and thwarted, is sometimes violent, while Mrs. Morel turns all her love towards her four children, particularly her two eldest sons, William and Paul. She struggles to keep herself and her family "respectable" and is determined that her boys will not become miners. William goes to London to work as a clerk, and Paul also gets a job as a clerk with Mr. Jorden, manufacturer of surgical appliances; William develops pneumonia and dies. Mrs. Morel, numbed by despair, is roused only when Paul also falls ill. She nurses him back to health, and subsequently their attachment deepens. Paul is friendly with the Leivers family of Willey Farm, and a tenderness grows between him and the daughter Miriam, a soulful, shy girl. Mrs. Morel fears that Miriam will exclude her and tries to break their relationship, while Paul, sickened at heart by Miriam's romantic love and fear of physical warmth, turns away and becomes involved with Clara Dawes, a married woman, separated from her husband Baxter, and a supporter of Women's Rights. Paul is made an overseer at the factory and he now begins to be noticed as a painter and designer. Clara returns to her husband. Meanwhile Mrs. Morel is ill with cancer. At last, unable to bear her suffering, Paul and his sister Annie put an overdose of morphine in her milk. Paul resists the urge to follow her "into the darkness" and, with a great effort, turns towards life.

Sons and Lovers is the first English novel with a truly working class background. It not only chronicles the domestic conflicts in Lawrence's own home between a coarse, inarticulate father and a self-consciously genteel mother, but also explores the theme of the demanding mother who exercises a strong emotional influence over her son and frustrates his relationships with other women. It is also, like several other novels of the time, a portrait of the birth of an artist.

The Rainbow traces the changes in a family and looks at how individuals come to terms with or rebel against the social and religious codes that govern their lives. In essence, the struggle is between conformity and freedom, which includes a form of sexual freedom. It is also a novel that starts to move on and forward, looking for something new, something to fill the void of modern life. The choice of the metaphoric title—the promise of something new after the destruction of the flood—indicates this, as does the emphasis on a new kind of woman in the figure of Ursula, a woman seeking independence and a life outside marriage.

The novel opens as a family chronicle relating the history of the long-established Brangwen family of March Farm, on the Derbyshire. Tom Brangwen marries the vicar's housekeeper, a Polish widow who already has a daughter, Anna, by her first marriage. Anna marries Will Brangwen, Tom's nephew, a craftsman and draughtsman at a lace factory; they produce a large family, of which the two oldest are Ursula and Gudrun. Ursula becomes the "child of her father's heart", and the interest of the novel gradually shifts to her developing consciousness. When she is about eight, her grandfather is drowned and she grows close to her grandmother Lydia at the March, intrigued by her Polish heritage; she meets Anton, son of a Polish friend of Lydia's and they fall in love, but he, a subaltern, departs for the Boer war. She then matriculates, and resolves to earn her living as a teacher. Will Brangwen is appointed Art and Handwork Instructor for the County of Nottingham, and the whole family move to Beldover. Ursula embarks on a three-year BA course. Anton returns, and they become engaged, and plan to go out to India together, but Ursula breaks away, and Anton abruptly marries his colonel's daughter. The novel ends with Ursula emerging from a spell of illness and suffering to contemplate a rainbow arching symbolically over the ugly industrial landscape.

Women in Love opens with an unanswerable question about marriage and ends with an unanswerable speculation about relationship beyond both the marital and the narrowly heterosexual. It explores a world which is fragmenting from a lack of coherence. The sisters Ursula and Gudrun Brangwen live in Beldover, Midlands colliery town. Ursula has been teaching at the Grammar School and Gudrun has just returned from art school in London. Ursula is in love with Rupert Birkin (a self-portrait of Lawrence), a school inspector involved in an unsatisfactory affair with Hermione Roddice, an eccentric and dominating literary hostess. Gudrun meets Gerald Crich, friend of Birkin and son of the local colliery owner. As a boy Gerald has accidentally killed his brother and now he feels responsible when his sister Diana is drowned. His father, Walter, is dying and he takes over management of the mine. Birkin breaks free from Hermione and hopes to find with Ursula the complete union between man and woman. Gerald suffers in his relationship with Gudrun, his mixture of violence and weakness arousing a destructive demon in her. Birkin offers Gerald love and friendship based on a new intimacy between men, but Gerald is unable to accept it. Ursula and Birkin are married. Both couples take a trip to the Alps where they meet the corrupt sculptor Loerke, the "wizard rat", with whom Gudrun flirts. While Ursula and Birkin move towards a real tenderness, Gudrun and Gerald become purely destructive until finally, in despair, Gerald wanders off into the snow and dies.

Lady Chatterley's Lover was privately printed in Florence in 1928 and was finally published in unexpurgated editions in the United States and England over 30 years later.

The delay was caused by its detailed and poetic descriptions of sexual union, and its uncompromising use of four-letter words. Constance Chatterley is married to Sir Clifford, writer, intellectual, and landowner, of Wragby Hall in the Midlands. He is confined to a wheelchair through injuries from the First World War. She has an unsatisfying affair with a successful playwright, Michaelis, followed by a passionate love relationship with gamekeeper Oliver Mellors. She becomes pregnant by him, goes to Venice with her sister Hilda partly to obscure the baby's parentage, but returns and tells her husband the truth, spurred on by the knowledge that Mellors's estranged wife Bertha has been stirring scandal in an effort to reclaim him. The novel ends with the temporary separation of the lovers, as they hopefully await divorce and a new life together.

8.5.7 James Joyce (1882–1941)

1. Life and Career

Joyce is the greatest novelist of the twentieth century, and has been credited as a pioneering example of the techniques of stream of consciousness. Joyce was born in Dublin, educated in Ireland and spent most of his life in Europe, mainly in France, Italy, and Switzerland. In Europe he was at the center of literary circles but he remained, throughout his life of voluntary exile from Ireland, a deeply Irish writer and he wrote only and always about Dublin. To write about Dublin and its people was for Joyce to write about all human experience. His first published work was a volume of verse, *Chamber Music* (1907), followed by *Dubliners* (1914), a volume of short stories published after great delay and difficulties. Joyce's play *Exiles* was published in 1918 and first performed in London in 1926. *A Portrait of the Artist as a Young Man* was published serially in the magazine *The Egoist*. His famous novel *Ulysses* was received as a work of genius by writers as varied as T. S. Eliot, Hemingway, and Arnold Bennett. This work, together with *Finnegans Wake* (1939), revolutionized the form and structure of the novel, decisively influenced the development of the "stream of consciousness", or "interior monologue", and pushed language and linguistic experiments to the extreme limits of communication.

2. Thought

Joyce's literary origins were in the main continental movements of the late nineteenth century, Naturalism and Symbolism. From the one he took the conviction that literature ought to present, relentlessly and exactly, the minute appearances of things, however banal or distasteful; from the other, the idea that the word and the world are separate and language ultimately offers not a representation of reality but reality itself. In the tradition of Flaubert, Joyce believed that life was one thing and art was another, and that it was the business of the writer to impose form and order on the chaos of raw experience. The theme of many of Joyce's works is the attempts of many of the citizens to free themselves from lives in which they feel paralyzed by relationships, by social, cultural, and religious traditions, or by their own natures.

3. Style

Joyce exploits the technique of stream of consciousness to extremes, often abandoning cohesion, syntax, and punctuation and lexical correctness which previously brought order and clarity to narration. In *Ulysses*, Bloom's stream of consciousness is made up of strange, inconsequential associations. Memories are prompted, unusual ideas connected, playful links created between words of similar sound or meaning. The style is kaleidoscopic and the language often ungrammatical, but rules are broken in order to represent the workings of Bloom's mind. Here is an extract from the famous interior monologue of Molly Bloom, Leopold Bloom's unfaithful wife. It is at the end of the day, and Molly Bloom is lying in bed, half-awake and half-asleep. Molly's monologue lasts for almost fifty pages and is totally without punctuation:

> Whatll I wear shall I wear a white rose or those fairy cakes in Liptons I love the smell of a rich big shop at 71/2d a lb or the other ones with the cherries in them and the pinky sugar lid a couple of lbs of those a nice plant for the middle of the table Id get that cheaper in wait wheres this I saw them not long ago I love flowers Id love to have the whole place swimming in roses God of heaven theres nothing like nature the wild mountains then the sea and the waves rushing...
>
> (*Ulysses*)

The stream of consciousness here is a freer, looser style and captures something of Molly's excited reverie. The lack of punctuation reflects the way in which thoughts and ideas merge into one another.

In the last work *Finnegans Wake*, Joyce's experiments with language are even more innovative and experimental. In the novel, devices of literary realism are replaced by a kind of dream language in which as many associations as possible are forced into words and combinations of words. In many ways, the novel is about language itself. Joyce uses puns and plays on words within and across both English and other languages. He pushes language to the absolute limits of experiment and for most readers the result is a very demanding, sometimes incomprehensible experience:

> Sobs they sighdid at Finnagain's chrissormiss wake, all the hoolivans of the nation, prostrated in their consternation and their duodisirnally profusive plethora of ululation. There was plumbs and grumes and cheriffs and citherers and raiders and cinemen too. Agog and magog and the round of them agrog. To the continuation of that celebration until Hanandhunihan's extermination!
>
> (Finnegans Wake)

The use of language suggests the merging of images in a dream. It enables Joyce to present history and myth in a single image with all the characters of history becoming a few eternal types, finally identified as Earwicker (the hero), his wife, and three children. This corresponds with a cyclical view of history which Joyce developed and in which the events of human life are like a river that flows into the sea from which rain clouds form to feed once again the source of the river. Thus, life is always renewed.

Dubliners is Joyce's collection of short stories. They depict the lives of the ordinary people of the city Dublin, which seemed to Joyce "the center of paralysis". This idea of cultural paralysis is stressed in the opening of the first story, *The Sisters*. There is a reference in the first line to the priest's fatal stroke and later in the first paragraph the narrator repeats the word as he gazes up highly at a window in the priest's house. Throughout the collection Dublin seems trapped by the mundane, the quotidian, and the historic. Its citizens are observed as bound up in private concerns and incapable of properly judging and quantifying their experience. Some are disillusioned, others lose vocations and illusions, and others are graceless. The best known of these stories—*The Dead*—is the final one in the sequence, to which many of the previous stories point. It is a story in which a husband is shocked out of his self-satisfaction and egotism by learning of his wife's love for a young man she had known many years before.

Chapter Eight
The Twentieth-Century Literature (1900–1945)

A Portrait of the Artist as a Young Man, Joyce's first major novel, is semi-autobiographical and tells the story of Stephen Dedalus from the earliest days of his life, showing him growing into adulthood and independence under the powerful influences of Irish national, political, and religious feelings. The novel shows how he gradually frees himself from those influences and decides to become an exile from Ireland and dedicate his life to writing. He also develops a view of the writer as necessarily alienated from the values of society and committed only to artistic values. Like T. S. Eliot in poetry, Stephen (who may represent Joyce's ideas) believes that the true artist has to be objective and not simply to give direct expression to his feelings. He compares the artist to the God of creation who remains within or behind or beyond or above his handiwork, invisible, refined, out of existence, indifferent, paring his fingernails.

Ulysses is the high point of Modernism, bearing the same relationship to the development of the novel as *The Waste Land* does to poetry. The novel deals with the events of one day in Dublin, 16 June, 1904 (the anniversary of Joyce's first walk with his wife). The principal characters are Stephen Dedalus (the hero *of A Portrait of the Artist as a Young Man*); Leopold Bloom, a Jewish advertisement canvasser and his wife Molly. The plot follows the wanderings of Stephen and Bloom through Dublin, and their eventual meeting. The last chapter is a monologue by Molly Bloom. The various chapters roughly correspond to the episodes of Homer's *Odyssey*: Stephen representing Telemachus, Bloom Odysseus, and Molly Penelope. In the course of the story a public bath, a funeral, a newspaper office, a library public house, a maternity hospital, and a brothel are visited. The style is highly allusive and employs a variety of techniques, especially those of the stream of consciousness and of parody and ranges from extreme realism to fantasy.

Finnegans Wake is written in a unique and extremely difficult style, making use of puns and portmanteau words, and a very wide range of illusion. The central theme of the work is a cyclical pattern of fall and resurrection.

This is presented in the story of Humphrey Chimpden Earwicker, a Dublin tavern keeper, and the book is apparently a dream sequence representing the stream of his unconscious mind through the course of one night. Other characters are his wife Anna Livia Plurabelle, their sons Shem and Shaun, and their daughter Isabel. In spite of its obscurity it contains passages of great lyrical beauty, and also much humor.

> **For Your Information**
>
> **Modern Women Novelists**
>
> After the flowering of female novelists such as the Brontë sisters, Elizabeth Gaskell and George Eliot in the nineteenth century, there was a flourishing of writing by women in the early years of the twentieth century when such very important figures as Virginia Woolf, Dorothy Richardson, May Sinclair, and Katherine Mansfield were writing.

8.5.8 Virginia Woolf (1882–1941)

Virginia Woolf is the most influential and probably the most widely studied woman writer and one of the most influential of all writers in the twentieth century. She was born into a large, talented, upper class, intellectual family in London. Her father, Leslie Stephen, was a famous Victorian biographer, critic, and philosopher. After her father's death, she and her sister and brothers moved to Bloomsbury where they formed the nucleus of the Bloomsbury group—an artistic and literary group renowned for their rebellion against Victorian Puritanism and which had great influence on British culture from 1920 to the 1940s. Mental illness affected Virginia Woolf throughout her life. In 1941, at a time of deep personal depression with the Second World War, and deeply dissatisfied with her own writing, she committed suicide.

Virginia Woolf's first novels were relatively traditional in form, but she later rebelled against what she called the "materialism" of novelists such as H. G. Wells, Arnold Bennett and John Galsworthy. Her characteristic method appears in her third novel, *Jacob's Room*, published in 1922, in which she renders the flow of experience through a stream of consciousness technique, but her work is also particularly characterized by an intensely poetic style. She utilizes poetic rhythms and imagery to create a lyrical impressionism in order to capture her characters' moods with great delicacy and detail. The novel shows her breaking free from traditional forms and has established her as a leading modernist writer, which is evident in her most famous works, *Mrs. Dalloway* (1925), *To the Lighthouse* (1927) and *The Waves* (1931).

Virginia Woolf was also a highly influential journalist and critic. In *A Room of One's*

Own (1928), she gives a unique account of why a woman must have money and a room of her own in order to write fiction. It has become a classic statement of feminism. Here lies Woolf's unique importance. Woolf has recognized that the traditional myths and structures have excluded women both from society and from writing in their own voice. Her works, both her novels and essays, demand to be recognized as constituting a highly significant feminist critique of the exclusion of women from economic independence and education.

Mrs. Dalloway is not only Woolf's most complete, but ambiguous, representation of the life of a woman character's mind, but also her most thorough experiment with the problem of an identity which is both multiple and singular, both public and private, and it gradually insists on the mutual dependence.

The action of the novel is restricted to the events of one day in central London, punctuated by the chimes of Big Ben; it opens on a June morning in Westminster as Clarissa Dalloway, wife of Richard Dalloway MP, sets off to buy flowers for her party that evening, the party which provides the culmination and ending of the book. Her interior monologue, interwoven with the sights and sounds of the urban scene, is handled with a technical confidence and bravura that herald a new phase in Woolf's mastery of the novel. Clarissa herself is captured in her many shifting moods and recollections, and contrasted with and seen through the eyes of many other characters. Her day is also contrasted with that of the shell-shocked Septimus Waren Smith, who hears the sparrows sing in Greek in Regent's Park, and who at the end of the day commits suicide by hurling himself from a window; news of his death intrudes upon Clarissa's party, brought by the Harley Street doctor whom he uselessly consults. Woolf insisted upon the mutual dependence of these two characters.

To the Lighthouse dispenses with plots and instead is organized around the symbols of the lighthouse and the painting. Like other modernist texts, it is much concerned with the nature of art and artistic creation, exemplified by the painter Lily Briscoe, whose art is clearly meant to be a metaphor for Virginia Woolf's own.

The novel is in three sections. The first, *The Window*, describes a summer holiday, with the Ramsays on holiday with their eight children and assorted guests, who include the plump and lethargic elderly poet Augustus Carmichael; the painter Lily Briscoe and the graceless lower-middle-class academic Charles Tansley. Family tension centers on the desire of the youngest child, James, to visit the lighthouse, and his father's apparent desire to thwart him.

The second section, *Time Passes*, records with laconic brevity the death of Mrs. Ramsay and of her son Andrew, killed in the war, and dwells with a desolate lyricism on the abandoning of the family home, and its gradual post-war reawakening; it ends with the arrival of Lily Briscoe and Mr. Carmichael. The last section, *The Lighthouse*, describes the exhausting but finally successful effort of Lily, through her painting, to recapture the revelation of shape-in-chaos which she owes to the vanished Mrs. Ramsay, and the parallel efforts of Mr. Ramsay, Camilla, and James to reach the lighthouse, which they also accomplish.

The Waves is regarded by many as Virginia Woolf's masterpiece. It traces the lives of a group of friends (Bernard, Susan, Rhoda, Neville, Jinny, and Louis) from childhood to late middle age, evoking their personalities through their reflections on themselves and one another. Their individuality is presented through a highly patterned sequence of recurring phrases and images, and what we learn of their daily lives (that Susan marries a farmer, that Bernard's ambitions as a writer are disappointed, and that Louis becomes a man of power and wealth). The main text is introduced and divided by sections of lyrical prose describing the rising and sinking of the sun over a seascape of waves and shore. There is one additional character, Percival: His death in India, halfway through the novel, becomes the focus for fears and defiance of death and mortality. One of the dominant images of the novel, used by phrasemaker Bernard, is that of a fin breaking from the water; this was, as Woolf's diary reveals, her starting-point for the work.

8.5.9 Dorothy Richardson (1872–1957)

Dorothy Richardson, as one of the leading women novelists in the twentieth century, has much in common with Virginia Woolf. They both explore the subjective experience of their heroines. It is more than coincidence that both use stream of consciousness in works that place women at their center. Both are concerned with the intricacies of personal relationships and how these can be rendered more truthfully in prose fiction, but more importantly, both are concerned with the position of women, their rights and their place in political and social life, and their complex identities.

Dorothy Richardson's masterpiece is *Pilgrimage*, a sequence of 13 novels published between 1913 and 1915. The novel explores her characters' psychology and motivations in a way that echoes Woolf, but with a more rigorous attention to detail. Richardson lately insisted that each volume was effectively only a chapter of the whole and that *Pilgrimage*

Chapter Eight
The Twentieth-Century Literature (1900–1945)

should be read as a single sequence. Her originality lay not merely in the shape and scope of her huge undertaking but in her determination to forge a technique expressive of an explicitly female consciousness, a style which stood in antithesis both to a received "masculine" tradition and to new male-dominated experiments in literature. She insisted that feminine prose should properly be unpunctuated, moving from point to point without formal obstructions. Her sentences are unanchored either by strict syntax or by formal reference to an exterior world. They fragment, drift, dissolve, and form themselves into new, ambiguous, and suggestive shapes. They allow for a representation of free association, for open-endedness, and for a perpetually varied interaction of the liberating inner consciousness (which Richardson particularly associated with the female) with an external world (whose control she saw as traditionally male). The eschewal of "formal obstructions" in both her style and her overall structures has, however, often rendered her an unapproachable, demanding, and difficult writer.

8.5.10 May Sinclair (1863–1946)

May Sinclair's use of stream of consciousness is more accessible than Dorothy Richardson's. She uses it to particularly good effect in her novels *Mary Olivior: A Life* (1919) and *The Life and Death of Harriet Trean* (1922), which chart the growth of a heroine from girlhood to unmarried middle age. May Sinclair had achieved great renown with the novel *The Divine Fire* (1904), and was a prominent figure in the literary life of her times, being a friend and associate of such diverse figures as Ezra Pound and Thomas Hardy. Seen as a Modernist, she was a keen supporter of women's suffrage, and was deeply interested in the psychoanalytical works of Freud and Jung; both the political and the psychological concerns are clear in her twenty-four novels. *The Three Sisters* (1914) echoes the lives of the Brontë sisters in its recounting of frustration and creativity. May Sinclair's work anticipates many of the trends of women's writing in the second half of the twentieth century, especially Doris Lessing's novels of psychological growth and Anota Brookner's novels exploring the lives of unmarried women.

8.5.11 Katherine Mansfield (1888–1923)

Katherine Mansfield, originally from New Zealand, is often associated with Virginia Woolf, although they were not particularly close, and their writing is very different. Mansfield is one of the greatest modern short story writers, catching in a scene, a glimpse, or a description of a day, as in *The Garden Party*, the essence of a relationship, the underlying sadness and solitude of the post-war era. Her earliest stories date from before the First World War (*In a German Pension*, 1911), but she preferred her later works, such as *Prelude* (1918). Mansfield died young, of tuberculosis, and her husband, the critic John Middleton Murry, built up her reputation as something of a tragic doomed young genius, publishing her stories, letters and journals after her death. Her best work appeared in *Bliss and Other Stories* (1920) and *The Garden Party and Other Stories* (1922). Her distinguishing feature is brevity, shot through with tragic humor. Mansfield's stories are impressionistic, witty, and, despite being very clearly set in her own times, they transcend their period and their social setting and provide an accessible, vivid introduction to several of the modes of modern writing. Many of her stories suggest the way in which Europe assumes increasing importance in almost every aspect of life in the early decades of the twentieth century: a wider world has displaced the old sense of domestic security and the insular convictions of English life. There is, consequently, something profoundly symbolic about a story such as *The Daughters of the Late Colonel* (1922), where two daughters watch their father die. On the surface, it seems slight enough, the story of a man dying, but the details imply that the old order is dying. The death of the colonel signals the death of a whole way of life which, looked back upon, now seems absurd in all its gestures and pomposity.

For Your Information

Novelists of the 1930s

The 1930s was a highly political decade. The General Strike of 1926 and the ensuing Great Depression resulted in a temporary loss of confidence. In 1933 Hitler was appointed Chancellor of Germany, and 1936 saw the outbreak of the Spanish Civil War. In 1938, the year of the Munich crisis, the British Prime Minister Neville Chamberlain agreed to Hitler's territorial demands on Czechoslovakia, but in 1939, following the German invasion of Poland, Britain declared war on Germany.

It is against this background of political, social and economic unrest that appeared such significant names W. H. Auden, Evelyn Waugh, Noel Coward, Henry Green, Aldous Huxley, George Orwell, and Christopher Isherwood. The decade also saw the publication of early poems by Dylan Thomas, the debut of Samuel Beckett,

Chapter Eight
The Twentieth-Century Literature (1900–1945)

> with *Murphy* (1938), and important works by Elizabeth Bowen, with *The Death of the Heart* (1938), and Graham Greene, with *Brighton Rock* (1938). Many of these authors are still known and widely read today, but it is noteworthy that the decade produced no writer, with the possible exception of Auden, of the reputation of Eliot, Joyce. A point that some critics would also make is that the new authors of this decade seem to have retreated from the kind of innovations that is associated with Modernism. Writing from this period tends, therefore, to be an attempt to engage with contemporary political tensions, rather than amounting to a fundamental reconsideration of the nature of writing.

8.5.12 Aldous Huxley (1894–1963)

Aldous Huxley was the grandson of T. H. Huxley, an eminent Victorian philosopher and writer who championed the ideas of Charles Darwin. In the 1920s, Aldous Huxley published a number of novels which satirized contemporary society. Among the best-known of them are *Crome Yellow* (1921), and *Antic Hay* (1923), which have many similarities with T. S. Eliot's *The Waste Land*, and *Point Counter Point* (1928). Huxley's best-known novel is *Brave New World*. The title is an ironic quotation from Shakespeare's *The Tempest*: "O brave new world, that has such people in it" —innocent and sincere words given to Miranda and used without irony. *Brave New World* is often compared with George Orwell's dystopia in *Nineteen Eighty-four*. The novel provides a prophecy of a world of test-tube babies, genetic engineering, and social control. It is a book which captures the particularly negative and destructive elements of the times. It is a fable about a world state in the seventh century, where social stability is based on a scientific caste system. Human beings, graded from highest intellectuals to lowest manual workers, hatched from incubators and brought up in communal nurseries, learn by methodical conditioning to accept their social destiny. The action of the story develops round Bernard Marx, an unorthodox and therefore unhappy Alpha-Plus (something had presumably gone wrong with his antenatal treatment), who visits a New Mexican Reservation and brings a Savage back to London. The Savage is at first fascinated by the new world, but finally revolts, and his argument with Mustapha Mond, World Controller, demonstrates the incompatibility of individual freedom and a scientifically trouble-free society.

Aldous Huxley became disillusioned with war in Europe and moved to California, where he became preoccupied with the kinds of visionary experience which hallucinogenic drugs can produce. *The Door of Perception* (1954) and *Heaven and Hell* (1956)—both titles that suggest links with the visionary Romantic poet William Blake—record these experiences. In 1962, Huxley wrote the novel *Island*, which appears to describe a society which is a genuine utopia—the opposite of *Brave New World*—where a good and optimistic life exists. This world is, however, eventually destroyed by a brutal and materialistic dictator, not only echoing the political threats of the 1920s and 1930s but also reflecting the terror of a post-war world which now possessed nuclear weapon.

8.5.13 Evelyn Waugh (1903–1966)

Evelyn Waugh's career as a novelist spanned the central years of the twentieth century—from the Jazz Age to the 1960s. Waugh's work may be divided into two periods: In the first period he wrote brilliant satires on the lives of the wealthy upper classes; in the second period he explores the place of Catholicism in the modern world with deep seriousness while always retaining a satirical eye for human absurdity. His best-known earlier novels are *Decline and Fall* (1928), *Vile Bodies* (1930), and *A Handful of Dust* (1934). *Decline and Fall* depicts the innocent adventures of a young man, Paul Pennyfeather, who becomes a schoolteacher in a seedy school in North Wales. The novel satirizes public school life (Paul's fellow teachers are either petty criminals or mad) by showing how the characters of the ruling classes are formed.

In *Vile Bodies* the emptiness and lack of values in the lives of the "bright young things"—the younger generation in the inter-war years—are cruelly exposed. *A Handful of Dust* is the story of the breakup of a marriage against the background of the dissolution of an ancient country estate. A contrast is established between a cynical and frivolous modern world and the gradual disappearance of a world of order and stability associated with an aristocratic past. Unlike Jane Austen or Henry Fielding, however, Waugh does not normally use irony and satire to judge or offer solutions, but presents the world as black comedy.

In the Second World War, Evelyn Waugh served in the Royal Marines and this provided him with material for a satirical trilogy about the English at war: *Men at Arms* (1952),

Officers and Gentlemen (1955), and *Unconditional Surrender* (1961), published together as *Sword of Honour* in 1965. In this trilogy, considered by some critics to be the best English fiction about the Second World War, the hero, Guy Crouchback, always tries to do his moral best but ends up doing something foolish or inconsequential. The publication of *Brideshead Revisited* (1945) had introduced a more sustained note of seriousness into Waugh's work. It is a novel about a fascinating but decadent aristocratic family and the powerful influence on them of the Roman Catholic faith. The house of Brideshead, similar to *Howard End* in the novel of the same name by E. M. Forster, represents a part of English society—the aristocracy—which was disappearing from the post-war world. Waugh is widely recognized as the preeminent novelist who charted that decline and fall.

8.5.14 Henry Green (1905–1973)

Henry Green, the pseudonym of Henry Vincent Yorke, was the son of a wealthy Birmingham industrialist. He, like his contemporary Ivy Compton-Burnett, is renowned for his dialogue. His most impressive achievement remains in the neutral study of the commonplaces of Birmingham factory life in *Living* (1929), for which he evolved a startlingly abbreviated narrative style, a style which eliminates definite articles and adjectives, which experiments with verbless sentences, and which allows for the flatness of much colloquial discourse. There is nothing exotic about *Living*. As Dupret, the son of the factory owner, walks through the artisan streets, he remarks on their air of "terrible respectability on too little money" and on a way of life that consists for all classes of the monotonies of being born, of going to school, of working, of being married, of bearing children, and of dying. *Living* was praised in its time for its evocation of the rhythms, repetitions, and deprivations of industrial life.

Many of Green's novels have one-word titles such as *Caught* (1943), *Loving* (1945), and *Nothing* (1950), which takes his colloquial, ungrammatical style to new heights, being written almost entirely in dialogue form. *Party Going* (1939), in which a group of rich young people are delayed at a railway station by fog, has been read as a highly symbolic examination of the decline of the class system. His style has been described as combining the upper class with the demotic, which is an accurate reflection of his concerns. In many ways, Green's novels mark the transition between the novel of upper-and-middle-class concerns and the working-class novels of the 1950s.

8.5.15 Graham Greene (1904–1991)

Graham Greene was a convert to Catholicism and in much of his work he explores problems of good and evil and the moral dilemmas these entail. In several of his novels, characters who are failures in life are shown to be closer to God as a result: Indeed, salvation in Greene's world can sometimes only be achieved through sin.

Greene's career before the Second World War culminates in *Brighton Rock*. For some critics, this remains his best novel, and it continues to be one of the most popular. It brings together the detective thriller genre, religious concerns and illusions to the post-Waste Land world. Greene's Catholicism is important in his portrayal of Pinkie, the young amoral "hero", who is one of the major anti-heroes of modern literature. He can be read as a personification of evil, a modern devil: Catholic belief in God implies belief in the Devil, and in many of his works Greene will examine the continuing presence of evil and corruption. In *Brighton Rock*, Pinkie's pleasure in killing and tormenting his victims, especially his girlfriend Rose, takes the reader into a new perception of unredeemed evil.

Graham Greene's most serious novels are *The Power and the Glory* (1940), *The Heart of the Matter* (1948), *The Quiet American* (1955) and *A Burnt out Case* (1961). Greene initially appeared to regard several of his novels as less serious, since he referred to them as "entertainments". In these novels he uses the popular conventions of the thriller or the spy story. These books include *The Confidential Agent* (1939), *The Third Man* (1950) and *Our Man in Havana* (1958). Throughout all his fiction he remained fascinated by people who are capable or incapable of judging between good and evil. His novels are carefully constructed, with powerful plots and a strong sense of place. As a whole, Greene's preoccupations with moral dilemma, his attempts to distinguish "good-or-evil" from "right-or-wrong", and his persistent choice of "seedy" locations give his work a highly distinctive and recognizable quality.

8.5.16 Christopher Isherwood (1904–1985)

Christopher Isherwood, a friend and collaborator with W. H. Auden, is best known for his Berlin novels *Mr. Norris Changes Trains* (1935) and *Goodbye to Berlin* (1939), the latter based on the author's own experience during the Nazi rise to power in Germany. Its narrator says "I am a camera" and proceeds to tell his stories with the kind of distanced objectivity a camera can lend. These novels remain valuable impressions of Germany at a crucial time in its history, and the lack of emotional involvement in the author's style takes on a highly ambiguous and chilling note as the 1930s moved rapidly towards the Second World War.

Besides the Berlin novels, Isherwood's first two stories are equally worthy of attention. *All the Conspirators* (1928) is patently the work of a very young man. Its subject is the futile revolt of brother and sister against a strong-willed bourgeois mother. *The Memorial* (1932) is a more ambitious study of a family disintegrating in the aftermath of the First World War. Isherwood's best late work is *A Single Man* (1964), the story of a day in the life of an aging homosexual grieving for his dead partner.

8.5.17 George Orwell (1903–1950)

George Orwell, whose real name was Eric Blair, came to prominence in the 1930s, commenting incisively on the social and political world of his day. He was born in Bengal and educated in England. He served with the Indian Imperial Police in Burma from 1922 to 1927, and his experiences are reflected in his first novel *Burmese Days* (1934). He returned to Europe, where he worked in Paris and London in a series of ill-paid jobs, reflected in *Down and Out in Paris and London* (1933). His novels include *A Clergyman's Daughter* (1935) and *Keep the Aspidistra Flying* (1936), which recount the literary aspirations, financial humiliations, and shotgun wedding of Gordon Comstock, bookseller's assistant. *The Road to Wigan Pier* (1937) is an impassioned documentary of unemployment and proletarian life. The Spanish Civil War produced *Homage to Catalonia* (1938). The threat of the coming war hung over his next novel, *Coming up for Air* (1939). By this stage Orwell saw himself primarily as a political writer, a democratic socialist who avoided party labels, and hated totalitarianism. His plain, colloquial style made him highly effective as a pamphleteer and journalist. His collections of essays include *Inside the Whale* (1940), *Critical Essays* (1946), and *Shooting an Elephant* (1950). But his most popular works are undoubtedly his political satires *Animal Farm* (1945) and *Nineteen Eighty-four*.

8.6 Reading

The Second Coming[1]

By W. B. Yeats

TURNING and turning in the widening gyre[2]

The falcon cannot hear the falconer[3]

Things fall apart; the center cannot hold;

Mere anarchy is loosed upon the world,

The blood-dimmed tide[4] is loosed, and everywhere

The ceremony[5] of innocence is drowned;

The best lack all conviction, while the worst

Are full of passionate intensity[6]

Surely some revelation is at hand;

Surely the Second Coming is at hand.

The Second Coming! Hardly are those words out

When a vast image out of *Spiritus Mundi*[7]

Troubles my sight: somewhere in sands of the desert

A shape with lion body and the head of a man,

A gaze blank and pitiless as the sun,

Is moving its slow thighs, while all about it

Reel shadows of the indignant desert birds.

The darkness drops again; but now I know

That twenty centuries[8] of stony sleep

Were vexed to nightmare by a rocking cradle[9],

And what rough beast, its hour come round at last,

Slouches towards Bethlehem[10] to be born?

Notes

1. The title is taken from Christian doctrine meaning the arrival of a new God. It blends Christ's prediction of this Second Coming and St. John's description of the beast of Apocalypse in *Revelation*. Yeats's combination of these two events vividly presents the potential crisis of Europe. The coming of the new era is not the peaceful world brought by Christ but a warring world brought by Apocalypse.

2. **widening gyre:** Gyre is an important symbol often used by Yeats to indicate the journey of life and history. Life and history start from a center. As time goes by, the circling is

Chapter Eight
The Twentieth-Century Literature (1900–1945)

spreading. When this outward movement is too powerful to be controlled by the center, everything is in confusion and the world and life are about to collapse. The declining of an old world and life foretells a new world and life starting from the center again. The widening gyre indicates the ending of an old world.

3. **The falcon cannot hear the falconer:** The hovering of the falcon is so far that the falcon is beyond the control of his master.

4. **blood-dimmed tide:** It perhaps refers to the First World War as well as the troubles in England.

5. **ceremony:** order.

6. **full of passionate intensity:** crazy.

7. ***Spiritus Mundi*:** the Spirit or Soul of the Universe, with which all individual souls are connected through the "Great Memory", which Yeats held to be universal subconsciousness in which the human race preserves its past memories.

8. **twenty centuries:** Yeats regards the Christian era as being of twenty thousand years.

9. **rocking cradle:** the cradle of the infant Christ.

10. **Bethlehem:** the birthplace of Christ.

Sons and Lovers
Chapter IV: The young Life of Raul

By D. H. Lawrence

...

All the children, but particularly Paul, were peculiarly against their father, along with their mother. Morel continued to bully and to drink. He had periods, months at a time, when he made the whole life of the family a misery. Paul never forgot coming home from the Band of Hope[1] one Monday evening and finding his mother with her eye swollen and discoloured, his father standing on the hearthrug, feet astride, his head down, and William, just home from work, glaring at his father. There was a silence as the young children entered, but none of the elders looked round.

William was white to the lips, and his fists were clenched. He waited until the children were silent, watching with children's rage and hate; then he said:

"You coward, you daren't do it when I was in."

But Morel's blood was up. He swung round on his son. William was bigger, but Morel was hard-muscled, and mad with fury.

"Dossn't I?" he shouted. "Dossn't I? Ha'e much more o'thychelp, my young jockey, an' I'll rattle my fist about thee. Ay, an' I sholl that, dost see?"

Morel crouched at the knees and showed his fist in an ugly, almost beast-like fashion. William was white with rage.

"Will yer?" he said, quiet and intense. "It'ud be the last time,though."

Morel danced a little nearer, crouching, drawing back his fist to strike. William put his fists ready. A light came into his blue eyes, almost like a laugh. He watched his father. Another word, and the men would have begun to fight. Paul hoped they would. The three children sat pale on the sofa.

"Stop it, both of you," cried Mrs. Morel in a hard voice. "We've had enough for ONE night. And YOU," she said, turning on to her husband, "look at your children!"

Morel glanced at the sofa.

"Look at the children, you nasty little bitch!" he sneered. "Why, what have I done to the children, I should like to know? But they're like yourself; you've put'em up to your own tricks and nasty ways—you've learned'em in it,you'ave."

She refused to answer him. No one spoke. After a while he threw his boots under the table and went to bed.

"Why didn't you let me have a go at him[2]?" said William, when his father was upstairs. "I could easily have beaten him."

"A nice thing—your own father," she replied.

"FATHER!" repeated William. "Call HIM MY father!"

"Well, he is—and so—"

"But why don't you let me settle him[3]? I could do, easily."

"The idea!" she cried. "It hasn't come to THAT yet."

"No," he said, "it's come to worse. Look at yourself. WHY didn't you let me give it him[4]?"

"Because I couldn't bear it, so never think of it," she cried quickly.

Chapter Eight
The Twentieth-Century Literature (1900–1945)

And the children went to bed, miserably.

When William was growing up, the family moved from the Bottoms[5] to a house on the brow of the hill, commanding a view of the valley, which spread out like a convex cockle-shell, or a clamp-shell, before it. In front of the house was a huge old ash-tree. The west wind, sweeping from Derbyshire, caught the houses with full force, and the tree shrieked again. Morel liked it.

"It's music," he said. "It sends me to sleep."

But Paul and Arthur and Annie hated it. To Paul it became almost a demoniacal noise. The winter of their first year in the new house their father was very bad. The children played in the street, on the brim of the wide, dark valley, until eight o'clock. Then they went to bed. Their mother sat sewing below. Having such a great space in front of the house gave the children a feeling of night, of vastness, and of terror. This terror came in from the shrieking of the tree and the anguish of the home discord. Often Paul would wake up, after he had been asleep a long time, aware of thuds downstairs. Instantly he was wide awake. Then he heard the booming shouts of his father, come home nearly drunk, then the sharp replies of his mother, then the bang, bang of his father's fist on the table, and the nasty snarling shout as the man's voice got higher. And then the whole was drowned in a piercing medley of shrieks and cries from the great, wind-swept ash-tree. The children lay silent in suspense, waiting for a lull in the wind to hear what their father was doing. He might hit their mother again.

There was a feeling of horror, a kind of bristling in the darkness, and a sense of blood. They lay with their hearts in the grip of an intense anguish. The wind came through the tree fiercer and fiercer. All the chords of the great harp hummed, whistled, and shrieked. And then came the horror of the sudden silence, silence everywhere, outside and downstairs. What was it? Was it a silence of blood? What had he done?

The children lay and breathed the darkness. And then, at last, they heard their father throw down his boots and tramp upstairs in his stockinged feet. Still they listened. Then at last, if the wind allowed, they heard the water of the tap drumming into the kettle, which their mother was filling for morning, and they could go to sleep in peace.

So they were happy in the morning—happy, very happy playing, dancing at night round the lonely lamp-post in the midst of the darkness. But they had one tight place of anxiety in their hearts, one darkness in their eyes, which showed all their lives[6].

Notes

1. **the Band of Hope:** an association of children for alcohol prohibition.

2. **have a go at him:** give him a sound beating.

3. **settle him:** give him a good lesson and make him behave himself.

4. **give it him:** give him a lesson.

5. **the Bottoms:** an area where coal miners live.

6. **which showed all their lives:** which affected them all their lives.

Mrs. Dalloway
Chapter 1 (Excerpt)

By Virginia Woolf

Mrs. Dalloway said she would buy the flowers herself.

For Lucy[1] had her work cut out for her. The doors would be taken off their hinges; Rumpelmayer's men were coming. And then, thought Clarissa Dalloway, what a morning—fresh as if issued to children on a beach.

What a lark! What a plunge! For so it had always seemed to her, when, with a little squeak of the hinges, which she could hear now, she had burst open the French windows[2] and plunged at Bourton into the open air. How fresh, how calm, stiller than this of course, the air was in the early morning; like the flap of a wave; the kiss of a wave; chill and sharp and yet (for a girl of eighteen as she then was) solemn, feeling as she did, standing there at the open window, that something awful was about to happen; looking at the flowers, at the trees with the smoke winding off them and the rooks rising, falling; standing and looking until Peter Walsh said, "Musing among the vegetables?"—was that it?—"I prefer men to cauliflowers"—was that it? He must have said it at breakfast one morning when she had gone out on to the terrace—Peter Walsh. He would be back from India one of these days, June or July, she forgot

Chapter Eight
The Twentieth-Century Literature (1900–1945)

which, for his letters were awfully dull; it was his sayings one remembered; his eyes, his pocket-knife, his smile, his grumpiness and, when millions of things had utterly vanished—how strange it was!—a few sayings like this about cabbages.

She stiffened a little on the kerb, waiting for Durtnall's van to pass. A charming woman, Scrope Purvis thought her (knowing her as one does know people who live next door to one in Westminster); a touch of the bird about her, of the jay[3], blue-green, light, vivacious, though she was over fifty, and grown very white since her illness. There she perched, never seeing him, waiting to cross, very upright.

For having lived in Westminster—how many years now? over twenty,—one feels even in the midst of the traffic, or waking at night, Clarissa was positive, a particular hush, or solemnity; an indescribable pause; a suspense (but that might be her heart, affected, they said, by influenza) before Big Ben strikes. There! Out it boomed. First a warning, musical; then the hour, irrevocable. The leaden circles dissolved in the air. Such fools we are, she thought, crossing Victoria Street. For Heaven only knows why one loves it so, how one sees it so, making it up, building it round one, tumbling it, creating it every moment afresh; but the veriest frumps, the most dejected of miseries sitting on doorsteps (drink their downfall) do the same; can't be dealt with, she felt positive, by Acts of Parliament for that very reason: They love life. In people's eyes, in the swing, tramp, and trudge; in the bellow and the uproar; the carriages, motor cars, omnibuses, vans, sandwich men shuffling and swinging; brass bands; barrel organs; in the triumph and the jingle and the strange high singing of some aeroplane overhead was what she loved; life; London; this moment of June.

Notes

1. **Lucy:** maid of the Dalloways.

2. **French windows:** a pair of casement windows extending to floor level and opening onto a balcony, garden.

3. **jay:** a bird of the crow family, with bright feathers and a noisy call.

Chapter Nine
English Literature (Since 1945)

9.1 Historical Background

The Second World War involved Britain and the British Empire and Commonwealth, France, America, Russia and China (the Allied powers) fighting Germany, Italy and Japan (the Axis powers). By the end of the war, the world had moved into the Atomic age with the dropping of bombs on Hiroshima and Nagasaki in 1945. With the atomic bomb, the world was a knife-edge: The world might end at any moment. This threat hung over the world until the end of the so-called cold war in the late 1980s.

The war accelerated the break-up of the British Empire, and financial and political leadership of the world now moved decisively to the United States. Great Britain had to reassess its place in the world. The wartime Prime Minister, Winston Churchill, after the labour government was elected in 1945, devoted much of his time to writing a six-volume history of *The Second World War* (1945–1954) and *A History of the English-Speaking Peoples* (1956–1958). He won the Nobel Prize for Literature in 1953.

The years since the end of the war have seen a decline in British influence and continuing failure to compete successfully with the newly developing economies of the world. Throughout the fifties, sixties and seventies, with the British economy continuing to decline, the country had to adjust to a sense of national decline and loss of national self-confidence; as sometimes happens, a sense of weakness can find expression in belligerence, lack of manners and aggression.

The last twenty years of the twentieth century—the years of Thatcher, Major and Blair governments—saw attempts to tackle some of Britain's fundamental problems. Two main stances could be identified in Britain politics in the last years of the century, both of which prioritized business; one group of politicians argued that the economy mattered, and that the benefits of greater prosperity would work their way down through society, while the other group maintained that economic prosperity could be the bedrock on which the government could gradually improve public services. The economic changes within Britain as a result of these policies, accompanied by a sustained boom in the world economy, meant that by the end of the twentieth century many people enjoyed a standard of living that they could never envisage twenty years earlier.

Yet at the same time, a feeling persisted that there was something fundamentally wrong in Britain. It was clear that the health and education services were far from satisfactory. Poverty in some areas of the country was as bad as ever. And people were worried about levels of crime and social discipline. These are, of course, concerns that are felt in all countries, but in Britain there was possibly the added feeling that the country had lost a sense of where it was heading; indeed, whether it was heading anywhere at all. The sense of the kind of mood of the nation is reflected in novels, poems and dramas of the time.

9.2 Literary Features

After the Second World War, the changes in society—in ways of thought and in literature—were every bit as deep and far-reaching as they were after the First World War. The sense of fragmentation developed into a sense of absurdity, of existential futility, which echoes and goes beyond the kind of futility expressed in the poems of Wilfred Owen. There was a veritable explosion of expression around the question of the atomic bomb, around the possibility that all life could end at a moment's notice.

For the novelist A. S. Byatt, there is, throughout this time, a new richness and diversity in English writing, a continuing of the search for a post-Darwinian security in creativity: A wonderful mix of realism, romance, fable, satire, parody, play with form and philosophical intelligence. Byatt notes an almost obsessive recurrence of Darwin in modern fiction. Where nineteenth-century writers—novelists in particular—wrote about the ending of certainty, especially religious certainty, late twentieth-century writers largely concerned themselves with (according to Byatt) what it means to be a naked animal, evolved over unimaginable centuries, with a history constructed by beliefs which have lost their power. This is much of the Modern or post-Modern perception of the world present.

Where "Modern" was a keyword for the first part of the twentieth century, the term "post-Modern" has been widely used to describe the attitudes and creative production which followed the Second World War. Post-Modernism almost defies definition. Rather, it celebrates diversity, eclecticism, and parody in all forms of art, from architecture to cinema, from music to literature. All the forms which represent experience are mediated, transformed, and the "truth" of experience thus becomes even more varied than it has ever been before.

The mix of "post-Darwin" and post-Modern is indicative of the binary linking of traditional and new elements in literature: The subject matter is still, essentially, the human condition, but the means and methods of exploring it are infinitely richer and more varied than ever before. There are no more heroes, as there might have been in the time of Beowulf. There is the individual: solitary, responsible for his or her own destiny, yet powerful when set against the ineluctable forces of the universe. This is one of the basic conflicts of the post-Modern condition, and one which gives rise to the immense variety of explorations of recent writings in English. Identity is a common theme: sexual identity, local identity, national identity, racial identity, spiritual identity, and intellectual identity. All of these, and more, recur.

It is almost impossible to classify post-Modern authors in terms of their lasting contribution to the literature of their time. A few figures have attained critical impregnability: Samuel Becket, John Osborne, Herald Pinter would seem to have a secure place among the major dramatists of the late twentieth century; Seamus Heaney's winning the Nobel Prize for Literature in 1995 assures his place in Irish poetry after Yeats. In the novel, it is much more problematic. For every exploration of history or myth, there will be forward-looking exploration of future novels in science fiction or a near-documentary examination of life in the streets today. Past, present and future coexist in literature today as never before.

It is an ongoing concern with humanity that keeps literature alive. The twenty-first century will no doubt see new treads, new forms of expression, a new literature to set beside the continuing story that began more than thirteen centuries ago.

9.3 Drama

The theater was dominated until the 1950s by well-made plays in standard English for middle-class audiences. However, the language of drama in the twentieth century underwent significant changes. From Oscar Wilde in the 1890s to Noël Coward from the 1920s to 1940s, it was consistently elevated and stylish, the formal elaborate speech modes matching the high social status of many of the characters. Shaw, Lawrence, Synge, and O'Casey

Chapter Nine
English Literature (Since 1945)

brought in dialect and lower-class accents and helped the transition to a more working-class voice which emerged in post-Second World War drama. The plays of Beckett, Osborne, Pinter, or Orton in the 1950s and 1960s are more colloquial and slangy, in keeping with the setting and the characters: tramps, gangsters, newspaper vendors and unemployed youth. Their language is more naturalistic and shows gaps, repetitions, silences, and incoherencies, modeled on normal conversation.

Modern dramatists since 1945 have turned their back on the dramatic tradition, and sought more radical forms appropriate for the chaotic period after the Second World War. A reaction set in the 1950s, when the "angry young man" appeared, most significantly in the figure Jimmy Porter in *Look Back in Anger* (1957) by John Osborne. Another dramatic response to the chaotic experience is the Theater of the Absurd, with Beckett's *Waiting for Godot* (1952) as its most representative. Beckett is the central figure in post-war drama. Around him are dramatists such as Pinter, Stoppard and a great many other well-known contemporary figures: John Arden, Arnold Wesker, Alan Ayckbourn, Edward Bond, David Hare, Trevor Griffiths, Howard Brenton, et al.

Many contemporary plays are, in fact, overtly political in intent and aimed at subverting their audience's comfortable illusions. Often they are deliberately shocking in their violence: In Bond's *Saved* (1965), a baby is stoned and punched to death; in Brebton's *The Romans in Britain* (1980), one male character rapes another. Informing of such plays is the idea that we live in an irrational anarchic world without any form of order or values.

In feminist theater, however, there has been a different response to the dilemma of modern life, a response no less political than that of Bond or Brenton, but interrogative of other issues. Feminist theater really began with the American dramatist Megan Terry in the 1960s. From then on, there has been a rapid increase in the number of feminist dramatists, including such central figures as Caryl Churchill, Pam Gems and Michelene Wandor, and acting and production companies such as the Women's Theater Group. The endeavor of both writers and actors has been to show how the achievements of women have been suppressed by history and society, and also to show how women have been made subordinate to men. The plays set out to make the audience review the past and present from a different perspective, to see that social or political order is not "natural" but constructed in favour of men by men.

9.3.1 Samuel Beckett (1906–1989)

Samuel Beckett, the most important dramatist in English in the later half of the twentieth century, is intriguingly an Anglo-Irish and a French writer. Born near Dublin, Beckett made his home in France in the 1930s where he wrote two full-length novels, *Murphy* and *Watt* (1953) in English, together with the trilogy *Molloy* (1951), *Malone Meurt* (*Malone Dies*, 1951) and *L'Innommable* (*The Unnamable*, 1953) in French. Like Joyce, by whom he was influenced, Beckett uses interior monologue as his major device to convey his sense of a bleak world in which all are isolated.

Although his novels had established Beckett as among the most discussed and respected of the avant-garde Parisian writers of the early 1950s, it was *Waiting for Godot* that gave him a wide international reputation. That reputation was cemented by his later work for the theater, notably plays known by their English titles as *Endgame* (1957), *Krapp's Last Tape* (1960), and *Happy Days* (1962). These plays belong to what, since Beckett, has been called the Theater of the Absurd, a term used to describe plays where the main feeling of the audience is one of bafflement as they face a world on stage where there is no logic to events or human behavior: Human life seems absurd in its disjointedness and meaninglessness. In these plays, especially in his masterpiece *Waiting for Godot*, Beckett conveys the deep sense of anxiety that marks the second half of the twentieth century.

In his later plays, Beckett reduces his theater to its essentials: from two acts in *Waiting for Godot* and *Happy Days*, to one, starting with *Endgame*; from five characters to four, then two, then one, and finally—in *Breath* (1970), which lasts only about thirty seconds—there are no characters at all. This move towards minimalism is really absurd. The setting is a "stage littered with miscellaneous rubbish", and the sounds of birth, breath and death are heard. This is the ultimate image of the Waste Lands of twentieth-century literature, where "we are born astride of a grave", and, "the light gleams an instant, then it's night once more", as Vladimir says in *Waiting for Godot*.

Beckett takes drama to new extremes, and pushes his characters to the limits of solitude, non-communication and hopelessness. Yet they all survive, and any thoughts of suicide are dispelled. Hamlet's age-old question, "To be or not to be", is answered in the affirmative, even though Beckett takes his characters closer to the extremes of despair and hopelessness of King Lear than any other writer since Shakespeare. In Beckett, there is no tragic climax; continuing the struggle to remain alive is offered as the unavoidable and necessary conclusion. His novel *The Unnamable* sums up the paradox of the "absurd" life humankind leads in the words, "Where I am, I don't know, I'll never know, in the silence you don't know, you must go on. I can't go on, I'll go on".

Waiting for Godot portrays two tramps, Estragon and Vladimir, trapped in an endless waiting for the arrival of a mysterious personage named Godot. They amuse themselves meanwhile with various bouts of repartee and word play, and are for a while diverted by the arrival of whip-cracking Pozzo, driving the oppressed and burdened Lucky on the end of a rope. Towards the end of each of the two acts, a boy arrives, heralding Godot's imminent appearance, but he does not come; each act ends with the interchange between the two tramps, "Well, shall we go?" "yes" "let's go", and the stage direction, "They do not move". There are strong biblical references throughout, but Beckett's powerful and symbolic portrayal of the human condition as one of ignorance, delusion, paralysis, and intermittent flashes of human sympathy, hope, and wit has been subjected to many varying interpretations.

9.3.2 John Osborne (1929–1994)

John Osborne made his name with *Look Back in Anger*. First staged in 1957, the year of Suez Crisis, which marked the end of British imperialism in the Middle East, the play created a tremendous stir. It was seen as the testament of a new generation, heralding a new spirit in drama, and, in culture in general. At the time, it was described as a "kitchen-sink" drama. Audiences at the Royal Court Theater where it was staged were used to polite drawing-room comedies, but Osborne, as was also the case in the plays of Arnold Weaker and Shelagh Delaney, put a new emphasis on domestic realism and everyday life and language. Suddenly the theater reflected, in a way that had not previously been the case, post-war life in ordinary Britain. The play explores the frustration and disappointment of the post-war generation and their rejection of the established values and social standards. Angrily, violently, and in an unadorned and colloquial dialogue, it reveals to the audience the psychological and social problems left unsolved, or even exacerbated by the society's so-called welfare state.

The play tells the story of the marital conflicts of Jimmy Portor and his wife Alison, which appear to arise largely from Jimmy's sense of their social incompatibility: He is a jazz-playing ex-student from a "white tile" university; she is a colonel's daughter. He is by turns violent, sentimental, maudlin, self-pitying and sadistic, and has a fine line in rhetoric. The first act opens as Alison stands ironing the clothes of Jimmy and their lodger Cliff. In the second act, Alison's friend Helena attempts to rescue her from her disastrous marriage; Alison departs with her father, and Helena falls into Jimmy's arms. The third act opens with Helena at the ironing board; Alison returns, having lost the baby she was expecting, and she and Jimmy find a manner of reconciliation through humiliation and game-playing fantasy. However, the plot of the play is not the main interest. Our attention focuses on the character of Jimmy, a new sort of hero. University-educated, he now works on a sweet stall, and much of the play consists of his attack on British society. His speeches, along with his education, position him outside the usual working-class stereotype; consequently, he seems to belong nowhere. For Jimmy, the old structure has disappeared, and the result is that he is an isolated figure without any place. But his bullying attitude towards women is revealing. Cut off from his own class, he seeks reassurance in the old-fashioned pattern of a gender relationship in which he can at least dominate women. The contradiction between Jimmy's analysis of social ills and his shocking treatment of his wife suggests something of the turmoil of the 1950s. Britain emerged from the war without any clear convictions about new directions or new forms of politics that might guide the country towards new ways of thinking about how to order society. Jimmy is foil of a certain kind of energy, but energy that is frittered away in empty speeches; he talks, but he is incapable of action.

Osborne followed *Look Back in Anger* with several plays, making the historical figure of *Luther* an angry young man, using the Austrian Empire as the setting for what is arguably his richest and most controversial play *A Patriot for Me* (1965), and giving the actor Sir Lawrence Oliver one of his most unusual roles, as a fading music-hall performer, in *The Entertainer* (1957). His later works (which include *West of Suez*, 1971; *A Sense of Detachment,* 1972; *Watch It Come Down,* 1976; *Deja Vu*, 1991) became increasingly vituperative in tone; his outbursts of rage against contemporary society frequently exhilarating remained one of his strongest theatrical weapons, but he also expressed from time to time an ambivalent nostalgic for the past that his work did so much to alter.

9.3.3 Harold Pinter (1930–2008)

Pinter's plays can be associated with the Theater of the Absurd, and clearly owe a debt to Beckett. Pinter's first play, *The Room*, was performed in 1957, followed by *The*

Birthday Party (1958), in which Stanley, an out-of-work pianist in a seaside boarding house, is mysteriously threatened and taken over by two intruders, an Irishman and a Jew, who present him with a Kafkaesque indictment of unexplained crimes, *The Caretaker* in 1960, and *The Homecoming* in 1965. Other plays have followed, but it is these early plays that are generally recognized as Pinter's special contribution to modern drama, in which menace and violence constantly threaten the characters' lives. Pinter's plays are oddly realistic in so far as they are concerned with social relationships and in their expression of the difficulties of communication between people. The characteristic Pinteresque exchange is one of silences and pauses, just as the characteristic Pinteresque setting is a room where people retreat from the world that threatens them, although the nature of this retreat is never clearly defined. There is, too, something characteristically Pinteresque about the obsessive behavior of his characters and their disturbed mental states. What Pinter presents is a world where people seem locked in their own non-communicating lines of thought, or in fantasies, so that there is never any chance of a sane or healthy society emerging. Rather, the sense is of individual trying to gain some assurance about their existence, but never able to articulate their needs. Their words, and language generally, become part of the menace and violence they are seeking to escape, but from which escape is impossible.

The Caretaker is one of Pinter's characteristically enigmatic dramas. It is built on the interaction of three characters, the tramp Davies and the brothers Aston and Mick. Aston has rescued Davies from a brawl and brought him back to a junk-filled room, in which he offers Davies a bed and eventually, an ill-defined post as caretaker, although it emerges that the flat actually belongs to his brother. The characters reveal themselves in inconsequential dialogue and obsessional monologue. In the end, both brothers turn on Davies, after he has tried to play the one off against the other, and evict him.

The Homecoming is a black Freudian family drama. The play presents the return to his North London home and ostentatiously womanless family of Teddy, an academic, and his wife of six years, Ruth, once a photographic model. The patriarch, Mac, a butcher, is alternately violent and cringing in manner, and the other two sons, Lenny and Joey, in a very short time make sexual overture to Ruth, who calmly accepts them; by the end of the play, Teddy has decided to leave her with the family, who intend to establish her as a professional prostitute.

9.3.4 Arnold Wesker (1932–)

Arnold Wesker was born in the East End of London into Jewish immigrant parents, and educated in Hackney. He worked at various jobs before making his name as a playwright. His three plays, *Chicken Soup with Barley* (1958), *Roots* (1959), and *I'm Talking About Jerusalem* (1960), are now grouped together as the Wesker Trilogy, which traces the attitude of a family of Jewish-socialist intellectuals from 1936 through the Second World War up to 1959. *The Kitchen* (1959) shows the stresses and conflicts of life behind the scenes in a kitchen, where men and women are imprisoned and dwarfed by grueling routine. It is a place of brief loveless attachments, of hard, unfulfilling work done by the many for the benefits of the few, and of vogue, hopeless dreams of escape. The play's use of the rhythms of the working life was highly innovative and did much to stimulate the growth of what was to be known as kitchen sink drama. Wesker's other plays include *Chips with Everything* (1962), *The Four Seasons* (1965), *The Merchant* (1977), and *Caritas* (1981). In addition to his plays for stage, television, and screen, Wesker has written criticism, essays, and short stories. *As Much As I Dare* is an autobiography, published in 1994.

Wesker, like Osborne, is one of the foremost of the New Wave dramatists of working class. He has a firm faith in the potential of the working class. He holds that there is a positive virtue in carrying on the moral and spiritual fight even if defeat is all but inevitable. Wesker's great strength lies in his realistic presentation of the Jewish working class and its problems without sentimentality or compromise. His plays focus on the conflict between individual and the pressures of society. By using the theater to portray a world which is falling apart, a world which is losing faith and hope, Wesker explores and demonstrates a cordial understanding of and a deep sympathy for the struggles of the working class people in London.

9.3.5 Joe Orton (1933–1967)

The comic tradition exemplified in Wilde and Coward reaches a high point in the subversive farce of Joe Orton. Homosexual, Orton allowed his sexual viewpoint to determine much of the satiric attack on society's hypocrisies. *Loot* (1966) is a black comedy, involving the taboo subject of death, hilariously mixed up with sex and money. *Entertaining Mr. Sloane* (1964) is a comedy of forbidden sexual attraction, a theme developed in Orton's last play *What the Butler Saw* (1969), which takes sexual and psychological subversion to new heights of farcical exploration. The climax of this play takes comedy back to its original Greek roots, and the "panic" which comic chaos can create.

9.3.6 Tom Stoppard (1937–)

Tom Stoppard was born in Czechoslovakia. His family settled in England after the war. He published a novel, *Lord Malquist and the Moon* (1965), and his play *Rosencrantz and Guildenstern Are Dead* (1966) attracted much attention. This was followed by many witty and inventive plays, including *The Real Inspector Hound* (1968); *Jumpers* (1972); *Travesties* (1974); *Dirty Linen* (1976, a satire of political life); *Every Good Boy Deserves Favour* (1977); *Night and Day* (1978), about the dangers of the "closed shop" in journalism; *The Real Thing* (1982), a marital tragic-comedy; *Arcadia* (1993, set in a country house); *Indian Ink* (1995). Stoppard has also written many works for film, radio, and television, including *Professional Foul* (TV, 1977). Stoppard's work displays a metaphysical wit, a strong theatrical sense, and a talent for pastiche which enables him to move from mode to mode within the same scene with great flexibility and rapidity; yet the plays appear far from frivolous in intention, increasingly posing considerable ethical problems.

Rosencrantz and Guildenstern Are Dead focuses on little men in a world beyond their comprehension. Rosencrantz and Guildenstern are the courtiers in Shakespeare's *Hamlet* who serve as spies on the prime for the King. Stoppard moves these peripheral characters to the leading players in a comedy of identity. Like Beckett's Vladimir and Estragon, Rosencrantz and Guildenstern are waiting for something to happen to give them a reason for existing. They exist, however, in "the irrational belief that somebody interesting will come on in a minute", finding their justification in what happens around them, over which they clearly have no control.

9.3.7 Alan Ayckbourn (1939–)

Alan Ayckbourn has written more than fifty plays, all of them comedies, from *Relatively Speaking* (1967) to *Comic Potential* (1999). Most of his plays have been very successful in the theater. Alan Ayckbourn is an observer of family behavior, and the conflicts of family life often provide the material for his plays. Over the years his plays have become darker and more serious, and he is now considered by many critics to be one of the most acute writers about middle class Britain in the late twentieth century.

Viewed by some as "traditional" comedies, Alan Ayckbourn's plays are seen by others as deeply serious observations on certain social malaises of the time. *Season's Greetings* (1980), *Absurd Person's Singular* (1973) and *Henceforward* (1987), along with the simultaneous-action comedies comprising *The Norman Conquests* (1973), are among his major plays in a prolific output during the 1970s and 1980s. Ayckbourn is probably the one dramatist who, like Greene as a novelist, has enjoyed great commercial success while retaining a following among the more intellectual or academic communities.

9.3.8 Edward Bond (1934–)

Edward Bond's best play is *Saved*, which caused considerable controversy because of the staged stoning to death of a baby, but *Saved* emerges as a key play in the recent political development of the theater. Bond's *Lear* (1971) takes Shakespeare's tragedy as a starting point for an examination of human cruelty; it is interesting that Edward Bond and Samuel Beckett should examine the geography of the human soul in divergent ways, concentrating on cruelty and on despair respectively—but with reference, direct or indirect, to the Shakespearean tragedy which critics have always seen as the most pessimistic.

Bond's *Bingo* (1973) actually puts the character of Shakespeare on stage, in an examination of the clash between artistic and capitalist values. The play shows Shakespeare in his retirement in Stratford, as a property owner rather than the cultural colossus history has made him. Bond's Marxist viewpoint makes Shakespeare a class enemy, an enemy of the people, in his support for the enclosures of common land. Bond's belief that violence occurs in "situations of injustice" and that it therefore flourishes under capitalism continues to arouse extreme responses from critics and audiences. His *The War Plays* (1985) portrays life after a nuclear holocaust.

9.3.9 David Hare (1947–)

David Hare was marked out by the play *Knuckle* (1974) as a powerful and original talent with a keen eye both for the iniquities of social privilege and the contradictions of radical idealism. Class antagonism at Cambridge is the subject of *Teeth "n" Smiles* (1976). In *Plenty* (1978), Hare provides a metaphor of the economic and ideological decline of post-war Britain through the experiences of a former courtier in occupied France. *Pravda* (1985), co-written with Howard Brenton, is a political satire concerning two national newspapers.

His acclaimed trilogy of plays on British institutions began with *Racing Demon* (1990), about four South London clergymen trying to make sense of their vocations. This was followed by *Murmuring Judges* (1991), a critique of the British criminal justice system, and *The Absence of War* (1993), about the Labour Party.

Skylight (1995) was Hare's most popular play. It brings together a highly successful businessman, a 1980s figure, and a socially conscious schoolteacher who has rejected his life-style to live and work in an economically deprived area of London. The play is Hare's most direct reflection on the 1990s—a world with quite different values. *Ary's View* (1997) then became Hare's most successful play. It is a play of an actress's memories and fantasies. Hare continues to explore the atmosphere of contemporary Britain *In My Zinc Bed* (2000) which brings together the contrasting world of an Internet entrepreneur and a poet he commissions to write about.

9.3.10 Howard Brenton (1942–)

One of the most controversial plays of the 1980s was Howard Brenton's *The Romans in Britain*, which, in a scene of homosexual rape, effectively paralleled the Roman occupation of Britain with the contemporary situation in Northern Ireland. Contrasting scenes of the two "occupations", Brenton draws on epic theater conventions: This is theater of war, but with a deeply human concern for history's victims. At the end of the play, we return to the aftermath of the Roman's departure from Britain, as the native characters try to identify something, maybe mythical, maybe real, that they can hold on to from the nightmare of their recent past.

9.3.11 Caryl Churchill (1938–)

Caryl Churchill's plays are predominantly radical and feminist in tone. Her best-known plays are *Top Girls* (1982) and *Serious Money* (1987), a satire on the Thatcher years. In *Top Girls*, women from history—for example, Pope Joan and Patient Griselda, the obedient wife from one of Chaucer's *The Canterbury Tales*—are brought into the everyday world of contemporary women to set up an extraordinary dialogue about oppression and the struggle waged by women across the years of recognition. In the "Top Girls" employment agency Louise is looking for a new job after twenty years in the same firm:

> I've spent twenty years in middle management. I've seen young men go on, in my own company or elsewhere, to higher things. Nobody notices me, I don't expect it, I

don't attract attention by making mistakes, everybody takes for granted that my work is perfect.

(Top Girls)

Louise's words seem to sum up the whole course of history for women: It is assumed that they will always play the role expected of them to perfection, but they are always seen as inferior to men and, consequently, denied opportunities for self-fulfillment. But Louise's desire to move on is a recognition of the way in which people, and especially women, in the late twentieth century can embrace a new position. Churchill, as such, articulates not just a sense of the past but also a sense of how the social order might be reconstructed differently.

9.4 Novel

The decades following the Second World War have seen a considerable increase in the numbers of novels published and in the variety of themes and subjects they cover. Several writers, such as Graham Greene, Augus Wilson, Fowles and Golding (on the more traditional side); Alan Sillitoe, the Armis (father and son) (on the more inventive side); Doris Lessing, Muried Spark, Angela Carter, Iris Murdoch, Margaret Drabble and A. S. Byatt (on the feminist side), made their distinction in their writing.

Among the voices which can be more clearly heard in the novel in recent years are those of the young and the lower classes, the voices of the new educated middle class, voices of women, racial minorities, gays and outsiders of many other types. Various sub-genres of novel have become bestsellers while retaining intellectual acceptability—for example, the working class novel, the academic novel, the Scottish novel, the women's novel and the magic realist novel.

At the same time there have been numerous bestsellers which have never reached intellectual acceptability—for example, romances, thrillers, and historical novels. Some genres, like the detective story and the spy story, have, however, begun to receive critical acclaim.

9.4.1 William Golding (1911–1993)

William Golding worked for many years as a teacher before achieving an instant success with his first novel *Lord of the Flies*. *The Inheritors* (1955) tells of man's brutal extermination of his gentler ancestors; the intrinsic cruelty of man is at the heart of many Golding's novels. *Pincher Martin* (1956), *The Brass Butterfly* (a play, 1958), *Free Fall* (1959), and *The Spire* (1964), were followed by a collection of essays, *The Hot Gates* (1965). His other novels are *The Pyramid* (1967), *The Scopion God* (three novellas, 1971), *Darkness Visible* (1979), *Rites of Passage* (1980), and *Paper Men* (1984). Golding often presents isolated individuals or small groups in extreme situations dealing with man in his basic condition, creating the quality of a fable. *Close Quarters* (1987) and *Fire Down Below* (1989) complete the historical trilogy begun with *Rites of Passage*. He was awarded the Nobel Prize in 1983 and knighted in 1988. His last novel, *The Double Tongue*, left in draft at his death, was published in 1995.

Lord of the Flies is Golding's best-known work. An aeroplane carrying a party of schoolboys crashes on a desert island. The boys' attempts, led by Ralph and Piggy, to set up a democratically new society quickly fail. Terror rules under the dictator Jack, and two boys are killed; it is only with the arrival of a shocked rescue officer that a mask of civilization returns.

The story reflects post-war disillusionment with human nature. With a combination of fantasy and psychological realism, Golding shows how, when the constraints of civilization are removed, the essential nature and original sin of man is revealed. Although based on the dynamics of a group of schoolboys, the novel confronts profound questions of innocence, evil and the fall of man, casting doubt on the possibility of any lasting social progress. Like George Orwell's *Nineteen Eighty-four* and Aldous Huxley's *Brave New World*, the novel has been described a dystopia.

Instead of showing an optimistic picture of a perfect world, Golding depicts a pessimistic picture of an imperfect world. The novel is also a revision of the desert-island myth originating in *Robinson Crusoe* and continued in *The Coral Island* (1857), a novel for boys written by R. M. Ballantyne. Ballantyne shows individuals who maintain their humanity in uncivilized places because of their innate goodness and virtue. Golding's novel shows the reverse.

9.4.2 John Fowles (1926–2005)

John Fowles's first novel *The Collector* (1963), a psychological thriller, was followed by *The Aristos* (1965), an idiosyncratic collection of notes and aphorisms, and *The Magus* (1966), a novel set largely on the Greek Island of "Phraxos", where British schoolmaster Nicholas Urfe is subjected to a series of mysterious apparitions which give the novel a narrative complexity and mythological dimension faintly suggestive of Magic realism. *The French Lieutenant's Woman* (1969) is a semi-historical novel, set largely in Lyme Regis in 1867; wealthy amateur palaeontologist Charles Smithton, engaged to conventional Ernestina Freeman, falls under the spell of Sarah Woodruff a lady's companion, who is believed to have been deserted by the French lover of the title. His pursuit of Sarah breaks his engagement, but Sarah eludes him, and when he finds her again she has become a New Woman. Fowles's other major novels include *The Ebony* Tower (1974), a collection of novellas; *Daniel Martin* (1977), a long, self-searching semi-naturalistic work about a screenwriter; *A Maggot* (1985), an eighteenth-century murder mystery; *The Tree* (1992), an exploration of the impact of nature on Fowles's work; *Tessera* (1993).

The influence of existentialism on Fowles's work is clear, especially with regard to his fascination with individual freedom and the desire to manipulate and control one's life. *The Collector*, *The Magus*, and *The French Lieutenants Woman* center on the power of repression and sex to mould the individual. The novels of John Fowles use magic and artifice to carry on the search for a truth of humanity. They have enjoyed great academic and commercial success in Europe and the U.S.A.: They are intellectual, self-conscious experiments with theme and form, and carry warnings for the reader about the nature of the reading experience. In *The French Lieutenant's Woman,* the Victorian novel form is used and questioned while the reader is left with a choice between two possible endings. For many readers and critics, this is a very good example of the post-Modern novel, innovative but questioning. It is, indeed, a major achievement, although the "alternative ending" idea had been tried out as early as Thackeray's *The Newcomes* in the 1850s.

9.4.3 Augus Wilson (1913–1991)

An academic, Wilson wrote about personal relationship in the upper middle classes with a range of characters, often in middle age, who try to balance the conflicting demands of the world they live in: the wild and the tame, the past and the present, conformity and difference. Wilson takes particular care to integrate homosexual characters into his fictional landscapes. His novels include *Hemlock and After* (1952), about the doomed attempts of a middle-aged novelist, Bernard Sands, to establish a writer's center in a country house; *Anglo-Saxon Attitudes* (1956), which also has a middle-aged protagonist, historian Gerald Middleton, who tries to reconstruct and understand the past, including the mystery of a possible archaeological forgery; *The Middle Age of Mrs. Eliot* (1958), about the reversed fortunes of Meg Eliot, who finds herself suddenly widowed in reduced circumstances; *The Old Men and the Zoo* (1961), which reflects Wilson's concern with conflicts between the wild and the tame, the disciplined and the free, and ends with a portrayal of Europe at war; *Late Call* (1964), set in a New Town; *No Laughing Matter* (1967), a family saga covering some fifty years in the history of the Matthews family, which marks a departure from the realism of earlier works, mingling parody and dramatization with direct narration in a rich and complex evocation of family politics and neuroses. Wilson has also written some short stories.

9.4.4 Alan Sillitoe (1928–2010)

Sillitoe's first work is a volume of verse, which was followed by his much-praised first novel *Saturday Night and Sunday Morning* (1958). The tiny story of *The Loneness of the Long Distance Runner* (1959) is the first-person portrait of a rebellious and anarchic Borstal boy who refuses both literally and metaphorically to play the games of the establishment. Many other works followed, including the novels *A Tree on Fire* (1967), *A Start in Life* (1970), *Raw Material* (1972), *Men, Women and Children* (1973), etc.

Saturday Night and Sunday Morning is the story of the anarchic young Arthur Seaton, lathe operator in a Nottingham bicycle factory, who provided a new prototype of the working-class Angry Young Man; rebellious, contemptuous towards authority, he unleashes his energy on women and drink, with quieter interludes spent fishing in the canal. His affair with Brenda, married to his workmate Jack, overlaps with an affair with her sister Winnie, inaugurated in the night that Brenda attempts a gin-and-hot-bath abortion recommended by his Aunt Ada; both relationships falter when he is beaten up by soldiers, one of them Winnie's husband, and he diverts his attention to young Doreen, to whom he becomes engaged in the penultimate chapter. A landmark in the development of the post-war novel, with its naturalism relieved by wit, high spirits, and touches of lyricism, the novel provided the screenplay for Karel Reisz's 1960 film.

9.4.5 Kingsley Amis (1922–1995)

Kingsley Amis achieved popular success with his first novel *Lucky Jim* (1954), whose hero, lower-middle-class radical lecturer Jim Dixon was hailed as an "angry young man". Its setting in a provincial university was also indicative of a new development in fiction (of choosing provincial, anarchic, but ambitious, lower-middle-class heroes, and a low-key realist tone as a reaction against Modernism), a movement that Amis confirmed in *That Uncertain Feeling* (1955) and *Take a Girl Like You* (1960). *I Like It Here* (1958), a novel set in Portugal, displays Amis's deliberate cultivation, for comic effect, of a prejudiced and Philistine pose which was to harden into an increasingly conservative and hostile view of contemporary life and manners. Amis is best known for satiric comedy: *One Fat Englishman* (1963), *Ending Up* (1974), *The Old Devils* (1986), and *You Can't Do Both* (1994). Amis also successfully attempted many other genres such as detective story and poem.

9.4.6 Martin Amis (1949–)

Martin Amis, the son of Kingsley Amis, published his first novel *The Rachel Papers* in 1973, the story of a sexually precocious teenager who plans the seduction of an older woman. Sex is treated both graphically and satirically in *Dead Babies* (1975). This was followed by *Success* (1978), *Other People* (1981), and *Money* (1984), memorable for its linguistic dexterity and inventiveness. *Einstein's Monsters* (1987), a collection of short stories, reflects a preoccupation with the threat of nuclear annihilation. *London Fields* (1988), part thriller, part surrealist fable, balances violent action with comedy. *Times Arrow* (1991), the story of a Nazi war criminal in which the normal chronological sequence of events is reversed, was followed by *The Information* (1995).

Martin Amis is a daring experimenter in form, style, and content, capable of shock, and capable of clear-sighted social observation. Perhaps more than any other English-born novelist, Martin Amis has forged a "new" language: going beyond "old" language, using new rhythms, incorporating American English, street English, and minority dialect Englishes, to hive a representation of some of the range of Englishes spoken in England at the end of the twentieth century.

9.4.7 Salman Rushdie (1947–)

Salman Rushdie was born in Bombay to a Muslim family, and educated at King's College, Cambridge. Rushdie's bicultural upbringing informs all his works. He draws on the allegorical, fable-making traditions of both East and West and is often classed among the exponents of Magic Realism (a movement in which the recognizably realistic mingles with the unexpected and the inexplicable, and in which elements of dream, fairy-story, or mythology combine with the everyday, often in a mosaic or kaleidoscopic pattern of refraction and recurrence). His first novel, *Grimus* (1975), was followed by *Midnight's Children* (1981), which won the Booker Prize (a prize founded in 1969 and financed by Booker McConnell, a multinational conglomerate company, awarded annually to the best full-length novel by a British or Commonwealth citizen published in the previous 12 months) and tells the story of Saleem Sinai, born on the stroke of midnight on the day that India was granted independence. In *Shame* (1983), the subject is Pakistan and the culture of shame and honour that oppresses women. *The Satanic Verse* (1988) is a jet-propelled panoramic novel which questions illusion, reality, and the power of faith. Certain passages were interpreted by some Muslims as blasphemous and brought upon Rushdie the notorious death sentence, which obliged him to seek police protection. After *Haroun and the Sea Stories* (1990), a novel for children, came his first collection of short stories, *East, West*, again between two imaginative traditions.

As a Magic realist, Rushdie recalls an oral tradition of storytelling applied in a modern context, evoking sights, sounds, and smells of the world in realistic terms, side by side with the spinning of wild fantasies and improbable tales.

For Your Information

Women Novelists

The flowering of writing of women authors since the 1950s has produced a very wide range of achievements. Their novels have absorbed and been shaped by the emergence of a feminist discourse over the past thirty years, providing the clearest examples of genuinely new voices in fiction.

9.4.8 Doris Lessing (1919–2013)

Doris Lessing's stature as one of the major writers of her time has been assured for many years. Her early stories and novels move between Africa and England. Her first novel *The Grass Is Singing* (1951), set in Southern Rhodesia (now Zimbabwe), focuses on the marriage of Mary and Richard Turner, and the murder of Mary by Moses, the African servant with whom she has been sleeping. The novel considers the essential frailty and emptiness of colonial power, conveying the sterility and hypocrisy of the lives of the settlers. Throughout the novel, there is a sense of a colonial order for the land or the native people.

Her quintet *Children of Violence* is a Bildungsroman (a novel of education), tracing the history of Martha Quest from her childhood in Rhodesia, through post-war Britain, to an apocalyptic ending in AD 2000 (*Martha Quest*, 1952; *A Proper Marriage*, 1954; *A Ripple from the Storm*, 1958; *Landlocked*, 1965; *The Four-Gated City*, 1969). *The Golden Notebook* (1962) is a lengthy and ambitious novel which was hailed as a landmark by the Women's Movement: Sections of conventional narrative ironically entitled "Free Women", enclose and intersperse the four experimental notebooks of writer Anna Wulf who is struggling with crises in her domestic and political life, and with a writer's block. The novel ends, after a period of breakdown, with release, union, and renewed creativity. Later novels, *Briefing for a Descent into Hell* (1971) and *Memoirs of a Survivor* (1975), enter the realm of "inner space fiction", exploring mental breakdown and the breakdown of society. The sequence collectively entitled *Canopus in Argos: Archives* (1975–1983, 5 volumes) marks a complete break with traditional realism, describing the epic and mythic events of a fictional universe with a remarkable freedom of invention. The first volume of her autobiography, *Under My Skin,* appeared in 1994. She has written many other works of fiction and non-fiction, displaying her concern with politics, with the changing destiny of women, and with a fear of technological disaster.

9.4.9 Antonia Susan Byatt (1936–2023)

A. S. Byatt is a former academic, whose novels are rich in historical, literary, and mythical allusions. *The Virgin in the Garden* (1978) portrays Yorkshire at the beginning of the new Elizabethan age in 1952, and is an ambiguous contrast of the sixteenth-century Elizabethan age with the present. Its sequel *Still Life* (1985) continues the rich observation of England in the 1950s. *Possession* (1990) brought Byatt wide acclaim, winning several major prizes. Once more it contrasts past and present, with the search for a Victorian poet's past illuminating a contemporary university researcher's life and times.

Byatt's *Angel and Insects* (1992) explores the background to Tennyson's *In Memoriam* in the context of travel, scientific discovery and inherited wealth. It became a successful film. *Byatt's Babel Tower* (1996) follows on from *The Virgin in the Garden* and *Still Life*. It is an ambitious, long, rather sprawling novel about the 1960s. The period is seen as a time of social and intellectual revolution, but in particularly English terms. It is a novel about words and ideas and contains within it a novel called "Babbletower" which is prosecuted for obscenity in an echo of the *Lady Chatterley's Lover* trial. Byatt takes post-Modern pastiche, intertextuality and contemporary history to new heights in this extended romp through recent fashions, preoccupations and intellectual concerns.

9.4.10 Muriel Spark (1918–2006)

Muriel Spark is a writer of Scottish-Jewish descent, born and educated in Edinburgh. After spending some years in Central Africa, which was to form the setting for several of her short stories, including the title story of *The Go-Away Bird* (1958), she returned to Britain. Her first novel, *The Comforters* (1957), was followed by many others such as *Memento Mori* (1959), a comic and macabre study of old age; her best-known work, *The Prime of Miss Lean Brodie* (1961); *The Driver's Seat* (1970), about a woman possessed by a death-wish; *The Take Over* (1976), set in Italy where she settled. Spark's novels are elegant and sophisticated, with touches of the bizarre and the perverse; many have a quality of fable or parable, and her use of narrative omniscience is highly distinctive. Her *Collected Poems* and *Collected Plays* were published in 1967, and a collected edition of her short stories in 1986. Spark continues to write prolifically. Her recent works include *Loitering with Intent* (1995), *Reality and Dreams* (1996) and *Aiding and Abetting* (2000).

The Prime of Miss Lean Brodie, set in Edinburgh during the 1930s, describes the career of eccentric and egotistical Miss Brodie, teacher at the Marcia Blaine School for Girls, and her domination of her "set" of 16-year-olds. With many flashes back and forward, it describes the manner in which Miss Brodie fascinates her disciples, who are particularly intrigued by her relationships with two male teachers, the married and Catholic art master, Mr. Lloyd, and the bachelor Church of Scotland Singing-master, Mr. Lowther, who, rejected after much dalliance by Miss Brodie, in despair marries the science mistress. Sandy, one of the set, has an affair with Mr. Lloyd while Miss Brodie is away in the summer of 1938 touring Hitler's Germany; the results of this are that Sandy becomes a Catholic and arranges the dismissal of Miss Brodie in the grounds of her sympathy with Fascism. Miss Brodie herself dangerous and compelling, is the center of the novel's considerable moral ambiguity and complexity.

9.4.11 Iris Murdoch (1919–1999)

Iris Murdoch, born in Ireland, is one of the most significant figures in the modern English novel. A philosopher by training, her work has always shown a more philosophical tendency than is usually found in English literature. Her first novel, *Under the Net* (1954), was followed by many other successful works, such as *The Bell* (1958); *The Red and the Green* (1965); *The Black Prince* (1973); *The Sea, The Sea* (1978, a novel about a theater director and his childhood love, which won the Booker Prize); *The Philosopher's Pupil* (1983). She has also written three plays.

Murdoch's novels, which have been described as psychological detective stories, portray complicated and sophisticated sexual relationships and her plots have an operatic quality, combining comic, bizarre, and macabre incidents in a highly patterned symbolic structure. Though clearly not intended as strictly realistic, her portrayal of the twentieth century middle-class and intellectual life shows acute observation as well as a wealth of invention, and has baffled critics by its evasion of recognized fictional genres. Murdoch revels in intertextuality—using or alluding to a wide range of other writings in her works. Her terms of reference are vast, covering literature, philosophy, and history, and this gives her works an unusual depth and richness of resonance, which few others can match.

9.4.12 Angela Carter (1940–1992)

Angela Carter's work often combines the macabre with the wittily surreal and draws heavily on symbolism and themes derived from fairy tales and folk myths. *The Magic Toyshop* (1967) associated her with the tradition of Magic Realism. Succeeding novels developed further a characteristic neo-Gothic ambience, often underpinned by a strong, but never intrusive, feminist sensibility. They included *Several Perceptions* (1968), *Heroes and Villains* (1969) and *The Infernal Desire Machines of Dr. Hoffman* (1972). *Night at the Circus* (1984), about a female Victorian circus performer called Fevers who can fly, confirmed her as a gifted literary fabulist, while her ability to evoke and adapt the darker resonance of traditional forms of fantasy was brilliantly deployed in *The Bloody Chamber and Other Stories* (1979), which includes her well-known "The Company of Wolves". Her last novel, *Wise Children* (1991), was an extravagant and bawdy chronicle of two theatrical families.

9.5 Poetry

The years after 1945 have seen both continuities and changes in English poetry. Some poets, despite Modernism, continued Romantic tradition, writing deeply personal responses to the world and engaging with "eternal" "elemental" themes. The central viewpoint in their poems is an "I", a single voice recording experiences directly and shaping them in generally traditional poetic forms. Other poets are not as clearly in the Romantic tradition. The "I" in their poems is more indirect, and experience is presented more ironically. The focus is restricted, concentrating more on the particulars of everyday life. However, no poet fits neatly into the categories of "Romantic" or "anti-Romantic". On the whole, there is a sheer diversity of poetry that followed the thirties, and poetry after the Second World War turned more and more away from the large issue of order in the world towards a more restricted sense of life. There is, for example, the war poetry of Keith Douglas, the exuberant poetry of Dylan Thomas, the bleak pastoral poetry of R. S. Thomas, the poetry of the 1950s' "The Movement", whose aim to rid poetry of high-flown Romanticism and bring it down to earth has been realized in the works (most notably) of Philip Larkin, and of Donald Davie, D. J. Enright, and Elizabeth Jennings, the "New Poetry" of the 1960s in which there is a move away from sobriety and tidiness towards the modernist innovativeness, with energetic poems of Thom Gunn, Sylvia Plath, and Ted Hughes.

The term post-Modern is used loosely to cover all literature written since the Second World War (the more precise use of the term limits to works characterized by fragmentation, discontinuity, indeterminacy, dislocation and self-consciousness). In poetry, it includes the poets named above and also contemporary poets such as Tony Harrison and Seamus Heaney. Their poetry is deeply influenced by, in the case of Heaney, the political problems in Ireland, and, in the case of Harrison, issues of class and a sense of alienation in society. Other significant figures in contemporary poetry include Tomlinson, Graig Raine, Geoffrey Hill, Edwin Morgan, Tom Paulin, Medbh McGuckian, Andrew Motion, and Paul Muldoon.

9.5.1 Dylan Thomas (1914–1953)

Dylan Thomas was born and brought up in Wales, and the Welsh traditions of the power of the spoken word, especially in matters of region, are present in his poetry. He writes with elegiac appreciation of natural forces, the forces of birth, sex, and death, and with a rhapsodic regret for all that is lost. His best poems affirm with great passion and vigor the joys and beauties of life, even in the midst of death. Much of modern poetry continues Dylan Thomas's affirmation of life over death, particularly poignant in the nuclear age of post-war writing.

Thomas's first volume of verse, *18 Poems*, appeared in 1934. He then embarked on a Grub Street career of journalism, broadcasting and filmmaking, rapidly acquiring a reputation for exuberance and flamboyance, as both poet and personality. Thomas's romantic, affirmative, rhetorical style gradually won a large following, and the publication of *Death and Entrances* (1946), which contains some of his best-known works (including *Fern Hill* and *A Refusal to Mourn the Death, by Fire, of a Child in London*), established him with a wide public: His *Collected Poems 1934–1952* (1952) sold extremely well. Thomas also wrote a considerable amount of prose, among which was his single famous work *Under Milk Wood*, a radio drama about the lives of the inhabitants in the Welsh seaside town of Llareggub, completed shortly before his death in 1953.

9.5.2 Philip Larkin (1922–1985)

Philip Larkin is perhaps the most distinctively English poet in the post-war period. His poetry plays with and against the Romantic tradition in poetry. Larkin does not assert the importance of his own personal experience. His version is realistic and unsentimental, preferring to be indirect and ironic. He continues, however, the tradition of Romantic poets such as Wordsworth and later poets, particularly Thomas Hardy, by exploring eternal themes of death and change within established rhythms and syntax, and he generally uses conservative poetic forms. Like Hardy, he writes about what appears to be normal and everyday, while exploring the paradox that the mundane is both familiar and limited. Larkin is also a Hardyesque poet in the way he presents experiences which many readers recognize and feel they can share. He is, however, more of a social poet than Hardy, frequently commenting on the tawdry and superficial aspects of modern urban living.

Chapter Nine
English Literature (Since 1945)

Larkin's early poems appeared in an anthology, *Poetry from Oxford in Wartime* (1944), and a collection, *The North Ship* (1945). His own voice became distinct in *The Less Deceived* (1955), where the colloquial bravura of a poem like *Toads* is offset by the half tones and somewhat bitter lyricism of other pieces. Many of his poems collected in *High Windows* (1974), notably *The Old Fools*, show a preoccupation with death and transience. Larkin's two novels are *Jill* (1946) and *A Girl in Winter* (1947).

9.5.3 Ted Hughes (1930–1998)

Ted Hughes succeeded John Betjeman as Poet Laureate in 1984. Hughes's poetry emphasized the pitiless and violent forces of nature. Many of his poems focus on animals that pursue their lives with a single-minded strength and power. Hughes makes his readers aware of the prehistory of the natural world, stressing its difference to man. His obsession with animals and his sense of the beauty and violence of the natural world appear in his first volume, *The Hawk in the Rain* (1957). This was followed by *Lupecal* (1960), *Wodwo* (1967, prose and verse), *Gaudete* (1977), and several books for children's use. *Crow* (1970) is a sequence of poems introducing the central symbol of the crow, who, as a creature born into a very particular nightmare, embodies the inner experience of modern man. Hughes retells the legend of creation and birth through the dark version of predatory, mocking, indestructible crow. Later volumes include *Cave Birds* (1975), *Season Songs* (1976), *Moortown* (1979), *River* (1983), *Wolfwatching* (1989), *Rain-Charm for the Duchy* (1992), and *New Selected Poems* (1995).

At the end of his death, Ted Hughes was enjoying immense popularity. Two volumes, *Birthday Letters* (1998) and *Tales from Ovid* (1997), became best-sellers and confirmed his status as a unique individual poetic voice that could reach a very wide audience. *Birthday Letters* courageously explores the relationship with his late wife, the American poet and novelist Sylvia Plath.

9.5.4 Tony Harrison (1937–)

Tony Harrison regards poetry as "the supreme form of articulation", and sees the poet's role as to "reclaim poetry's publicunction". His writing, often set in his home county of Yorkshire, as in *V* (1985–1988), uses colloquial forms, natural speech, and local dialect in perfectly scanning rhymes to explore matters like education and class, violence and language, questions of social conflicts. The letter V stands for "Versus", punning on "verses" and the traditional V for victory.

The Gaze of the Gorgon (1992), a long poem for television written in the wake of the Gulf War, has shown that his energy and creativity are constantly developing, making Harrison one of the most accessible and exciting poets now writing. He is also an accomplished translator, especially from classical Latin and Greek. The range of poetic and dramatic reference in his works is immense. *A Kumquat for John Keats* (1981) finds the fruit to celebrate the famous poet; *U.S. Martial* (1981) punningly transposes the Latin epigrammatist Martial into 1980s New York.

Tony Harrison refused to be considered for the appointment as Poet Laureate after the death of Ted Hughes (which was given to Andrew Motion in 1999), and wrote polemically about it, describing the role as "rat-catcher to our present Queen". His most recent collection takes its title from that text: *"Laureates Block" and Other Occasional Poems* (2000).

9.5.5 Seamus Heaney (1939–2013)

The most interesting British poetry of the last quarter of the twentieth century has originated from Northern Ireland, with three quite outstanding poets, Seamus Heaney, Derek Mahon and Paul Muldoon.

Seamus Heaney is a poet who writes directly and obliquely about politics, speaking in a clearly personal voice. As an Irishman, many of his poems deal with the horrors which continue to afflict Northern Ireland. In his early poems, Heaney writes of the countryside and the national world in ways which suggest the influence of D. H. Lawrence and Ted Hughes. In one of his earliest poems, *Digging* (1966), he establishes a metaphor which recurs in different ways in several subsequent poems:

> Between my finger and my thumb
> The squat pen rests
> I'll dig with it.

(Digging)

He digs into his own memory, into the lives of his family, into the past of Irish history and into the deeper levels of legend and myth which shape the character of the people of his

Chapter Nine
English Literature (Since 1945)

country. Heaney attempts to go beyond the terrible daily events of life in Northern Ireland to discover the forces beneath the history of that country which might restore hope and comfort. But he does not hide the deep-rooted tribal passions of revenge and honour which endure in contemporary society.

In 1967, his political preoccupations were brought into sharper focus by his reading of *The Bog People* by P. V. Glob, a Danish archaeologist. This opened his eyes to deeper levels of mythic and historical congruence. His perception that the Irish "bog is a memory bank" in that it preserves everything thrown into it produced the powerful bog poems of *North* (1975), which established his fame and popularity.

The award of the Nobel Prize for Literature to Seamus Heaney in 1995 set the seal on his worldwide reputation as the major Irish poet of the second half of the twentieth century, and indeed, as one of the finest poets writing in the English language. His more recent collections of verse have examined the "bog people", the poet's own relationships, and the complex relationships between individual and society, cult and history. The subtle beauty of his poetry derives from his strong respect for, and love of words.

Heaney's first volume after winning the Nobel Prize was *The Spirit Level* (1996). The title brings together his spiritual side and his practical nature, and the volume consolidates his position as a poet of nature, politics and humanity who can make major poetry out of the essentially mundane. *Opened Ground* (1998) collected his poems from between 1966 and 1996, and the translation of *Beowulf* (1999) brought him great popular and critical acclaim, followed by *Electric Light* (2000).

9.6 Reading

Punishment[1]

By Seamus Heaney

I can feel the tug
of the halter at the nape
of her neck, the wind
on her naked front.

It blows her nipples
to amber beads,
it shakes the frail rigging
of her ribs.

I can see her drowned
body in the bog,
the weighing stone
the floating rods and boughs.

Under which at first
she was a barked sapling
that is dug up
oak-bone, brain-firkin[2]:

her shaved head
like a stubble of black corn,
her blindfold a soiled bandage,
her noose a ring

to store
the memories of love.
Little adulteress,
before they punished you

you were flaxen-haired,
undernourished, and your
tar-black face was beautiful.
My poor scapegoat,

I almost love you
but would have cast, I know,
the stones of silence.
I am the artful voyeur

Chapter Nine
English Literature (Since 1945)

of your brain's exposed

and darkened combs,

your muscles' webbing

and all your numbered bones:

I who have stood dumb

when your betraying sisters,

cauled in tar,

wept by the railings,

who would connive

in civilized outrage

yet understand in the exact

and tribal, intimate revenge.

Notes

1. It is one of Heaney's bog poems. In 1951, the peat-stained body of a young girl, who lived in the late first century A. D., was recovered from a bog in Windeby, Germany. As P. V. Glob describes in *The Bog People*, she "lay naked in the hole in the peat, a bandage over the eyes and a collar round the neck. The band across the eyes was drawn tight and had cut into the neck and the base of the nose. We may feel sure that it had been used to close her eyes to the world. There is no mark of strangulation on the neck, so that it had not been used for that purpose". Her hair "had been shaved off with a razor on the left side of the head… When the brain was removed the convolutions and folds of the surface could be clearly seen. … this girl of only fourteen had had an inadequate winter diet. … To keep the young body under, some birch branches and a big stone were laid upon her". According to the Roman historian Tacitus, the Germanic peoples punished adulterous women by shaving off their hair and then scourging them out of the village or killing them. Today, her "betraying sisters" are sometimes shaved, stripped, tarred, and handcuffed by the IRA to the railings of Belfast in punishment for keeping company with British soldiers.

2. **firkin:** small cask.

Waiting for Godot
Act I: A country road. A tree. Evening

By Samuel Beckett

[*Estragon, sitting on a low mound, is trying to take off his boot. He pulls at it with both hands, panting. He gives up, exhausted, rests, tries again. As before.*]

[*Enter Vladimir.*]

Estragon: [*Giving up again.*] Nothing to be done.

Vladimir: [*Advancing with short, stiff strides, legs wide apart.*] I'm beginning to come round to that opinion. All my life I've tried to put it from me, saying, Vladimir, be reasonable, you haven't yet tried everything. And I resumed the struggle. [*He broods, musing on the struggle. Turning to Estragon.*] So there you are again.

Estragon: Am I?

Vladimir: I'm glad to see you back. I thought you were gone forever.

Estragon: Me too.

Vladimir: Together again at last! We'll have to celebrate this. But how? [*He reflects.*] Get up till embrace you.

Estragon: [*Irritably.*] Not now, not now.

Vladimir: [*Hurt, coldly*] May one inquires where His Highness[1] spent the night?

Estragon: In a ditch.

Vladimir: [*Admiringly.*] A ditch! Where?

Estragon: [*Without gesture.*] Over there.

Vladimir: And they didn't beat you?

Estragon: Beat me? Certainly they beat me.

Vladimir: The same lot[2] as usual?

Estragon: The same? I don't know.

Vladimir: When I think of... all these years... but for me... where would you be...
[*Decisively.*] You'd be nothing more than a little heap of bones at the present minute, no doubt about it.

Estragon: And what of it?

Vladimir: [*Gloomily.*] It's too much for one man. [*Pause. Cheerfully.*] On the other hand what's the good of losing heart now, that's what I say. We should have thought of it a million years age, in the nineties.

Estragon: Ah, stop blathering[3] and help me off with this bloody thing.

Vladimir: Hand in hand from the top of the Eiffel Tower, among the first. We were respectful in those days. Now it's too late. They wouldn't even let up. [*Estragon tears at his boot.*] What are you doing?

Estragon: Taking off my boot. Did that never happen to you?

Vladimir: Boots must be taken off every day. I'm tired telling you that. Why don't you listen to me?

Estragon: [*Feebly.*] Help me.

Vladimir: It hurts?

Estragon: [*Angrily*] Hurts! He wants to know if it hurts[4]!

Vladimir: [*Angrily*] No one ever suffers but you. I don't count. I'd like to hear what you'd say if you had what I have.

Estragon: It hurts?

Vladimir: [*Angrily*] Hurts! He wants to know if it hurts!

Estragon: Charming spot. [*He turns, advances to front, halts facing auditorium.*] Inspiring prospects.

[*He turns to Vladimir.*] Let's go.

Vladimir: We can't.

Estragon: Why not?

Vladimir: We're waiting for Godot.

Estragon: [*Despairingly.*] Ah! [*Pause.*] You're sure it was here?

Vladimir: What?

Estragon: That we were to wait.

Vladimir: He[5] said by the tree. [*They look at the tree.*] Do you see any others?

Estragon: What is it?

Vladimir: I don't know. A willow.

Estragon: Where are the leaves?

Vladimir: It must be dead.

Estragon: No more weeping.

Vladimir: Perhaps it's not the season.

Estragon: Looks to me more like a bush.

Vladimir: A shrub.

Estragon: A bush.

Vladimir: A—. What are you insinuating[6]! That we've come to the wrong place?

Estragon: He should be here.

Vladimir: He didn't say for sure he'd come.

Estragon: And if he doesn't come?

Vladimir: Well come back tomorrow.

Estragon: And then the day after tomorrow.

Vladimir: Possibly.

Estragon: And so on.

Vladimir: The point is—

Estragon: Until he comes.

Vladimir: You're merciless.

Estragon: You came here yesterday.

Vladimir: Ah no, there you're mistaken.

Estragon: What did we do yesterday?

Vladimir: What did we do yesterday?

Estragon: Yes.

Vladimir: Why... [*Angrily.*] Nothing is certain when you're about.

Estragon: In my opinion we were here.

Vladimir: [*Looking rounds.*] You recognize the place?

Estragon: I didn't say that.

Vladimir: Well?

Estragon: That makes no difference.

Vladimir: All the same... that tree... [*Turning towards auditorium.*] that bog...

Estragon: You're sure it was this evening?

Vladimir: What?

Estragon: That we were to wait.

Vladimir: He said Saturday. [*Pause.*] I think.

Estragon: You think.

Vladimir: I must have made a note of it. [*He fumbles in his pockets, bursting with miscellaneous rubbish.*]

Estragon: [*Very insidious.*] But what Saturday? And is it Saturday? Is it not rather Sunday? [*Pause.*] Or Monday? [*Pause.*] Or Friday?

Vladimir: [*Looking wildly about him, as though the date was inscribed in the landscape.*] It's not possible!

Estragon: Or Thursday?

Vladimir: What'll we do?

Estragon: If he came yesterday and we weren't here you may be sure he won't come today.

Vladimir: But you say we were here yesterday.

Estragon: I may be mistaken. [*Pause.*] Let's stop talking for a minute, do you mind?

Vladimir: [*Feebly.*] All right. [*Estragon sits down on the mound. Vladimir paces agitatedly to and fro, hatting from time to time to gaze into distance off. Estragon falls asleep. Vladimir halts finally before Estragon.*] Gogo!... Gogo[7]!

... GOGO!

[*Estragon wakes with a start.*]

Estragon: [*Restored to the horror of his situation.*] I was asleep! [*Despairingly*] Why will you never let me sleep?

Vladimir: I felt lonely.

Estragon: I had a dream.

Vladimir: Don't tell me!

Estragon: I dreamt that—

Vladimir: DON'T TELL ME!

Estragon: [*Gesture towards the universe.*] This one is enough for you? [*Silenced.*] It's not nice of you, Didi[8]. Who am I to tell my private nightmares to if I can't tell them to you?

Vladimir: Let them remain private. You know I can't bear that.

Estragon: [*Coldly.*] There are times when I wonder if it wouldn't be better for us to part.

Vladimir: You wouldn't go far.

Notes

1. **Highness:** here it refers to Estragon.

2. **lot:** fortune, fate.

3. **blathering:** talking foolishly and meaninglessly.

4. **He wants to know if it hurts:** It's self-evident that my boots hurt me.

5. **He:** Godot.

6. **What are you insinuating:** What on earth do you mean?

7. **Gogo:** Estragon.

8. **Didi:** Vladimir.

References

Abrams, M. H. 1986. *The Norton Anthology of English Literature*. London: W. W. Norton & Company.

Bell, M. 1986. *The Context of English Literature*. London: Methuen & Co.

Branet, S. 1993. *An Introduction to Literature*. New York: Harper Collins College Publishers.

Carter, R. & McRae, J. 2001. *The Routledge History of Literature in English*. London and New York: Routledge.

Drabble, M. & Stringer, J. 1996. *The Concise Oxford Companion to English Literature*. Oxford: Oxford University Press.

Fowler, A. 1987. *A History of English Literature*. Oxford: Basil Blackwell Ltd.

Groom, B. 1999. *A Literary History of England*. London: Longmans, Green & Co.

Harvey, P. 1978. *The Oxford Companion to English Literature*. Oxford: Oxford University Press.

Hawthorn, J. 1997. *Studying the Novel*. London: Arnold.

Peck, J. & Coyle, M. 1993. *Literary Terms and Criticism*. London: Macmillan.

Rogers, P. 1987. *The Oxford Illustrated History of English Literature*. Oxford: Oxford University Press.

Sanders, A. 1994. *The Short Oxford History of English Literature*. Oxford: Clarendon Press.

Stewart, J. I. M. 1963. *Eight Modern Writers*. Oxford: Oxford University Press.

Ward, C. A. 1981. *Longman Companion to Twentieth Century Literature*. London: Longman.

教师服务

感谢您选用清华大学出版社的教材！为了更好地服务教学，我们为授课教师提供本学科重点教材信息及样书，请您扫码获取。

▶ 最新书目

扫码获取 2024 **外语类**重点教材信息

▶ 样书赠送

教师扫码即可获取样书